UNIVERSITIES AND THE ENTREPRENEURIAL ECOSYSTEM

Wherever possible, the articles in these volumes have been reproduced as originally published using facsimile reproduction, inclusive of footnotes and pagination to facilitate ease of reference.

For a full list of published and future titles in this series and a list of all Edward Elgar published titles visit our website at www.e-elgar.com

Universities and the Entrepreneurial Ecosystem

Edited by

David B. Audretsch

Distinguished Professor
and Ameritech Chair of Economic Development
Indiana University, Bloomington, USA

Albert N. Link

Virginia Batte Phillips Distinguished Professor of Economics
University of North Carolina at Greensboro, USA

Edward Elgar
PUBLISHING

Cheltenham, UK • Northampton, MA, USA

Published by
Edward Elgar Publishing Limited
The Lypiatts
15 Lansdown Road
Cheltenham
Glos GL50 2JA
UK

Edward Elgar Publishing, Inc.
William Pratt House
9 Dewey Court
Northampton
Massachusetts 01060
USA

A catalogue record for this book
is available from the British Library

Library of Congress Control Number: 2017931744

This book is available electronically in the **Elgar**online
Economics subject collection
DOI 10.4337/9781786432797

ISBN 978 1 78643 278 0 (cased)
ISBN 978 1 78643 279 7 (eBook)

Printed and bound in Great Britain by TJ International Ltd, Padstow

Contents

Acknowledgements

The editors and publishers wish to thank the authors and the following publishers who have kindly given permission for the use of copyright material.

American Economic Association for articles: Zoltan J. Acs, David B. Audretsch and Maryann P. Feldman (1992), 'Real Effects of Academic Research: Comment', *American Economic Review*, **82** (1), March, 363–7; David B. Audretsch and Paula E. Stephan (1996), 'Company–Scientist Locational Links: The Case of Biotechnology', *American Economic Review*, **86** (3), June, 641–52.

Elsevier Ltd for articles: Albert N. Link and John T. Scott (2003), 'U.S. Science Parks: The Diffusion of an Innovation and its Effects on the Academic Missions of Universities', *International Journal of Industrial Organization*, **21** (9), November, 1323–56; Albert N. Link and John T. Scott (2005), 'Opening the Ivory Tower's Door: An Analysis of the Determinants of the Formation of U.S. University Spin-off Companies', *Research Policy*, **34** (7), September, 1106–12; David B. Audretsch, Erik E. Lehmann and Susanne Warning (2005), 'University Spillovers and New Firm Location', *Research Policy*, **34** (7), September, 1113–22; T. Taylor Aldridge and David Audretsch (2011), 'The Bayh–Dole Act and Scientist Entrepreneurship', *Research Policy*, **40** (8), October, 1058–67; Marco Guerzoni, T. Taylor Aldridge, David B. Audretsch and Sameeksha Desai (2014), 'A New Industry Creation and Originality: Insight from the Funding Sources of University Patents', *Research Policy*, **43** (10), December, 1697–706.

Oxford University Press via the Copyright Clearance Center's RightsLink service for article: Albert N. Link, Donald S. Siegel and Barry Bozeman (2007), 'An Empirical Analysis of the Propensity of Academics to Engage in Informal University Technology Transfer', *Industrial and Corporate Change*, **16** (4), August, 641–55.

President and Fellows of Harvard College and the Massachusetts Institute of Technology for article: Bronwyn H. Hall, Albert N. Link and John T. Scott (2003), 'Universities as Research Partners', *Review of Economics and Statistics*, **85** (2), May, 485–91.

Springer Science and Business Media BV for articles: Albert N. Link and John Rees (1990), 'Firm Size, University Based Research, and the Returns to R&D', *Small Business Economics*, **2** (1), March, 25–31; Albert N. Link and John T. Scott (2006), 'U.S. University Research Parks', *Journal of Productivity Analysis*, **25** (1), April, 43–55; Ahmed Alshumaimri, Taylor Aldridge and David B. Audretsch (2010), 'The University Technology Transfer Revolution in Saudi Arabia', *Journal of Technology Transfer*, **35** (6), December, 585–96; Dennis Patrick Leyden and Albert N. Link (2013), 'Knowledge Spillovers, Collective Entrepreneurship, and

Economic Growth: The Role of Universities', *Small Business Economics*, **41** (4), December, 797–817; T. Taylor Aldridge, David Audretsch, Sameeksha Desai and Venkata Nadella (2014), 'Scientist Entrepreneurship Across Scientific Fields', *Journal of Technology Transfer*, **39** (6), December, 819–35.

Taylor & Francis Group for article: David B. Audretsch, Dennis P. Leyden and Albert N. Link (2012), 'Universities as Research Partners in Publicly Supported Entrepreneurial Firms', *Economics of Innovation and New Technology*, **21** (5–6), September, 529–45 (available online, http://wwww.tandfonline.com/ http://dx.doi.org/10.1080/10438599.2012.656523).

Introduction

David B. Audretsch and Albert N. Link

Universities have been around for longer than most things we observe in our modern, contemporary world. By contrast, the concept of entrepreneurial ecosystems is new. That such an old and new concept should collide is sufficiently surprising that their intersection constitutes the topic of this book.

Just because the university is such an established and revered institution does not mean that it is widely understood, particularly when it comes the role of the university in the economy. For centuries, universities were subject to the power, scrutiny and whims of the church and state. We all know the resistance from the church that the famed mathematician and astronomer, Nicolaus Copernicus, met from the Catholic Church when he dared to posit that the earth revolves around the sun.

It took the giant of a philosopher and linguist, Wilhelm von Humboldt, to liberate the university from the dictates of the church and state, freeing it to pursue knowledge for its own sake. Humboldt's revolutionary vision for the university was: 'The purpose of the universities is to cultivate learning in the deepest and broadest sense of the word, not for some practical or utilitarian end, but for its own sake as preparatory material of spiritual and moral education (*Bildung*).'[1]

With enactment of the Morrill Act in the United States, which was signed into law by President Abraham Lincoln in 1862, selected land grant universities were given the mandate not just to pursue knowledge for its own sake but rather knowledge to support and promote the agriculture community of that particular state. In fact, research, teaching and outreach undertaken at the land grant universities helped to propel U.S. agriculture to the highest levels of productivity and competitiveness in global markets.

The role of the university in society was further expanded following the second world war. In his highly influential report, *Science: the Endless Frontier*, Vannevar Bush (1945) posited a new and bold mandate for American universities to include not just the inward-looking values of the traditional and scholarly academic disciplines, but also the outward-looking social values.

However, it was not until the advent of contemporary globalization that the role of the university became firmly and decidedly an institution not just to anchor cherished social and political values but also to promote economic ones. As knowledge and ideas emerged as driving forces in the globalized economy, the university came into focus as a key source of competitiveness and growth.

The advent of entrepreneurial ecosystems in the last several years reflects the widespread recognition that entrepreneurship plays a key role in enabling knowledge investments, by the universities but also by private companies, non-profit organizations and research institutions, in commercializing new ideas and ultimately transforming them into innovations. Entrepreneurship has become increasingly viewed as the conduit taking ideas from the research laboratory, shop floor, and classroom and implementing them in the market, ultimately triggering the coveted economic growth, new jobs and competitiveness in global markets (Hébert and Link, 2009).

The English poet, John Donne, observed in 1624 that 'no man is an island'. It was not until more recently that both scholars as well as thought leaders in business and policy similarly concluded that entrepreneurs are similarly not an island. Rather, entrepreneurs, along with their start-ups, ventures, organizations and companies, have a strikingly greater propensity to be innovative when they are embedded in a community of other complementary entrepreneurs, institutions, and organizations, or what has become referred to as an entrepreneurial ecosystem. Because of their multiple roles of not just generating valuable knowledge and ideas, but also as a source of entrepreneurial behavior, universities have emerged as a cornerstone of entrepreneurial ecosystems.

Just as Michael Porter (1985) demonstrated that established companies generate a strong performance within the context of what he termed as a *cluster*, so too, entrepreneurs and the ventures also exhibit a stronger performance within the context of an entrepreneurial ecosystem. Thus, the title of our collection, *Universities and the Entrepreneurial Ecosystem*, is intended to suggest two things. First, it emphasizes the primary topic of the collection, namely the university; second, it suggests that universities are an element of the ecosystem that affects entrepreneurial behavior.

As with most titles, different readers might have differing interpretations about the scope of a book. Regarding *universities*, the scholarship that we have selected for this volume views universities as homogeneous agents of change. That is, we, like many others, have treated empirically the university as an independent variable that affects the behavior of entrepreneurial firms. Of course, universities are not homogeneous in their resource base; but we, like others in our field, have yet to delve into what are surely relevant distinguishing characteristics of one university over another. Regarding *ecosystem*, the articles in this volume assume that it consists of multiple enterprises, organizations, institutions, and individuals. And, those interact in such a manner as to elevate their own economic performance as well as those with whom they interact.

In order to decipher the interaction between universities and the entrepreneurial ecosystem, four main focus areas have emerged. The first involves university entrepreneurship. The second is concerned with university technology transfer. The third has a focus on the complementary nature of university-based research, and the fourth on universities as research partners. We have grouped the chapters included in this volume according to these four salient themes.

The articles assembled in the first two parts of this volume – University Entrepreneurship and University Technology Transfer – emphasize the unique characteristics of the behavior of universities, and it is that behavior that is the genesis of understanding the role and impact of universities in an entrepreneurial ecosystem and on its members. The first chapter in Part I on University Entrepreneurship, 'U.S. Science Parks: The Diffusion of an Innovation and its Effects on the Academic Missions of Universities', was selected to kick off the volume because it explains how the role and mission of the university has been changing over time. The focus is narrowed to a specific analysis of start-ups emanating from universities in the second chapter, 'Opening the Ivory Tower's Door: An Analysis of the Determinants of the Formation of U.S. University Spin-off Companies'. In the third chapter, a different aspect of university entrepreneurship is considered in 'U.S. University Research Parks'. The final two papers provide an explicit analysis of the impact of policy on university entrepreneurship. In particular, the impact of the Bayh–Dole Act, enacted by the United States Congress in 1981, on university entrepreneurship is analyzed in the fourth chapter, 'The Bayh–Dole Act and Scientist Entrepreneurship', and in Chapter 5, 'Scientist Entrepreneurship across Scientific Fields'.

Part II of the volume focuses on University Technology Transfer. The spatial and geographic dimension of technology transfer is analyzed in Chapter 6, 'University Spillovers and New Firm Location'. In Chapter 7 the technology transfer behavior of scientists and researchers is the focus in 'An Empirical Analysis of the Propensity of Academics to Engage in Informal University Technology Transfer'. Technology transfer is considered within the developing country context in Chapter 8, 'The University Technology Transfer Revolution in Saudi Arabia'.

The remaining two parts – Complementary Nature of University-Based Research and Universities as Research Partners – discuss and quantify how universities, as an element of an ecosystem, affect the behavior of entrepreneurial firms within the ecosystem. The first article included in the third section, Chapter 9, provides a meticulous analysis of 'Firm Size, University Based Research and the Returns to R&D'. Similarly, in 'Real Effects of Academic Research: Comment' (Chapter 10), the spatial dimension of knowledge spillovers from university research are analyzed. Knowledge spillovers from university research for the specific context of biotechnology are the focus of Chapter 11. The impact of knowledge spillovers emanating from university research on economic growth is the focus of Chapter 12, 'Knowledge Spillovers, Collective Entrepreneurship, and Economic Growth: The Role of Universities'.

The first chapter included in the final part, Chapter 13, provides an explicit analysis of 'Universities as Research Partners'. Similarly, Chapter 14 has a focus on 'Universities as Research Partners in Publicly Supported Entrepreneurial Firms'. The final paper of the volume, Chapter 15, provides an analysis of 'New Industry Creation and Originality: Insight from the Funding Sources of University Patents'.

Taken together as an integrated body of research offering a variety of perspectives about the intersection between universities and the entrepreneurial ecosystem, this volume provides a starting point for fleshing out the rich and nuanced details of the role of the university in the entrepreneurial ecosystem and vice versa. Our hope is that this collection of scholars will be a seed motivating how scholars think about the economic role and impact of universities. We also hope that seed will stimulate more research on this important topic.

Note

1   Cited from Fallon (1980, p. 5), from Audretsch and Lehmann (2016).

References

Audretsch, David B. and Erik E. Lehmann (2016), *The Seven Secrets of Germany: Economic Resilience in an Era of Global Turbulence*, New York: Oxford University Press.
Bush, Vannevar (1945), *Science: the Endless Frontier*, Washington, DC: US Government Printing Office.
Fallon, Daniel (1980), *The German University: A Heroic Ideal in Conflict with the Modern World*, Boulder: University of Colorado Press.

Hébert, Robert F. and Albert N. Link (2009), *A History of Entrepreneurship*, London: Routledge.
Porter, Michael E. (1985), *Competitive Advantage: Creating and Sustaining Superior Performance*, New York: Free Press.

PART I

UNIVERSITY ENTREPRENEURSHIP

ELSEVIER

International Journal of Industrial Organization
21 (2003) 1323–1356

International Journal of
Industrial
Organization

www.elsevier.com/locate/econbase

U.S. science parks: the diffusion of an innovation and its effects on the academic missions of universities

Albert N. Link[a], John T. Scott[b],*

[a]Department of Economics, University of North Carolina at Greensboro, Greensboro, NC 27402, USA
[b]Department of Economics, Dartmouth College, Hanover, NH 03755, USA

Abstract

The paper is an exploratory study of science parks in the United States. It models the history of science parks as the diffusion of an innovation that was adopted at a rapid and increasing rate in the early 1980s, and since then at a decreased rate. It models the growth of a science park once established, showing significant effects on growth for the proximity to universities and other resources. The paper also reports university administrators' perceptions about the impact of their science parks on the academic missions of their universities. Statistical analyses show there is a direct relationship between the proximity of the science park to the university and the probability that the academic curriculum will shift from basic toward applied research.
© 2003 Elsevier B.V. All rights reserved.

JEL classification: I2; L31; O32; R1

Keywords: Science parks; Innovation; University/industry relationships

1. Introduction

While there is a growing body of knowledge regarding university–industry

*Corresponding author. Tel.: +1-603-646-2941; fax: +1-603-646-2122.
E-mail addresses: al_link@uncg.edu (A.N. Link), john.t.scott@dartmouth.edu (J.T. Scott).

0167-7187/03/$ – see front matter © 2003 Elsevier B.V. All rights reserved.
doi:10.1016/S0167-7187(03)00085-7

1324   *A.N. Link, J.T. Scott / Int. J. Ind. Organ. 21 (2003) 1323–1356*

research partnerships,[1] there are few studies of university–industry strategic alliances in science parks. In this paper, we first describe the establishment and growth of a prominent sample of science parks that were among those operating in the United States at the end of the twentieth century. We then characterize, using survey data collected from a sample of major research universities in the United States, the perceptions of university administrators about the impact of science parks on various dimensions of the academic mission of a university. We relate those data about perceptions statistically to university and science park characteristics. Those characteristics include the distance of the park from the university and the formality of the relationship between the park and the university. Other characteristics are the R&D budget of the university and the percentage of its faculty engaged in research with science park organizations, the percentage of total academic R&D financed by industry, whether the university is public or private, the age of the park, and the technologies pursued by faculty associated with the park.

Surprisingly, given their long history in the United States as well as in other countries, there is no generally accepted definition of a science park. One definition has been posited by the Association of University Related Research Parks (AURRP).[2] As stated in their *Worldwide Research & Science Park Directory, 1998* (AURRP, 1997, p. 2):[3]

---

[1] Much of this literature is reviewed in Hall et al. (2000, 2003), forthcoming) and in the papers in Siegel et al. (2001). Formal university participation in industrial research joint ventures has increased steadily since the mid-1980s (Link, 1996), the number of university–industry R&D centers has increased by more than 60 percent during the 1980s (Cohen et al., 1997), and a recent survey of U.S. science faculty revealed that many desire even more partnerships with industry (Morgan, 1998). Mowery and Teece (1996, p. 111) contend that such growth in strategic alliances in R&D is indicative of a "broad restructuring of the U.S. national R&D system."

[2] In 2002, the Association was renamed the Association of University Research Parks (AURP).

[3] More narrowly, the U.S. General Accounting Office (GAO, 1983, p. ii) defines university-related research parks as "clusters of high technology firms or their research centers located on a site near a university, where industry occupancy is limited to research-intensive organizations." The lack of a standard definition of a science park is not unique to the United States. As Monck et al. (1988, p. 62) point out: "There is no uniformly accepted definition of a Science Park [in Britain] and, to make matters worse, there are several terms used to describe broadly similar developments—such as 'Research Park,' 'Technology Park,' 'Business Park,' 'Innovation Centre,' etc." The United Kingdom Science Park Association (UKSPA, 1985, p. ii) defines a science park in terms of the following features: "A science park is a property-based initiative which: has formal operational links with a university or other higher education or research institution; is designed to encourage the formation and growth of knowledge-based businesses and other organizations normally resident on site; has a management function which is actively engaged in the transfer of technology and business skills to the organizations on site."

A.N. Link, J.T. Scott / Int. J. Ind. Organ. 21 (2003) 1323–1356 1325

The definition of a research or science park differs almost as widely as the individual parks themselves. However, the research and science park concept generally includes three components:

- A real estate development
- An organizational program of activities for technology transfer
- A partnership between academic institutions, government and the private sector.

'Science park' has evolved to become a generic term which refers to parks with some or all of the foregoing characteristics. Included under this rubric are—and these designations are subjective—research parks with a majority of tenants that are heavily engaged in basic and applied research. As well, science parks include technology parks with a majority of tenants that are heavily engaged in applied research and development. Technology or innovation parks often house new start-up companies and incubator facilities.[4] Finally, commercial or industrial parks typically have tenants that add value to R&D-based products through assembly or packaging, rather than do R&D. However, we prefer the generic term science park since each of the classifications above does include some of the characteristics noted in the AURRP definition.

Fig. 1, based on the 1998 *Directory*, the most complete directory published by AURRP to date, illustrates the historical growth for the AURRP's U.S. science parks, as defined by the date at which each park was founded.[5] The AURRP *Directory*'s set of parks is just one sample of U.S. science parks.[6] Notable in Fig. 1 are the following parks: Stanford Research Park (established in 1951), Cornell Business & Technology Park (established in 1952), and the Research Triangle Park of North Carolina (established in 1959). We examine the foregoing set of science parks that have been formed in the United States since 1950—the AURRP membership—to establish a few simple facts about the establishment and growth of science parks.

---

[4] Incubator facilities house pre-start-up companies. Often, when the science park is tied to a state university, the state underwrites the cost of operating the incubator facility as part of a regional economic development strategy.

[5] Year of establishment is only one metric for dating the age and subsequent growth of science parks in the United States. It, like other metrics, is less than perfect since the date of establishment of a park may not be the date at which the first organization established itself in the park. In the case of the Research Triangle Park of North Carolina, the first tenant committed to the Park in 1965 (Link, 1995, 2002; Link and Scott, 2003) six years after the Park was formally established.

[6] Without an accepted definition of what a park is, without the complete population, and without a field-tested taxonomy of science parks, however, we do not know if the characterization of the establishment and growth of science parks that comes from examining the AURRP membership is a characterization of science parks more generally.

1326   *A.N. Link, J.T. Scott / Int. J. Ind. Organ. 21 (2003) 1323–1356*

Science Parks in the United States from 1951-1998

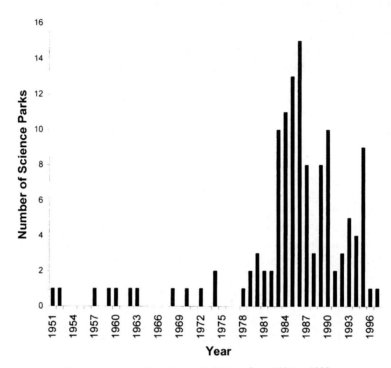

Fig. 1. Science Parks in the United States from 1951 to 1998.

Few scholars or researchers have studied science parks in any systematic manner.[7] A number of studies have examined the influence of being in a science

---

[7] There have, however, been a number of important and carefully done historical studies of the formation and/or growth of science parks. Castells and Hall (1994) and Saxenian (1994) describe the Silicon Valley (California) and Route 128 (around Boston) phenomenon; Luger and Goldstein (1991), Link (1995, 2002), and Link and Scott (2003) detail the history of Research Triangle Park (North Carolina); Gibb (1985), Grayson (1993), Guy (1996a,b), and Vedovello (1997) summarize aspects of the science park phenomenon in the United Kingdom; Gibb (1985) also chronicles the science park phenomenon in Germany, Italy, Netherlands, and selected Asian countries; and Chordà (1996) reports on French science parks, Phillimore (1999) on Australian science parks, and Bakouros et al. (2002) on the development of Greek science parks.

A.N. Link, J.T. Scott / Int. J. Ind. Organ. 21 (2003) 1323–1356   1327

park on various aspects of firm performance (e.g., growth and R&D productivity).[8] However, after describing the U.S. experience with the establishment and growth of the modern science park, this paper provides, in an exploratory manner, the first systematic insights into the influence of industry in science parks on the academic missions of universities.

2. Emergence and growth of U.S. science parks

2.1. Diffusion of the science park innovation

If the cumulative total for the science parks shown in Fig. 1 is plotted against time, the familiar logistic curve results.[9] In this section we offer an analytical model to characterize the 'lazy-S,' S-shaped pattern of the cumulative total of parks through time. We argue that the observed pattern of the establishment of science parks should be interpreted in terms of a model of the adoption of an innovation. Specifically, we posit the appearance of a new park as a new adoption of the innovative environment of a science park. We demonstrate that the establishment of science parks can be seen in terms of a simple model of diffusion, thereby offering support for this conceptualization and for how one might think of, and possibly forecast, the growth of the numbers of science parks in existence.

We have chosen a Gompertz survival-time model for our analytical demonstration because the model is quite simple and yet more general than a model using the exponential distribution that has a constant hazard rate. Geroski (2000)

---

[8] See Monck et al. (1988); Sternberg (1990); Westhead and Storey (1994); Westhead and Cowling (1995); Westhead et al. (1995); Westhead (1997); Westhead and Batstone (1998); Löfsten and Lindelöf (2002); and Siegel et al. (2003). Implicitly, policy makers assume that science parks do add value to firm performance, as well as to local community development, as evidenced by the recent National Research Council studies of the proposed Sandia Science Park and Ames Research Center (Wessner, 1999, 2001). As Massey et al. (1992, p. 56) point out, the 'environmental focus' that others have taken has merit:

At the core of the science-park phenomenon lies a view about how technologies are created. This view is that scientific activities are performed in academic laboratories [and Massey et al. assume that at the core of a science park is a university] isolated from other activities. The resulting discoveries and knowledge are potential inputs to technology. Science provides break-throughs from which new technological goods may spring. ... The argument goes that universities have many brilliant people making new discoveries but that they lack the means or the will to reach out to the market. *Science parks constitute a channel by which academic science may be linked to commerce* [*emphasis added*]. Thus science parks are there to promote, not 'science,' but its application in technology.

[9] Danilov (1971) attributes the relatively long period from about 1960 to the early 1970s, during which the science park movement seemingly stalled, to a number of park efforts that failed as well as to restraints on corporate R&D growth because of a lackluster economy.

1328   *A.N. Link, J.T. Scott / Int. J. Ind. Organ. 21 (2003) 1323–1356*

discusses many distinct reasons for S-shaped diffusion curves, and he observes that different reasons suggest different distributions for describing adoptions of innovation. For example, when there are asymmetries in the speed of diffusion among different groups in the population of adopters, the Gompertz distribution has been used.[10] The Gompertz survival-time model allows the data to represent a monotonically increasing or decreasing hazard rate for the adoption of the innovation—the appearance of a group of research companies in the innovative environment of a new science park. We hypothesize that as understanding of the science park innovation and the importance of interaction between industry and university science increased over the last half century, the hazard rate (described fully below) for adopting the science park innovation has increased.

The Gompertz model we estimate describes the adoption of the science park innovation as a stochastic diffusion process with an increasing hazard rate. Alternatively, the Weibull distribution could be used with the survival time model and also allow estimation of a hazard rate that increases or decreases through time. The log–normal or log–logistic distributions could be used for data with hazard rates that initially increase and then decrease, and the generalized gamma model would allow for even more flexibility in the hazard function.[11] For our purposes, the Gompertz model offers the appropriate flexibility with a simple functional form to describe the S-shaped diffusion curve where the hazard rate for the population of adopters of the innovative environment increased over time.[12]

Our time series of adoptions of the science park innovation, for our sample of AURRP members in the United States, runs from 1951 when the first park was established until the most recent adoptions in our data that occurred in 1997. In the absence of any particular event that precipitated the awareness of the concept of a science park, we assume that in 1950 potential adopters of the science park concept are made aware of the possibilities. Then, through time science parks appear with appearances being most likely in the environments most favorable to the success of a science park.

The probability that an adoption of the innovation—the establishment of a

---

[10] See Geroski (2000); in particular, see his discussion there of Dixon (1980) and Davies (1979).

[11] StataCorp (2001), pp. 343–75) describes the alternative distributions, and the implementation of the Gompertz distribution for use as an estimable parametric survival-time model. Rather than using maximum likelihood techniques to estimate survival-time models using various distributions as we do here, the early literature on the diffusion of innovations imposed the logistic S-curve for the diffusion of an innovation using appropriate transformations to reach a functional form that could be estimated with relatively simple estimation techniques. See Geroski (2000) for a tracing of the literature from the pioneering studies to the later ones that have modeled hazard rates.

[12] The implementation of the Gompertz distribution for use as an estimable parametric survival model is described in StataCorp (2001, p. 351–2), and we provide a brief explanation here as well. Our estimation uses the procedures and software described in StataCorp (2001, pp. 343–75).

A.N. Link, J.T. Scott / Int. J. Ind. Organ. 21 (2003) 1323–1356   1329

science park—will have occurred by time t is:

$$F(t) = 1 - S(t). \tag{1}$$

$S(t)$ is the probability that for a particular adopter, the adoption has not occurred by time t:

$$S(t) = e^{(-e^{\lambda}/\gamma)(e^{\gamma t}-1)} \tag{2}$$

The hazard rate for the adoption is:

$$h(t) = F'(t)/(1 - F(t)), \tag{3}$$

where

$$F'(t) = -S'(t) = e^{(\lambda + \gamma t)-(e^{\lambda}/\gamma)(e^{\gamma t}-1)}. \tag{4}$$

Substituting (1), (2), and (4) into (3), the hazard rate for adoption is then:

$$h(t) = e^{\lambda + \gamma t} = e^{\lambda}e^{\gamma t}, \tag{5}$$

and the hazard rate is increasing, decreasing, or constant as γ is $>$, $<$, or $= 0$.

The hazard rate is the conditional probability density for adoption of the science park innovation. Conditional on an incipient group of potential investors not yet having adopted the innovative environment of a science park, the probability that it will adopt the innovation and establish a park during the small interval of time dt is given by $h(t)dt$. The parameter λ determines the base level of the hazard rate throughout the history of the second half of the twentieth century, while the parameter γ determines the rate at which that base level grows through time. The survival-time model that we use to describe the history of science parks as the diffusion of an innovation treats the parameter λ as a constant plus a linear combination of explanatory variables that have had an impact on the diffusion of science parks.

For the Gompertz diffusion model that we estimate, we have a proportional hazard model where the hazard $h(t_j)$ for the jth adopter is:

$$h(t_j) = e^{x_j\beta}e^{\gamma(t_j)}. \tag{6}$$

The vector of explanatory variables for the jth observation is denoted as x_j. The parameters in the vector β and the ancillary parameter γ are estimated from the data with a maximum likelihood estimator. We find that the ancillary parameter γ is significantly greater than zero; thus, the hazard rate for adoption has increased throughout the fifty-year period.

Using the data provided in AURRP (1997), we estimate the model to describe the historical experience in the United States. The presence of a medical center or the park having aerospace/aeronautics among its technologies has a significant positive effect on the hazard rate. Park technology in the biotechnology/bio-

1330   *A.N. Link, J.T. Scott / Int. J. Ind. Organ. 21 (2003) 1323–1356*

medical area significantly reduces the hazard rate, reflecting the historical fact that while aerospace emerged relatively early in the half century of science park emergence, biotechnology emerged as an important area for industrial investment more recently. On the whole, the hazard rate for a park in the South or the Northeast exceeded that for a park in the West or the Midwest.[13]

To help intuition about the model, we present the results of the model as hazard ratios for each variable. The hazard ratio for an explanatory variable shows the effect on the hazard rate given a one-unit change in the variable while all other variables remain unchanged. From Eq. (6), the hazard ratio for variable z among the several in $\mathbf{x}_j$ is then:

$$(h(t_j|z+1) = e^{x_j\beta}e^{\gamma(t_j)}e^{\beta_z})/(h(t_j) = e^{x_j\beta}e^{\gamma(t_j)}) = e^{\beta_z} \tag{7}$$

The model is estimated using the 77 science parks for which data about the technologies were available. The model is estimated with robust standard errors, accounting for the fact that the same 'subjects' appear repeatedly in the pools of 'subjects at risk'.[14] With the interpretation we provide, the statistics in Table 1 show the historical picture for the emergence of science parks. Note that the z

Table 1
Gompertz survival time model of the diffusion of science parks[a]

Explanatory Variable	Hazard Ratio	Robust Std. Error	z^b	Prob. $> \|z\|^b$
Medical Center	1.93	0.519	2.45	0.014
t1	1.74	0.467	2.08	0.038
t4	0.649	0.157	−1.79	0.073
South	1.36	0.302	1.37	0.170
Northeast	1.61	0.465	1.66	0.097
gamma	0.180	0.0215	8.35	0.000

Number of subjects = 77, number of observations = 77, number of failures = 77, time at risk = 2607, Wald chi-squared (5) = 10.6, log likelihood = 8.38, probability > chi-squared = 0.0594.

[a] The dependent variable or outcome is analytical time of the establishment of the park ('failure time' or 'analysis time when record ends'—thus, for the model, analysis time begins in 1950, and a science park that was established in 1983 has an analytical time of establishment of 33). The term 'failure' refers to traditional applications of the survival-time model and the 'survival' function, S. As long as a 'subject at risk' has not adopted the innovation by establishing a science park, it 'survives' in the data, but on adoption it ceases to 'survive' and leaves the set of potential adopters. *t1* = aerospace/aeronautics; *t4* = biotechnology/biomedical; the remaining technology categories (in the intercept here in Table 1) provided in AURRP (1997) are provided in the note to Table 2 below where they are used.

[b] The z statistics and probability statements are for each of the underlying coefficients, rather than for the hazard ratios.

---

[13] The U.S. Census definitions for regions of the United States were used to assign states to one of the four regions—West, Midwest, South, and Northeast.

[14] StataCorp (2001, p. 281, p. 345).

statistics and probability statements are for each of the underlying coefficients in β, the vector of coefficients, rather than for the hazard ratios that are formed using those coefficients.[15]

The hazard ratios in Table 1 show that holding other things constant the hazard rate increases by 1.9 times if a medical center is present and by 1.7 times given aerospace/aeronautics technology. Reflecting its emergence later in the history of science parks, the hazard rate is 65 percent as great if biotechnology/biomedicine is indicated, other things the same. Because the model is estimated over the entire half of the century of the science park experience, the technology effects on the hazard rate, for the long-term historical S-curve for the diffusion of science parks, reflect the fact that aerospace investments were more likely earlier in the history, while biotechnology is more likely to be reported by parks formed later in the history. The model also shows that over the entire half of the century, the hazard rates for science parks are about 1.4 times as great in the South and 1.6 times as great in the Northeast as in the West and the Midwest. The AURRP (1997) data of course provide much more information about technologies and various other characteristics of parks, but for our statistical summary of the history, we have reported a very simple specification with just the effects that are statistically significant (or, in the case of the geographic effects, somewhat significant) in the presence of other effects. Our purpose at this point is not to document all of the detail of the history, but to use the simple model to provide a formal description that illustrates science parks as an innovation that diffused throughout the second half of the twentieth century.

The graph shown in Fig. 2 uses the estimated model to predict, for a science park with the characteristics of the average park in our sample, the probability that the innovation (the science park) will not have occurred by time t, where time is measured along the x-axis in analytic time from 0 to 47 which corresponds to calendar time from 1950 to 1997. Fig. 3 shows the predicted hazard rate for the park with average characteristics.[16] Subtracting from 1 the probability shown in Fig. 2 gives the probability that the innovation (the science park) has occurred by each time.[17] Multiplying that probability by the number of science parks in our population gives the model's fitted logistic curve, shown in Fig. 4, that corresponds to the actual curve that could be plotted by cumulating the appearance of the parks as shown in Fig. 1. Instead of the actual result, the model is predicting the expected number of parks at each time, illustrating that their appearance has

---

[15] StataCorp (2001, pp. 354–355).

[16] The statistics show that the gamma parameter is significantly greater than zero, so the hazard rate is increasing over time. Thus, the Gompertz model is appropriate rather than the simple exponential model where the hazard rate is constant. The plot of the hazard rate against time for the average science park is shown in Fig. 3.

[17] Using the model's average estimation of lambda, -8.43 is the average for the sample of the linear combination of the estimated coefficients and the explanatory variables, and gamma, estimated to be 0.180, we then have the probability of occurrence for the average park through time.

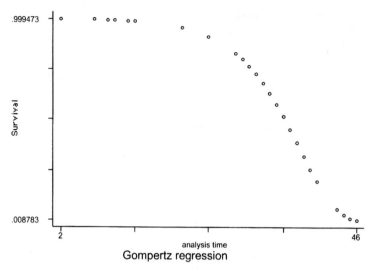

Fig. 2. The probability that the average science park would not have appeared by time *t* for *t* from 1950 to 1997.

followed the S-shaped logistic curve often associated with the diffusion of an innovation.

Using the date at which each new science park is established, we have a list of the 77 parks' arrival times starting with the earliest ones appearing in the early

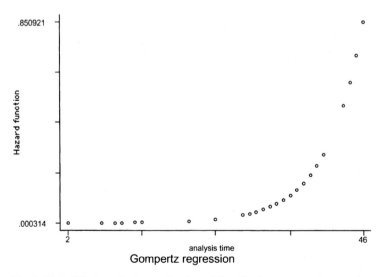

Fig. 3. Plot of the hazard rate as a function of time for the average science park.

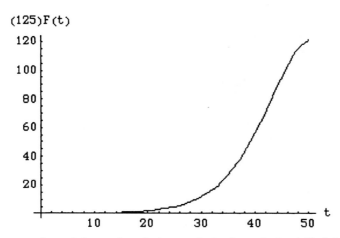

Fig. 4. The expected cumulative number of science parks by time *t* for last half of the twentieth century.

1950s, and ending with those appearing in the late 1990s. With that information, we were able to estimate λ and γ for the diffusion model showing the adoption of the science park research environment by successive groups of investors. On average for those groups, the model shows that λ is estimated to be -8.43 and γ is estimated to be 0.18 for the diffusion of the innovation—the science park. Thus, from Eq. (5), in 1950 at $t=0$ the hazard rate on average across the 77 groups of investors is $e^{-8.43}=0.00022$, and the hazard rate grows at the rate of 18 percent per year.

Fig. 4 raises a question that is important for the formation of technology policy. Has the adoption of the innovation of the science park run its course? Would public policy make possible the beginning of a new logistic curve, rising from the flat portion that both actual adoptions in Fig. 1 and the simulated ones in Fig. 4 suggest has followed half of a century of growth?[18] The actual establishments of research parks as shown in Fig. 1 as well as our diffusion model's tracking of the history as shown in Fig. 4, suggest that public policy can have a large impact on the formation of science parks. From both Fig. 1 and Fig. 4, we see that the acceleration in the formation of science parks occurred after the passage of several technology initiatives in the early 1980s. These policies included, in chronological order, the Bayh–Dole Act of 1980 which reformed federal patent policy by providing increased incentives for the diffusion of federally-funded innovation results; the research and experimentation (R&E) tax credit of 1981 which underwrote, through tax credits, the internal cost of increases in R&E in firms; and

---

[18] Price (1963, Chapter 1) provides a seminal discussion of the appearance of new logistic curves in the history of science.

the National Cooperative Research Act of 1984 which encouraged the formation of research joint ventures, as well as numerous state policies that coincided with the adoption of science parks.[19] These technology policies, and others, were a public sector reaction to both the productivity growth slowdown that began in the early 1970s and to the associated precipitous decrease in the competitive position of many U.S. technology-based industries. Of course, the public policies, being more or less coincident with the growth in science parks, could reflect public policies that followed the actions of industry rather than policies that stimulated those actions.

New public policies that encouraged interactions between universities and industry could stimulate a new logistic curve, perhaps even a new fifty-year cycle of growth for science parks. Would such public policy be desirable? The answer is not obvious, but any new policies that foster partnerships between universities and research organizations—private, public, or non-profit—would certainly enhance the environment conducive for partnering within science parks. As for the social desirability of such an environment, that depends on the costs of the new policies and on the size of the net benefits from cooperation, benefits that might include shortened research time and reduced research costs. Are the effects of newly directed commercial interests within science parks in the public interest? The answer will require developing understanding of the sources of growth for science parks, the effects that the parks have on both the economy and on the academic missions of universities, and the role of science parks in the U.S. innovation system.

2.2. Growth of science parks

Science parks are an innovation that reorganizes the method of applying scarce research resources to the production and application of knowledge by combining university and industry resources in a new way. As discussed in the introduction, Fig. 1 shows the adoption of science parks—reflecting the establishment and formation of the science park concept—throughout the last half of a century. We have modeled that adoption as the diffusion of an innovation, with the model estimating the logistic curve in Fig. 4.

In this section, we address the question: Once each park is established, how can we explain its growth over time? In particular, we are interested in developing initial stylized facts about the growth of science parks. To that end, we estimate a model describing the growth of a science park once the basic innovation of the park for combining and applying research resources has been adopted.

Our growth model is:

$$y(t) = ae^{gt}e^{\varepsilon} \tag{8}$$

---

[19] These initiatives are discussed in detail in Audretsch et al. (2002).

A.N. Link, J.T. Scott / Int. J. Ind. Organ. 21 (2003) 1323–1356   1335

where $y(t)$ is the science park's employment t years after it was established, a is the minimum efficient start-up scale for a science park, g is the annual growth rate of the park, and ε is random error.

The growth rate for the park is a function of various explanatory variables, x_1 to x_k:

$$\frac{\dot{y}}{y} = g = b_0 x_0 + b_1 x_1 + \cdots + b_k x_k \tag{9}$$

We then have:

$$\ln y(t) = \ln a + gt + \varepsilon \tag{10}$$

Substituting, we have an estimable model:

$$\ln y(t) = \ln a + b_0 t + b_1 x_1 t + \cdots + b_k x_k t + \varepsilon \tag{11}$$

Estimation of the growth model for the U.S. data is presented in Table 2. The coefficient on t (the length of time that a park has been in existence) shows the annual growth rate for science parks to be 0.084 or 8.4 percent for the parks in the Northeast when none of the qualitative variables in our model are 'turned on'. The annual growth rates for the West, Midwest, and South do not differ significantly, ceteris paribus.

The coefficient on each of the remaining variables (each being the interaction of an explanatory variable and the time that the science park has existed) gives the variable's effect on the annual growth rate. The growth rate of science parks has varied with technologies and with park characteristics. There are controls for all technology effects (leaving 'other technologies' in the intercept) and all regional effects (leaving Northeast in the intercept).[20]

The variable *tp* is a dummy variable that equals 1 if a park was established in 1980 or later during the period of technology policy initiatives. Thus, the coefficient on its interaction with the time a park has been in existence shows the difference in the annual average rate of growth for parks established after the passage of the aforementioned new technology policies. The coefficient is statistically significant and equal to 0.102; parks established after the passage of the new technology policies have annual growth rates that are higher by 10.2 percentage points, other things being the same.

Three park characteristics are robustly significant. (1) A knowledge environment variable: the driving distance (in miles) between the park and the nearest university, which has a negative effect on growth. For smaller mileage, the growth rate per year falls by the amount of about 10 percentage points for every 100 miles distance between the park and the nearest university. The effect diminishes as

---

[20] The technology areas are those reported to the AURRP, and the regional areas are again those described by the Census for the U.S.—Northeast, West, Midwest, and South.

1336   *A.N. Link, J.T. Scott / Int. J. Ind. Organ. 21 (2003) 1323–1356*

Table 2
Explaining the growth of science parks*

Variable	Coefficient (standard error)
t	0.0842 (0.0480)*
$t \times West$	− 0.0194 (0.0358)
$t \times Midwest$	− 0.0302 (0.0385)
$t \times South$	0.00800 (0.0309)
$t1 \times t$	− 0.0433 (0.0373)
$t2 \times t$	− 0.0837 (0.0458)*
$t3 \times t$	0.0635 (0.0354)*
$t4 \times t$	0.0160 (0.0350)
$t5 \times t$	− 0.148 (0.0415)***
$t6 \times t$	−0.0346 (0.0275)
$t7 \times t$	0.0875 (0.0385)**
$t8 \times t$	0.00817 (0.0252)
$t9 \times t$	0.121 (0.0313)***
$t10 \times t$	0.0331 (0.0394)
$t11 \times t$	− 0.0266 (0.0305)
$t12 \times t$	0.0113 (0.0445)
$t13 \times t$	− 0.0236 (0.0304)
$t14 \times t$	0.115 (0.0383)***
$t15 \times t$	− 0.0309 (0.0313)
$t16 \times t$	− 0.00146 (0.0341)
$t17 \times t$	0.0796 (0.0310)**
$Lease \times t$	− 0.0662 (0.0258)**
$Venture\text{-}capital \times t$	0.0692 (0.0284)**
$Miles \times t$	− 0.00104 (0.000374)***
$Miles^2 \times t$	1.29×10^{-6} (6.99×10^{-7})*
$tp \times t$	0.102 (0.0363)***
constant	3.21 (0.604)***

Number of observations = 51; $F(26, 24) = 5.14$***; $R^2 = 0.848$; adjusted $R^2 = 0.683$.
*The dependent variable, ln *emp*, is the natural logarithm of employment. The observations are for all science parks in the U.S. for which the data were available. The park technology categories are from AURRP (1997): $t1$ = aerospace/aeronautics; $t2$ = agriculture; $t3$ = animal science; $t4$ = biotechnology/biomedical; $t5$ = chemical; $t6$ = communication; $t7$ = computer; $t8$ = electronics/microelectronics; $t9$ = engineering; $t10$ = environmental; $t11$ = information technology; $t12$ = food processing; $t13$ = life science; $t14$ = medical related; $t15$ = pharmaceutical; $t16$ = software; $t17$ = telecommunications; $t18$ = other. Significance levels are denoted by * (10 percent), ** (5 percent), and *** (1 percent).

mileage increases.[21] (2) A financial environment variable: 1 if venture capital funds are available and 0 otherwise, which has a positive effect on growth. The

---

[21] The negative sign on mileage and the positive sign on mileage squared imply the negative effects on growth of more miles bottoms out (and then turns up, but we believe the upturn is really outside the range of anything interesting or sensible). With $y = a + bx + cx^2 + \ldots$, the first order condition $dy/dx = b + 2cx = 0$ implies that the negative effect will bottom out at $-b/2c$ miles. So, for the growth model in Table 2, the strong negative effect for low mileage gradually diminishes until miles = $0.00104/0.0000026 = 400$ miles. There is only one observation among the 51 observations in the model for which a science park is more than 400 miles from the associated university.

A.N. Link, J.T. Scott / Int. J. Ind. Organ. 21 (2003) 1323–1356   1337

growth rate per year increases by the amount of 6.9 percentage points per year if the park reports that venture capital funds are available. (3) A real-estate management variable: having sites for lease only (=1) as contrasted with having sites for sale and lease (=0), which has a negative effect on growth. The annual growth rate is lower by 6.6 percentage points when parks report sites are leased rather than leased and sold.

Additionally, there are technology effects. Across technologies reported by the AURRP, the strongest statistically significant growth has come from computers, engineering, medical, and telecommunications technologies. The technologies showing the most pronounced negative growth rates are agriculture and chemicals.

The model also provides a stylized fact for the base size for a park. The constant term gives a stylized, initial estimate of the log of the minimum efficient start-up scale for a research park. Looking at the model in that way, we see that the minimum efficient scale is a park with 25 employees (the base to the natural logarithms raised to the power 3.21).

These are exploratory results; future research should consider other explanatory variables such as the extent and nature of faculty and university administration involvement with the university-related science park and whether clusters of universities affect the performance of science parks. Further, growth is just one metric for the success of a park, but it is probably not a bad metric for success. Presumably growth would be correlated with many other metrics for success that would be less easy to quantify (positive externalities affecting the regional economy or the entire economy, successful transfer to industry of university research, placement of university graduates, and so on).

3. Science parks and the academic missions of universities

3.1. Sample of U.S. universities and the data collection process

The population sample of U.S. universities selected for this study consists of the 88 academic institutions that are categorized *both* in the top 100 academic institutions as measured by R&D expenditures and as defined by the National Science Board (2000), and in the Carnegie extensive classification of doctoral/ research universities (Carnegie Foundation, 2001). Our priors were that this sample would contain a large segment of academic institutions located in or near science parks that have a research or technology park character, and that have significant interactions with park organizations. The population sample is shown in Table 3.

A brief survey was designed, pretested, and then sent electronically in 2001 to the provost's office at each of these 88 universities. The purpose of the 10 percent pretest ($n=9$) was to ensure that a provost could answer our survey questions in

Table 3
Sample of U.S. universities ($n = 88$)

Auburn U	SUNY Buffalo	NYU
U of Alabama at Birmingham	SUNY Stony Brook	U of Rochester
U of Arizona	North Carolina State	Yeshiva U
UC-Berkeley	U of North Carolina	Duke
UC-Davis	Ohio State	Case Western
UC-Irvine	U of Cincinnati	Carnegie Mellon
UCLA	U of Oklahoma	U of Pennsylvania
UC-San Diego	Oregon State	Vanderbilt
UC-Santa Barbara	Penn State	
Colorado State	U of Pittsburgh	
U of Colorado	Clemson U	
U of Connecticut	U of Tennessee	
Florida State	Texas A&M	
U of Florida	U of Texas-Austin	
U of South Florida	U of Utah	
Georgia Tech	Utah State	
U of Georgia	U of Virginia	
U of Hawaii	Virginia Tech	
U of Illinois, Chicago	U of Washington	
U of Illinois, Urbana-Champaign	Washington State	
Indiana U	U of Wisconsin	
Purdue U	Cal Tech	
Iowa State	Stanford	
U of Iowa	U of Southern California	
U of Kansas	Yale	
U of Kentucky	Georgetown	
LSU	U of Miami	
U of Maryland, Baltimore County	Emory U	
U of Maryland, College Park	Northwestern	
U of Massachusetts	U of Chicago	
Michigan State	Tulane	
U of Michigan	Johns Hopkins	
Wayne State	Boston U	
U of Minnesota	Harvard	
Mississippi State	MIT	
U of Missouri	Tufts	
U of Nebraska	Washington U	
Rutgers	Princeton	
New Mexico State	Columbia	
U of New Mexico	Cornell	

an informed manner and to ensure that questions were phrased in an unambiguous manner. Follow-up telephone surveys were made to all non-respondents.

A variety of information was requested (discussed below), but the primary goal of the survey was to collect qualitative information regarding the provost's

A.N. Link, J.T. Scott / Int. J. Ind. Organ. 21 (2003) 1323–1356   1339

perception of the impact of the university's involvement with science parks on the following six academic missions:[22]

- research output, measured in terms of publications
- research output, measured in terms of patents
- extramural research funding
- applied versus basic nature of the curriculum
- placement of doctoral graduates
- ability of the university to hire preeminent scholars.

Motivating this inquiry is not only the conspicuous void of information about science parks in general and about technology flows from organizations into universities in particular, but also the need to understand how those flows affect fundamental academic behavior. Nelson (2001), for example, has asked if universities can take on the role of 'commercial enterprises' (e.g., licensing and patenting) without jeopardizing their more traditional roles such as their commitment to publish in the public domain and contribute to public science.

We received 47 responses (electronic and telephone), representing an initial response rate of 53.4 percent. However, 18 universities responded that they currently have no relationship with a science park and that the survey was therefore not relevant to them. Our final sample, which is analyzed in this paper, consists of the remaining 29 of the 47 responding universities, representing an overall usable response rate of 33.0 percent. Each of the 29 science parks is either a research park or a technology park, using the taxonomy above.

Table 4 shows the distribution of responses to statements about the influence of science parks on the academic missions of the university. Two general patterns are clear from the distribution of responses. First, there is more agreement than disagreement (e.g., more 4 and 5 responses than 1 and 2 responses) that involvement with a science park positively affects the research output and extramural research funding of universities. Second, there is more disagreement than agreement that such involvement affects the placement of doctoral graduates and improves the ability of the university to hire preeminent scholars.

---

[22] A concern prior to administering the survey was whether a provost (including the resources the provost could draw upon) could meaningfully provide such information. During the pretest phase of the study we specifically explored this issue and found in all cases that there was institutional knowledge about the university–science park relationship, even in cases where the provost was only recently appointed. Further, during the follow-up telephone interviews, each respondent was asked whether non-response to the electronic survey was in any way because of ambiguity in the survey or an inability to respond accurately to the survey statements. Also, we discussed with the provosts involved in the pretest stage the appropriateness of the six academic mission statements.

3.2. Quantitative analysis of the impact of science parks on the academic missions of universities

To address the general question of how a science park relationship affects the academic missions of a university, we estimated six ordered probit models using the data collected from our survey. The left-hand-side variable in each of the models is a Likert-scale response variable; hence, the ordered probit model is the appropriate statistical technique. Each model was specified to explain inter-university differences in the extent to which provosts agreed or disagreed with the academic mission statements referenced in Table 4. Greater agreement with a mission statement is associated with a higher score; for example, a higher score for the first question means greater enhancement of the university's academic mission of creating research publications. The extent of agreement is modeled as a function of characteristics of both the university and the science park with which the university is affiliated.

Our models initially focused on the same set of independent variables as represented in the model:

$$academic\ mission = f\ (relationship, mileage, rd, \mathbf{X}) \tag{12}$$

where *academic mission* represents each provost's response to each of the six academic mission statements, and where the independent variables will be discussed below. Thus, we estimated six versions of Eq. (12), one corresponding to each survey statement summarized in Table 4.[23]

Regarding the independent variables in Eq. (12), *relationship* dichotomizes the structure of each university's relationship with its science park. The variable *formal* equals one when the relationship is formal, and it equals zero if it is informal. Two questions on the survey quantify this: "Does your university have a *formal* relationship with a science park? (By 'formal' we intend any institutionally recognized arrangements, such as contractual arrangements of various sorts between your university and the science park.)"[24] Or, "Does your university have an *informal* relationship with a science park? (By 'informal' we intend individual rather than institutional relationships, for example, contract research between faculty members and the science park that is not contracted through the university

---

[23] Alternative econometric approaches to the general question of how a university's relationship with organizations in a science park affects the academic missions of the university were considered. Those alternatives are discussed in the Appendix.

[24] Following this question we asked: If YES, what is the name of the science park and what is the nature of your formal relationship (e.g., joint research with selected organizations, joint appointments of faculty at a research institute, own the land the park is on, lease buildings to research companies in the park, etc.)?

Table 4
Percent distribution of responses by provosts to mission statements ($n = 29$)

Mission statement	Response scale ($1 =$ 'strongly disagree' and $5 =$ 'strongly agree')				
	1	2	3	4	5
'As a result of my university's involvement with organizations in a science park, the ....'					
overall research output, measured in terms of publications, by faculty has increased.	28%	7%	21%	21%	24%
overall research output, measured in terms of patents, by faculty has increased.	24%	10%	21%	24%	21%
overall extramural research funding by faculty has increased.	21%	10%	28%	17%	24%
research curriculum has become more applied.	24%	10%	31%	7%	28%
placement of doctoral graduates has improved.	24%	14%	28%	28%	7%
ability of the university to hire preeminent scholars has improved.	24%	28%	21%	17%	10%

Note: The rows may not add to 100% due to rounding.

but treated as individual consulting.)"[25] We hypothesize that a formal relationship between a university and a science park leads to greater control over the interaction between faculty and the organizations in the park, much like in a centralized decision-making firm. Thus, where formal relationships exist the university may be able to exercise greater influence over the entrepreneurial direction that faculty take and how organizations in the park interact with the university as a whole. To the extent that a formal relationship overcomes barriers to faculty–organization interactions, it may reveal itself as greater faculty research output, greater placement of doctoral graduates, and a greater ability for the university to hire preeminent scholars.

The variable *mileage*—the miles between a university and its associated science park—quantifies the geographical relationship between the university and the science park.[26] Adams and Jaffe (1996) suggest that communication costs related to collaborative R&D activity increase with distance. Wallsten (2001) shows that geographical proximity to other successful innovative firms, as evidenced by the firm receiving a Small Business Innovation Research (SBIR) award, is associated with a firm's own success. These papers, as well as the works of Feldman (1999), Feldman and Lichtenberg (2002), and Adams (2002) motivate the inclusion of the variable *mileage*; we hypothesize that the closer a science park is to the university the more innovative the university. In the context of our model, *mileage* should thus enter negatively in the research output and extramural research equations. We also expect it to enter negatively in the curriculum equation, expecting a closer science park to have a bigger impact on a university's applied research since that is the research area common to both the university and the organizations in the park.

The variable *rd* is a scale variable, distinguishing universities in terms of their total research and development budget in millions of dollars.[27] Following Cohen and Levinthal (1989), we conjecture that more R&D-active universities may have a greater capacity to absorb the knowledge gained through research relationships with organizations in a science park. Thus, we hypothesize that such universities will benefit, in a research sense, relatively more from a relationship with a science park, and this absorption will show itself in more basic research and related research output.

Vector **X** controls for other university and firm characteristics. Two technology dummy (i.e., set to equal either one or zero) variables are included in the empirical

---

[25] Following this question we asked: If YES, what is the name of the science park and what is the nature of your informal relationship (e.g., joint research or faculty members who have consulting positions with selected businesses or a research institute; have an incidental, real estate relationship with the science park but no formal joint effort between the university and the tenants to develop the park in ways that integrate the tenants' activities with the university's research resources; etc.)?

[26] Data on mileage between a university and its named science park came from Internet information about the university or about the park.

[27] These data came from National Science Board (2000, p. A-315).

A.N. Link, J.T. Scott / Int. J. Ind. Organ. 21 (2003) 1323–1356   1343

specifications. Each provost was asked on the survey what technology(ies) are being investigated by faculty involved in research with science park organizations. The variable *dIT* equals 1 if information technology was mentioned, and *dbiotech* equals 1 if biotechnology was mentioned. Multiple technologies were generally mentioned; however, no significance was given to the order in which they were mentioned.

Provosts were also asked to approximate the percentage, *perinresrch,* of faculty who are routinely involved in research with science park organizations. That percentage is a scale variable approximating the proportion of faculty who could be the recipients of a reverse knowledge flow from industry into the university. The reverse flow of knowledge could have an impact on the university's academic missions.

The variable *agepark* is the age of the science park with which each university interacts, measured as the number of years between the time of the survey (in late 2000 with telephone follow-ups well into 2001) and the year that the named science park was formed.[28] This variable is designed to control for the development over time of park organizations with which the university could interact as well as the development of the quality of the interactions—a process that takes time. However, it is an imperfect control for this purpose, although no better information is available, since a park may not begin to have organizations enter immediately upon its formation.

In addition to the university and park characteristics described above, we also control for response bias. As seen in Table 5, the sample of 29 responding and reporting universities does not perfectly mirror the population sample of 88 universities in terms of the selected key characteristics. To control for differences in the probability of responding to the survey, we estimated the probability of responding and completing the survey, that is, the probability of selection into the

Table 5
Selected mean values, by sample of universities

University characteristics	Population sample ($n=88$)	Responding sample ($n=29$)
Park on campus (*parkoncampus*)	54.55%	65.52%
Total academic R&D (*rd*)	$198.41M	$207.07M
% of total academic R&D from industry (*indrd*)	13.57%	15.00%
% public universities (*pubpriv* = 1 if public; 0 otherwise)	69.32%	79.31%

---

[28] In 27 of 29 parks we could identify the year the park was formed using information from the Internet and from AURRP (1997).

sample of 29, *prob*8829.[29] That probability is then used as a control variable in Eq. (12).[30] We believe that this variable is doing more than simply controlling for the effect of a correlation in random errors in the model of response and complete models of the provosts' perceptions about the effects of science parks on academic missions. Our model of perceptions is exploratory and unlikely to be complete with just the variables other than *prob*8829. We view the variable *prob*8829 as capturing substantive effects of the complete model that otherwise would be left in the error term and that are related to the probability of responding to the survey.

Table 6 shows the econometric results for the six ordered probit models to assess the determinants of inter-university differences in the impact of science park relationships on the academic missions of universities. The specifications presented are for the parsimonious models that include (apart from the response control) only the explanatory variables that had coefficients at least as great as their standard errors when each model was estimated with all of the explanatory variables. As we have presented in the conference versions of this paper, remarkably (given the small number of observations and the large number of explanatory variables) the full specifications with every one of the explanatory variables included show essentially the same results regarding the significant variables presented in Table 6. The variables omitted in Table 6 had insignificant coefficients, but their inclusion in the all-inclusive models did not eliminate the significance or change the signs of the other variables as presented in Table 6's parsimonious models. Given the small number of observations and the exploratory

---

[29] The probit estimates used to calculate *prob*8829 came from a model of the probability of selection into the sample of 29 respondents among the 88 universities surveyed. The explanatory variables for the probit model of selection were *parkoncamp*, *indrd*, and *pubpriv*. Each explanatory variable had a positive impact on the probability of response to the survey. Although the coefficients were not very significant individually, the probabilities predicted by the model are important in explaining the provosts' responses to some of the mission statements.

[30] Alternatively, the hazard rate from the probability of response model can be used to control for systematic components in the error that are associated with selection into the sample. Results are similar using the hazard rate rather than the probability of selection. We prefer to control for the possibility that something in the error is associated with the selection into the sample by using the probability of response directly. The specifications for our models are exploratory, and Maddala (1983, p. 269) points to evidence "that the normal selection-bias adjustment is quite sensitive to departures from normality." The use of the probability of response rather than the hazard rate has straightforward, intuitive meaning that is not dependent on an assumption of joint normally distributed disturbances for the response probit and the ordered probit models. Further, the standard approach to selection bias of course depends on complete models for response and for the substantive model of interest—here the model of university administrators' perceptions. The response term in the later model then captures the effect of correlation in the random errors in the two models. As discussed in the text, we view the variable *prob*8829 as completing our substantive model, capturing systematic effects on the academic missions that vary with characteristics of universities that are associated with the probability of response. Those ultimate causal characteristics may not be those in our response model, but rather associated with them and therefore with response.

A.N. Link, J.T. Scott / Int. J. Ind. Organ. 21 (2003) 1323–1356   1345

nature of the models, our preferred specifications are the parsimonious ones shown in Table 6.

Ceteris paribus, universities with a formal relationship with a science park realize greater benefits from that relationship as quantified through increased publication and patenting activity, greater extramural funding success, and through an enhanced ability to hire preeminent scholars and to place doctoral graduates.

The closer geographically a university is to the science park, ceteris paribus, the greater the university's success obtaining extramural funding, the greater the influence of park tenants on the applied versus basic research nature of the university's curriculum, and the greater the ability of the university to place its doctoral graduates. The effects are stronger the closer the university and the science park are to one another, and the attenuation of the effect associated with increasing mileage should be considered for ranges reasonably near the sample means. The finding about the applied research curriculum is revisited below.[31]

The total R&D budget of the university, *rd*, enters significantly in three cases. It enters positively in the patenting equation meaning that, ceteris paribus, more R&D-active universities have their patenting activity positively influenced by their association with a science park, supporting the hypothesis about absorptive capacity. It enters negatively in the extramural funding equation, as well as in the hiring equation. We interpret the latter two findings to suggest that the R&D activity of the university, rather than its science park affiliation, drives its academic reputation as reflected through enhanced funding and hiring. The effect of *rd* is explored further below.

The results in Table 6 also suggest (keeping in mind the caveats associated with *agepark*) that older parks have an applied influence on the university's research curriculum, perhaps also explaining the positive effect of age on patenting. Older parks are also more likely to have a positive influence on the hiring of preeminent scholars. The percentage of faculty engaged in university/science park activities, which like *rd* is a scale variable, also enters significantly in the publications equation.

The probability of responding to the academic mission statements, *prob*8829, enters somewhat significantly in the publications model, the patents model, and the

---

[31] Note that there are two models with the nonlinear mileage effect, and the negative effect in the first case—for extramural funding—bottoms out at $0.0951/0.005 = 19$ miles, but recall that the sample mean for the sample of responding firms is only 5.7 miles. For the range around the mean where it is sensible to simulate the effect, the effect is negative. In the second case, the effect bottoms out at $0.942/0.034 = 28$ miles. The effect estimated is negative and diminishing. Think of a negatively sloped curve that gradually bottoms out and approaches an asymptote. It is very sensible that as distance gets bigger, the marginal negative effect would diminish, but we think that mathematical upturn is not of interest empirically given the sample means. Just 4 of the 29 responding parks are further than 19 miles and just 2 of the 29 (and of the 27 used in the applied research model) are further than 28 miles.

Table 6
Ordered probit estimates of agreement with mission statements

Variable	Mission statement coefficient (robust standard error)					
	Publications	Patents	Extramural research funding	Applied research curriculum	Placement of doctoral graduates	Hiring of preeminent scholars
formal	3.31 (0.832)***	2.57 (0.753)***	1.01 (0.618)*	1.39 (0.601)**	1.10 (0.622)*	1.92 (0.644)***
mileage		-0.0354 (0.0293)	-0.0951 (0.0573)*	-0.942 (0.176)***	-0.0327 (0.0257)	
mileage²			0.00252 (0.00125)**	0.0175 (0.00369)***		
rd		0.0120 (0.00541)**	-0.00431 (0.00267)#	-0.00618 (0.00506)		-0.00510 (0.00307)*
dIT	-2.33 (0.807)***		-1.09 (0.446)**	-1.06 (0.603)*		
dbiotech						-0.798 (0.441)*
perinresrch	0.159 (0.0714)**					
agepark		0.0301 (0.0190)#		0.0876 (0.0288)***	0.0236 (0.0173)	0.0455 (0.0195)**
prob8829	5.77 (3.21)*	6.67 (3.15)**	3.19 (3.07)	-6.96 (3.95)*	0.131 (1.58)	1.70 (2.65)
Number of observations	28	27	29	27	27	27
Log likelihood	-19.99	-24.21	-35.72	-17.30	-34.59	-32.46
Pseudo-R^2	0.519	0.420	0.212	0.569	0.157	0.231
Wald Chi-squared (df)	20.0 (4) ***	36.2(5)***	24.8 (6)***	62.8 (7)***	14.1 (4)***	23.6 (5)***
cut1	2.16 (1.04)	5.33 (1.48)	-0.779 (1.34)	-6.75 (1.98)	0.030 (0.613)	0.192 (1.06)

cut2	2.47 (1.12)	5.99 (1.55)	−0.141 (1.42)	−4.19 (1.79)	0.682 (0.622)	1.59 (1.04)
cut3	4.42 (1.36)	7.30 (1.65)	0.909 (1.52)	−1.38 (1.51)	1.62 (0.704)	2.46 (1.14)
cut4	6.20 (1.64)	8.77 (1.83)	1.49 (1.54)	−0.988 (1.60)	2.91 (0.895)	3.41 (1.28)
Mean formal (n=29)	0.655					
Mean mileage (n=29)	5.741					
Mean rd (n=29)	207.07					
Mean dIT (n=29)	0.345					
Mean dbiotech (n=29)	0.414					
Mean perinresrch (n=28)	3.750					
Mean agepark (n=27)	19.185					
Mean prob8829 (n=29)	0.363					

Notes: Significance levels denoted by #(15 percent), *(10 percent), **(5 percent), ***(1 percent).
From the sample of 29 responding universities, 2 listed science parks for which we were unable to determine the year in which the park began, thus we were unable to calculate the variable agepark, defined as (2000−year started). Also, a third university did not report a value for perinresrch.

1348   *A.N. Link, J.T. Scott / Int. J. Ind. Organ. 21 (2003) 1323–1356*

applied research model. It remains an open question whether the effect reflects a substantive effect of unobserved explanatory variables associated with response, or instead is simply the result of correlation of the errors in the model of response and the models of university administrators' perceptions.

3.3. Interpretation of statistical results for perceptions of science parks' effects on academic missions of universities

Universities seek external research relationships in an effort to enrich both the knowledge in their research base and the financial value of that knowledge. Herein, we explored how university research relationships with clusters of industrial firms in a science park affect six academic missions. While our sample is relatively small and the information collected from university provosts is qualitative, this study is, to our knowledge, the first to address such impacts in a systematic manner.

The statistical relationships that we found are interesting for a general understanding of science parks and associated knowledge flows. However, the relationships also show how universities that are considering establishing a science park might benchmark their planned activities and structure their relationship with their science park to control the influence of the relationship on academics at the university. Our survey did not apply to 18 of the 47 universities that returned our survey. Five of those 18 universities reported that they are currently planning a science park or are in the process of building one. While we may not see a resurgence of the creation of new science parks as observed in the mid- to late 1980s (see Fig. 1), our survey data and informal discussions with science park directors suggest that the science park phenomenon is again on the rise. Put differently, in terms of our model as illustrated in Fig. 4, a new logistic curve may be taking off from the plateau attained after the first half century of science park growth. As university administrators deal with collaborative research relationships in science parks, our results suggest the following expectations.

First, the organizational nature of the university–park relationship is important. Our measures of a formal versus an informal relationship apparently capture important differences in how universities form a research relationship with their science park. When the relationship is formal, specific impacts will follow including enhanced research output (e.g., publications and patents), increased extramural funding, and improvements in hiring and placement capabilities.

Second, proximity of the science park to the university has an impact on various aspects of the university's academic mission. Proximity, other things held constant, increases success in obtaining extramural funding. Further, other factors held constant, a science park located on or very close to the university campus confers greater employment opportunities for doctoral graduates. But, this nexus also has a curricular influence by causing a more applied research curriculum other things being the same.[32]

Third, ceteris paribus, more R&D-active universities are more likely to report that their interaction with science park organizations positively affects their propensity to patent. They are less likely to report science park effects on their extramural funding activity or on their ability to hire preeminent scholars. The R&D activity within the university is considered in more detail below.

Fourth, as measured by the percentage of faculty, the intensity with which university faculty are engaged in research with science park organizations appears to have little measurable impact on the effect of science parks on the academic missions of universities except on publications.

Fifth, the influence of university-park research interactions may change over the life of the interaction. Over time, the impact that science parks have on academic missions changes. Initially, that impact may not influence patenting activity or curriculum, but over time it will. Similarly, over time the reputation of the science park will confer a hiring advantage to the university, ceteris paribus.[33]

Reemphasizing the caveats associated with this study, namely that we rely on the provosts' perceptions of effects (rather than time-series data about the effects) and that our sample is small, the results in Table 6 may nevertheless be useful for guiding aspects of university decision making. The results may inform the decision making of universities that have science parks and are trying to understand the full extent of the university–park relationship. Also, the results may inform universities that are contemplating establishing a science park or planning one. We illustrate this with two examples, both focusing on the effect of a university's involvement with a science park on the applied nature of the university's research curriculum. That dimension of curricular focus has gained attention in recent years. As noted previously, Nelson (2001) has warned that as universities take on commercial activities, often in conjunction with industry, their commitment to public science may be endangered. Stephan (2001) as well has noted that there is the potential that technology transfer activities—likely to occur from university/ science park interactions—will divert faculty away from students and curriculum and towards commercial activities such as the quest for extramural research funding. If such funding comes from industrial firms, then it is reasonable to be concerned that commercial influences will spill over to influence the character of the university's research and hence its research curriculum.

---

[32] Nelson (2001) is concerned that commercialization of university research may have a detrimental effect on its 'public science.' Stephan (2001) observes that university/industry research partnerships have a potential to have a detrimental affect on the university's basic research curriculum. This issue is discussed in more detail in Poyago-Theotoky et al. (2002).

[33] We did investigate the possibility of a nonlinear age of park effect, but that variable never entered at even a marginally significant level.

1350   *A.N. Link, J.T. Scott / Int. J. Ind. Organ. 21 (2003) 1323–1356*

First, consider a university that has an ongoing relationship with organizations in a science park; consider also the ordered probit results presented in Table 6 for the applied research curriculum mission of the university. Ceteris paribus, as *rd* increases, there is a decrease in the probability of agreement with the mission statement that the university's research curriculum has become more applied as a result of its involvement with organizations in a science park. The point is that university R&D activity is an instrument that the university can use to control the impact that its involvement with its science park has on its curricular mission. As well, university R&D activity is an instrument useful in predicting, in a benchmarking sense, what impact to expect from its science park involvement. Interpreted slightly differently, the research culture of the university—and we suggest that the 'strength' of that culture may be related to the intensity of the university's R&D activity—that also confers an academic reputation on the university, offsets outside (e.g., through science park relationships) influences that push the academic curriculum away from basic research toward applied research.

Second, consider a university planning a science park. Again, using the estimated coefficients in Table 6, ceteris paribus, for a reasonable range around the sample mean, as mileage increases, the probability of agreement with the mission statement that the university's research curriculum has become more applied as a result of its involvement with organizations in a science park decreases. Proximity does matter. When planning an on-campus science park, *mileage* = 0, provosts should expect over time a significant applied influence in the research curriculum from that relationship. Ceteris paribus, the probability of such an influence decreases rapidly when the cluster of industrial firms is off campus.

4. Conclusions

There is much to be learned about science parks, in general, and their influence on university activity, in particular. This exploratory paper is only a first step in the new learning about science parks and their effects on the academic missions of universities. We have in our paper modeled the appearance of science parks throughout the last half of a century as the diffusion of an innovation—the innovation of the modern science park. With the model, we could describe the hazard rate for the appearance of new science parks through time, and we could observe the initial increase in the rate of new park formations about the time of the Bayh–Dole Act's passage, the enactment of the R&E tax credit, and the rise in research joint venture activity encouraged through the National Cooperative Research Act, and then the eventual decline in that rate. Understanding the determinants of the rate of formation can inform public policy toward science parks as we enter a new era of growth in the formation of science parks. We have provided initial insights about the forces that stimulate the growth of a science

A.N. Link, J.T. Scott / Int. J. Ind. Organ. 21 (2003) 1323–1356 1351

park once it has been established. We tentatively identified sources of growth from knowledge, financial, and real estate resources, holding constant the types of technologies associated with the science park and its geographic region and the apparent effect of the technology policies. Further development of the model will be important to inform public policy toward science parks. Finally, we surveyed university administrators to discover their perceptions about the impacts of science parks on their universities' academic missions. Formal association with a science park tends to be perceived by the university administrators as increasing research outputs as measured by publications and patents, as increasing extramural funding, as improving their universities' prospects for hiring preeminent scholars and for placing doctoral graduates. Proximity to a science park improves success in obtaining extramural funding, and proximity improves a university's doctoral graduates' prospects for jobs. However, the applied nature of the university's research curriculum increases with such proximity; R&D spending at the university reduces that impact.

Future research can extend and develop the findings of this exploratory paper. Regarding the diffusion of the innovation of science parks, the underlying determinants of our model's gamma and lambda can be further developed and explored with data describing the resources available in the geographical environments that host the science parks. For future research about adoptions of the science park concept, samples should include not only established science parks, but as well entrepreneurial groups considering establishment of a park yet never adopting the science park innovation within the sample period. That is, the sample would include entrepreneurial groups that 'survive' throughout the sample period—hence do not 'fail' in the language of the survival time model—and do not adopt the science park innovation. Further, the samples could include parks that were established—adopted the science park concept—but then failed as science parks. Our preliminary work with the growth of science parks once they are established suggests the importance of the knowledge, financial, and real estate resources available to a science park, but future research is needed to develop our exploratory findings.

Our initial look at the perceptions of university administrators is only a beginning in developing understanding about the impact of science parks on the academic missions of universities. The sample size is necessarily small when the unit of observation is the university itself, and a useful extension of our exploratory study could focus on multiple respondents for each university. Multiple respondents could be developed with interviews of faculty members as well as university administrators, and with respondents representing industry participants in the science park. The multiple responses—combined with additional data (including data about the geographic and economic areas in which the parks are located and including qualitative historical data) about the universities and the science parks—will allow future research to develop further the understanding of the interactions between the university and the associated science

1352   *A.N. Link, J.T. Scott / Int. J. Ind. Organ. 21 (2003) 1323–1356*

park.[34] In particular, our findings suggest that the proximity of the science park to the university has no discernable impact on two of the six dimensions of the academic mission. We expect that the reason may simply be the small size of our sample, but future research should explain why, and it should also develop the timing of science park impacts on the academic missions of universities.

Further, in addition to working with the perceptions of those involved with the university/science park interactions, quantitative measures of the interactions' effects should be evaluated in future research. For example, future work could attempt to assess quantitatively a university's success in basic research as a function of the degree of involvement with a science park, measuring success with citation counts or ranking of graduate programs in science and engineering. Additionally, our exploratory study focused on the experience in the United States with its patent law, its mix of public and private universities, and so forth; one expects different experiences in different countries, and future research will develop those differences and thereby increase knowledge about the science park/university interactions.

Acknowledgements

Earlier versions of parts of this paper were presented at the University of Nottingham's Institute for Enterprise and Innovation/National Academy of Sciences' Board of Science, Technology and Economic Policy Collaborative Conference on "Policies to Promote Entrepreneurship in a Knowledge-Based Economy: Evaluating Best Practices from the U.S. and U.K," September 18–19, 2000; at the Industrial Organization Society's session on "Innovations in Industrial Organization of R&D and Technology Transfer" at the Allied Social Sciences Association's meetings in New Orleans, January 5, 2001; at the Georgia Institute of Technology Roundtable for Engineering Entrepreneurship Research Conference, March 21–23, 2002; and at two workshops at the University of North Carolina at Greensboro — the National Science Foundation Workshop on Science Park Indicators, November 14, 2002, and the Workshop on the Economics of Intellectual Property at Universities, November 15, 2002. We appreciate comments from the participants at those conferences, especially those from Irwin Feller and Donald Siegel, as well as comments from Richard Arnott regarding the directions

---

[34] The details that distinguish science parks may be crucial to understanding the perceptions that we have documented in our exploratory study. Future research should develop those details. Richard Arnott has suggested (personal correspondence, July 26, 2002) questions such as the following ones. "Do most faculty who have an association with a research park consult or are they part owners of start-up companies? If a professor develops a product in a science park that derives from basic research performed at the university, who has the patent rights? Do the professor's research students at the university routinely get involved in their science park activities?"

A.N. Link, J.T. Scott / Int. J. Ind. Organ. 21 (2003) 1323–1356   1353

for future research. We also appreciate the generous funding provided by the National Science Foundation to conduct this study.

Appendix A

In this Appendix, we discuss alternative econometric approaches to the question of how a university's relationship with a science park affects the academic missions of the university. One alternative to exploring inter-university differences in perceived effects of a science park on academic missions would have been to collect quantitative data on aspects of university activity (e.g., publications, patents, extramural funds, curriculum, student placements, and hiring) and estimate for each university a time series model, controlling for the date that the university began its relationship with the science park. Such a model as

$$academic\ activity_{t=0\ to\ t=n} = f\ (science\ park\ interaction_{t=0\ to\ t=n}) \qquad (A.1)$$

has the benefit of relying on objective data to quantify academic activity on the left. However, the error in the equation may be correlated (causing biases in the estimates of the model's coefficients) with the errors in the observations of the independent variables—errors that may be severe because there is no meaningful way to date when a university began to have relationship with a park. Parks evolve over time from a concept to a development project to an infrastructure housing research partners. Research Triangle Park is a case in point. Faculty from Duke University, University of North Carolina, and North Carolina State University (then State College) were involved with the Park before the Park became a park. That is, faculty were integrally involved in research relationships with companies as far back as the late 1950s, although the first tenant did not commit to the Park until 1965 and began research operations more than a year later. In other cases, there have been long standing relationships between the university and the park, but the park has yet to move from a land development corporation to one with research tenants. Or, we could have created a matched sample of universities with and without a science park relationship and compared the performance of each group of universities. Such a model as

$$academic\ activity_{university\ A\ vs.\ university\ B}$$
$$= f\ (science\ park\ interaction_{university\ A\ vs.\ university\ B}) \qquad (A.2)$$

also has the advantage of objective data on the left, but there is not a meaningful (as opposed to systematic) way to create a matched sample of universities that do not have a science park relationship. Again, we expect correlation between the error in equation and the errors in the explanatory variables. There are two main reasons for those errors. One, the relationship between a university and park is an

1354   *A.N. Link, J.T. Scott / Int. J. Ind. Organ. 21 (2003) 1323–1356*

evolving one, as just discussed, and, even controlling for age of park, the sample of universities with park relationships would still have a degree of heterogeneity that could not be matched in the sample of universities without park relationships. And two, we would have had no way to hold constant in such an experiment other industry influences on the university that occurred as a result of research or other interactions outside of the geographic park setting. As compared with our approach, the alternative approaches represented by Eqs. (A.1) and (A.2) have some advantages despite the potentially bias-inducing errors in variables difficulties we have identified. Just as clearly, however, our approach has its own advantages, and the perceptions of the universities' provosts about the effects of the science park affiliations on the universities' missions are important in themselves. Although the dependent variables in the versions of Eq. (12) that were estimated clearly reflect perceptions, we are convinced, as a result of our pretests, that provosts reported well-informed perceptions. And, given that the dependent variable reflects perceptions, ordered probit is the appropriate econometric technique. The alternative models noted above would also have contained judgmental information, but would have done so in a manner that would be likely to create an important errors in variables problem. Although there are econometric approaches to dealing with the errors in variables problem, the errors introduced in the two alternative models would be central to the time series investigation and especially intractable.

References

Adams, J.D., 2002. Comparative localization of academic and industrial spillovers. Journal of Economic Geography 2, 253–278.

Adams, J.D., Jaffe, A.B., 1996. Bounding the effects of R&D: An investigation using matched establishment-firm data. Rand Journal of Economics 94, 700–721.

Association of University Related Research Parks (AURRP), 1997, Worldwide Research & Science Park Directory 1998. BPI Communications.

Audretsch, D.B., Bozeman, B., Combs, K.L., Feldman, M.P., Link, A.N., Siegel, D.S., Stephan, P.E., Tassey, G., Wessner, C., 2002. The economics of science and technology. Journal of Technology Transfer 27, 155–203.

Bakouros, Y.L., Mardas, D.C., Varsakelis, N.C., 2002. Science park, a high tech fantasy?: An analysis of the science parks of Greece. Technovation 22, 123–128.

Carnegie Foundation for the Advancement of Teaching, 2001. The Carnegie Classification of Institutions of Higher Education, 2000 Edition. Carnegie Foundation, Menlo Park, California.

Castells, M., Hall, P., 1994. Technopoles of the World. Routledge, London.

Chordà, I.M., 1996. Towards the maturity state: An insight into the performance of French technopoles. Technovation 16, 143–152.

Cohen, W.M., Levinthal, D.A., 1989. Innovation and learning: The two faces of R&D. Economic Journal 99, 569–596.

Cohen, W.M., Florida, R., Randazzese, L., Walsh, J., 1997. Industry and the academy: Uneasy partners in the cause of technological advance. In: Noll, R. (Ed.), Challenge to the University. Brookings Institution Press, Washington, D.C.

A.N. Link, J.T. Scott / Int. J. Ind. Organ. 21 (2003) 1323–1356 1355

Danilov, V.J., 1971. The research park shake-out. Industrial Research 13, 1–4.

Davies, S., 1979. The Diffusion of Process Innovations. Cambridge University Press, Cambridge.

Dixon, R.J., 1980. Hybrid corn revisited. Econometrica 48, 145–146.

Feldman, M., 1999. The new economics of innovation, spillovers and agglomeration: A review of empirical studies. Economics of Innovation and New Technology 8, 5–25.

Feldman, M., Lichtenberg, F., 2002. Innovation, imitation and distance in the pharmaceutical industry. Mimeograph, Johns Hopkins University.

Geroski, P.A., 2000. Models of technology diffusion. Research Policy 29, 603–625.

Gibb, M.J., 1985. Science Parks and Innovation Centres: Their Economic and Social Impact. Elsevier, Amsterdam.

Grayson, L., 1993. Science Parks: An Experiment in High Technology Transfer. The British Library Board, London.

Guy, I., 1996a. A look at Aston Science Park. Technovation 16, 217–218.

Guy, I., 1996b. New ventures on an ancient campus. Technovation 16, 269–270.

Hall, B.H., Link, A.N., Scott, J.T., 2000. Universities as research partners. NBER Working Paper 7643.

Hall, B.H., Link, A.N., Scott, J.T., 2003. Universities as research partners. Review of Economics and Statistics 85, 485–491.

Link, A.N., 1995. A Generosity of Spirit: The Early History of the Research Triangle Park. University of North Carolina Press for the Research Triangle Park Foundation, Research Triangle Park.

Link, A.N., 1996. Research joint ventures: Patterns from Federal Register filings. Review of Industrial Organization 11, 617–628.

Link, A.N., 2002. From Seed To Harvest: The History of the Growth of the Research Triangle Park. University of North Carolina Press for the Research Triangle Park Foundation, Research Triangle Park.

Link, A.N., Scott, J.T., 2003. The growth of Research Triangle Park. Small Business Economics 20, 167–175.

Löfsten, H., Lindelöf, P., 2002. Science parks and the growth of new technology-based firms— Academic-industry links, innovation and markets. Research Policy 31, 859–876.

Luger, M.I., Goldstein, H.A., 1991. Technology in the Garden. University of North Carolina Press, Chapel Hill.

Maddala, G.S., 1983. Limited Dependent and Qualitative Variables in Econometrics. Cambridge University Press, Cambridge.

Massey, D., Qunitas, P., Wield, D., 1992. High-tech Fantasies: Science Parks in Society, Science and Space. Routledge, London.

Monck, C.S.P., Porter, R.B., Quintas, P., Storey, D.J., Wynartczyk, P., 1988. Science Parks and the Growth of High Technology Firms. Croom Helm, London.

Morgan, R.P., 1998. University research contributions to industry: The faculty view. In: Blair, P., Frosch, R. (Eds.), Trends in Industrial Innovation: Industry Perspectives & Policy Implications. Sigma Xi, The Scientific Research Society, Research Triangle Park, pp. 163–170.

Mowery, D.C., Teece, D.J., 1996. Strategic alliances and industrial research. In: Rosenbloom, R., Spenser, W. (Eds.), Engines of Innovation: U.S. Industrial Research at the End of an Era. Harvard Business School, Boston, pp. 111–129.

National Science Board, 2000. Science & Engineering Indicators—2000. National Science Foundation, Arlington, Virginia.

Nelson, R.R., 2001. Observations on the post-Bayh–Dole rise of patenting at American universities. Journal of Technology Transfer 26, 13–19.

Phillimore, J., 1999. Beyond the linear view of innovation in science park evaluation: An analysis of Western Australian Technology Park. Technovation 19, 673–680.

Poyago-Theotoky, J., Beath, J., Siegel, D.S., 2002. Universities and fundamental research: Reflections on the growth of university–industry partnerships. Oxford Review of Economic Policy 18, 10–21.

Price, D.J. de Solla, 1963. Little Science, Big Science. Columbia University Press, New York.

Saxenian, A.L., 1994. Regional Advantage. Harvard University Press, Cambridge.

Siegel, D.S., Thursby, J.G., Thursby, M.C., Ziedonis, A.A., 2001. In: Symposium On Organizational Issues in University–Industry Technology Transfer. Journal of Technology Transfer, Vol. 1–3.

Siegel, D.S., Westhead, P., Wright, M., 2003. Science parks and the performance of new technology-based firms: A review of recent U.K. evidence and an agenda for future research. Small Business Economics 20, 177–184.

StataCorp, 2001. Stata Statistical Software: Release 7.0, Vol. 3. Stata Corporation, College Station, Texas.

Stephan, P.E., 2001. Educational implications of university–industry technology transfer. Journal of Technology Transfer 26, 199–205.

Sternberg, R., 1990. The impact of innovation centres on small technology-based firms: The example of the Federal Republic of Germany. Small Business Economics 2, 105–118.

United Kingdom Science Park Association (UKSPA), 1985. Science Park Directory. UKSPA, Sutton Coldfield.

U.S. General Accounting Office, 1983. The Federal Role in Fostering University–Industry Cooperation. GAO, Washington, D.C.

Vedovello, C., 1997. Science parks and university–industry interaction: Geographical proximity between the agents as a driving force. Technovation 17, 491–502.

Wallsten, S., 2001. An empirical test of geographic knowledge spillovers using geographic information systems and firm-level data. Regional Science and Urban Economics 31, 571–599.

Wessner, C.W. (Ed.), 1999. A Review of the Sandia Science and Technology Park Initiative. National Research Council, Washington, D.C.

Wessner, C.W. (Ed.), 2001. A Review of the New Initiatives at the NASA Ames Research Center: Summary of A Workshop. National Research Council, Washington, D.C.

Westhead, P., 1997. R&D 'inputs' and 'outputs' of technology-based firms located on and off science parks. R&D Management 27, 45–62.

Westhead, P., Batstone, S., 1998. Independent technology-based firms: The perceived benefits of a science park location. Urban Studies 35, 2197–2219.

Westhead, P., Cowling, M., 1995. Employment change in independent owner-managed high-technology firms in Great Britain. Small Business Economics 7, 111–140.

Westhead, P., Storey, D.J., 1994. An Assessment of Firms Located On and Off Science Parks in the United Kingdom. HMSO, London.

Westhead, P., Storey, D.J., Cowling, M., 1995. An exploratory analysis of the factors associated with the survival of independent high-technology firms in Great Britain. In: Chittenden, F., Robertson, M., Marshall, I. (Eds.), Small Firms: Partnerships For Growth. Paul Chapman, London, pp. 63–99.

[2]

ELSEVIER

Research Policy 34 (2005) 1106–1112

www.elsevier.com/locate/econbase

Opening the ivory tower's door: An analysis of the determinants of the formation of U.S. university spin-off companies

Albert N. Link [a,*], John T. Scott [b,1]

[a] *Department of Economics, University of North Carolina at Greensboro, Greensboro, NC 27412, USA*

[b] *Department of Economics, Dartmouth College, Hanover, NH 03755, USA*

Abstract

This paper presents findings from an analysis of the determinants of the formation of university spin-off companies within the university's research park. We find that university spin-off companies are a greater proportion of the companies in older parks and in parks that are associated with richer university research environments. We also find that university spin-off companies are a larger proportion of companies in parks that are geographically closer to their university and in parks that have a biotechnology focus.

© 2005 Elsevier B.V. All rights reserved.

Keywords: University spin-offs; Research park; Biotechnology

1. Introduction

Since the passage of the Bayh–Dole Act in 1980 in the United States, technology transfer activities at universities have taken center stage. The extant literature has focused on patenting activities as a general trend and as a university-specific response to the Act (Nelson, 2001; Hall, 2005; Mowery and Sampat, 2005), and on the establishment and operations of university technology transfer offices (Siegel et al., 2003). One technology transfer activity that has received lit-

tle attention, either in the United States or in other industrialized countries, is the formation of university spin-off companies on university research parks.[2] This is surprising because technology transfer has become a dominant strategy in U.S. universities over the past 25 years.[3] To emphasize further the economic importance of technology transfer associated with new firms located in parks, the Science Park Administration Act

---

[2] A second area that has received little attention, and however, is beyond the scope of this paper, is the impact of university spin-off companies on both the revenue growth of the university and the economic growth of the region.

[3] Deuker (1997) makes a case that the development of biomedical technologies was the genesis of technology transfer activity in U.S. universities.

---

* Corresponding author. Tel.: +1 336 334 5146.
 E-mail addresses: al_link@uncg.edu (A.N. Link), john.t.scott@dartmouth.edu (J.T. Scott).
 [1] Tel.: +1 603 646 2941.

0048-7333/$ – see front matter © 2005 Elsevier B.V. All rights reserved.
doi:10.1016/j.respol.2005.05.015

A.N. Link, J.T. Scott / Research Policy 34 (2005) 1106–1112   1107

of 2004, S.2737, decrees that high technology clustering "... is in the best interest of the Nation ..." (U.S.
Congress, 2004).

In the United States, the preponderance of related
research has been case-based, focusing almost exclusively on spin-off activity in high technology cluster areas such as Silicon Valley, Route 128 around
Boston, and Research Triangle Park (Kennedy, 2000;
Lee et al., 2000; Link, 1995, 2002; Link and Scott,
2003a; Roberts, 1991; Saxenian, 1994).[4] This paper
departs from the case-based approach and investigates,
in a systematic yet exploratory manner, characteristics associated with university differences in the formation of spin-off companies, specifically university-
based companies that locate in the university's research
park.

Our specific focus on university research parks is
important because they contribute critically to the U.S.
national innovation system. Parks enhance knowledge
spillovers between universities and tenant firms, and
parks enhance regional economic growth and make
markets more competitive (Link, 2002).

In Section 2, we posit a model of the determinants
of the formation of university spin-off companies. The
data used to estimate the model are described and the
estimates are presented in Section 3. The paper concludes with summary observations in Section 4 along
with a call for future work on this previously neglected
topic.

Spin-off companies are found to be concentrated
more in older parks and in parks that are associated
with richer university research environments. We also
find that spin-off companies are concentrated more in
parks that are geographically closer to their university
and in parks that have a biotechnology focus.

2. A Model of spin-off company formation in university research parks

We proffer the following definition of a university
research park:[5]

A university research park is a cluster of technology-
based organizations that locate on or near a university
campus in order to benefit from the university's knowledge base and ongoing research. The university not
only transfers knowledge but expects to develop knowledge more effectively given the association with the
tenants in the research park.

Generally, if the park is on or adjacent to a university campus, the university owns the park land and
either oversees, or at least advises on, aspects of the
activities that take place in the park as well as on the
strategic direction of the park's growth. When the park
is located off campus, it is often the case that the park
land is owned by a private venture – and sold or leased
to tenants – but the university has typically contributed
financial capital to its formation and/or intellectual capital to its operation; therefore, there are elements of an
administrative relationship between the university and
such research parks.

Universities are motivated to develop a research
park by the possibility of financial gain associated with
technology transfer, the opportunity to have faculty and
students interact at the applied level with technology-
based organizations, and by their responsibility of contributing to a regional-based economic development
effort. Research organizations are motivated to locate
in a research park to gain access to faculty, students, and
research equipment, and to foster research synergies.

Based on the definition above, the population of
81 currently active research parks, as defined in the
National Science Foundation database on university
research parks, through 2002 is shown in Fig. 1.[6]
Notable in the figure are the following parks: Stanford
Research Park (established in 1951), Cornell Business & Technology Park (established in 1952), and the
Research Triangle Park of North Carolina (established
in 1959). Also notable in the figure is the increase in
park formation that began in the late-1970s and accelerated in the early 1980s in response to the increase in

---

[4] See also the excellent reviews of the literature in Clarysse et al.
(2005), Degroof and Roberts (2004), and Johansson et al. (in press).
[5] This is the definition that will be used by the National Science
Board in its forthcoming *Science and Engineering Indicators*, 2006.
This section draws directly from Link and Scott (in press); therein is
a more detailed explanation of the development of this definition.

[6] The genesis for the construction of this database came from
recommendations at the National Science Foundation-sponsored
Research Park Indicators Workshop, convened at the University of
North Carolina at Greensboro in November 2002. Based on the findings from the workshop, the National Science Foundation set forth
an initiative for Link to develop a national database on university
research parks.

A.N. Link, J.T. Scott / Research Policy 34 (2005) 1106–1112

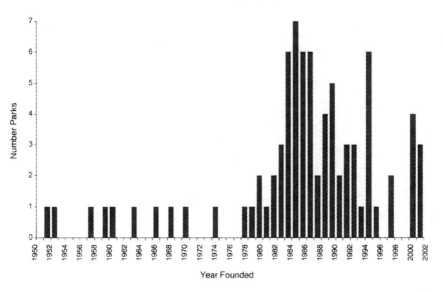

Fig. 1. Population of university research parks, by year founded (1951–2002) (*n* = 81).

real R&D performed in industry in the late 1970s and to several public policies designed to stimulate R&D and thus possibly park formations – the Bayh–Dole Act of 1980, the R&E tax credit in 1981 and its subsequent renewal, and the National Cooperative Research Act of 1984.

Danilov (1971) attributes the relatively long period from about 1960 to the early 1970s, during which the research park formation movement seemingly stalled, to a number of park efforts that failed as well as to the restraints on corporate R&D growth that coincided with a lackluster economy.

We view the formation of university spin-off companies as an output of university research related activity and an outcome of the university's purposive technology transfer efforts.[7] Our hypothesis is that there are two relevant sets of inputs to spin-off formations: the

research environment of the university and the characteristics of the research park to which the spin-off companies locate:

spin-offs $= f$(university research environment,

research park characteristics)   (1)

We offer two hypotheses about relationship (1). First, we hypothesize that the more research intensive the university, the greater the probability that faculty will innovate, and the more innovative the faculty, the greater the probability that technologies will develop around which a spin-off company could be based. Regarding the research environment of the university, DiGregorio and Shane (2003) emphasize that intellectually eminent universities generate more start-up companies.[8] To the extent that the university's research environment relates to its broader social network – especially an industrial social network – the research of Lockett et al. (2003) also supports our first hypothesis.

---

[7] Not all university spin-off companies are the result of the purposive activity of the university. It is also the case that faculty may establish a spin-off company because they cannot reach an intellectual property (IP) agreement with university administrators. As Hall et al. (2001) and Hertzfeld et al. (2003) have shown, IP issues associated with university research can be pronounced.

[8] Shane and Stuart (2002) argue that the overall resource environment of a university is important for the survival of start-ups, regardless of their location (See also Lerner, 2005).

A.N. Link, J.T. Scott / Research Policy 34 (2005) 1106–1112

Table 1
Description of variables ($n = 51$)

Name	Description	Mean	Range
Spin-offs	Percentage of park organizations that are university spin-off companies in year 2002	9.58	0–40
RD100	=1 if the university is a top 100 university in terms of R&D spending in 1999 (latest year of data available from the National Science Foundation)	0.61	0–1
Age	Age of the park in years from the date it was founded	16.80	0–50
Mileage	Miles from the university to the park	4.31	0–35
Prstate	=1 if university is private; 0 if university is state	0.18	0–1
Oper	=1 if the park is operated by the university; 0 if the park is operated by a foundation or private contractor	0.31	0–1
Techit	=1 if IT is the advertised dominant technology of park tenants; 0 otherwise	0.25	0–1
Techbio	=1 if bioscience is the advertised dominant technology of park tenants; 0 otherwise	0.27	0–1
Region[a]	$s = 1$ if the park is in the south, 0 otherwise; mw $= 1$ if the park is in the midwest, 0 otherwise; $w = 1$ if the park is in the west, 0 otherwise	$s = 0.33$; mw $= 0.24$; $w = 0.22$	0–1

[a] Following the U.S. Bureau of the Census classification, the northeast includes: Maine, Vermont, New Hampshire, Massachusetts, Rhode Island, Connecticut, New York, Pennsylvania, and New Jersey. The south includes: Delaware, Maryland, West Virginia, Virginia, Kentucky, Tennessee, North Carolina, South Carolina, Georgia, Alabama, Mississippi, Florida, Louisiana, Arkansas, Oklahoma, Texas, and the District of Columbia. The midwest includes: North Dakota, South Dakota, Nebraska, Kansas, Minnesota, Iowa, Missouri, Wisconsin, Illinois, Michigan, Indiana, and Ohio. And the West includes: Alaska, Washington, Oregon, California, Montana, Idaho, Nevada, Wyoming, Utah, Arizona, Colorado, New Mexico, and Hawaii.

Radosevich (1995) and Franklin et al. (2001) argue that an entrepreneurial environment is conducive for the formation of spin-off companies. To the extent that universities with older research parks have, over time, developed such an environment where entrepreneurial-like perception of opportunities is part of the park's culture,[9] then we hypothesize that the formation of university spin-off companies into the university's park will occur more often in older parks than in newer ones.

3. The dataset and the empirical findings

As part of the dataset on university research parks that we have developed for the National Science Foundation (Link and Scott, 2003b), information was collected on the percentage of current (in year 2002) park organizations that were university spin-off companies. This information was collected through interview surveys for 51 of the 81 U.S. research parks in the United

States (Fig. 1). Thus, with reference to Eq. (1), this information forms the dependent variable in our analysis.

We approximate the research environment of the university qualitatively. Each of the 51 universities in our dataset is classified as being one of the top 100 universities in terms of the level of R&D spending from all sources, or not. We approximate the age of the park as the number of years since its formation. We control for other university and park characteristics, such as: the distance, in miles, between the university and its research park; if the university is a private or a state university; if the research park is operated by the university or by a foundation or private contractor; the technology focus of the park if it has one; and the region of the country of the university and its park.

Thus, for estimation purposes, Eq. (1) becomes:

$$\text{spin-offs} = f(\text{RD100, age, mileage, prstate, oper,}$$
$$\text{techit, techbio, region}) \qquad (2)$$

Each of the variables is described in Table 1.
As noted in Table 1, spin-offs is a truncated variable between 0 and 100 although the dataset only contains

---

[9] See Hébert and Link (1998) for a discussion of the perception characteristic of an entrepreneur.

Table 2
Tobit Estimates from Eq. (2), $n = 51$ (standard errors in parentheses)

Variables	(1)	(2)	(3)
RD100	3.56* (1.82)	3.78** (1.78)	3.49* (1.80)
Mileage	0.65 (0.65)	–	–
Mileage^2	−0.10* (0.05)	−0.055*** (0.017)	−0.057*** (0.017)
Prstate	3.50 (3.17)	2.39 (2.21)	–
Oper	1.47 (1.88)	2.00 (1.86)	2.58 (1.79)
Age	0.76*** (0.09)	0.76*** (0.09)	0.80*** (0.08)
Techit	2.40 (2.15)	1.66 (2.11)	–
Techbio	4.82** (2.17)	4.46** (2.07)	3.86** (1.92)
South	1.15 (3.19)	–	–
Midwest	−0.74 (3.22)	–	–
West	1.93 (3.34)	–	–
Constant	−9.34** (3.78)	−7.58*** (2.24)	−7.22*** (2.17)
Tobin's sigma	5.27 (0.58)	5.38 (0.59)	5.49 (0.61)
Pseudo R^2	0.229	0.223	0.216
χ^2 (d.f.)	77.28 (11)***	75.17 (7)***	73.11 (5)***
log likelihood	−130.28	−131.34	−132.37

Note: There are 10 left-censored observations at spin-offs = 0 and 41 uncensored observations.
* Denotes significance at the 0.10 level.
** Denotes significance at the 0.05 level.
*** denotes significance at the 0.01 level. Tobin's sigma is the ancillary parameter σ for the Tobit model (Greene, 2003, pp. 764–766).

multiple observations at 0, thus Tobit is the appropriate econometric procedure.[10]

The Tobit estimates corresponding to three variations of Eq. (2) are in Table 2.[11] The results in column (1) are the full specification, while those in columns (2) and (3) delete insignificant variables. All three specifications are overall significant; our discussion focuses on the parsimonious specification in column (3) with comparisons to the other specifications.

The research environment of the university is significant, as hypothesized. More research-oriented universities, as measured by RD100, have within their research parks a greater proportion of tenants that are university spin-off companies. In alternative regressions, we dropped RD100 and included variables that alternatively distinguished research orientation by dividing the sample into top 10 R&D universities versus all others, and top 50 R&D universities and all others. These alternative R&D environment variables were never significant.[12]

Also, as hypothesized, older parks do have a greater percentage of tenants that are university spin-off companies. The variable *age* is highly significant.

[10] Tobit analysis allows us to model the need for an appropriate environment before any spin-offs at all appear. Without the appropriate circumstances, the dependent variable is 0; with the right environment, then the spin-offs' share exceeds 0, with the share being a function of the explanatory variables. Greene (2003, pp. 764–766) provides a general discussion of the Tobit model and its use with limited dependent variables such as our variable for the percentage of tenants that are university spin-off companies. Also, we do not have information for all parks on the number of tenants in the park. Thus, Eq. (2) is specified as a share equation because information on the number of spin-offs was not available.

[11] Selection from the population of 81 universities with research parks into our sample of 51 university research parks was not considered empirically. Either we were told by park directors that information on spin-offs was not available because it had not been collected, or we were unable to identify a park individual who could provide the requested information. Those variables – information was available or not, and an individual was available or not – of course predict response perfectly and cannot be used to explain the differences in the probability of response with the sample of 51 respondents. Our paper leaves for future research the specification of an underlying model of the determinants of response (factors that make it more or less likely that the information or a responding individual would be available) and the determination of whether the error in the probit model of response is correlated with the error in the Tobit model of the percentage of spin-off companies.

[12] These results are available on request from the authors. Also, we do not have consistent information on the level of R&D performed at universities. Selected data on this innovation measure are available from the National Science Foundation for those universities in the top 100, but for the other universities their websites generally report contradictory numbers. Thus, we chose to control for research environment of each university dichotomously.

A.N. Link, J.T. Scott / Research Policy 34 (2005) 1106–1112   1111

Our findings also indicate that distance matters. Those universities with research parks closer to their campus (i.e., mileage decreases) have a greater percentage of university spin-off companies, and this effect is non-linear. The empirical results suggest that technology also matters. The percentage of university spin-off companies is greater in research parks that have a biotechnology focus than in parks with either an information technology focus or in parks with no specific technology focus.

Finally, the above findings do not differ significantly across the different regions.

4. Summary observations and policy implications

Because this study is the first effort to quantify university spin-off formations into a university research park, our findings should be interpreted cautiously. However, our results are important not only because of their general descriptive interest, but also because they validate our conceptual arguments and signal university and research park characteristics associated with an aspect of technology transfer, namely technology that is transferred from the university as manifested in the form of companies rather than simply in the form of licensing fees to be paid to the university.

Interpreting our dependent variable as a signal of technology transfer embodied in companies raises the possibility that our model may omit at least one important explanatory variable, namely a variable capturing differences among universities' administrative incentives to appropriate technology returns simply with licensing fees as opposed to appropriating the technology returns through a start-up company in which the university could have an interest. Describing such different incentive structures is certainly one area for future research.[13]

Further, our analysis did not consider characteristics of spin-off companies other than whether each was

an information technology or biotechnology company. Describing spin-off company characteristics is a second area for future research. In addition to descriptions of the technologies, company ownership characteristics (e.g., is the spin-off company owned and managed by a faculty member or by a venture capitalist?) are possibly important. Also, are there important and systematic performance differences for university spin-off companies, and are those differences related to the company's location within or outside a research park?

These caveats aside, our finding that the percentage of university spin-off companies is relatively greater in research parks that have a biotechnology focus has important policy implications—regional economic development policy implications in particular. As noted by Link (2005), and others, the success of biotechnology clusters within several regions of the United States, and other industrialized nations, has led economic development planners in other regions to focus on biotechnology as a strategic technology for stimulating growth in their region. Of course, fundamental to such an imitative policy strategy being successful is a clear understanding of how established clusters were developed, the research capabilities of the university(ies) or institute(s) in the planning regions, and the ability of such university(ies) or institute(s) in the planning regions to emulate what others have done.

What others have done is spin-off dedicated biotechnology firms into juxtaposed areas or parks in order to take critical advantage of the tacit knowledge that resides in the university(ies) or institute(s) scientists. Thus, understanding characteristics of university research parks conducive for spin-off formations is a critical first step, or planning guideline, especially relevant to a regional biotechnology growth strategy or policy. Perhaps the findings in this paper will provide the seeds for such an understanding.

Acknowledgement

We gratefully acknowledge the National Science Foundation for financial support to develop the database used herein. We also appreciate comments and suggestions from Don Siegel, Andy Lockett, Mike Wright, two anonymous referees and selected participants at the Technology Transfer Society meetings in Albany, N.Y., September 2004.

---

[13] It was suggested that Eq. (2) should control for the physical opportunity of parks to house spin-off companies and for the relative incentive of parks to encourage or even invite spin-off companies to locate. This is a reasonable issue, but unfortunately our data do not allow us to test these ideas. We have no measures of acres available or tenant space that is vacant. Controlling for park size per se will not address this point.

References

Clarysse, B., Wright, M., Lockett, A., van de Velde, E., Vohora, A., 2005. Spinning out new ventures: a typology of incubation strategies from European research institutions. Journal of Business Venturing 20, 183–216.

Danilov, V.J., 1971. The research park shake-out. Industrial Research 13, 1–4.

Degroof, J., Roberts, E.B., 2004. Spinning-off new ventures from academic institutions in areas with weak entrepreneurial infrastructure: insights on the impact of spin-off policies on the growth-orientation of ventures. Journal of Technology Transfer 29, 327–352.

Deuker, K.S., 1997. Biobusiness on campus: commercialization of university-developed biomedical technologies. Food and Law Journal 52, 453–509.

DiGregorio, D., Shane, S., 2003. Why do some universities generate more start-ups than others? Research Policy 32, 209–227.

Franklin, S., Wright, M., Lockett, A., 2001. Academic and surrogate entrepreneurs in university spin-out companies. Journal of Technology Transfer 26, 127–141.

Greene, W.H., 2003. Econometric Analysis. Prentice Hall, Upper Saddle River, New Jersey.

Hall, B.H., 2005. Exploring the patent explosion. Journal of Technology Transfer 30, 35–48.

Hall, B.H., Link, A.N., Scott, J.T., 2001. Barriers inhibiting industry from partnering with universities: evidence from the Advanced Technology Program. Journal of Technology Transfer 26, 87–98.

Hébert, R.F., Link, A.N., 1998. The Entrepreneur: Mainstream Views and Radical Critiques. Praeger Publishers, New York.

Hertzfeld, H., Link, A.N., Vonortas, N., 2003. Intellectual property protection mechanisms in research partnerships. Mimeograph.

Johansson, M., Jabob, M., Hellström, T., in press. The strength of strong ties: university spin-offs and the significance of historical relations. Journal of Technology Transfer.

Kennedy, M., 2000. Understanding Silicon Valley. The Anatomy of an Entrepreneurial Region. Stanford Business Books, Stanford, CA.

Lee, C.M., Miller, W.F., Hancock, M.G., Rowen, H.S., 2000. The Silicon Valley Hedge: A Habitat for Innovation and Entrepreneurship. Stanford University Press, Stanford, CA.

Lerner, J., 2005. The university and the start-up: lessons from the past two decades. Journal of Technology Transfer 30, 49–56.

Link, A.N., 1995. A Generosity of Spirit: The Early History of the Research Triangle Park. The Research Triangle Foundation, Research Triangle Park, NC.

Link, A.N., 2002. From Seed to Harvest: The Growth of the Research Triangle Park. The Research Triangle Foundation, Research Triangle Park, NC.

Link, A.N., 2005. Economic Factors Related to the Development and Commercialization of Biotechnologies. Technical Report 05-0204, Center for Applied Economics, University of Kansas.

Link, A.N., Scott, J.T., 2003a. The growth of Research Triangle Park. Small Business Economics 20, 167–175.

Link, A.N., Scott, J.T., 2003b. U.S. science parks: the diffusion of an innovation and its effects on the academic missions of universities. International Journal of Industrial Organization 21, 1323–1356.

Link, A.N., Scott, J.T., in press. U.S. university research parks. Journal of Productivity Analysis.

Lockett, A., Wright, M., Franklin, S., 2003. Technology transfer and universities' spin-out strategies. Small Business Economics 20, 185–200.

Mowery, D.C., Sampat, B.N., 2005. The Bayh–Dole Act of 1980 and university-industry technology transfer: a model for other OECD governments? Journal of Technology Transfer 30, 115–127.

Nelson, R.R., 2001. Observations on the post Bayh–Dole rise of patenting at American universities. Journal of Technology Transfer 26, 13–19.

Radosevich, R., 1995. A model for entrepreneurial spin-offs from public technology sources. International Journal of Technology Management 10, 879–893.

Roberts, E.B., 1991. Entrepreneurs in High Technology: Lessons from MIT and Beyond. Oxford University Press, New York.

Saxenian, A., 1994. Regional Advantage: Culture and Competition in Silicon Valley and Route 128. Harvard University Press, Cambridge, MA.

Shane, S., Stuart, T., 2002. Organizational endowments and the performance of university start-ups. Management Science 48, 154–170.

Siegel, D., Waldman, D., Link, A.N., 2003. Assessing the impact of organizational practices on the productivity of university technology transfer offices: an exploratory study. Research Policy 32, 27–48.

U.S. Congress, Science Park Administration Act of 2004. S.2737, introduced in the Senate of the United States, July 22, 2004.

[3]

J Prod Anal (2006) 25:43–55
DOI 10.1007/s11123-006-7126-x

U.S. university research parks

Albert N. Link · John T. Scott

Abstract University research parks are important as a mechanism for the transfer of academic research findings, as a source of knowledge spillovers, and as a catalyst for national and regional economic growth. We develop a model to describe the growth, or productivity, of research parks, and we test this model using the newly constructed National Science Foundation database on university research parks. We find that parks closer to the university, operated by a private organization, and with a specific technology focus — information technology in particular — grow faster than the average of 8.4% per year.

JEL Classification O33, O31

Keywords Research park · Science park · University research · Technology transfer

A. N. Link (✉)
Department of Economics,
University of North Carolina,
Greensboro,
Greensboro, NC 27412
E-mail: al_link@uncg.edu

J. T. Scott
Department of Economics,
Dartmouth College,
Hanover, NH 03755
E-mail: John.t.scott@dartmouth.edu

Introduction

University research parks (URPs) are important as a mechanism for the transfer of academic research findings, as a source of knowledge spillovers, and as a catalyst for national and regional economic growth.[1] Despite these contributions, there are few managerial benchmarks to follow to ensure the growth and possible success of university research parks; and, more generally, the place of URPs in the U.S. innovation system is not well understood. In large part, this gap in understanding stems from the lack of well-defined constructs about what constitutes a university research park, the variety of goals of a research park, and the general lack of clear metrics for measuring their success.[2] This paper, using the newly constructed national database on

---

[1] This generalization follows from the rich economics literature on the impact of basic research, which is performed in universities for the large part, on the productivity growth of firms that use that research (Griliches 1986; Link 1981; Link and Siegel 2003; Mansfield 1980) and the economic development literature on the impact of research clusters on regional economic growth (Porter 2001; Swann et al. 1998).

[2] These points were recently emphasized at the National Science Foundation-sponsored science park indicators workshop, convened at the University of North Carolina at Greensboro in November 2002. Based on the findings from the workshop, the National Science Foundation set forth an initiative to develop a national database on university research parks. This database, constructed for the National Science Foundation by Link, forms the basis for the analysis presented herein.

 Springer

J Prod Anal (2006) 25:43–55

university research parks, represents, in our opinion, an initial step in filling this void.

In the following section, we posit a synthesized definition of a URP. Then, in section 'The growth of university research parks', we develop a model of park growth, where park growth is widely accepted as a measure of park productivity or success.[3] We test the model using the newly constructed National Science Foundation database on university research parks. Finally, in section 'Discussion of the findings', we conclude the paper with a discussion of the potential usefulness of our findings for university and research park administrators who are strategically involved in the development of parks, and with an initial discussion of university research parks as an element of our national innovation system.

A definition of a university research park

A number of definitions of a research or science park have been proffered by various institutions or associations. See the Appendix for such definitions. In this paper, we proffer the following succinct definition of a university research park:[4]

> *A university research park is a cluster of technology-based organizations that locate on or near a university campus in order to benefit from the university's knowledge base and ongoing research. The university not only transfers knowledge but expects to develop knowledge more effectively given the association with the tenants in the research park.*

Generally, if the park is on or adjacent to a university campus the university owns the park land and either oversees, or at least advises on, aspects of the

activities that take place in the park as well as on the strategic direction of the park's growth.[5,6] When the park is located off campus, it is often the case that the park land is owned by a private venture — and sold or leased to tenants — but the university had contributed financial capital to its formation and/or intellectual capital to its operation; therefore, there are elements of an administrative relationship between the university and these research parks.[7]

Universities are motivated to develop a research park on their own or in partnership by the possibility of financial gain associated with technology transfer, the opportunity to have faculty and students interact at the applied level with technology-based organizations, and by the responsibility of contributing to a regional-based economic development effort.[8,9] Research organizations are motivated to locate in a research park to gain access to faculty, students, and research equipment, and to foster research synergies.

Based on the definition above, the population of currently active URPs, as defined in the National Science Foundation database on university research parks, is

---

[3] Link and Link (2003), based on extensive interviews with URP directors, and Link and Scott (2003b), based on extensive interviews with university provosts, conclude that employee growth is the dominant metric that those associated with a university research park use to quantify its productivity or success over time. Emphasis on employment is intuitive, since most research parks are associated with a state university (discussed below), and a part of the motivation for the university to establish the park is regional economic growth. Technology transfer-related metrics (e.g., university start-ups or licensed technologies to park tenants) or student placements are important, but are rarely considered as productivity or success measures.

[4] This is the definition that will be used by the National Science Board in its forthcoming *Science and Engineering Indicators, 2006.*

[5] Such oversight may include tenant criteria for leasing space in the park (Link and Link 2003). Such criteria may specify particular technologies or state that the tenant must maintain an active research relationship with university departments and their students.

[6] Approximately 6% of existing parks are formally affiliated with more than one university (e.g., Duke University, North Carolina State University, and University of North Carolina have a formal relationship with Research Triangle Park.)

[7] The form of the relationship between the university and the research park can be very explicit, as in the case when the university owns the park land and buildings and leases space to criteria-specific tenants; or very implicit, as in the case when the privately owned park is juxtaposed to the university and the university owns and operates buildings on park land. Certainly, a physical relationship between the university and the park does not necessarily imply an administrative or strategic relationship. The inability to quantify all of the dimensions of the dynamics of such relationships is an issue suggesting cautious interpretation of the quantitative analysis below.

[8] In most cases, regional economic development is one justification of the creation of a university-related research park. Based on information from university websites and from surveys of park directors, in approximately 11% of the cases the research park's location was in either a distressed urban area or on an abandoned public-sector area (e.g., Yale University's Science Park is located in what had been an abandoned Winchester gun factory in New Haven).

[9] Just over 50% of university-related research parks were initially funded with public moneys. Of those, the public sector supported about 70% of the initial park cost.

Springer

J Prod Anal (2006) 25:43–55

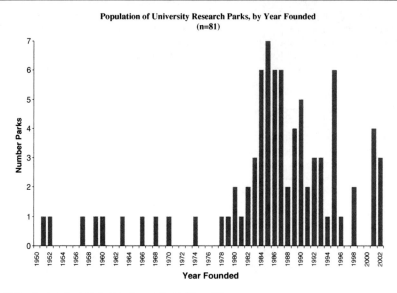

Fig. 1 Population of university research parks, by year founded ($n = 81$)

shown in Fig. 1. Notable in the figure are the following parks: Stanford Research Park (established in 1951), Cornell Business & Technology Park (established in 1952); and the Research Triangle Park of North Carolina (established in 1959). Also notable in the figure is the increase in park formation that began in the late-1970s and accelerated in the early 1980s.[10]

During the early and mid-1970s, real industrial R&D spending decreased. Based on National Science Foundation data reported in the National Science Board's (2002) *Science and Engineering Indicators, 2002*, the real R&D performed in industry decreased in 1970 and 1971, and then again in 1974 and 1975.[11] It was not until 1977 that real R&D performed in industry was able to return to its 1969-pre-decline level, and relatedly, in 1978 park formations began to increase. It is reasonable to hypothesize that private sector demand for

research park space increased during this R&D growth period because firms were looking for cooperative research partnerships to expand their research portfolios, as opposed to development portfolios.

The period of the relatively rapid increase in park formation corresponds to a period of significant public policy initiatives to encourage university-with-industry relationships, increases in industrial R&D spending, and the formation of cooperative research partnerships. The Bayh-Dole Act was passed in 1980, the R&E tax credit was enacted in 1981, and the National Cooperative Research Act was legislated in 1984.[12] All of these public initiatives fostered additional private sec-

---

[10] Danilov (1971) attributes the relatively long period from about 1960 to the early 1970s, during which the research park movement seemingly stalled, to a number of park efforts that failed as well as to the restraints on corporate R&D growth because of a lackluster economy.

[11] R&D can be financed directly or indirectly from firm debt, equity, cash flow, and the federal government. See National Science Board (2002), Appendix Table 4.4.

[12] The University and Small Business Patent Procedure Act of 1980, known as the Bayh-Dole Act, reformed federal patent policy by providing increased incentives for the diffusion of federally funded innovation results. In particular, universities were permitted to obtain titles to innovations developed with government funds. The R&E tax credit of 1981 provided a tax incentive (originally 25% and today 20%) to firms that increased their R&D expenditures over those made in previous years. And, the National Cooperative Research Act of 1984 encouraged the formation of research joint ventures (RJVs) among U.S. firms — and universities were partners in many of those ventures. RJVs, if subjected to criminal or civil antitrust action, would be evaluated under a rule of reason, and if found to fail a rule of reason, they would be subjected to actual rather than treble damages.

🍎 Springer

J Prod Anal (2006) 25:43–55

tor R&D activity, which could have stimulated states and universities to establish potentially beneficial locations for that R&D to take place.

Not shown in the figure, but important for an overall understanding of the trend in the establishment of university research parks is the fact that there are an additional 27 parks — 30% of the existing population — in the planning stage.[13] These parks are being structured by both leading research universities and universities that have traditionally had teaching as a primary mission. Our interpretation of this renewed growth in parks is influenced by discussions with park directors from both established parks and from planned parks. Increasingly, universities are adopting alternative strategies for the transfer of their own technologies, and success will increase the universities' revenues.

The growth of university research parks

The growth model

Based on the data underlying Fig. 1, we model the growth of URPs over time as:

$$y(t) = ae^{gt}e^{\varepsilon} \quad (1)$$

where $y(t)$ is the research park's employment t years after it was established, a is the minimum efficient start-up scale for a research park, g is the annual rate of growth of the park, and ε is a random error term.

The growth rate for a park is hypothesized to be a function of various explanatory variables, x_1 to x_k, as

$$(\partial y(t)/\partial t)/y(t) = g = b_0 + b_1 x_1 + \cdots + b_k x_k \quad (2)$$

From Eq. (1):

$$\ln y(t) = \ln a + gt + \varepsilon \quad (3)$$

Substituting Eq. (2) for g into Eq. (3):

$$\ln y(t) = \ln a + b_0 t + b_1 x_1 t + \cdots + b_k x_k t + \varepsilon \quad (4)$$

Equation (4) is the growth model estimated in this paper.[14]

---

[13] Only two of the 27 planned parks are at private universities.

[14] Our approach yields a sensible, estimable growth rate. An alternative to the growth model in Eq. (1) is a production function representation of park output. If employment, y, is interpreted as park output, and if inputs include park age, t, and a vector of other institutional variables, $\mathbf{X}$, then:

$$y_t = f(t, \mathbf{X})$$

The definition of variables

The variables, x_1 to x_k, are motivated by previous empirical research and economic reasoning; the variables are described in Table 1 and discussed below.

Data used in the estimation of Eq. (4) came from a number of sources. Published data from associations and park web sites were used initially to identify the population of university research parks. However, neither of these sources was complete, and, in most cases, not current. The information was then supplemented through survey interviews (mail and telephone) with park directors and university research administrators or designates.[15] Whenever contradictory information was discovered, it was assumed that the interview information was correct.

The growth model above is formulated in terms of time, t, which is the age of the park. Data on park employment was generally available for 2 years, 1997 and 2002. In most instances, t is the number of years since the park was founded to year 2002.[16] In those cases when only

---

If this functional form is Cobb-Douglas:

$$y_t = t^{\alpha} X_1^{\beta_1} \cdots X_k^{\beta_k}$$

then after taking logarithms:

$$\ln y_t = \alpha \ln t + \beta_1 \ln X_1 + \cdots + \beta_k \ln X_k$$

While this production function could be estimated, it does not yield a sensible estimate of park growth because of the constraint that the functional form imposes on employment as a function of time. The functional form posits an elasticity (α) of employment with respect to time. The use here of elasticity with respect to time is not sensible, because the percentage change in time is not a meaningful concept in this context. The growth rate (α/t in the production function model of this footnote) in employment would therefore be constrained to fall as time increases. One could use the model to derive growth rates for each different age (the variable t) for a park. If one had a sample for which all parks were the same age, t would be dropped from the model and the estimated intercept term would be the estimate of $\alpha \ln t$, from which an estimate of the parameter α could be derived. Alternatively, the model could include the variable $\ln t$, but be fitted without an intercept, with the coefficient estimated for $\ln t$ being the estimate of α. For the usual samples with parks of many different ages (many different values for t), dummy variables could theoretically be used to estimate a different value of α for the parks of each different age. However, degrees of freedom will typically not be sufficient to allow the estimation, so as a practical matter the approach is not feasible.

[15] Link and Link (2003) and Link and Scott (2003b) report findings from a portion of this field research.

[16] Data are sporadically available on the year that the first tenant entered the park. We know from numerous interviews and park

J Prod Anal (2006) 25:43–55   47

Table 1 Description of Variables ($n = 81$)	Name	Description	Mean	Range
	y_t	Employment level in either 1997 or 2002, depending on latest data availability	2805.57	1–45,000
	t	Age of the park measured by the number of years since the park was founded; this variable is constructed to correspond to y_t	15.05	0–51
	mile	Miles from park to university; 4 of 81 parks are associated with more than one university and in those cases mileage is to the nearest university	4.56	0–35
	oper	=1 if the park is operated by the university; 0 if park operated by a foundation or private contractor	0.33	0–1
	nouniv	Number of universities associated with the park	1.10	1–4
	techit	=1 if IT is the advertized dominant technology of park tenants; 0 otherwise	0.17	0–1
	techbio	=1 if bioscience is the advertized dominant technology of park tenants; 0 otherwise	0.20	0–1
	regw	=1 if university is in West; 0 otherwise	0.22	0–1
	regne	=1 if university is in Northeast; 0 otherwise	0.21	0–1
	regmw	=1 if university is in Midwest; 0 otherwise	0.23	0–1
Note: In the context of our growth model, each of the above variables is weighted by the age, t, of the park	*incub*	=1 if incubator located in the park; 0 otherwise	0.56	0–1
	statepr	=1 if university is state; 0 if university private	0.83	0–1

1997 data were available, *t* was calculated as the number of years since the park was founded to year 1997.[17]

The variable *mile* quantifies the geographical relationship between the university and the park. Twenty-eight parks from the population of 81 university research parks (see Fig. 1) are located on the university campus. Another eight are juxtaposed to the university campus (within 1 mile of the campus). Adams and Jaffe (1996) suggest that communication costs related to collaborative R&D activity increase with distance. Wallsten (2001) shows geographic proximity to other successful innovating firms, as evidenced by firms receiving a Small Business Innovation Research

(SBIR) award, is associated with a firm's own success. These papers, as well as the works of Feldman (1999), Feldman and Lichtenberg (2002), and Adams (2002) motivate the inclusion of the mileage variable. We hypothesize that the closer a park is to the university the greater the knowledge flows among park tenants and the university and thus the more attractive the park for new tenants and employment growth. In the context of our growth model, mileage, represented in the interaction term *mile*$^*t$, should enter negatively.

Twenty-seven of the 81 parks are operated by the university, and the remaining parks are operated by a non-university related foundation or a private contractor. Bozeman and Crow (1991); Bozeman (2000); Hall et al. (2001, 2003); and Siegel et al. (1999, 2003) suggest that the red tape associated with a bureaucracy, a state university in particular, is often an insurmountable barrier. As such, private sector firms could be deterred from entering the park for lack of willingness, or an ability, to cope. We hypothesize that parks operated by the university will experience slower growth because of, among other things, organizational bottlenecks created in the park by the university and a general lack of expertise on the part of the university in economic development activities. Alternatively, university oper-

---

histories, that there is a long and variable lag between a park's founding and its first tenant. For example, the first tenant located in Research Triangle Park, NC in 1965, 6 years after the park was founded (Link 1995; Link and Scott 2003a).

[17] As shown in Fig. 1, three parks were founded in 2002; however, employment in those parks in that year was 0. Of the four parks founded in 2001, employment in one was 0 in 2002. And, one park founded in 1992 had 0 employees in 1997 and no information could be obtained for employment in 2002. For those five cases, employment was set at 1 to account for the known fact that there was a park director in each. This is seen in Table 1 in the range of values for y_t, and in the text's discussion of the various samples used in Table 2.

🍃 Springer

ations may be associated with more challenging technology transfer and hence slower overall growth of the park. The alternative interpretation here is controlled to some extent by the variable *incub* as discussed below. With either interpretation, in the context of our growth model, the variable indicating whether or not the park is operated by a university, in the interaction term *oper*t*, should enter negatively.

Four of the 81 parks are associated with more than one university. If the number of universities proxies economies of scale and scope in gaining access to faculty, students, and research equipment, and in fostering research synergies, then *nouniv* t* should enter positively in our model.

It is not uncommon for newly founded parks to have a technology focus. This, according to park directors, is a competitive strategy to lure new companies away from more established infrastructures.[18] Among the population of parks, 30 are either focused on building a cluster of information technology (*it*) or bioscience companies (*bio*). We offer no hypothesis about how such a technology-focused strategy has affected the productivity of parks. Thus, the interaction terms *techit*t* and *techbio*t* are viewed as control variables.

Also held constant are regional dummies interacted with time, *t*: *regw*t, regne*t, regmw*t*;[19] if there is an incubator facility located in the park, *incub* t*;[20]

[18] The majority of the 27 planned parks tentatively state a technology focus.

[19] Following the U.S. Bureau of the Census classification, the Northeast includes: Maine, Vermont, New Hampshire, Massachusetts, Rhode Island, Connecticut, New York, Pennsylvania, and New Jersey. The South, captured statistically in the intercept term, includes: Delaware, Maryland, West Virginia, Virginia, Kentucky, Tennessee, North Carolina, South Carolina, Georgia, Alabama, Mississippi, Florida, Louisiana, Arkansas, Oklahoma, Texas, and the District of Columbia. The Midwest includes: North Dakota, South Dakota, Nebraska, Kansas, Minnesota, Iowa, Missouri, Wisconsin, Illinois, Michigan, Indiana, and Ohio. And the West includes: Alaska, Washington, Oregon, California, Montana, Idaho, Nevada, Wyoming, Utah, Arizona, Colorado, New Mexico, and Hawaii.

[20] Nekar and Shane (2003) show that newly founded firms are more likely to survive in the presence of an incubator, but to our knowledge there is no literature on how incubators are associated with the growth of clusters of organizations. We do know, however, that incubators are established to assist newly established firms and university spin-offs, both of which are small in size and are likely to grow very slowly while within the research park. As discussed in section 'The empiral results', success and rapid growth for companies initially assisted by incubators may come after they leave the park.

and if the university is state or private, *statepr* t*.[21] These variables are included in our model to control for alternative park and university characteristics. We offer no set hypotheses about the direction or magnitude of their impact on park growth, although we have noted the possibilities that (1) state universities may be more accountable for research and technology transfer (with positive effects on productivity) and — in part for that reason — may have more bureaucratic red tape (with negative effects on productivity) and (2) incubators are associated with newly established firms of types that are likely to demonstrate slow *within-park* growth. However, we do note that, *a priori*, we expect *different* opportunities and resources for parks in different regions, parks with incubator facilities as contrasted to those without them, and parks affiliated with state universities rather than private ones. Conventional two-tailed tests for the significance of the coefficients for the control variables will reveal if the differences are associated with different rates of growth for the parks.

The empirical results

The regression results associated with alternative specifications of Eq. (4) are in Table 2. Results are reported for the population of 81 parks and for two sub-samples. The first sub-sample deletes the three parks founded in 2002 because insufficient time has passed for them to attract tenants. The second sub-sample also deletes the one park founded in 2001 and the one park founded in 1992 for which no employees have yet located. As discussed above and as noted in Table 1, y_t for these five parks is set at 1. The essential results — as seen in columns (1) through (3) — are robust across the different samples. In the discussion to follow we use the results in column (3).

Column (3) shows the annual rate of growth for university research parks located on campus (*mile* = 0) and with one associated university (*nouniv* = 1) to be $0.1025 + 0.0186$ or 12.1% for parks in the South when none of the qualitative variables in the model are 'turned on.' The annual rate of growth for parks in the Northeast, Midwest, or West does not differ significantly, *ceteris paribus*.

[21] State universities receive state funding and may be more accountable for research activities and technology transfer activities than private universities.

Table 2 Regression results for Eq. (4) dependent variable: ln y_t

Variable	(1)	(2)	(3)	(4)	(5)	(6)
t	0.1309***	0.1117***	0.1025***	0.1356***	0.1157***	0.1068***
	(0.0341)	(0.0302)	(0.0285)	(0.0336)	(0.0298)	(0.0282)
$mile*t$	−0.0100***	−0.0088***	−0.0078***	−0.0088***	−0.0079***	−0.0067***
	(0.0030)	(0.0027)	(0.0025)	(0.0029)	(0.0028)	(0.0025)
$mile^2*t$	0.0003**	0.0002**	0.0002**	0.0002**	0.0002**	0.0002*
	(0.0001)	(0.0001)	(0.0001)	(0.0001)	(0.0001)	(0.0001)
$nouniv*t$	0.0101	0.0153*	0.0186**	0.0087	0.0141*	0.0174**
	(0.0097)	(0.0085)	(0.0076)	(0.0096)	(0.0084)	(0.0075)
$oper*t$	−0.0538**	−0.0580***	−0.0534***	−0.0864***	−0.0851***	−0.0822***
	(0.0218)	(0.0206)	(0.0192)	(0.0348)	(0.0318)	(0.0307)
$regw*t$	−0.0142	−0.0145	−0.0199	−0.0194	−0.0188	−0.0246
	(0.0266)	(0.0253)	(0.0248)	(0.0275)	(0.0261)	(0.0254)
$regne*t$	0.0280	0.0157	0.0032	0.0288	0.0164	0.0039
	(0.0278)	(0.0265)	(0.0247)	(0.0278)	(0.0267)	(0.0250)
$regmw*t$	−0.0045	−0.0083	−0.0131	−0.0071	−0.0104	−0.0154
	(0.0270)	(0.0213)	(0.0178)	(0.0261)	(0.0207)	(0.0172)
$techbio*t$	0.0266	0.0227	0.0167	0.0274	0.0234	0.0174
	(0.0208)	(0.0208)	(0.0214)	(0.0209)	(0.0205)	(0.0210)
$techit*t$	0.0429**	0.0457***	0.0436***	0.0492***	0.0509***	0.0492**
	(0.0202)	(0.0181)	(0.0170)	(0.0219)	(0.0198)	(0.0188)
$incub*t$	−0.0288*	−0.0259*	−0.0268*	−0.0218	−0.0202	−0.0207
	(0.0160)	(0.0146)	(0.0141)	(0.0170)	(0.0158)	(0.0155)
$statepr*t$	0.0511*	0.0304	0.0155	0.0378	0.0195	0.0038
	(0.0265)	(0.0238)	(0.0213)	(0.0285)	(0.0261)	(0.0232)
$(oper*statepr)*t$				0.0511	0.0424	0.0453
				(0.0459)	(0.0433)	(0.0412)
constant	4.2093***	4.8398***	5.2847***	4.185***	4.8167***	5.2603***
	(0.5096)	(0.4165)	(0.2717)	(0.5092)	(0.4153)	(0.2675)
R^2	0.51	0.51	0.56	0.51	0.51	0.57
F value	12.38***	11.15***	15.23***	10.48***	9.96***	13.57***
n	81	78	76	81	78	76

Note: Robust standard errors in parentheses. Significance levels denoted by* (10%), ** (5%), *** (1%). Coefficients and standard errors in column (3) are discussed within the text

The coefficient on each of the variables other than time, t, each variable being interacted with t, gives the variable's effect on the annual growth rate. The growth rate of research parks does vary by park and technology characteristics. The coefficient on the driving distance (in miles) from the university to the park is negative, as hypothesized. For smaller mileage, the annual growth rate decreases by about 8% for every 10 miles between the university and the park. This effect diminishes as mileage increases.[22]

The number of universities formally affiliated with the park has a positive effect on growth. Going from 1 university to 2 universities increases growth by nearly 2% per year.

One-third of all parks are operated by the university, and the rest of the parks are operated by a private sector organization. As hypothesized, either the park operational skills of the university are less effective, at least in terms of park growth, or universities operate parks that on the whole undertake more commercially challenging technology transfer. University operated research parks grow on average about 5% per year slower than parks operated by a private sector organization.

Those parks that specialize in attracting information technology companies grow faster than other parks, either bioscience specialty parks or parks with heterogeneous technologies represented by the tenant mix, by slightly more than 4% per year.

Just over one-half of all parks have incubators within the park.[23] The negative coefficient on that variable shows that research parks with incubator facilities grow nearly 3% slower per year than parks without. This finding could mean, from an institutional perspective based on our discussions with park directors and university provosts, that incubator facilities assist with the growth of small companies, and then those small companies leave the park and rarely ever develop research synergies with other park tenants.

Finally, the ownership of the university — private university or public state university — has no statistical

effect on park growth. Further, we investigated whether university ownership affects the efficiency with which state university operated parks grow. As the results in columns (4)–(6) show, university ownership is not statistically important in our model.

Using Eq. (2) from section 'The Growth of University Research Parks' and the estimates from column (3) of Table 2, the predicted growth rate for a park is:

$$\hat{g} = 0.1025 - 0.0078(mile) + 0.0002(mile^2)$$
$$+0.0186(nouniv) - 0.0534(oper)$$
$$-0.0199(regw) + 0.0032(regne)$$
$$-0.0131(regmw) + 0.0167(techbio)$$
$$+0.0436(techit) - 0.0268(incub)$$
$$+0.0155(statepr) \tag{5}$$

The average value of $\hat{g}$ in the sample of 76 parks used in the model of column (3) is 0.0840 or 8.40%.[24]

Discussion of the findings

As the first systematic investigation of U.S. university research parks, our level of inquiry provides some new and interesting findings about the growth or productivity of research parks in the United States, but also it has several limitations, which we hope that researchers will address in the future. Before discussing the limitations of our study, we offer some additional insights into the direct usefulness of our findings.

Those involved in the 81 existing research parks as well as those associated with the planning and implementation of the 27 additional parks currently in the planning stage could use our statistical findings for benchmarking themselves against the population as a whole. Our findings may also be useful for guiding

---

[22] The strong negative effect for low mileage gradually diminishes until miles= 0.0078/0.0004 = 19.5 miles. The functional form allows capturing the diminishing of the negative effect, and the eventual upturn in the effect over high mileage is probably not of interest. The range for $mile$ is 0–35 miles, but only three parks have $mile > 19.5$. The median value for $mile$ is 2.0, and 44% of the 81 parks are closer than 2 miles from their university.

[23] Unfortunately, we do not have data on the age of the incubator facility or its size.

[24] Equation (5) is our prediction model. One might reasonably expect that some of the right-hand-side variables, in particular whether ($oper = 1$) or not ($oper = 0$) a university operates the park, may be associated with the number of miles, $mile$, between the university and the park. For that reason, especially given the large number of explanatory variables, multicollinearity might conceivably make the estimation of the model difficult. As it turns out, although $mile$ and $oper$ are negatively correlated, the correlation coefficient is just -0.11 and is not significant. The equation (5) follows from our theoretical growth model. We did not experiment, nor do we think that we should, with exploratory specifications. Collinearity is not a problem in this particular sample; the estimation is stable, with the variables' coefficients the partial derivatives well estimated with relatively small standard errors.

🍃 Springer

J Prod Anal (2006) 25:43–55

university and park administrators in making strategic decisions about their park.

Many of the variables in our growth model are not discretionary — an off-campus park cannot easily relocate on campus, and a university cannot change its ownership affiliation from being private to being public. But there are strategic options at the discretion of administrators. The first is who operates the park — the university or a private organization; the second is if the park is technology focused — information technology or biosciences. For illustrative purposes, Table 3 shows the average annual growth rates predicted by our models, based on column (3) in Table 2, for alternative distances between the university and the park, and for each form of operational structure. This experiment, which is also illustrated in Fig. 2, is based on the following assumptions: the single university ($nouniv = 1$) is a state university ($statepr = 1$) in the Northeast ($regne = 1$); there is no incubator facility in the park ($incub = 0$); and the park has a focus on information technology ($techit = 1$). Clearly, those involved in developing park growth strategy can locate the distance between their university and park and see the predicted growth differences associated with who operates the park. The predicted average annual rate of growth decreases for both private and university operated parks as mileage increases, and the rate of growth is significantly less in the university operated park.

These predictions, in particular, and the analysis presented in this paper, in general, must be interpreted cautiously. First, our analysis is subject to data limitations. For example, we were able to control for whether or not a university operates the park, but we could not control for the experience of those who operate the park. An experienced university management staff may well outperform, in terms of park growth, an inexperienced private organization's management staff. Further, we have not controlled for the age or expertise of the university's technology transfer office/officer, nor have we controlled for the research expertise of faculty. Also, given the alternative interpretation above of *oper*'s negative effect on growth, the results may reflect more commercially challenging technology transfer for university operated parks. Second, and this point relates to data limitations, our analysis is based on a rather simple growth model. Certainly, more insights about the growth of research parks could be gleaned when the growth process is modeled more completely by taking into account lags and simultaneous effects. But, even

with these limitations, our analysis does begin to fill the conspicuous void about the growth of university research parks.

That said, we are aware that there are broader issues associated with university research parks than growth. Specifically, for a policy perspective, an overarching question relates to how university research parks fit within our national innovation system. Drawing on Cohen (2002),[25] a relevant question is whether university research parks increase R&D efficiently — both tenant R&D and university R&D — by enhancing information flows. If so, then it is not unreasonable to think of university research parks as an infrastructural component of our national innovation system.

Unfortunately, our analysis in this initial inquiry into university research parks is insufficient to answer the broader question about the efficiency of URPs.[26] However, we have offered a suggestive argument that park formations do increase R&D efficiency. In particular, the rise in park formation in the late 1970s when real industrial R&D was also increasing, and when the public sector introduced incentives to stimulate industrial and university innovation-related relationships, is consistent with firm and university strategies for purposive information sharing from which both parties benefit.[27] That, taken in conjunction with the fact that there are 27 new university research parks in the planning stage at a time when technology transfer is burgeoning, suggests to us that as technology transfer activities at universities continue to increase there will be more and more universities that are eager to imitate the infrastructural successes of other universities with established parks.

Still, the broad topic of university research parks is relatively new to the research domain of econom-

---

[25] And Cohen's (2002) discussion builds on the work of Nelson (1993).

[26] This is because of the factors noted above and the fact that our dataset does not include information about research parks that may have failed and, if so, are no longer active or observable.

[27] These trends are not consistent with the findings that firm-with-firm (in separate geographical locations) RJVs are a countercyclical strategic response (Brod and Link 2001; Hagedoorn et al. 2000). The demand for park locations appears to increase during periods when industrial R&D activity is also increasing, and the supply of parks appears to increase during periods when firm R&D activity is growing and when incentives exist for technology transfers from universities. That observed increase in demand — R&D spending — reflects, in our opinion, a greater ability on the part of firms to take advantage of the juxtaposed synergies with other firms and the university that a park location affords.

Table 3 Predicted annual growth rates, by mileage and operational structure (in percentages)

Note: The predicted average annual growth rates come from the regression coefficients in column (3) of Table 2 given: $nouniv = 1$, $statepr = 1$, $regne = 1$, $incub = 0$, $techbio = 0$, and $techit = 1$

Miles	$\hat{g}$ Park Operated by Private Organization	$\hat{g}$ Park Operated by University
0	18.34	13.00
1	17.58	12.24
2	16.86	11.52
3	16.18	10.84
4	15.54	10.20
5	14.94	9.60
6	14.38	9.04
7	13.86	8.52
8	13.38	8.04
9	12.94	7.60
10	12.54	7.20

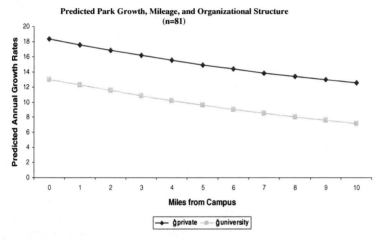

Fig. 2 Predicted park growth, mileage, and organizational structure ($n = 81$)

ics; and therefore, scholars in the future will certainly refine our analysis and begin to address the broader question about parks within our national innovation system.

Acknowledgements This paper has benefited from the comments and suggestions of the editors of the *Journal of Productivity Analysis* and two anonymous referees. Also, we gratefully acknowledge the National Science Foundation, Division of Science Resources Statistics, for its financial support of this study.

Appendix A

A number of definitions of a research park have been proffered in recent years. Beginning with the international definitions, the International Association of Science Parks (IASP) offers the following:[28]

---

[28] http://www.iaspworld.org/information/definitions.php

A Science Park (or Technology Park, or Technopole or Research Park) is an organisation managed by specialised professionals, whose main aim is to increase the *wealth of its community* [emphasis added] by promoting the culture of innovation and the competitiveness of its associated businesses and knowledge-based institutions.

To enable these goals to be met, a Science Park stimulates and manages the flow of knowledge and technology amongst universities, R&D institutions, companies and markets; it facilitates the creation and growth of innovation-based companies through incubation and spin-off processes; and provides other value-added services together with high quality space and facilities.

J Prod Anal (2006) 25:43–55

The United Kingdom Science Park Association's (UKSPA) definition is more focused:[29]

> A science park is essentially a cluster of knowledge-based businesses, where support and advice are supplied to assist in the growth of the companies. In most instances, science parks are associated with a center of technology such as a university or research institute. In more detail, they are business support and technology transfer initiatives that:
>
> • Encourage and support the start up, incubation and further *growth of innovative businesses with good growth potential* [emphasis added].
> • Provide an environment where larger, frequently international businesses can develop scientific and close interactions with a particular center of technology for their mutual benefit.
> • Usually have a formal and operational link with such a reservoir of technology.

The United Nations Educational, Scientific and Cultural Organization (UNESCO) defines a science park as:[30]

> … an economic and technological development complex that aims to foster the development and application of high technology to industry. Research facilities, laboratories, business incubator, as well as training, business exchange and service facilities are located in the complex. It is formally linked (and usually physically close) to a centre of technological excellence, usually a university and/or research centre. Most science parks focus on information technology (including electronics and computers), telecommunication, biotechnology and new materials.
> The general characteristic of a science park is as follows:
>
> • promote research and development by the *university in partnership with industry* [emphasis added], assisting in the growth of new ventures, and promoting economic development;

• facilitate the creation and growth of innovation-based companies through incubation and venturing; and
• stimulate and manage the flow of knowledge and technology amongst universities, R&D institutions, companies and markets;
• provide an environment where knowledge-based
  enterprises can develop close interactions with a particular centre of knowledge creation for their mutual benefit.

More specific to the United States, the Association of University Related Research (AURRP) parks defined a research park in the following terms:[31]

> The definition of a research or science park differs almost as widely as the individual parks themselves. However, the research and science park concept generally includes three components:
>
> • A real estate development
> • An organizational program of activities for technology transfer
> • A partnership between academic institutions, government and the private sector

The AURRP recently changed its name to the Association of University Research Parks (AURP), and it set forth the following definition for a university research park.[32]

> A university research *park or technology incubator* [emphasis added] is defined by AURP as a property-based venture which has:
>
> • Existing or planned land and buildings designed primarily for private and public research and development facilities, high technology and science based companies, and support services.
> • A contractual and/or formal ownership or operational relationship with one or more universities or other institutions of higher education, and science research.
> • A role in promoting research and development by the university in partnership with

---

[29] http://www.ukspa.org.uk/htmlfiles/index1.htm

[30] http://www.unesco.org/pao/s-parks/what.htm

[31] AURRP (1997).

[32] http://www.aurp.net/whatis/

industry, assisting in the growth of new ventures, and promoting economic development.

- A role in aiding the transfer of technology and business skills between the university and industry tenants.

The park or incubator may be a not-for-profit or for-profit entity owned wholly or partially by a university or a university related entity. Alternatively, the park or incubator may be owned by a non-university entity but have a contractual or other formal relationship with a university, including joint or cooperative ventures between a privately developed research park and a university.

A priori, each of the above definitions had limitations, and based on previous research none of these definitions is an accurate characterization of the U.S. phenomenon.[33] In particular, the IASP definition only emphasizes the regional economic growth aspects associated with park activity, but in some European countries that is the founding objective of many of the parks. The UKSPA definition appropriately emphasizes technology transfer from the university, but it is narrow in that it focuses on park company growth. Although the recognition of "mutual benefit" suggests a two-way flow of knowledge, the UNESCO definition like that of the UKSPA emphasizes a one-way knowledge flow from the university to the private sector. The AURP definition appropriately acknowledges that knowledge does flow in two directions between park tenants and the university. The AURP definition is appealing and formed the foundation for our working definition of a university research park.

References

Adams JD (2002) Comparative localization of academic and industrial spillovers. J Econ Geogr 2:253–278

Adams JD, Jaffe AB (1996) Bounding the effects of R&D: an investigation using matched establishment-firm data. Rand J Econ 94:700–721

Association of University Related Research Parks (AURRP) 1997. Worldwide Research & Science Park Directory 1998. BPI Communications

Bozeman B (2000) Technology transfer and public policy: a review of research and theory. Res Policy 29:627–656

Bozeman B, Crow M (1991) Red tape and technology transfer in U.S. government laboratories. J Technol Transf 16:29–37

Brod AC, Link AN (2001) Trends in cooperative research activity. In Feldman MP, Link AN (eds) Innovation policy in the knowledge-based economy. Kluwer Academic Publishers, Boston

Cohen W (2002) Thoughts and questions on science parks, presented at the National Science Foundation Science Parks Indicators Workshop, University of North Carolina at Greensboro, November 2002 (Also in A.N. Link, Final Report to the National Science Foundation on Science Park Indicators Workshop, January 2003.)

Danilov VJ (1971) The Research park shake-out. Ind Res 13: 1–4

Feldman MP (1999) The new economics of innovation, spillovers and agglomeration: a review of empirical studies. Econ. Innovation New Technol 8:5–25

Feldman MP, Lichtenberg F (2002) Innovation, imitation and distance in the pharmaceutical industry. Johns Hopkins University, mimeographed

Griliches Z (1986) Productivity growth, R&D, and basic research at the firm level in the 1970s. Am Econ Rev 76:141–154

Hagedoorn J, Link AN, Vonortas NS (2000) Research partnerships Res Policy 29:567–586

Hall BH, Link AN, Scott JT (2001) Barriers inhibiting industry from partnering with universities: evidence from the advanced technology program. J Technol Transf 26:87–98

Hall BH, Link AN, Scott JT (2003) Universities as research partners. Rev Econ Stat 85:485–491

Link AN (1981) Basic research and productivity increase in manufacturing: some additional evidence. Am Econ Rev 71:1111–1112

Link AN (1995) A Generosity of spirit: The early history of the Research Triangle Park. University of North Carolina Press for the Research Triangle Park Foundation: Research Triangle Park NC

Link AN (2002) From seed to harvest: the history of the growth of the research triangle park. University of North Carolina Press for the Research Triangle Park Foundation: Research Triangle Park NC

Link AN, Link KR (2003) On the growth of U.S. science parks. J Technol Transf 28:81–85

Link AN, Siegel DS (2003) Technolgical change and economic performance, Routledge, London.

Link AN, Scott JT (2003a) The growth of Research Triangle Park. Small Bus Econ 20:167–175

Link AN, Scott JT (2003b) U.S. science parks: the diffusion of an innovation and its effects on the academic mission of universities. Int J Ind Org 21:1323–1356

Mansfield E (1980) Basic research and the productivity increase in manufacturing. Am Econ Rev 70:863–873

National Science Board (2002) Science and engineering indicators, 2002. Government Printing Office, Arlington, VA

Nekar A, Shane S (2003) When do start-ups that exploit patented academic knowledge survive. Int J Ind Org 21:1391–1410

Nelson RR (1993) National innovation systems: a comparative analysis. Oxford University Press New York.

Porter M (2001) Clusters of innovation: regional foundations of U.S. competitiveness. Council on Competitiveness Washington, DC

Siegel DS, Waldman D, Link AN (1999) Assessing the impact of organizational practices on the relative productivity of uni-

[33] See in particular Link (1995, 2002), Link and Link (2003), Link and Scott (2003a, 2003b). As one park director noted to us in a personal interview: "If you've seen *one* research park … you've seen *one* research park."

J Prod Anal (2006) 25:43–55   55

versity technology transfer offices. NBER Working Paper 2756, July 1999

Siegel DS, Waldman D, Link AN (2003) Assessing the impact of organizational practices on the relative productivity of university technology transfer offices: an exploratory study. Res Policy 32:27–48

Swann GMP, Prevezer M, Stout D (1998) The dynamics of industrial clustering. Oxford University Press, Oxford

Wallsten S (2001) An empirical test of geographic knowledge spillovers using geographic information systems and firm-level data. Reg Sci Urban Econ 31:571–599

[4]

Research Policy 40 (2011) 1058–1067

Contents lists available at ScienceDirect
Research Policy

ELSEVIER

The Bayh-Dole Act and scientist entrepreneurship

T. Taylor Aldridge [a,b,*], David Audretsch [a,b]

[a] Indiana University, King-Saud University, Riyadh, Saudi Arabia
[b] WHU Otto Beisheim School of Management, Vallendar, Germany

ARTICLE INFO

Article history:
Received 30 July 2010
Received in revised form 31 January 2011
Accepted 28 April 2011

JEL classification:
M13
O38

Keywords:
Bayh-Dole Act
Entrepreneurship

ABSTRACT

Much of the literature examining the impact of the Bayh-Dole Act has been based on the impact on patenting and licensing activities emanating from offices of technology transfer. Studies based on data generated by offices of technology transfer, suggest a paucity of entrepreneurial activity from university scientists in the form on new startups. There are, however, compelling reasons to suspect that the TTO generated data may not measure all, or even most of scientist entrepreneurship. Rather than relying on measures of scientist entrepreneurship reported by the TTO and compiled by AUTM, this study instead develops alternative measures based on the commercialization activities reported by scientists. In particular, the purpose of this paper is to provide a measure of scientist entrepreneurship and identify which factors are conducive to scientist entrepreneurship and which factors inhibit scientist entrepreneurship. This enables us to compare how scientist entrepreneurship differs from that which has been established in the literature for the more general population. We do this by developing a new database measuring the propensity of scientists funded by grants from the National Cancer Institute (NCI) to commercialize their research as well as the mode of commercialization. We then subject this new university scientist-based data set to empirical scrutiny to ascertain which factors influence both the propensity for scientists to become an entrepreneur. The results suggest that scientist entrepreneurship may be considerably more robust than has generally been indicated in studies based on TTO data.

© 2011 Elsevier B.V. All rights reserved.

1. Introduction

The enormous investment in physical plant and equipment propelled the United States to unprecedented post World War II prosperity. In the new era of globalization, both scholars and policy makers have been looking towards the country's unrivaled investment in research and knowledge to generate economic growth, employment and competitiveness in internationally linked markets for continued prosperity. However, it has been long recognized that investment in scientific knowledge and research alone will not automatically generate growth and prosperity. Rather, these new knowledge investments must penetrate what has been termed "the knowledge filter" in order to contribute to innovation, competitiveness and ultimately economic growth (Acs et al., 2010). In fact, the knowledge filter impeding the commercialization of investments in research and knowledge can be formidable. As Senator Birch Bayh warned, "A wealth of scientific talent at American colleges and universities – talent responsible for the development of numerous innovative scientific breakthroughs each year – is going to

waste as a result of bureaucratic red tape and illogical government regulations, ..."[1] It is the knowledge filter that stands between investment in research on the one hand, and its commercialization through innovation, leading ultimately to economic growth, on the other.

Seen through the eyes of Senator Bayh, the magnitude of the knowledge filter is daunting, "What sense does it make to spend billions of dollars each year on government-supported research and then prevent new developments from benefiting the American people because of dumb bureaucratic red tape?"[2]

In an effort to penetrate such a formidable knowledge filter, the Congress enacted the Bayh-Dole Act in 1980 to spur the transfer of technology from university research to commercialization.[3] The goal of the Bayh-Dole Act was to facilitate the commercialization of university science (Kenney and Patton, 2009; Link et al., 2005, 2007). Assessments about the impact of the Bayh-Dole Act on penetrating the knowledge filter and facilitating the commercialization

* Corresponding author at: Indiana University, King-Saud University, Riyadh, Saudi Arabia.
E-mail address: aldridge@econ.mpg.de (T.T. Aldridge).

---

[1] Introductory statement of Birch Bayh, September 13, 1978, cited from the Association of University Technology Managers Report (AUTM) (2004, p. 5).
[2] Statement by Birch Bayh, April 13, 1980, on the approval of S. 414 (Bayh-Dole) by the U.S. Senate on a 91-4 vote, cited from AUTM (2004, p. 16).
[3] Public Law 98-620

T.T. Aldridge, D. Audretsch / Research Policy 40 (2011) 1058–1067   1059

of university research have bordered on the euphoric,[4] "Possibly the most inspired piece of legislation to be enacted in America over the past half-century was the Bayh-Dole Act of 1980. Together with amendments in 1984 and augmentation in 1986, this unlocked all the inventions and discoveries that had been made in laboratories through the United States with the help of taxpayers' money. More than anything, this single policy measure helped to reverse America's precipitous slide into industrial irrelevance. Before Bayh-Dole, the fruits of research supported by government agencies had gone strictly to the federal government. Nobody could exploit such research without tedious negotiations with a federal agency concerned. Worse, companies found it nearly impossible to acquire exclusive rights to a government owned patent. And without that, few firms were willing to invest millions more of their own money to turn a basic research idea into a marketable product."[5]

An even more enthusiastic assessment suggested that, "The Bayh-Dole Act turned out to be the Viagra for campus innovation. Universities that would previously have let their intellectual property lie fallow began filing for – and getting patents at unprecedented rates. Coupled with other legal, economic and political developments that also spurred patenting and licensing, the results seems nothing less than a major boom to national economic growth."[6]

The mechanism or instrument attributed to facilitating the commercialization of university scientist research has been the university technology transfer office (TTO). While the TTO was not an invention of the Bayh-Dole Act, its prevalence exploded following passage of the Act in 1980. Not only does the TTO typically engage in painstaking collection of the intellectual property disclosed by scientists to the university but also the extent of commercialization emanating from the TTO. The Association of University Technology Managers (AUTM) collects and reports a number of measures reflecting the intellectual property and commercialization of its member universities. A voluminous and growing body of research has emerged documenting the impact of TTOs on the commercialization of university research (Lockett et al., 2003, 2005; O'Shea and Rory, 2008; Phan et al., 2005; Siegel et al., 2007). Most of these studies focus on various measures associated with university TTOs (Mustar et al., 2006; Mosey and Wright, 2007; Shane 2004; Powers and McDougall, 2005; Phan and Siegel, 2006; Di Gregorio and Shane, 2003; Mowery et al., 2004) By most accounts, the impact on facilitating the commercialization of university science research has been impressive.

However, in terms of scientist entrepreneurship, measured by new ventures started by university scientists, the data reported by university TTOs and collected by AUTM suggests a paucity of commercialization spilling over from universities. In the first years of this century, which also pre-dated the financial and economic crises, the number of startups emanating from U.S. universities reported by AUTM averaged 426 per year from 1998 to 2004. Given the magnitude of research budgets and investments in knowledge at American universities, an estimated total between 1998 and 2004 funded by the United States government granting agencies, this measure of university startups is both startling and disappointing.

Similarly, O'Shea et al. (2008) report that, for all its research prowess and headlines as an engine of the Route 128 high tech entrepreneurial cluster around Boston (Saxenien, 1994), the technology transfer office at MIT registered only 29 startups emanating from the university in 2001. Its counterpart, which is generally considered to have fuelled the Silicon Valley high-tech cluster (Saxenien, 1994), Stanford University, registered just six startups. Based on the TTO data measuring scientist entrepreneurship at universities compiled by AUTM, the Bayh-Dole does not seem to have had much of an impact on the economy.

However, there are compelling reasons to suspect that measuring and analyzing the commercialization of university research by relying solely upon data collected by the TTOs may lead to a systematic underestimation of commercialization and innovation emanating from university research. The mandate of the TTO is not to measure and document all of the intellectual property created by university research along with the subsequent commercialization. Rather, what is measured and documented are the intellectual property and commercialization activities with which the TTO is involved. This involvement is typically a subset of the broader and more pervasive intellectual property being generated by university research and its commercialization which may or may not involve the TTO office (Thursby and Thursby, 2005; Mosey and Wright, 2007). For example, in his exhaustive study on academic spinoffs, Shane (2004, p. 4) warns "Sometimes patents, copyrights and other legal mechanisms are used to protect the intellectual property that leads to spinoffs, while at other times the intellectual property that leads to a spinoff company formation takes the form of know how or trade secrets. Moreover, sometimes entrepreneurs create university spinoffs by licensing university inventions, while at other times the spinoffs are created without the intellectual property being formally licensed from the institution in which it was created. These distinctions are important for two reasons. First it is harder for researchers to measure the formation of spinoff companies created to exploit intellectual property that is not protected by legal mechanisms or that has not been disclosed by inventors to university administrators. As a result, this book likely underestimates the spin-off activity that occurs to exploit inventions that are neither patented nor protected by copyrights. This book also underestimates the spin-off activity that occurs "through the back door", that is companies founded to exploit technologies that investors fail to disclose to university administrators."

There is little empirical evidence supporting Shane's (2004) admonition that relying solely upon the data registered with and collected by the TTO will result in a systematic underestimation of commercialization and ownership of university research (Thursby et al., 2009; Aldridge and Audretsch, 2010). Such an underestimation of commercialization of university research may lead to an underestimation of the impact that spillovers accruing from investment in university research have on innovation and ultimately economic growth.

If the spillover of knowledge generated by university research is viewed as essential for economic growth, employment creation, and international competitiveness in global markets, the systematic underreporting of university spillovers resulting from the commercialization of scientist research concomitantly may lead to severe policy distortions. Thus, rather than relying on measures of scientist entrepreneurship reported by the TTO and compiled by AUTM, this study instead develops alternative measures based on the commercialization activities reported by scientists. Some of this intellectual property is co-owned by the university; some is completely owned by the scientist In particular, the purpose of this paper is to provide a measure of scientist commercialization of university research and identify which factors are conducive to scientist entrepreneurship and which factors inhibit scientist entrepreneurship. We do this by developing a new database mea-

---

[4] Mowery (2005, p. 40–41) argues that such a positive assessment of the impact on Bayh-Dole is exaggerated, "Although it seems clear that the criticism of high-technology startups that was widespread during the period of pessimism over U.S. competitiveness was overstated, the recent focus on patenting and licensing as the essential ingredient in university-industry collaboration and knowledge transfer may be no less exaggerated. The emphasis on the Bayh-Dole Act as a catalyst to these interactions also seems somewhat misplaced."
[5] "Innovation's Golden Goose," *The Economist*, 12 December, 2002.
[6] Cited in Mowery (2005, p. 64).

suring the propensity of scientists funded by grants from the National Cancer Institute (NCI) to commercialize their research as well as the mode of commercialization. We then subject this new university scientist-based data set to empirical scrutiny to ascertain which factors influence the propensity for scientists to become an entrepreneur. This enables a comparison of the factors conducive to scientist entrepreneurship to what has already been solidly established in the literature for the more general population. We should emphasize that in this paper we are considering a specific context for scientist entrepreneurship – the creation of a new firm. While this fits within the broader definition of scientist entrepreneurship stated in the introductory paper for this special issue, it should be recognized that we are only focusing on this sole aspect and measure of scientist entrepreneurship.

Section 2 of the paper develops the main hypotheses about why some university scientists engage in entrepreneurship while others abstain from entrepreneurial activities, and why the entrepreneurial behavior of scientists may either emulate or not emulate the entrepreneurial behavior that has been identified in the literature for the more general population, enabling us to posit seven main hypotheses about what influences scientist entrepreneurship. In Section 3 the data base for university scientists funded by the National Cancer Institute of the National Institutes of Health (NIH) is explained. The main hypotheses for scientist entrepreneurship are tested in Section 4 and the results are presented. The findings are discussed and highlighted in Section 5. Finally, a summary and conclusions are presented in Section 6. In particular, by asking scientists what they do rather than the university technology transfer offices, this paper finds that the Bayh-Dole Act has resulted in a strikingly robust and vigorous amount of scientific entrepreneurship. We find that one-quarter of patenting scientists have commercialized their research by starting a firm. In addition, the results suggest that in some aspects scientist entrepreneurship emulates what the literature has found to exist for the broader population. However, in other aspects, scientist entrepreneurship diverges from what the literature has established for the more general population.

2. The scientist entrepreneurial decision

A compelling literature has been developed, both theoretically, as well as being substantiated with robust empirical evidence, explaining why some people choose to become an entrepreneur, in the form of starting a new firm, while others do not (Parker, 2010). However, a review of Parker's comprehensive and exhaustive review of the literature reveals that virtually none of these studies have focused on the decision by university scientists to become an entrepreneur. What is known about entrepreneurial scientist startups originating from universities has normally been inferred from data where the unit of analysis was the university.

Thus, the starting point for analyzing the decision by a scientist to become an entrepreneur is the extensive literature on the entrepreneurial choice for the context of a broad population. To this we will add specific considerations for the scientist context. Five types of factors have been found to shape the individual decision to become an entrepreneur – characteristics specific to the individual, human capital, social capital, the institutional context, and access to financial capital.

2.1. Individual characteristics

A vast and extensive literature has accumulated linking the characteristics of individuals to the propensity to become an entrepreneur (McClelland, 1961; Roberts, 1991; Brandstetter, 1997; Gartner, 1990). While McClelland (1961) undertook pioneer-

ing work, Zhao and Seibert (2006) summarize a more focused series of studies on personality characteristics conducive to becoming an entrepreneur. For example, Reynolds et al. (2004) use the PSID to identify the key role that personality characteristics play in becoming an entrepreneur.

A particular focus for framing the decision to become an entrepreneur has been on entrepreneurial intentions (Wright et al., 2006; Ajzen, 1991; Gaglio and Katz, 2001) However, none of these studies is concerned with the particular type of individuals which are the focus in this present studies – university scientists. Thus, it is not clear whether the consistent findings concerning entrepreneurship and entrepreneurial intentions for the more general population also hold for scientists. In fact, there are reasons to suspect that the main influences underlying entrepreneurial intentions may differ for scientists when compared to the more general population. For example, studies by Levin and Stephan (1991) and Stephan and Levin (1992), posited and found empirical evidence supporting a life cycle model of scientist commercialization, which suggested that, in particular, that age may have a different impact on the propensity for a scientist to engage in entrepreneurial behavior than for the overall population. While the preponderance of studies based on the overall population tend to find that age is negatively related to the likelihood of an individual becoming an entrepreneur, Levin and Stephan (1991) and Stephan and Levin (1992) found that age is positively related to scientist entrepreneurship. Their empirical results were consistent with their life-cycle framework, which predicted that in the early stages of their career, scientists are the most productive and have the greatest incentives to invest in creating knowledge which is public in nature, in an effort to enhance their scientific reputation. As they mature and have achieved prominence, they then have an incentive to invest in knowledge which is private and can be commercialized, so that they are more likely to become entrepreneurs as they mature rather than when they are starting out in their careers.

The scientist life cycle prediction is consistent with the focus of Wright et al. (2006), Shapero and Sokol (1982) and Ajzen (1991) on entrepreneurial intentions. Such entrepreneurial intentions and the propensity to be sensitive to entrepreneurial opportunities may increase as a scientist evolves over her life cycle. Based on the life-cycle framework of Levin and Stephan (1991) and Stephan and Levin (1992) we postulate

Hypothesis 1. Age is positively related to the propensity for scientists to become an entrepreneur.

2.2. Gender

An important individual specific characteristic that has consistently been found to influence the decision to become an entrepreneur is gender (Minniti and Nardone, 2007). Studies have consistently found that females have a lower propensity to become entrepreneurs (Allen et al., 2007). For example, in 2003, the U.S. self employment rate of females was about 55% as high as the male self-employment rate; and 6.8% of women in the labor force were self-employed, compared with 12.4% of men. Similarly, according to Allen et al. (2007), the results from the Global Entrepreneurship Monitor (GEM) identify 10.73% prevalence rate of entrepreneurial activity by U.S. females, measured in terms of owning a business, as compared to 18.45% by U.S. males.

There is also at least some evidence that female scientists and engineers have a lower propensity to engage in commercialization activities, such as entrepreneurship. Elston and Audretsch (2010, 2011) find that gender is the most significant determinant of using an Small Business Innovation Research (SBIR) grant to start a firm, and that, female applicants were far less likely than males to report SBIR grants as their primary source of start-up capital. The nega-

T.T. Aldridge, D. Audretsch / Research Policy 40 (2011) 1058–1067   1061

tive effect of being female on probability of receiving SBIR funding was robust and persistent even after controlling for age, race, education, and wealth. Similarly, Link and Scott (2009) find that only 17.5% of the SBIR firms in their sample from the NIH SBIR program were owned by females, with the remaining 82.5% owned by males. Thus, the evidence suggests not only is there low participation of females in the SBIR program, but it is significantly lower than the prevalent rates for U.S. female entrepreneurs. This suggests

Hypothesis 2.   Female scientists will have a lower likelihood of being entrepreneurs.

2.3. Human capital

A large literature has emerged examining the link between human capital and entrepreneurship (Bates, 1995; Evans and Leighton, 1989; Gimeno et al., 1997; Davidsson and Benson, 2003). Higher levels of human capital facilitate the ability of individuals to recognize entrepreneurial opportunities as well as to act on them through entrepreneurial action. Studies have typically found a positive relationship between human capital and entrepreneurship. The human capital of the individual, typically measured in terms of years of education, has been found to have a positive impact on the decision to become an entrepreneur.

There is no reason to suspect that the relationship between human capital and scientist entrepreneurial behavior differs from that of the more general population, which would suggest a positive relationship. However, an important caveat is that scientists represent a highly truncated part of the overall distribution of human capital. All scientists exhibit very high levels of human capital. Still, with this caveat in mind, we propose

Hypothesis 3.   The propensity for a scientist to become an entrepreneur is positively related to human capital.

2.4. Social capital

Social capital refers to meaningful interactions and linkages the scientist has with others. While *physical capital* refers to the importance of machines and tools as a factor of production (Solow, 1956), the endogenous growth theory (Romer, 1986, 1990; Lucas, 1988) puts the emphasis on the process of knowledge accumulation, and hence the creation of *knowledge capital*. The concept of *social capital* (Putnam, 1993; Coleman, 1988) can be considered a further extension because it adds a social component to those factors shaping economic growth and prosperity. According to Putnam (2000, p.19), "Whereas physical capital refers to physical objects and human capital refers to the properties of individuals, social capital refers to connections among individuals – social networks. By analogy with notions of physical capital and human capital – tools and training that enhance individual productivity – social capital refers to features of social organization, such as networks that facilitate coordination and cooperation for mutual benefits."

Similarly, social capital is considered by Coleman (1988) to be "a variety of entities with two elements in common: they all consist of some aspect of social structure, and they facilitate certain actions of actors, …, within the structure." A large and robust literature has emerged attempting to link social capital to entrepreneurship (Mosey and Wright, 2007; Aldrich and Martinez, 2010; Shane and Stuart, 2002; Davidsson and Benson, 2003). According to this literature, entrepreneurial activity should be enhanced where investments in social capital are greater. Interactions and linkages, such as working together with industry, are posited as conduits not just of knowledge spillovers but also for the demonstration effect providing a flow of information across scientists about how scien-

Table 1
Technology transfer office mission statements.

Primary objectives of the UTTO	Percentage of times appeared in mission statement (%)
Licensing for royalties	78.72
IP protection/management	75.18
Facilitate disclosure process	71.63
Sponsored research and assisting inventors	56.74
Public good (disseminate information/technology)	54.61
Industry relationships	42.55
Economic development (region, state)	26.95
Entrepreneurship and new venture creation	20.57

N = 128 TTOs

Source: Markman et al. (2005).

tific research can be commercialized (Thursby and Thursby, 2002). This leads us to

Hypothesis 4.   Social capital is positively related to the propensity for a scientist to become an entrepreneur.

2.5. Institutional influences

In addition to individual specific characteristics, the entrepreneurship literature has identified the institutional context within which the decision to become an entrepreneur is made. Henrekson and Stenkula (2010) and Karlsson and Karlsson (2002) suggest that certain institutional features are more conducive to individuals recognizing and acting on entrepreneurial opportunities, while other institutions are actually impediments to entrepreneurship. There are additional considerations that are special or unique to the scientist context. One of these is the role played by the technology transfer office (Mustar et al., 2006; Chapple et al., 2005). Studies provide evidence that offices of technology transfer are not homogeneous across universities and are likely to impact scientific entrepreneurship in different ways. In particular, some offices of technology transfer simply are larger, and have great resources, both human and financial, at their disposal (Mowery, 2005). Presumably, better endowed offices of technology transfer can offer scientists greater assistance in commercialization activities.

A second dimension of the offices of technology transfer is that some may put a higher priority on licensing of intellectual property rather than on facilitating scientist startups. For example, as shown in Table 1, Markman et al. (2005) illustrate how the mission statements of 128 university TTOs prioritize licensing intellectual property over scientist startups. Similarly, O'Shea et al. (2005), and Lockett et al. (2005) show that characteristics of the TTO influence the propensity for scientists to become an entrepreneur.

This leads us to posit two hypotheses concerning the institutional context in which the scientist is working

Hypothesis 5.   Scientist entrepreneurship is positively related to the resources available to the technology transfer office.

Hypothesis 6.   Scientist entrepreneurship is negatively related to the extent to which the TTO devotes resources to licensing.

2.6. Financial resources

Having access to financial resources to facilitate starting a new firm is one of the biggest issues confronting nascent entrepreneurs. As Kerr and Nanda (2009, p. 1) point out, "Financing constraints are one of the biggest concerns impacting potential entrepreneurs around the world." Similarly, Gompers and Lerner (2010) emphasize that such financing constraints may be even more severe for scientists, where the ideas generating entrepreneurial ventures are highly uncertain, asymmetric and characterized by high costs of transaction. This suggests

Hypothesis 7. Access to additional financial resources is positively related to scientist entrepreneurship.

In addition, Roberts and Malone (1996) and Breznitz et al. (2008) emphasize that the external environment external may also influence the propensity for scientists to start a new firm. While this paper will not posit any explicit hypotheses linking the external environment to scientist entrepreneurship, we explain in Section 3 that several control variables are included to at least control for several external influences.

3. Measurement

While AUTM collects and makes available data identifying TTO sponsored and approved scientist startups, the data are aggregated at the level of the university TTO. In fact, no large-scale, systematic data base measuring scientist entrepreneurship for the disaggregated level of the individual scientist exists.

Thus, in order to analyze scientist entrepreneurship at the level of the individual scientist, rather than at the level of the aggregated university TTO, we had to create a unique and new data base. The starting point for creating a data base measuring the entrepreneurial activity, in terms of scientist startups, was to identify those scientists awarded a research grant by the National Cancer Institute between 1998 and 2002. Of those research grant awards, the largest 20%, which corresponded to 1693 scientist awardees, were taken to form the database used in this study. The National Cancer Institute (NCI) awarded a total of $5,350,977,742 to the 1693 highest funded quintile of United States-based scientists from 1998 to 2002.

The second step in creating the scientist entrepreneurship data base was to identify which of the scientists receiving funding to support basic research from The National Cancer Institute subsequently received patent protection for an invention. This suggested a sub-set of scientists receiving support for basic research that had potential commercialization applications. NCI award scientists being granted a patent was identified by obtaining patent data from the United States Patent and Trademark Office (USPTO).

To match the patent records with the 1692 NCI recipient scientists, Structured Query Language (SQL) and Python programming languages were written to extract and manipulate data. A match between the patent and NCI databases was considered to be positive if all four of the following necessary conditions were met:

The first necessary condition was that a positive match was made with the first, middle, and last name. If, for example, the scientist did not have a middle name listed on either the NCI award database or the patent database, but did have a positive first and last name, this first condition was considered to be fulfilled.

The second criterion involved matching the relevant time periods between the two databases. Observations from both databases were matched over the time period 1998–2004, which corresponds to the initial year in which observations were available from the NCI database (1998–2002) and the final year in which patents were recorded in the patent database (1975–2004). Because applications of patents may take anywhere from 3 months to 2 years to be issued, the 2003 and 2004 USPTO patent records were included in our query. Issued patents from 1998 to 2004 by NCI scientists fulfilled the second criterion.

The third criterion was based on location. If the patentee resided within an approximate radius of 60 miles from the geographic location of the university, the third condition was fulfilled. The fourth criterion was based on USPTO patent classification. Using the USPTO patent classification code, all patents were separated into respective coding groups. Patents which did not fall under

the traditional categories of biotechnology were identified. All non biotech patents were evaluated and patents such as "Bread Alfalfa Enhancer" were rejected as an NCI scientist. Based on these four match criteria, a subset of 398 distinctly issued patentees were identified between 1998 and 2004 with a total of 1204 patents.

While the patent records identify which of the NCI Award scientists have been awarded a patent to protect the intellectual property representing an invention, they provide no indication whether or not the scientist has started a business. To identify whether a scientist had started a firm, we implemented a survey of the NCI scientists with a patent. The survey instrument was designed with two main criteria. The first was to maximize information without overly burdening the nation's top medical scientists. Reducing the time and input burden imposed on the scientist was considered to have a favorable impact on the response rate. The second was to maximize information revealing the creation of intellectual property and its subsequent commercialization through licensing and entrepreneurial activity, while at the same time respecting the need for scientist confidentiality and not confronting the scientist with information requests that might compromise such confidentiality.

Based on these two criteria, an interview instrument was designed probing four subgroups of issues: licensing, entrepreneurship, social capital and the role of the TTO. The question in the licensing section asked if the scientist has licensed their intellectual property. The question contained in the entrepreneurship section identified whether the scientist started a new firm. The questions concerning social capital asked the scientist if she sat on any industry science advisory boards (SAB) or board of directors, the extent to which the NCI grant award facilitated commercialization, along with other sources of major funding received from a governmental agency. The questions concerning the influence of the TTO asked whether the university's TTO "directly helped you to commercialize your research between 1998 and 2004".

The 398 patenting scientists were "Googled" to obtain their e-mail and telephone information. The records could, generally, be found by typing their full name, university and the word "oncology". The ensuing patentee e-mail accounts and telephone numbers were then collected and registered in the scientist database. Of those 398 scientists identified in the database, 146 responded. Six respondents indicated that they had not patented the ascribed patents, therefore reducing the number of patentees to 392. The number of respondent, therefore, reflects a response rate of 36%. Of these respondents, one in four reported that they had, in fact, started a firm. This is a strikingly high degree of entrepreneurial activity exhibited by these high profile scientists, and certainly reflects a much more robust and extensive degree of entrepreneurship than has been indicated by the TTO data collected by AUTM.

Section 2 identified from the literature five different types of factors shaping the decision by a scientist to become an entrepreneur – personal characteristics, human capital, social capital, financial resources, and TTO characteristics. These factors are empirically operationalized through the following measures:

3.1. Personal characteristics

Two measures reflecting the personal characteristics of scientists are included. The first is the age of the scientist, measured in terms of years, which was obtained from the scientist survey. Hypothesis 1, which is based on the life-cycle framework for scientists posited by Levin and Stephan (1991) and Stephan and Levin (1992), suggests that age will be positively related to scientist entrepreneurship.

The second measure is gender. This is a dummy variable assigned the value of one for males (1310) of the overall 1693 included in the NCI database. The gender of each scientist was obtained by "Googling" their names, i.e. pictures. The estimated

T.T. Aldridge, D. Audretsch / Research Policy 40 (2011) 1058–1067   1063

coefficient will reflect whether the gender of the scientist influences the propensity to commercialize research. Hypothesis 2 suggests a positive relationship between gender and scientist entrepreneurship.

3.2. Scientist human capital

A unique computer program was used to measure scientist citations over the period 1998–2004, using the "Expanded Science Citation Index." Higher levels of human capital were inferred by a greater citation count divided by the number of publications. This measure has been used elsewhere to reflect the human capital of scientists. As Hypothesis 3 suggests, a positive relationship is expected to emerge between scientist human capital and the propensity of a scientist to start a new firm.

3.3. Social capital

Two different measures were used to reflect the extent of a scientist's social capital in the context of linkages with private industry. Such linkages are hypothesized to be conducive to generating both entrepreneurial opportunities and the access to expertise and experience in commercializing those opportunities through entrepreneurship. The first measure a binary variable taking on the value of one if the scientist has been a member of a scientific advisory board or the board of directors of a firm. A positive coefficient would indicate that social capital, as reflected by board membership, is conducive to the commercialization of university research. The second measure is *industry co-publications*, which reflects social capital and linkages between university scientists and their counterparts in industry and is measured as co-authorship between a university scientist and an industry scientist in the Science Citation Index using the Institute for Scientist Information (ISI) Web of Science citation database. The total count of papers co-authored with an industry scientist between the years of 1998 and 2004 was estimated using several search queries on the ISI database. Using the address fields within each publication value in the ISI database, co-publications were identified as a private sector address if the terms *Co., Co. Ltd., Inc.*, or *LLC*, were found. Also, in order to not misidentify the University of Colorado as a company, for example, the query forced the previously mentioned search terms to be standalone words, and not part of larger words. Hypothesis 4 suggests that the coefficient is expected to be positive, which would reflect that university–industry scientist interactions are conducive to scientist entrepreneurship.

3.4. Characteristics of the technology transfer office

Hypotheses 5 and 6 involve the relationship between the technology transfer office and scientist entrepreneurship. Two dimensions of the technology transfer office at the university are included. The first is *TTO employees*, which measures the mean number of employee. The measure is taken from the AUTM data base. A positive relationship would suggest that a greater commitment of TTO employee resources yields a higher propensity for scientists to become an entrepreneur. The second measure is *TTO licensing*, which is obtained by dividing the number of employees dedicated to licensing technology by the number of administrative employees. This variable reflects the commitment of the TTO to licensing relative to other TTO functions. This measure is derived from the AUTM data base. A positive relationship would suggest that allocating a greater share of TTO employees to licensing would increase scientist entrepreneurship.

3.5. Financial resources

There are two measures reflecting financial resources available to the scientist. The first is NCI grant, which is the mean total NCI awarded to the scientist between 1998 and 2002. The award amount was obtained from the original NCI award excel sheet. If external funding of scientific research is conducive to scientific entrepreneurship, a positive coefficient of the NCI grant would be expected. The second measure reflects the extent to which the NCI grant helped the scientist commercialize by obtaining patent protection of her invention. This measure was obtained from the survey of scientists. A positive coefficient would be consistent with Hypothesis 7, which suggests a positive relationship between additional financial resources and scientist entrepreneurship.

3.6. Control variables

Several other measures were included to control for the external context in which the scientist was working. The first is *NCI center*, which is a binary variable taking on the value of one if the scientist is employed at one of the 39 nationally recognized cancer centers, and zero otherwise. A comprehensive cancer integrates research activities across the three major areas of laboratory, clinical and population-based research. The comprehensive cancer centers generally have the mission to support research infrastructure, but some centers also provide clinical care and service, reflecting the priority that community outreach and dissemination play at the centers. A positive coefficient would reflect that being located at a comprehensive cancer center facilitates scientist entrepreneurship. The second measure is *Ivy league*, which is a binary variable taking on the value of one for all scientists employed at Brown University, Cornell University, Columbia University, Dartmouth College, Harvard University, Princeton University, the University of Pennsylvania and Yale University. The third variable is *public universities*, which is a binary variable taking on the value of one for scientists employed at public universities and zero otherwise. Because they are at least partially financed by the public, state universities tend to have a stronger mandate for outreach and commercialization of research. This may suggest a positive coefficient.

The final control variable includes a dummy variable taking on the value of one if the patent was licensed. This may preclude entrepreneurial activity by the scientist, at least in the form of a start up, so that a negative relationship would be expected.

The independent variables are summarized and described in Table 2. The mean and standard deviation of each variable is given in Table 3. The means and standard deviations are provided for three different samples – the top grant recipients from the National Cancer Institute, those top funded scientists with a patent, and those who were interviewed. There are some differences across these groups. For example, the number of citations per scientist is considerably greater for those scientists with a patent, than those who did not patent their intellectual property. The patenting scientists have a greater propensity of being male and of co-authoring an article with a scientist from industry.

The correlation coefficients for the variables are listed in Table 4. These variables do not exhibit high levels of correlation. The highest correlation coefficient is 0.292, between the scientist working at a public institution and the TTO commitment to licensing. Most of the correlation coefficients are below 0.20.

4. Model and results

The purpose of the analysis is to identify factors which are conducive to scientist entrepreneurship and those which impede it. The dependent variable, which was obtained from the interviews,

T.T. Aldridge, D. Audretsch / Research Policy 40 (2011) 1058–1067

Table 2
Description of independent variables.

Independent variables	Description
Board	Binary variable, for scientists indicating that they sat on either a board of directors or science advisory board, board = 1
Industry co-publications	The number of publications an NCI scientist shared with a private industry scientist
NCI helpful	Binary variable, for scientists indicating that the NCI grant was helpful for patenting, NCI helpful = 1
Scientist age	The age of the scientist
Male	Binary variable, where a male = 1
NCI grant	Total amount of funding received by the scientist
NCI center	Binary variable, for a scientist whose institution is recognized by NCI as a comprehensive center for cancer research, NCI center = 1
Public institution	Binary variable, for a scientist whose institution is a public institution, public institution = 1
Ivy league	Binary variable, for a scientist whose institution is an Ivy league university, Ivy league = 1
Average citation per publication	Aggregate number of ISI citations divided by the number of ISI publication a scientist received from 1998 to 2004
TTO employees	The mean annual number of TTO employees dedicated to licensing and patenting
TTO licensing commitment	The number of TTO employees dedicated to licensing and patenting divided by administrative employees
Scientist patent licensed	Binary variable, for scientists indicating that the at least one of their patents were licensed, scientist patent licensed = 1

Table 3
Means and standard deviations.

Variable	NCI scientist N = 1693	Patent scientist N = 392	Interviewed scientist N = 140
Patent (%)	23.35 (0.42)	100.00	100.00
Startup (%)	–	–	25.71 (0.44)
Industry co-publications	1.83 (3.57)	3.01 (4.89)	2.56 (3.73)
Board (%)	–	–	58.00 (0.50)
TTO employees	8.66 (11.44)	9.14 (11.6)	8.95 (11.65)
TTO licensing commitment	1.68 (2.29)	1.31 (1.45)	1.22 (1.24)
NCI grant (Dollars)	3,161,943 (3,196,918)	3,484,128 (3,795,993)	3,053,465 (2,674,288)
Gender (%)	77.87 (0.42)	87.85 (0.33)	88.57 (0.32)
NCI helpful (%)	–	–	45.04 (0.50)
Scientist age	–	–	56.76 (8.40)
Scientist citations	1316.44 (2472.29)	1741.19 (2441.07)	1500.34 (1603.49)
NCI center (%)	55.86 (0.50)	56.50 (0.50)	50.70 (0.50)
Public institution (%)	53.91 (0.50)	48.10 (0.50)	49.29 (0.50)
Ivy league (%)	10.24 (0.30)	12.15 (0.33)	15.00 (0.36)

takes on a value of one if the scientist started a firm and zero if she did not. Because of the binary nature of the dependent variable, a probit regression model is appropriate.

The results from the probit estimation are provided in Table 5. The results suggest considerable support for Hypothesis 4. Both measures of social capital, the scientist serving on a scientific advisory board, and co-authoring a publication with a scientist employed in private industry are positively related to the likelihood of that scientist starting a new firm. These results for the entrepreneurial behavior of scientists are certainly consistent with

those found for the more general population by Davidsson and Benson (2003), among others, and suggest that the entrepreneurial behavior of top university scientists emulates the entrepreneurial behavior of the general behavior, at least in terms of the important role played by social capital.

The positive and statistically significant coefficient of NCI helpful is consistent with Hypothesis 7. The financial resources provided

Table 4
Correlation coefficients of variables.

	Startup	Industry Co-pubs	Board	TTO employees	TTO Commit	NCI grant	NCI helpful
Startup	1						
Industry Co-pubs	0.166	1					
Board	0.346	0.031	1				
TTO employee	−0.015	0.143	0.091	1			
TTO commit	0.006	0.126	0.089	0.983	1		
NCI grant	−0.053	0.073	0.12	0.15	0.134	1	
NCI helpful	0.277	−0.01	0.213	0.205	0.2	0.106	1
Scientist age	−0.137	−0.166	−0.066	−0.038	−0.041	0.041	0.004
Gender	0.157	−0.017	0.315	−0.015	−0.007	−0.058	0.086
Avg citation per Pub	−0.066	0.066	0.104	0.07	0.078	0.193	0.09
NCI center	−0.057	0.237	−0.093	0.232	0.268	−0.089	0.079
Public institution	−0.075	−0.067	−0.031	0.278	0.292	0.073	0.132
Ivy league	−0.007	0.048	−0.1	−0.152	−0.138	0.015	0.122

	Scientist age	Gender	Average Citation per Pub	NCI center	Public institution	Ivy league
Scientist age	1					
Gender	0.056	1				
Average citation per pub	−0.103	0.053	1			
NCI center	−0.099	−0.145	0.022	1		
Public institution	0.259	0.181	−0.193	−0.108	1	
Ivy league	−0.214	−0.007	0.127	0.175	−0.376	1

T.T. Aldridge, D. Audretsch / Research Policy 40 (2011) 1058–1067   1065

Table 5
Probit regression results estimating scientist commercialization – startups.

Independent variables	1	2	3	4
Board	**1.277***** [3.747]	**1.502***** [4.456]	**1.525***** [4.517]	**1.488***** [4.628]
Industry co-publications	6.425* [3.401]	8.687** [3.997]	9.083** [4.094]	9.404** [4.229]
NCI helpful	**8.284***** [3.212]	9.148** [3.682]	9.277** [3.704]	8.965** [3.787]
Scientist age		-2.102 [2.487]	-2.190 [2.496]	-2.123 [2.499]
Male		5.649 [1.006]	5.718 [1.008]	5.997 [1.018]
NCI grant		-8.558 [9.982]	-8.601 [1.004]	-8.289 [9.929]
NCI center		-2.277 [3.966]	-2.013 [3.886]	-1.875 [3.909]
Public institution		-2.652 [3.995]	-2.675 [3.998]	-2.963 [4.008]
Ivy league		-6.405 [8.085]	-6.739 [8.131]	-7.586 [8.396]
Average citation per publication		-1.197 [1.011]	-1.168 [1.012]	-1.160 [1.013]
TTO employees		-4.721 [9.528]		
TTO licensing employees			-1.286 [1.705]	-1.389 [1.748]
Scientist patent licensed			1.580	-1.076 [4.046]
Constant	**-2.247***** [4.519]	-9.534 [1.715]	-9.366 [1.720]	-1.076 [1.768]
Observations	91	82	82	82
chi^2	27.66	33.43	33.77	33.93

Standard errors in brackets. *Note*: all units have been multiplied by 10,000. The bold values mean that the coefficient is statistically significant for a two-tailed test at the 95 percent level of confidence.
  * $p < 0.1$.
  ** $p < 0.05$.
  *** $p < 0.01$.

by the NCI grant are conducive to scientist entrepreneurship. Those scientists who suggested that the grant from the National Cancer Institute facilitated patenting their intellectual property exhibited a higher propensity to start a new firm. This would suggest that the NCI is enhancing scientist entrepreneurship. These findings are consistent with the findings for the more general population that a lack of access to financial resources tends to constrain entrepreneurial activity (Kerr and Nanda, 2009).

The empirical results are not consistent with Hypotheses 1 and 2. In contrast to the consistent findings in the literature for entrepreneurship for the general population (Reynolds et al., 2004), in the case of university scientists, age and gender have no impact on the propensity for the scientist to become an entrepreneur. While both gender and age are consistently found to influence the decision to become an entrepreneur for the population at large (Reynolds et al., 2004), these are not found to have any statistically significance impact for the scientists included in this study.

Similarly, there is no statistical evidence supporting Hypothesis 3. Human capital apparently has no statistically significant impact on the propensity for scientists to start a new firm. This is a contrast to the findings for the more general population (Davidsson and Benson, 2003; Bates, 1995). One interpretation of this disparity may be that this sample consists of scientists with exceptionally high levels of human capital. Variations in human capital for these scientists apparently have no additional impact on the decision

to become an entrepreneur. By contrast, studies focusing on the broader population include observations with a much greater variance in levels of human capital, as well as a much lower mean level of human capital, so that human capital has consistently been found to influence entrepreneurial activity.

The main hypotheses focusing on the impact of the institutional context on scientist entrepreneurship, Hypotheses 5 and 6, are not supported by the empirical evidence. Neither the resources of the technology transfer office, as measured by number of full-time employees, nor the share of TTO employees dedicated to licensing and patenting has a statistically significant on the likelihood of a scientist starting a new firm.

None of the control variables have any statistically significant impact on the likelihood of a scientist starting a new firm.

5. Discussion

The empirical results presented in Section 4 from analyzing why some scientists become entrepreneurs, while other colleagues do not, point to the importance of relationships and linkages forged through social capital, and in particular, to other scientists working in industry, as well as experiences gained by serving on a company scientific advisory board. The measures of social capital are found to be the most important influences in the decision of a scientist to become an entrepreneur. Those scientists with higher levels of social capital, in that they are members of a scientific advisory board of a company, or they have co-authored articles with scientists working for a company, exhibit a systematically higher propensity to become an entrepreneur.

Some of the more traditional explanations of entrepreneurship, and in particular, personal characteristics such as gender and age, but also human capital do not seem to play an important role.

Thus, in some aspects, scientist entrepreneurship appears to emulate the entrepreneurial behavior exhibited by the more general population. In particular, the validation of Hypotheses 4 and 7, highlighting the key roles that social capital and access to financial resources play in facilitating entrepreneurship, are also consistent with the empirical results found for the general population (Davidsson and Benson, 2003; Aldrich and Martinez, 2010; Kerr and Nanda, 2009; Gompers and Lerner, 2010). However, in other important aspects, and in particular age, gender and human capital, scientist entrepreneurship diverges from the results found for the more general population (Minniti and Nardone, 2007; Davidsson and Benson, 2003; Bates, 1995). While Blanchflower and Oswald (1998), pose the question, "What makes an entrepreneur?" the answer does not seem to be exactly identical for scientist entrepreneurship.

6. Conclusions

A number of indications suggest that the Bayh-Dole has not had much of an impact on generating entrepreneurial activity by scientists in the form of starting a new firm. Based on the respected and often cited data collected by the technology transfer offices at universities, and assembled by AUTM in a systematic and comprehensive manner, it would appear that even the most entrepreneurial universities generate only a handful of startups by scientists each year.

However, in this study, by asking scientists rather than the technology transfer offices of universities what entrepreneurial activities they actually engage in, a very different picture emerges. In fact, based on a data base of high profile scientists receiving large-scale funding from the National Cancer Institute, we find that university scientist entrepreneurship is robust and dynamic. The empirical results from this study suggest that around one in four scientists has engaged in entrepreneurial activity in the form of starting a new firm.

In addition, while most of the previous literature on scientist has been restricted to focusing on characteristics of the technology transfer offices and universities, due to the nature of the data being aggregated to the level of the university, in this study we are able to analyze the decision of a scientist to engage in entrepreneurial activity at the level of the individual scientist. The empirical results suggest that the decision to become an entrepreneur does not exactly mirror what has been found in the extensive literature for studies analyzing the broader population. Neither personal characteristics nor human capital seem to play an important role in the decision of a scientist to become an entrepreneur, as they do for the broader population. Rather, it is the levels of social capital, as measured by linkages to private industry that increase the propensity of a scientist to become an entrepreneur.

An important qualification of the findings from this paper is that they are based on a special sample of highly successful top scientists in a narrow scientific field. Whether they hold across broader groups of scientists and for other scientific fields is an important issue that needs to be addressed in future research. There is no a priori reason to expect the results from this exceptionally high performing group of scientists in a very narrow, specific scientific field to hold across other scientific fields. Subsequent research needs to identify both the prevalence and determinants of scientific entrepreneurship across a broad spectrum of scientific fields. In addition, future research could make a valuable contribution by

analyzing the post-startup performance of scientist startups. For example, do the growth and survival of new firms started by university scientists emulate the growth and survival patterns that have been well documented in the literature for firms more generally? It would also be desirable to expand the analysis to include a third typology of university startups, such as those new companies founded by surrogate academic entrepreneurs, based on university owned technologies without the involvement of the inventor of the technology (Clarysse et al., 2005; Franklin et al., 2001). Thus, while the findings of this study would indicate that scientist entrepreneurship is robust and prevalent in the Bayh-Dole era, and is certainly more prevalent than previous studies have suggested, there are important research opportunities to understand how and why scientist entrepreneurship differs from entrepreneurship for the more general population.

Acknowledgements

We thank Don Siegel, Mike Wright, participants of the Conference on "30 Years after Bayh-Dole: Reassessing Academic Research," held on October 29 at the National Academy of Sciences, Washington, DC, and an anonymous referee for their valuable comments. Any errors or omissions are our responsibility.

References

Acs, Z., Audretsch, D.B., Braunerhjelm, P., Carlsson, B., 2010. The missing link: the knowledge filter and entrepreneurship in endogenous growth. Small Business Economic 34 (2), 105–125.
Ajzen, I., 1991. The theory of planned behavior. Organizational Behavior and Human Decision Processes 50, 179–211.
Aldrich, H., Martinez, M., 2010. Entrepreneurship as social construction. In: Acs, Z.J., Audretsch, D.B. (Eds.), Handbook of Entrepreneurship. Springer, New York.
Aldridge, T.T., Audretsch, D., 2010. Does policy influence the commercialization route? Evidence from National Institutes of Health funded scientists. Research Policy 39 (5), 583–588.
Allen, I.E., Langowitz, N., Minitti, M., 2007. 2006 Report on Women and Entrepreneurship. Global Entrepreneurship Monitor.
Association of University Technology Managers, 2004. Recollections: Celebrating the History of AUTUM and the Legacy of Bayh-Dole.
Bates, T., 1995. Self-employment entry across industry groups. Journal of Business Venturing 10, 143–156.
Blanchflower, D., Oswald, A.J., 1998. What makes an entrepreneur? Journal of Labor Economics 16 (1), 26–60.
Brandstetter, H., 1997. Becoming an entrepreneur – a question of personality structure? Journal of Economic Psychology 18, 157–177.
Breznitz, S.M., O'Shea, R.P., Allen, T.J., 2008. University commercialization strategies in the development of regional bioclusters. Journal of Product Innovation Management 25, 129–142.
Chapple, W., Lockett, A., Siegel, D., Wright, M., 2005. Assessing the relative efficiency effects of UK University Technology Transfer offices: a comparison of parametric and non-parametric approaches. Research Policy 34 (3), 369–384.
Clarysse, B., Wright, M., Lockett, A., Van de Velde, A., Vohora, A., 2005. Spinning out new ventures: a typology of incubation strategies from European research institutions. Journal of Business Venturing 20 (2), 183–216.
Coleman, J., 1988. Social capital in the creation of human capital. American Journal of Sociology Supplement 94, 95–120.
Davidsson, P., Benson, H., 2003. The role of social and human capital among nascent entrepreneurs. Journal of Business Venturing 18 (3), 301–331.
Di Gregorio, D., Shane, S., 2003. Why some universities generate more TLO start-ups than others? Research Policy 32 (2), 209–227.
Elston, J., Audretsch, D.B., 2010. Risk attitudes, wealth and sources of entrepreneurial start-up capital. Journal of Economic Behavior and Organization 76 (1), 82–89.
Elston, J., Audretsch, D.B., 2011. Financing the entrepreneurial decision: an empirical approach using experimental data on risk attitudes. Small Business Economics 36 (2), 209–222.
Evans, D., Leighton, L., 1989. Some empirical aspects of entrepreneurship. American Economic Review 79, 519–535.
Franklin, S., Wright, M., Lockett, A., 2001. Academic and surrogate entrepreneurs and university spin-out companies. Journal of Technology Transfer 26 (1–2), 127–141.
Gaglio, C.M., Katz, J.A., 2001. The psychological basis of opportunity identification: entrepreneurial alertness. Small Business Economics 16 (2), 95–111.
Gartner, W., 1990. What are we talking about when we talk about entrepreneurship? Journal of Business Venturing 5 (1), 15–28.
Gimeno, J., Folta, T.B., Cooper, A.C., Woo, C.Y., 1997. Survival of the fittest? Entrepreneurial human capital and the persistence of underperforming firms. Administrative Science Quarterly 42, 750–783.

66   Universities and the Entrepreneurial Ecosystem

Gompers, P., Lerner, J., 2010. Equity financing. In: Acs, Z.J., Audretsch, D.B. (Eds.), Handbook of Entrepreneurship Research. Springer Publishers, New York, pp. 183–216.

Henrekson, M., Stenkula, M., 2010. Entrepreneurship and public policy. In: Acs, Z.J., Audretsch, D.B. (Eds.), Handbook of Entrepreneurship Research. Springer, New York.

Karlsson, C., Karlsson, M., 2002. Economic policy, institutions and entrepreneurship. Small Business Economics 19 (2), 163–171.

Kerr, W., Nanda, R., 2009. Financing constraints and entrepreneurship. National Bureau of Economic Research Working Paper no. 15498.

Kenney, M., Patton, D., 2009. Reconsidering the Bayh-Dole Act and the current university invention ownership model. Research Policy 38 (9), 1407–1422.

Levin, S.G., Stephan, P.E., 1991. Research productivity over the life cycle; evidence for academic scientists. American Economic Review 81 (4), 114–132.

Link, A., Scott, J.T., 2009. Private investor participation and commercialization rates for government-sponsored research and development: would a prediction market improve the performance of the SBIR programme? Economica 76 (302), 264–281.

Link, A., Siegel, D., Bozeman, B., 2007. An empirical analysis of the propensity of academics to engage in informal university technology transfer. Industrial and Corporate Change 16 (4), 641–655.

Link, A., Siegel, N., Donald, S., 2005. University-based technology initiatives: quantitative and qualitative evidence. Research Policy 34 (3), 253–257.

Lockett, A., Wright, M., Franklin, S., 2003. Technology transfer and universities' spin-out strategies. Small Business Economics 20 (2), 185–201.

Lockett, D.S., Wright, M., Ensley, M., 2005. The creation of spin-off firms at public research institutions: managerial and policy implications. Research Policy 34 (7), 981–993.

Lucas, R., 1988. On the mechanics of economic development. Journal of Monetary Economics 22, 3–39.

Markman, G., Phan, P., Balkin, D., Gianiodis, P., 2005. Entrepreneurship and university-based technology transfer. Journal of Business Venturing 20 (2), 241–263.

McClelland, D., 1961. The Achieving Society. Van Nostrand, Princeton.

Minniti, M., Nardone, C., 2007. Being in someone else's shoes: the role of gender in nascent entrepreneurship. Small Business Economics 28 (2–3), 223–238.

Mosey, S., Wright, M., 2007. From human capital to social capital: a longitudinal study of technology based academic entrepreneurs. Entrepreneurship Theory and Practice (31), 909–935.

Mowery, D.C., 2005. The Bayh-Dole Act and high-technology entrepreneurship in U.S. universities: chicken, egg, or something else? In: Gary, L. (Ed.), University Entrepreneurship and Technology Transfers. Elsevier, Amsterdam, pp. 38–68.

Mowery, D., Nelson, R., Sampat, B., Ziedonis, A., 2004. Ivory Tower and Industrial Innovation: University-Industry Technology Transfer before and after the Bayh-Dole Act. Stanford University Press, Stanford, CA.

Mustar, P., Reanault, M., Columbo, M., Piva, E., Fontes, M., Lockett, A., Wright, M., Clarysse, B., Moray, N., 2006. Conceptualizing the heterogeneity of research-based spin-offs: a multi-dimensional taxonomy. Research Policy 35 (2), 289–308.

O'Shea, R., Allen, T., Chevalier, A., Roche, F., 2005. Entrepreneurial orientation, technology transfer and spinoff performance of U. S. universities. Research Policy 34 (7), 994–1009.

O'Shea, R.P., Chugh, H., Allen, T.J., 2008. Determinants and consequences of university spinoff activity: a conceptual framework. Journal of Technology Transfer 33, 653–666.

O'Shea, R., 2008. University commercialization strategies in the development of regional bioclusters. Journal of Product Innovation Management 25 (2), 129–142.

Parker, S., 2010. The economics of entrepreneurship. Cambridge University Press, New York.

Phan, P., Siegel, D.S., 2006. The effectiveness of university technology transfer: lessons learned, managerial and policy implications, and the road forward. Foundations and Trends in Entrepreneurship 2 (2), 77–144.

Phan, P., Siegel, D., Wright, M., 2005. Science parks and incubators: observations, synthesis and future research. Journal of Business Venturing 20 (2), 165–182.

Powers, J.B., McDougall, P., 2005. University start-up formation and technology licensing with firms that go public: a resource-based view of academic entrepreneurship. Journal of Business Venturing 20 (3), 291–311.

Putnam, R., 2000. Bowling Alone: The Collapse and Revival of American Community. Simon and Schuster, New York.

Putnam, R., 1993. Making Democracy Work. Civic Traditions in Modern Italy. Princeton University Press, Princeton, NJ.

Reynolds, P., Carter, N., Gartner, W., Greene, P., 2004. The prevalence of nascent entrepreneurs in the United States: evidence from the panel study of entrepreneurial dynamics. Small Business Economics 23, 263–284.

Roberts, E., Malone, R., 1996. Policies and structures for spinning off new companies from research and development organizations. R&D Management 26 (1), 17–48.

Roberts, E., 1991. Entrepreneurs in High-Technology: Lessons from MIT and Beyond. Oxford University Press, Oxford.

Romer, P., 1986. Increasing returns and long-run growth. Journal of Political Economy 94 (5), 1002–1037.

Saxenien, A., 1994. Regional Advantage. Harvard University Press, Cambridge, MA.

Shane, S., 2004. Academic Entrepreneurship: University Spinoffs and Wealth Creation. Cheltenham, Edward Elgar.

Shane, S., Stuart, T., 2002. Organizational endowments and the performance of university start-ups. Management Science 48 (1), 154–171.

Shapero, A., Sokol, L., 1982. The social dimensions of entrepreneurship. In: Kent, C.A., Sexton, D.L., Sexton, D.L., Vesper, K.H. (Eds.), Encyclopedia of Entrepreneurship. Prentice-Hall, Englewood Cliffs, NJ, pp. 72–88.

Siegel, D.S., Veugelers, R., Wright, M., 2007. Technology transfer offices and commercialization of university intellectual property: performance and policy implications. Oxford Review of Economic Policy 23 (4), 640–660.

Solow, R., 1956. A contribution to the theory of economic growth. Quarterly Journal of Economics 70, 65–94.

Stephan, P., Levin, S., 1992. Striking the Mother Lode in Science: the Importance of Age, Place, and Time. Oxford University Press, New York (1992).

Thursby, J., Thursby, M., 2005. Gender patterns of research and licensing activity of sciences and engineering faculty. Journal of Technology Transfer 30 (4), 343–353.

Thursby, J., Fuller, A., Thursby, M., 2009. US faculty patenting: inside and outside the university. Research Policy 38 (1), 14–25.

Thursby, J., Thursby, M., 2002. Who is selling the ivory tower? Sources of growth in university licensing. Management Science 48, 90–104.

Wright, M., Westhead, P., Ucbasaran, D., 2006. Habitual Entrepreneurship. Edward Elgarm, Aldershot.

Zhao, H., Seibert, S., 2006. The big five personality dimensions and entrepreneurial status: a meta-analytic review. Journal of Applied Psychology 91 (2), 259–271.

[5]

J Technol Transf (2014) 39:819–835
DOI 10.1007/s10961-014-9339-x

Scientist entrepreneurship across scientific fields

T. Taylor Aldridge · David Audretsch · Sameeksha Desai ·
Venkata Nadella

Published online: 28 May 2014
© Springer Science+Business Media New York 2014

Abstract Knowledge generated in universities can serve as an important base for the commercialization of innovation. One mechanism for commercialization is the creation of a new company by a scientist. We shed light on this process by examining the role of scientist characteristics, access to resources and key university conditions in driving the likelihood of a scientist to start a company. Our sample comprises 1,899 university scientists across six different scientific fields. We make a methodological contribution by using self-reported data from the scientists themselves, whereas most previous research relied on university or public data. Our consideration of six scientific fields is a substantive contribution and reveals that scientist startups are heterogeneous in nature. Our findings are largely consistent with extant research on the role of individual and university variables in scientist entrepreneurship; in addition, we uncover the novel finding that the type of research field is also a key driver of scientist startup activity.

Keywords Scientist entrepreneurship · Commercialization · Startup · University · Research

JEL Classification L26 · M13 · O30

T. T. Aldridge
Leibniz Institute for Regional Development & Structural Planning, Flaksenstraße 28-31, 15537 Erkner, Germany
e-mail: aldridge@irs-net.de

D. Audretsch · S. Desai (✉) · V. Nadella
School of Public & Environmental Affairs, Indiana University, 1315 E. 10th Street, Bloomington, IN 47405, USA
e-mail: desai@indiana.edu

D. Audretsch
e-mail: daudrets@indiana.edu

V. Nadella
e-mail: vnadella@indiana.edu

 Springer

1 Introduction

University contributions to economic growth have long been acknowledged, such as by playing a role in supporting research which could later lead to innovation (Dosi 1988; Nelson 1959). Scholars and policymakers tend to agree that universities are an important hub for knowledge creation, and can serve as a base for commercialization of innovations.

A key question in understanding this process is scientist entrepreneurship—specifically, why some scientists, and not others, start companies. We shed light on this question by examining self-reported data on commercialization from scientists across six fields of research. Using survey data from 1,899 scientists in six research fields which received National Science Foundation (NSF) funding between 2005–2012(Q1), we examine the role of scientist characteristics, access to resources, and university conditions in explaining the likelihood of starting a company. In doing so, we leverage the methodological advantage of directly surveying scientists and we improve upon previous research on the drivers of scientist entrepreneurship by examining multiple scientific fields. Our findings indicate that scientist startup activity is heterogeneous in nature, and varies according to scientist and university characteristics, as established by previous research, and also by the research field.

The remainder of the paper is as follows. We discuss the relevant literature next. We describe our sample and method in the third section, and present our empirical findings in the fourth section. We employ a two-part empirical strategy, first testing six hypotheses on our full sample of 1,899 scientists and second, providing a disaggregated picture of trends in scientist startups across six fields of science. We discuss our findings in the fifth section, followed by a brief conclusion.

2 Scientist entrepreneurship

Entrepreneurial activities undertaken by university scientists have important implications for the scientists themselves, their universities, funding agencies, regional economic development, and innovation processes and discovery more broadly (Dosi 1988). Assessing entrepreneurial activity by university scientists is difficult and can produce inconsistent results depending on the type, source and quality of data used (Aldridge and Audretsch 2011). The use of some measures are potentially problematic (see Pakes and Griliches 1980; Griliches 1990), such as patents (see Henderson et al. 1998) which reflect the extent to which innovative activities are taking place but do not necessarily capture commercialization activities more comprehensively. Patents could be problematic because they capture one mechanism for protecting innovations, rather than measuring innovation more broadly or the market value of innovations. For example, some patented innovations simply do not make it to the market. In this way, studying only patents does not always capture the scale, scope and breadth of scientist entrepreneurship. Further, scientists could have multiple modes of commercialization, such as by providing consulting services, other innovative products and the like. We therefore focus on a broad measure of scientist entrepreneurship, the *scientist startup*, defined as the founding of a new legal company, which could in fact be providing many types of economic activity.

Previous research examining scientist entrepreneurship has provided insights specifically on the founding of a new company by scientists. Aldridge and Audretsch (2011) study scientist startups among 400 National Cancer Institute (NCI) grant recipients and 1,200 matched patents in the period 1998–2004. They find that roughly one in four

 Springer

scientists started new businesses. However, they examined scientists in only one field, they examined scientists in only one field of research (cancer research) and second, their sample was limited to high-performing scientists (all of whom had patents in cancer research and received on average $3.5 million in grant money from the National Cancer Institute between 1998 and 2002). In order to examine entrepreneurial activity among a more representative scientist population, we examine all NSF-funded scientists in six research fields (civil, mechanical and manufacturing innovation; environmental biology; computer and network systems; physical oceanography; particle and nuclear astrophysics; biological infrastructure). We now turn to our hypotheses about scientist characteristics (human capital and social capital), resources, and university conditions.

2.1 Scientist characteristics

2.1.1 Scientist human capital

Greater human capital could mean scientists also gain greater access and ability to exploit opportunities, as well as more chances to recognize opportunities to begin with. Scientists represent a well-educated and highly accomplished subsection of the general population and are exceptional in many ways, but there is no apparent indication to consider human capital would impact scientists differently than the general population (Aldridge and Audretsch 2010). Human capital has been found to improve entrepreneurial activity in the general population (Davidsson and Honig 2003; Bates 1995; Evans and Leighton 1989).

Most research scientists are highly specialized and hold multiple advanced degrees and educational qualifications. In some fields, scientists follow a traditional academic path, completing doctorates and becoming professors. Their professional academic status (i.e. assistant, associate, full professor) could be an important reflection of educational qualifications and experience. In other fields, a scientist's career trajectory could include several years of working in a lab before becoming faculty or finding employment outside the university; in this case, a scientist may have accumulated significant experience before leading substantial NSF-funded projects and overseeing large research teams. It could be then that the overall amount of experience, regardless of tenure status, could reflect the amount of time the scientist has been able to establish a reputation by publishing and being cited (Audretsch and Stephan 2002; Aldridge and Audretsch 2011). We thus hypothesize on both the role of academic rank and the role of experience:

H1   Scientist academic rank is positively associated with scientist startup.

H2   Scientist experience is positively associated with scientist startup.

2.1.2 Scientist social capital

Scientist social capital refers to the scientist's potential to derive tangible and intangible benefits from interactions and cooperative activities with other individuals and groups. Social capital could be an important determinant of scientist entrepreneurship because it enhances existing resources (like human capital) through social ties and networks. Social capital could affect a scientist's likelihood of starting a new company in several ways. First, interactions and linkages among scientists working across different institutional contexts, such as industry in private labs, could function as conduits of knowledge spillovers and allow for information about entrepreneurship to transfer. Second, interactions and linkages with industry, such as participation on scientific boards of companies in

Universities and the Entrepreneurial Ecosystem

industry, could facilitate flow of knowledge and information about the demand, potential and likelihood for successful entrepreneurship. Agarwal and Henderson (2002) posit that industry interaction can encourage university scientists to commercialize, and Lawson (2012) finds evidence for the importance of collaboration with industry in academic patenting. Social capital has in fact been found to enhance entrepreneurial activity in the general population (Mosey and Wright 2007; Aldrich and Martinez 2010; Shane and Stuart 2002; and Davidsson and Honig 2003) and among scientists specifically (see Karlsson and Wigren 2012; Thursby and Thursby 2002; Aldridge and Audretsch 2011). Thus, we expect scientists with more networks and industry ties to have greater propensity to start a new company:

H3   Scientist social capital is positively associated with scientist startup.

2.2 Resources

In his model of knowledge production function, Griliches (1979) proposed that investments in knowledge-generating inputs have the greatest effect on innovative outputs. A central role for resources has been identified in productive capacity and in aggregate innovative output. Though much of the existing research focuses on the role of resources in driving the innovative capacity of firms, it could also be that individual scientists harness resources in a similar manner as firms. Scientists are agents who use resources, ranging from their own human and social capital to external financial resources, for knowledge creation and to transform scientific knowledge into innovative outputs (Aldridge and Audretsch 2010, 2011).

We consider two types of resources relevant in this context. First, *human resources* refer to a set of knowledge and intellectual resources available to the scientist, such as students working in the lab, pre- and post-doctoral researchers and other scientists. A larger number and higher quality of human resources could support scientist entrepreneurship by helping speed up the innovative process and improve the efficiency of the scientific research activity. In addition, human resources available to the scientist could also improve opportunity recognition by expanding the scope and applications of the ongoing research. The amount and availability of financial resources are expected to positively influence scientist startup propensity in several ways. Second, *financial resources* support research activity by providing funds for technological, infrastructure and labor inputs. Second, financial resources support research activity by providing funds for technological, infrastructure and labor inputs and increase the scope of research by increasing knowledge creation. Further, greater financial resources could lead to greater experimentation and expand opportunities to transform scientific knowledge into innovative outputs. This leads us to posit the following about the role of human resources and the role of financial resources:

H4   Human resources are positively associated with scientist startup.

H5   Financial resources are positively associated with scientist startup.

2.3 University conditions

The scientist could be affected by her immediate work (departmental) environment as well as broader work (university) conditions. Support from within the department could encourage scientific entrepreneurship in several ways. First, interactions with scientists in the same department could provide knowledge about starting a new company. This could

 Springer

lead to awareness and interest in entrepreneurship among scientists who might have otherwise not known or considered the possibility. In addition, the exchange of knowledge about the entrepreneurial process could take place within the department. Second, departmental support, particularly from leadership such as deans or department chairs, could demonstrate that becoming an entrepreneur is also rewarded or at least not discouraged. This could be especially applicable for younger or untenured scientists.

The broader university context could also be important. For example, a university could implicitly or explicitly place a positive emphasis on innovations with market value and on bringing the fruits of research to the market. Such an emphasis could be communicated by a strong university TTO office, whose successes are known across the institution. The support of the university TTO could mean better resources for scientist commercialization (Mowery 2005) and provision of knowledge about the opportunities and process of commercialization for the scientist. For example, university TTO offices have been found to influence the scientist's mode of commercialization depending on their organizational priorities (O'Shea et al. 2005; Lockett and Wright 2005). An effective TTO could help lower risk for scientists with technical and scientific training but not the kind of legal, financial or managerial training useful to start and grow a new company. The importance of institutional conditions which shape the scientist's work environment (Henrekson and Stenkula 2010; Karlsson and Karlsson 2002) leads us to posit:

H6   A supportive immediate working environment (department) is positively associated with scientist startup.

H7   A supportive broader working environment (university) is positively associated with scientist startup.

3 Sample and method

Our method in this paper consists of two sets of empirical analyses. First, we test our seven hypotheses using a large sample of 1,899 university scientists. Second, we explore the determinants of field-specific variation and analyze the drivers of scientist startups in six scientific fields.

3.1 Sample

In order to analyze scientist entrepreneurship at the scientist level and across different fields of research, we used primary survey data from scientists to create a database[1] which measures entrepreneurial activity in terms of scientist commercialization through startups. Most empirical investigations of scientist entrepreneurship used information from university TTOs, other university units or data from the Association of University Technology Managers (AUTM). However, in their study of scientists funded by the National Cancer Institutes (NCI), Aldridge and Audretsch (2011) bypassed university and official sources of data and surveyed scientists directly. They concluded that the rate of scientist entrepreneurship, as reported by the scientists themselves, is higher than previously thought when using TTO or AUTM data.

---

[1] The database used in this study comes from Small Business Administration (SBA) Report No. 409, and the project is funded under the contract SBAHQ-11-M-0212. The full report and research summary can be accessed at http://www.sba.gov/advocacy/7540/586391.

For this reason, we use data based on surveying scientists directly. We identified 9,361 scientists that received NSF funding between 2005 and 2012(Q1) and worked in six different fields of research: (1) CMMI: Civil, mechanical and manufacturing innovation (2) DEB: Environment biology (3) CNS: Computer and network systems (4) OCE: Physical ocean-ography (5) PHY: Particle and nuclear astrophysics (6) DBI: Biological infrastructure.

An online survey questionnaire was directed to the entire population of 9,361 scientists in the first round of survey administration. We detected that 30 scientists were on sab-batical, 9 scientists were inactive, and email addresses of 172 scientists were returned since they were incorrect/incomplete. Thus, we administered the survey questionnaire to a sample of 9,150 scientists (97.75 % of the population). We achieved a response rate of 20.75 % for a total of 1,899 individual scientists in the database.

The survey questionnaire was designed to capture scientist entrepreneurship through startups (key dependent variable, with a response rate of 99.5 %), as well as scientist characteristics, access to resources, university characteristics, and other institutional context.

3.2 Dependent variable

To test the hypotheses presented in the previous section, we use a dependent variable defined as the likelihood of startup of a new legal company by a scientist. This is based on the survey question "Have you started a legally recognized company?" and is a binary variable, with a value of 1 identifying a "yes" response and a value of 0 identifying a "no" response.

Considerable variation is apparent in the propensity for a scientist to start a firm in different scientific fields, as depicted in Fig. 1. This ranges from 4.6 % in environmental biology to 23.8 % in computer and network systems. Scientists in the fields of physical oceanography, biological infrastructure, particle and nuclear astrophysics and environ-mental biology are less likely to commercialize their research through startups. This variation could have several explanations. First, it is possible that scientists in the fields of biological, physical and environmental sciences need greater human capital (access to a large number of prior patents, collaboration from a large number of field experts) to commercialize their research. Second, due to the basic nature of their research, it is possible that scientists in these fields need greater access to financial and infrastructure resources to commercialize their research. Third, it could be that the technology transfer offices in their universities are not competent in understanding their area of research, and hence less successful in surpassing the knowledge filer to commercialize research through startups. Finally, it could be possible that scientists in these fields select other modes of commercializing their research without founding a new company. Description of variables used in the study are shown in Table 1; descriptive statistics are shown in Table 2.

3.3 Explanatory variables

Our key explanatory variables relate to scientist characteristics (demographic, human capital, social capital), access to human and financial resources, and the scientist's insti-tutional context. We use measures from Audretsch et al. (2013) scientist entrepreneurship database, reflecting self-reported responses from each individual scientist who participated in the adaptive online survey.

For human capital, we use two measures. First, we use *academic rank* of the scientist, based on the scientist's self-identification as: Non-tenured, assistant professor, associate professor, endowed professor and emeritus professor. We measure academic rank as full

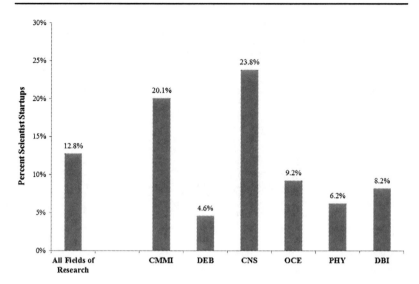

Fig. 1 Scientist startups by field of research. *CMMI* Civil, mechanical and manufacturing innovation, *DEB* Environmental biology, *CNS* Computer and network systems, *OCE* Physical oceanography, *PHY* Particle and nuclear astrophysics, *DBI* Biological infrastructure

professorship, defined as 1 if the scientist indicated that their tenure status is a full professor and 0 otherwise. Second, we use *scientist experience*, measured as the number of years since the scientist made tenure. We measure scientist social capital as board membership (Aldridge and Audretsch 2011), defined as 1 if the scientist indicated that they sat on a scientific advisory board and 0 otherwise.

We consider two types of resources important—human resources and financial resources. We measure human resources as the number of student collaborators that worked closely with the scientist during the duration of research. We measure financial resources using two measures: the amount of NSF research grant funding received by the scientist (continuous variable), and whether the scientist reported receiving substantial amount of funding (greater than $750,000) from other sources such as nonprofits, university, government organizations, industry and others (binary variable).

We use two measures to capture the immediate institutional context in which the scientist works. First, we measure the entrepreneurial orientation of the department head as 1 if the department head of the scientist's institution is an entrepreneur (started a firm). Second, we measure the extent to which the department encourages commercialization on a 7-point likert scale. In order to measure the broader university context in which the scientist works, we measure the scientist's perception of the TTO's success in commercializing research in her field. This variable is created on a 7-point likert scale based on the scientist's answer to the question: "My Technology Transfer Office is successful at commercializing my field of research". We consider scientist perception of the TTO appropriate to understand the broader university context as this also reflects relevance to the scientist.

 Springer

Table 1 Variable definitions and description

Variable	Description
Startup	Binary dependent variable, for scientists indicating that they started a firm = 1 and 0 otherwise
Board membership	Binary variable, for scientists indicating that they sat on a scientific advisory board = 1 and 0 otherwise
Award amount	Continuous variable indicating the scientist's NSF funding amount received between 2005 and 2012-Q1
Other funding (>750 K)	Binary variable, for scientists indicating that they received other sources of funding greater than 750,000 USD = 1 and 0 otherwise
# Student collaborators	Count variable indicating the number of students that worked on the scientist's project funded by the NSF
Tenure experience	Count variable indicating the number of years in tenure status
Full professor	Binary variable, for scientists indicating if the scientist's tenure status is a full professor = 1 and 0 otherwise
Dept. Commercialize	7-point likert scale, for scientists whose department's encourage commercialization of research
Dept Head E.O.	7-point likert scale, for scientists whose department head is an entrepreneur
Univ TTO Success	7-point likert scale, for scientists who consider their university technology transfer office to be successful
Male	Binary variable, for male scientists = 1 and 0 for female scientists
Midwest	Binary variable, for scientists affiliated to institutions located in the midwest region = 1 and 0 otherwise
South	Binary variable, for scientists affiliated to institutions located in the south region = 1 and 0 otherwise
West	Binary variable, for scientists affiliated to institutions located in the west region = 1 and 0 otherwise

3.4 Control variables

We control for gender because of previous findings on its importance (Elston and Audretsch 2010, 2011). Previous research on scientist entrepreneurship points to a lower propensity for females to start new companies (Link and Scott 2009), and Aldridge and Audretsch (2010, 2011) argue that gender could also play a role through other mechanisms, such as propensity to patent an innovation and access to financial resources. We include gender to account for demographic characteristics of the scientist. This is a dummy variable where a value of 1 represents a "male" scientist and a value of 0 represents a "female" scientist.

Additionally, we control for region of the United States to account the spillover of knowledge within geographically bounded regions (Jaffe 1989; Audretsch and Feldman 1996; Jaffe et al. 1993; Glaeser et al. 1992): Location could play a role in driving investment in new knowledge, access to technological infrastructure, and even in shaping scientist behavioral norms and attitudes towards entrepreneurship (Louis et al. 1989). We use dummy variables to control for Midwest, South and West regions with Northeast as the reference group. Correlations for our variables are reported in Table 3.

4 Empirical results

The purpose of this analysis is to identify factors that are predictive of scientist entrepreneurship. Our main dependent variable of interest takes on a value of 1 if the scientist

 Springer

Table 2 variable descriptive statistics

	Mean	SD	Min	Max
Scientist startups	0.13	0.33	0	1
Award amount (in Millions USD)	0.95	5.58	0	166.27
Other sources of funding (>750 K)	0.41	0.49	0	1
Number of student collaborators	15.54	16.13	0	250
Non-Tenured	0.10	0.29	0	1
Assistant professor	0.09	0.29	0	1
Associate professor	0.27	0.45	0	1
Full professor	0.44	0.50	0	1
Endowed professor	0.09	0.29	0	1
Emeritus professor	0.02	0.14	0	1
Years of tenure	16.08	9.00	0	52
Board of directors	0.34	0.47	0	1
Dept. Head Entrepreneurial Orientation	0.40	0.49	0	1
Dept. Encourages Research Commercialization	4.47	1.77	1	7
Univ. TTO Competent in Understanding Research	4.71	1.74	1	7
Univ. TTO Successful in Commercialization	5.13	1.64	1	7
Male scientist	0.79	0.41	0	1
North east region	0.24	0.43	0	1
Midwest region	0.20	0.40	0	1
South region	0.28	0.45	0	1
West region	0.26	0.44	0	1

started a firm and 0 if she did not. We use probit regression estimation as appropriate for our binary dependent variable, to analyze the role of scientist characteristics, access to resources, and university conditions in explaining scientist startup propensity. We first present probit estimation results for our full sample (all six research fields together) and then for each research field separately.

4.1 Hypothesis testing and probit models for the full sample

The probit regression results for our full sample are reported in Table 4. Model 1 is the base model and Model 2 includes scientist experience and TTO success. The negative and statistically insignificant coefficients on scientist years in tenure and academic rank (dummy for full professor) do not provide support for H1 and H2. These results indicate that human capital does not play an important role in determining the likelihood of scientist startup.

However, the results for social capital provide support for H3. Social capital, measured as the scientist's membership on a scientific advisory board, is positively related to the likelihood of that scientist starting a firm. These results are consistent with previous findings for scientists (Aldridge and Audretsch 2011) and with the importance of social capital for the general population (Davidsson and Honig 2003).

With respect to access to human resources, the negative and statistically significant coefficient for the number of student collaborators is surprising. However, the practically insignificant magnitude of the coefficient is insufficient in providing substantial support for

 Springer

Table 3 Correlation Matrix of Variables

	Startup	Board membership	Award amount	Other funding (>750 K)	# Student collaborators	Tenure experience	Full Professor	Dept. Commercialize	Dept Head E.O.	Univ TTO Success	Male
Startup	1										
Board membership	0.2291	1									
Award amount	0.0714	-0.0215	1								
Other funding (>750 K)	0.158	0.134	0.0599	1							
# Student collaborators	-0.0411	0.0101	0.0213	0.0335	1						
Tenure experience	-0.0233	0.0566	0.013	-0.0695	-0.0087	1					
Full Professor	-0.0574	-0.1069	0.0205	-0.0589	-0.0194	-0.282	1				
Dept. Commercialize	-0.225	-0.0547	-0.0278	-0.1514	0.05	-0.0382	-0.0414	1			
Dept Head E.O.	0.1824	0.0497	-0.0424	0.1091	-0.0316	-0.0025	-0.0289	-0.2022	1		
Univ TTO success	-0.0965	-0.0289	-0.0256	-0.1431	0.0488	-0.0782	-0.0455	0.5144	-0.1886	1	
Male	0.0729	-0.0208	0.0305	-0.0126	-0.0074	0.1377	-0.0105	-0.0887	-0.0431	-0.0788	1

Springer

Table 4 Probit regression results estimating likelihood of scientist starting a firm

Independent variables	(1)	(2)	(3)	(4)
Grant amount (in millions)–*Fin Res.*	0.011	0.013	0.011	0.011
	(2.07)**	(2.58)***	(2.07)**	(2.16)**
Other funding (> 750 K)–*Fin Res.*	0.296	0.173	0.282	0.304
	(2.42)**	(1.84)*	(2.27)**	(2.39)**
# of Students–*Human Res.*	−0.001	0	−0.001	−0.001
	(−2.08)**	(−1.57)	(−1.88)*	(−2.03)**
Years in tenure–*Human Capital*	−0.006		−0.011	−0.01
	(−0.88)		(−1.45)	(−1.39)
Full Professor–*Human Capital*			−0.209	−0.212
			(−1.33)	(−1.34)
Board membership–*Social Capital*	0.668	0.706	0.66	0.687
	(5.31)***	(7.44)***	(5.26)***	(5.40)***
Dept. Encourages Commercialization	−0.163	−0.152	−0.161	−0.183
	(−4.18)***	(−5.23)***	(−4.07)***	(−4.32)***
Dept. Head Entrepreneurial Orientation	0.514	0.37	0.512	0.513
	(4.11)***	(3.82)***	(4.04)***	(3.98)***
Univ. TTO success				0.051
				−1.22
Male	0.412	0.561	0.469	0.478
	(2.23)**	(3.93)***	(2.51)**	(2.55)**
Midwest *region*	−0.056	0.072	−0.034	−0.026
	(−0.31)	−0.52	(−0.19)	(−0.14)
South *region*	0.041	−0.037	0.054	0.056
	−0.25	(−0.29)	−0.32	−0.33
West *region*	−0.014	−0.021	−0.019	−0.006
	(−0.09)	(−0.16)	(−0.11)	(−0.04)
Constant	−1.311	−1.587	−1.125	−1.322
	(−4.12)***	(−6.92)***	(−2.95)***	(−3.12)***
Number of observations	793	1517	786	766
Wald Chi–sq.	75.97	124.22	76.1	80.25

Absolute z values in parentheses

* Denotes significant at the 10 % level; ** significant at the 5 % level; *** significant at the 1 % level

H4. This result could be interpreted to indicate that projects which require a large number of student collaborators, in the sciences, tend to be applied and hence indicate the incremental nature of scientific contributions geared at academic contributions. With respect to financial resources, the results provide strong support for H5. The positive and statistically significant coefficient for other significant sources of funding, and magnitude of the grant amount, indicates that scientists with more financial resources for research have a greater propensity to start a firm.

When it comes to the role of the department head's entrepreneurial orientation, we find a positive and statistically significant coefficient. However, we find a negative and statistically significant coefficient for department encouragement to commercialize scientific

🖄 Springer

research. This surprising finding could be interpreted as a substitution effect between department encouragement and the department head's entrepreneurial orientation in providing a more conducive environment for the scientist in starting a firm. Since the net effect between these two measures is positive, our results overall support H6.

We find that a broader supportive university technology transfer office does not improve the likelihood of scientist's starting a firm, which does not support H7. We find that male scientists have greater propensity to start a company.

4.2 Probit models by research field

We tested our hypotheses on the full sample of 1,899 scientists without considering specialization of research fields. Now, we turn to our findings in six different research fields. When our sample is disaggregated in this manner, we find that the overall trend changes according to the specialization of the scientist and our results are heterogeneous.

We run the same probit regression model individually for each of our six research fields: Civil, mechanical and manufacturing innovation (CMMI), Environment biology (DEB), Computer and network systems (CNS), Physical oceanography (OCE), Particle and nuclear astrophysics (PHY), Biological infrastructure (DBI). For all fields, we report our results from the model which includes scientist experience and TTO success. Findings are reported in Table 5.

The results for Civil, Mechanical, and Manufacturing Innovation (CMMI) are consistent with the overall sample of scientists in providing evidence for H3 indicating that greater social capital increases the scientist's likelihood in starting a firm. The positive and statistically significant coefficient on department head's entrepreneurial orientation also indicates evidence supporting H6. Interestingly, the co-efficient on scientist tenure experience is negative and statistically significant, indicating that older CMMI scientists are less likely to start firms than younger untenured-scientists. The magnitude of the coefficient is small compared to the effect from social capital and departmental-environment. The positive and statistically significant co-efficient for the Midwest variable indicates that CMMI scientists with university affiliations in the Midwest have a greater likelihood in starting new firms compared to scientists affiliated to universities in the northeast region.

The results for Environmental Biology (DEB) do not provide support to any of the seven hypotheses. The general directionality of the results is consistent with the overall sample; however none of the measures are statistically significant at the 5 % level. We find a positive and statistically significant coefficient for scientists with other sources of funding at the 10 % level, providing support for H5.

The results for Computer and Network Systems (CNS) are consistent with the overall sample of scientist in providing evidence for H3 on the positive role of social capital in propensity for a scientist to start a firm. The positive and statistically significant coefficient on department head's entrepreneurial orientation and the negative and statistically significant coefficient for department encouragement to commercialize scientific research indicate support for H6. Consistent with the results for the overall scientist population, the positive and statistically significant coefficient for male scientists indicates that male CNS scientists are more likely to start new firms as compared to female CNS scientists.

The results for Physical oceanography (OCE) are consistent with the overall sample of scientists in providing evidence for H5, indicating that other sources of funding increases the scientist's likelihood in starting a firm. The positive and statistically significant coefficient on years in tenure indicates evidence supporting H2. Unlike any other field of research, the positive and statistically significant coefficient of technology transfer office

 Springer

Table 5 Probit regression results estimating likelihood of scientist starting a firm, by field of research

Independent variables	CMMI	DEB	CNS	OCE	PHY	DBI
Grant amount (in millions)–*Fin Res.*	0.111 (0.69)	−0.499 (−1.33)	0.204 (1.25)	0.009 (1.64)	−1.103 (−2.57)**	0.139 (1.59)
Other funding (> 750 K)–*Fin Res.*	0.043 (0.16)	0.54 (1.5)	−0.2 (−0.70)	0.857 (2.06)**	0.767 (1.48)	0.839 (2.11)**
# of students–*Human Res.*	−0.001 (−0.53)	−0.001 (−0.87)	−0.001 (−1.13)	−0.002 (−1.11)	0.006 (1.1)	−0.004 (−2.03)**
Years in Tenure–*Human Capital*	−0.036 (−2.10)**	0.016 (0.83)	0.012 (0.77)	0.041 (1.78)*	−0.101 (−2.52)**	−0.007 (−0.39)
Full professor–*Human Capital*	−0.075 (−0.23)	0.518 (0.88)	−0.205 (−0.45)	0.222 (0.34)	−1.98 (−3.31)***	0.282 (0.67)
Board membership–*Social Capital*	1.078 (4.07)***	0.113 (0.33)	1.058 (3.75)***	−0.593 (−1.22)	3.165 (3.52)***	0.994 (3.00)***
Dept. Encourages commercialization	−0.081 (0.89)	0.012 (0.11)	−0.255 (−2.55)**	−0.493 (−2.55)**	−0.072 (−0.53)	−0.146 (−1.30)
Dept. Head Entrepreneurial Orientation	0.447 (1.69)*	−0.436 (−0.85)	0.446 (1.67)*	−0.251 (−0.43)	0.171 (0.25)	0.591 (1.36)
Univ. TTO Success	−0.073 (−0.71)	0.039 (0.25)	0.041 (0.48)	0.558 (3.02)***	−0.142 (−0.82)	0.151 (1.19)
Male	0.503 (1.43)		0.792 (1.74)*		0.974 (1.24)	−0.089 (−0.21)
Midwest region	0.797 (1.79)*		−0.164 (−0.38)		1.956 (2.28)**	−0.573 (−1.02)
South region	0.694 (1.51)	0.122 (0.27)	−0.189 (−0.51)	−0.797 (−1.22)	−0.125 (−0.22)	−0.169 (−0.37)
West region	−0.038 (−0.07)	0.669 (1.49)	0.012 (0.04)	−1.177 (−2.31)**	−0.744 (−0.73)	0.11 (0.27)
Constant	−1.297 (−1.40)	−2.641 (−2.06)**	−1.349 (−1.24)	−2.798 (−1.88)*	−0.939 (−0.72)	−2.306 (−2.06)**
Number of observations	157	113	138	89	100	104
Wald Chi–sq.	35.27	16.11	40.44	31.31	23.71	24.64

Absolute z values in parenthesis

* Denotes significant at the 10 % level; ** significant at the 5 % level; *** significant at the 1 % level

(TTO) success indicates that OCE scientists in universities with successful TTO offices are more likely to commercialize research than OCE scientists in other offices.

The results for Particle and Nuclear Physics (PHY) are consistent with the overall sample of scientists in providing evidence for H3, indicating that greater social capital increases the likelihood to start a firm. Unlike any other field of research, the coefficient on grant amount is negative and statistically significant, providing preliminary evidence against H5. This result in particle and nuclear physics could be related to basic (and theoretical) research requiring more initial funding, but the results could be subject to a larger knowledge filter before they can be commercialized through startups. Similar to

 Springer

CMMI scientists, the coefficients for full-professor and years in tenure variables are negative and statistically significant, indicating preliminary evidence against H4. Also, the positive and statistically significant coefficient for the Midwest variable indicates that PHY scientists with university affiliations in the Midwest have a greater likelihood in starting new firms compared to scientists affiliated to universities in the northeast region.

The results for Biological Infrastructure (DBI) are consistent with the overall sample of scientists in supporting H3, indicating the positive role of social capital in scientist propensity to start a firm. Consistent with the results for the overall scientist population, the positive and statistically significant coefficient of other sources of funding provide support for H5, and negative and statistically significant co-efficient for number of student collaborators provides preliminary evidence against H4 (however, the magnitude of the effect is insignificant).

5 Discussion

When we consider the heterogeneity of scientific research by disaggregating our sample into six research fields, the results provide a much richer picture than could be obtained from the simple hypotheses testing conducted using the full sample. Table 6 provides a summary of statistically significant effects for the full sample and for each of the six research fields.

The empirical results demonstrate key differences in scientist propensity to start a firm across fields. First, we observe that scientist human capital and human resources are not strong consistent predictors of scientist entrepreneurship for the overall sample and for scientists in each of the six fields of research. We find that scientist social capital, measured as membership in scientific advisory board, is a strong predictor for the likelihood to start a new firm. Second, with the exception of Physical Oceanography, financial resources measured primarily as an indicator of other sources of funding is a factor conducive to scientist entrepreneurship. Third, we find that university conditions, measured at the departmental level (department encouraging commercialization and department head's entrepreneurial orientation) and university level (success of the university technology transfer office), are strong predictors of a scientist's propensity to start a new firm.

Future research can also build upon this paper by expanding and enhancing data sources, and examining the differences between data reported by university TTOs and self-reported data from scientists. This could help university administrators and policymakers better understand how to assess the contribution of universities to innovative activity and commercialization.

Another agenda is to broaden the spectrum of scientific and academic contexts being analyzed. Thus far, most studies have examined one field but our findings point to the need to understand the drivers of important differences across fields. We uncover a strongly nuanced picture of scientist entrepreneurship for which heterogeneity of scientific field is important. The propensity for a university scientist to commercialize knowledge varies considerably across scientific fields. In some fields, such as Computer and Network Systems, the rate of entrepreneurship is remarkably high at almost 24 %; similarly, more than 20 % of scientists in Civil, Mechanical, and Manufacturing Innovation start a firm. In contrast, scientist startups are lower in other fields: Less than 5 % in Environmental Biology and just over 6 and 8 % in Particle and Nuclear Astrophysics and Biological Infrastructure, respectively. Further, we find that many of our variables do not have consistent effects across six fields of research. For example, scientist experience, measured as

 Springer

Table 6 Summary of key determinants of scientist entrepreneurship by field of research

	All fields	CMMI	DEB	CNS	OCE	PHY	DBI
Financial resources	+				+	−	+
Grant amount	+					−	+
Other funding (>750 K)	+				+		+
Human resources	−						−
# of students	−						−
Human capital		−			+	−	
Years in tenure		−			+	−	
Full professor						−	
Social capital	+	+		+		+	+
Board membership	+	+		+		+	+
Institutional factors	+	+		+	+		
Dept. Encourages Commercialization	−			−	−		
Dept. Head Entrepreneurial Orientation	+	+		+	−		
Univ. TTO Success					+		
Scientist demographics							
Male	+			+			
Midwest region		+				+	
South region							
West region					−		

The signs indicate directionality of the coefficients that are statistically significant in the models

CMMI civil, mechanical, and manufacturing innovation, *DEB* environmental biology, *CNS* computer and network systems, *OCE* physical oceanography, *PHY* particle and nuclear astrophysics, *DBI* biological infrastructure

years in tenure, is positively associated with startups for Physical Oceanography scientists but negatively for Particle and Nuclear Astrophysics scientists. Our findings caution against generalizations across fields of science, as both the prevalence and determinants of startup vary. An important question for future research is not only to understand how, but also why, scientific fields are different. This could help advance understanding of how best to help scientists in some fields commercialize their research, if for example, they work in fields which are systematically characterized by less commercialization.

6 Conclusion

We analyzed scientist entrepreneurship by examining the drivers of scientist startup propensity among 1,899 scientists across six research fields. Our approach is novel because we collected primary survey data from scientists rather than use data collected by sources such as university TTOs or AUTM. We use a two-part empirical approach, first testing six hypotheses on our full sample. Second, we examined differences in the drivers of scientist startups in each field individually. Our findings suggest that approximately 13 % of scientists have started a new company, indicating spillovers of knowledge from universities for commercialization, innovation and ultimately economic growth, employment creation and global competitiveness.

 Springer

Acknowledgments   Our paper uses data collected and presented in Small Business Administration Report # 409, funded under the contract SBAHQ-11-M-0212. SBA Report #409 can be accessed at http://www.sba. gov/advocacy/7540/586391.

References

Acs, Z., Audretsch, D., & Lehmann, E. (2013). The knowledge spillover theory of entrepreneurship. *Small Business Economics, 41,* 757–774.

Agarwal, A., & Henderson, R. (2002). Putting patents in context: Exploring knowledge transfer from MIT. *Management Science, 48*(1), 44–60.

Aldrich, H., & Martinez, M. (2010). Entrepreneurship as social construction: A multilevel evolutionary approach. *Handbook of Entrepreneurship Research* (pp. 387–427). New York: Springer.

Aldridge, T., & Audretsch, D. (2010). Does policy influence the commercialization route? Evidence from National Institutes of Health funded scientists. *Research Policy, 39,* 583–588.

Aldridge, T., & Audretsch, D. (2011). The Bayh-Dole act and scientist entrepreneurship. *Research Policy, 40,* 1058–1067.

Arrow, K. (1962). The economic implications of learning by doing. *The Review of Economic Studies, 29,* 155–173.

Audretsch, D., Aldridge, T., & Nadella, V. (2013). University science faculty ventures into entrepreneurship, Report No. 409, Small Business Administration.

Audretsch, D., & Feldman, M. (1996). R&D spillovers and the geography of innovation and production. *The American Economic Review, 86,* 630–640.

Audretsch, D., & Stephan, P. (2002) Knowledge spillovers in biotechnology: sources and incentives. In: Economic evolution, learning, and complexity, Physica, HD, pp. 127–137.

Bates, T. (1995). Self-employment entry across industry groups. *Journal of Business Venturing, 10,* 143–156.

Bonaccorsi, A., Colombo, M., Guerini, M., & Rossi-Lamastra, C. (2014). The impact of local and external university knowledge on the creation of knowledge-intensive firms: Evidence from the Italian case. *Small Business Economics* (forthcoming).

Davidsson, P., & Honig, B. (2003). The role of social and human capital among nascent entrepreneurs. *Journal of Business Venturing, 18,* 301–331.

Dosi, G. (1988). Sources, procedures, and microeconomic effects of innovation. *Journal of Economic Literature, 26*(3), 1120–1171.

Elston, J., & Audretsch, D. (2010). Risk attitudes, wealth and sources of entrepreneurial start-up capital. *Journal of Economic Behavior & Organization, 76,* 82–89.

Evans, D., & Leighton, L. (1989). Some empirical aspects of entrepreneurship. *American Economic Review, 79,* 519–535.

Fryges, H., & Wright, M. (2014) The origin of spin-offs: A typology of corporate and academic spin-offs. *Small Business Economics* (forthcoming).

Glaeser, E., Kallal, H., Scheinkman, J., & Shleifer, A. (1992). Growth in cities. *Journal of Political Economy, 100*(6), 1126–1152.

Griliches, Z. (1979). Issues in assessing the contribution of R&D to productivity growth. *Bell Journal of Economics, 10,* 92–116.

Griliches, Z. (1990). Patent statistics as economic indicators: A survey. *Journal of Economic Literature, 28,* 1661–1707.

Henderson, R., Jaffe, A., & Trajtenberg, M. (1998). Universities as a source of commercial technology: A detailed analysis of university patenting, 1965–1988. *Review of Economics and Statistics, 80,* 119–127.

Henrekson, M., & Stenkula, M. (2010). Entrepreneurship and public policy. *Handbook of Entrepreneurship Research* (pp. 595–637). New York: Springer.

Jaffe, A. (1989). Real effects of academic research. *American Economic Review, 79*(5), 957–970.

Jaffe, A., Trajtenberg, M., & Henderson, R. (1993). Geographic localization of knowledge spillovers as evidenced by patent citations. *The Quarterly Journal of Economics, 108,* 577–598.

Karlsson, C., & Karlsson, M. (2002). Economic policy, institutions and entrepreneurship. *Small Business Economics, 19,* 163–171.

Karlsson, T., & Wigren, C. (2012). Start-ups among university employees: The influence of legitimacy, human capital and social capita. *Journal of Technology Transfer, 37*(3), 297–312.

Kerr, W., & Lincoln, W. (2010) The supply side of innovation: H-1B visa reforms and US ethnic invention, Number W15768, National Bureau of Economic Research.

 Springer

Kerr, W., & Nanda, R. (2009). Democratizing entry: Banking deregulations, financing constraints, and entrepreneurship. *Journal of Financial Economics, 94,* 124–149.

Lawson, C. (2012). Academic patenting: The importance of industry support. *Journal of Technology Transfer, 38*(4), 509–535.

Levin, S., & Stephan, P. (1991). Research productivity over the life cycle: Evidence for academic scientists. *American Economic Review, 81*(1), 114–132.

Link, A., & Scott, J. (2009). Private investor participation and commercialization rates for government-sponsored research and development: Would a prediction market improve the performance of the SBIR programme? *Economica, 76,* 264–281.

Lockett, A., & Wright, M. (2005). Resources, capabilities, risk capital and the creation of university spin-out companies. *Research Policy, 34,* 1043–1057.

Louis, K., Blumenthal, D., Gluck, M., & Stoto, M. (1989). Entrepreneurs in academe: An exploration of behaviors among life scientists. *Administrative Science Quarterly, 34,* 110–131.

Markman, G., Gianiodis, P., & Phan, P. (2008). Full-time faculty or part-time entrepreneurs. *IEEE Transactions, 55,* 29–36.

Minniti, M., & Nardone, C. (2007). Being in someone else's shoes: The role of gender in nascent entrepreneurship. *Small Business Economics, 28,* 223–238.

Mosey, S., & Wright, M. (2007). From human capital to social capital: A longitudinal study of technology-based academic entrepreneurs. *Entrepreneurship Theory and Practice, 31,* 909–935.

Mowery, D. (2005). The Bayh-Dole Act and high-technology entrepreneurship in US universities: Chicken, egg, or something else? *Advances in the Study of Entrepreneurship, Innovation & Economic Growth, 16,* 39–68.

National Economic Council (NEA) (2011) A strategy for American innovation: Security our economic growth and prosperity. Council of economic advisors, office of science and technology policy, The White House: Washington, DC, February; available online at http://www.whitehouse.gov/sites/default/files/uploads/InnovationStrategy.pdf; date last accessed: June 15, 2013.

Nelson, R. (1959). The simple economics of basic scientific research. *Journal of Political Economy, 67,* 297–306.

O'Shea, R., Allen, T., Chevalier, A., & Roche, F. (2005). Entrepreneurial orientation, technology transfer and spinoff performance of US universities. *Research Policy, 34*(7), 994.

Pakes, A., & Griliches, Z. (1980). Patents and R&D at the firm level: A first report. *Economics Letters, 5,* 377–381.

Reynolds, P., Carter, N., Gartner, W., & Greene, P. (2004). The prevalence of nascent entrepreneurs in the United States: Evidence from the panel study of entrepreneurial dynamics. *Small Business Economics, 23,* 263–284.

Shane, S., & Stuart, T. (2002). Organizational endowments and the performance of university start-ups. *Management Science, 48,* 154–170.

Thursby, J., & Thursby, M. (2002). Who is selling the ivory tower? Sources of growth in university licensing. *Management Science, 48,* 90–104.

🕗 Springer

PART II

UNIVERSITY TECHNOLOGY TRANSFER

[6]

ELSEVIER

Research Policy 34 (2005) 1113–1122

research policy

www.elsevier.com/locate/econbase

University spillovers and new firm location[☆]

David B. Audretsch[a,*], Erik E. Lehmann[b], Susanne Warning[c]

[a] *Indiana University and CEPR, Entrepreneurship, Growth and Public Policy, Max Planck Institute Jena,*
Kahlaische Strasse 10, D-07745 Jena, Germany
[b] *University of Augsburg, Universitaetstrasse 16, 86159 Augsburg, Germany*
[c] *IAAEG, University of Trier, Behringstrasse, 54296 Trier, Germany*

Abstract

This paper examines the impact of locational choice as a firm strategy to access knowledge spillovers from universities. Based on a large dataset of publicly listed, high-technology startup firms in Germany, we test the proposition that proximity to the university is shaped by different spillover mechanisms—research and human capital—and by different types of knowledge spillovers—natural sciences and social sciences. The results suggest that spillover mechanisms as well as spillover types are heterogeneous. In particular, the evidence suggests that new knowledge and technological-based firms have a high propensity to locate close to universities, presumably in order to access knowledge spillovers. However, the exact role that geographic proximity plays is shaped by the two factors examined in this paper—the particular knowledge context, and the specific type of spillover mechanism.
© 2005 Elsevier B.V. All rights reserved.

JEL classification: M13; L20; R30

Keywords: University spillovers; New firm location; Spillover mechanisms

1. Introduction

The assets that really count are those accountants cannot count.

(T.A. Stewart 1995, in Fortune 137 (7), p. 157)

[☆] Large parts of the paper were written while the second two authors were at the University of Konstanz.
* Corresponding author.
E-mail addresses: audretsch@mpiew-jena.mpg.de
(D.B. Audretsch), Erik.Lehmann@wiwi.uni-augsburg.de
(E.E. Lehmann), warning@iaaeg.de (S. Warning).

In proposing a new theory of economic geography, Krugman (1991) asks, "What is the most striking feature of the geography of economic activity? The short answer is surely concentration [...] production [...] which is remarkably concentrated in space." As for other fields of economics, the impact of geography has not escaped the attention of scholars of entrepreneurship. Recent studies have focused on the locational decision of new-firm startups (Sorenson and Audia, 2000; Baum and Sorenson, 2003). Indeed, an important finding of this literature is that the impact of geographic characteristics on locational choice is

1114   *D.B. Audretsch et al. / Research Policy 34 (2005) 1113–1122*

anything but neutral. For example, the collection of European-country studies included in the special issue of *Regional Studies*, on "Regional Variations in New Firm Formation" (Reynolds et al., 1994), identified a number of geographic-specific characteristics that impact the location of new firms. These characteristics were generally based on factors identified in earlier studies by Carlton (1983) and Bartik (1985).

However, none of these studies focused on the role of accessing knowledge spillovers in the locational choice decision of new firms. This oversight is surprising, given that the growing literature on technology management and the economics of innovation has found that knowledge spillovers play an important role in fostering entrepreneurship and innovative activity (Sorenson and Audia, 2000; Baum and Sorenson, 2003). In addition, spillovers from universities, as well as from private firms, have been identified as key sources promoting firm innovation and performance (Stuart and Sorenson, 2003; Hall et al., 2003).

The purpose of this paper is to address these significant gaps in the literature that relates locational choice as a strategic decision by firms to knowledge externalities in general and spillovers from universities in special. We do this by linking the locational choice of firms, in terms of proximity to a university, to both the type of knowledge produced at universities, as well as the actual spillover mechanism transmitting that knowledge. In particular, the importance of locational proximity to a university is analyzed in terms of two distinct types of knowledge and two distinct spillover mechanisms in order to identify whether the role of geographic proximity to a knowledge source is heterogeneous with respect to the type of knowledge as well as the actual spillover mechanism. Thus, we assume that location is a strategic choice of an entrepreneur and that the locational decision is influenced by both research activities and the provision of human capital of universities.

In Section 2, we explain why proximity to a university should yield benefits to knowledge-based startups. In Section 3, the different types of knowledge outputs and different mechanisms used by firms to access knowledge spillovers from universities are discussed. Not only are the types of knowledge and spillover mechanisms heterogeneous, but also the capacity to generate knowledge spillovers varies considerably across universities. Thus, in Section 4, a new database

consisting of 281 publicly listed firms in German high-technology and knowledge industries is used to identify empirically in Section 5 how locational choice varies for different types of knowledge and spillover mechanisms. In Section 6, a summary and conclusion are provided. In particular, the evidence suggests that, in general, new knowledge and technological-based firms have a high propensity to locate close to universities, presumably in order to access knowledge spillovers. However, the exact role that geographic proximity plays is shaped by the two factors examined in this paper—the particular knowledge context, and the specific type of spillover mechanism.

2. Proximity to universities as a locational strategy

There are two streams of literature linking locational choice as a strategic decision to access and absorb knowledge spillovers. The first strand of the literature focuses on the existence and geographic distribution of university spillovers. The second set of studies deals with the impact of location on the entrepreneurial choice to start and sustain a new firm. While the first strand of literature establishes that knowledge not only has spillovers from universities but is also spatially bounded, an implication for the model of entrepreneurial choice is that the prospects for a new firm are greater in locations conducive to accessing and absorbing those knowledge spillovers. Thus, the major premise of the location argument is that new firms would like to reduce their knowledge acquisition costs by locating close to the knowledge source, the university. However, those benefits must bear the higher costs of locational proximity to a university (see also Link and Scott, in press).

The prevalent theoretical framework analyzing the decision to start a firm has been the general model of entrepreneurial choice. The model of entrepreneurial choice dates back at least to Knight (1921), but was more recently extended and updated by Khilstrom and Laffont (1979), Holmes and Schmitz (1990), Jovanovic (1994), Lazear (2002), Alvarez and Barney (2004) among others. None of the above models or studies consider the role of location in the context of the entrepreneurial choice framework. However, geographic location should influence the

D.B. Audretsch et al. / Research Policy 34 (2005) 1113–1122 1115

entrepreneurial decision by altering the expected return from entrepreneurial activity.

The theory of localized knowledge spillovers suggests that profits will be greater in agglomerations and spatial clusters, since access to tacit knowledge is easier. Because firms access external knowledge at a cost that is lower than the cost of producing this value internally or of acquiring it externally from a geographic distance (Harhoff, 2000), they will exhibit higher expected profits. The cost of transferring such knowledge is a function of geographic distance and gives rise to localized externalities (Siegel et al., 2003). Thus, the empirical analysis of university spillovers assumes that the geographical dimension is a significant factor explaining the innovative activities of firms.

University spillovers could be defined by externalities towards firms, for which the university is the source of the spillover but is not fully compensated (Harris, 2001). Some models assume that geography plays no role in the cost of accessing that knowledge (Spence, 1984; Cohen and Levinthal, 1990). However, theories of localization suggest that just because universities are the sources of knowledge, spillovers do not mean that knowledge transmits costlessly across geographic space. In particular, these theories argue that geographic proximity reduces the cost of accessing and absorbing knowledge spillovers. Thus, a basic tenet in the literature is that university spillovers lower the costs of firms accessing and absorbing knowledge spillovers. If an entrepreneur decides to locate nearby a university, the benefits must outweigh the costs. Locating close to universities, mostly in city center, is associated with high costs of living, housing, and others. Thus, firms also have to pay higher wages to their employees. If the basic resources gathered from a university are not essential to bear those costs, it is more advantageous to locate outside such a metropolitan area.

There are both theoretical reasons and empirical evidence to believe that such knowledge spillovers generated by universities are not accessed and absorbed at costs that are invariant to geographic location (Bottazzi and Peri, 2003). Rather, because university spillovers tend to be spatially bounded, the costs of absorbing spillovers increases with distance from a university. An implication of the geographic distribution of knowledge spillovers is not only that they are spatially clustered around universities, but also that the entrepreneurial opportunities to start a new firm are also geographically linked to the spatial distribution of knowledge spillovers. The limited geographic reach of such channels for the exchange of information and know-how is one of the leading causes of the impact of geographical proximity. Or, with the words of Marshall (1890) more than a century ago, "the mysteries of the industry are in the air". Thus, a key hypothesis of this paper is that the value of locating within close geographic proximity to a university will depend upon the university output. In particular, the locational strategy of firm geographic proximity to a university should be greater when the knowledge output of the university is high.

3. Spillover mechanisms—research and human capital

There are at least two principle mechanisms facilitating the knowledge spillovers from universities to firms. The first one involves scientific research published in scholarly journals. Such published research is codified knowledge. This is because knowledge provided by articles can be transferred and transmitted with low cost, or with costs which are independent from the location. Academic papers can be downloaded from the Internet, obtained from publishers or found in libraries. This suggests that an important testable hypothesis is that the amount of scientific articles published by a university has no effect on firm location, since accessing (codified) knowledge is more or less invariant to locational distance from the university producing that knowledge.

However, an important qualification is that not all university knowledge is the same. In fact, the knowledge output of a university is heterogeneous. One useful distinction differentiates natural and social science knowledge. Social science knowledge is not based on a unified and established scientific methodology, but it rather is idiosyncratic to very specific disciplines, sub-disciplines and even research approaches. Compared to the natural sciences, research in the social sciences is considerably less codified. Thus, geographic proximity to high output universities may be more important for accessing social science research than for accessing natural science research.

The second type of spillover mechanism involves human capital embodied in students graduating from the university. As Saxenian (1994) points out, one of the important mechanisms facilitating knowledge spillovers involves the mobility of human capital, embodied in graduating students, as they move from the university to a firm. Spatial proximity to universities can therefore generate positive externalities that can be accessed by the firm through the spillover mechanism of human capital. As Varga (2000) shows, university graduates may be one of the most important channels for disseminating knowledge from academia to the local high-technology industry. In addition, other related externalities may result from close geographic proximity. For example, local proximity lowers the search costs for both firms and students. This may lead to some competitive advantage over similar firms, which are not located close to universities, especially when high skilled labor is a scarce resource and there is intense competition about high potentials.[1]

Central to the theories of localized knowledge, spillovers is the distinction between codified and tacit knowledge (Kogut and Zander, 1992). Tacit knowledge needs oral communication and reciprocity, which may be ineffective or infeasible over longer distances. Such elements of know-how and operations cannot be codified easily in a blueprint or a contractual document (Mowery and Ziedonis, 2001). Thus, technology transfer or exchange is associated with personal contacts. Such spillovers could be transmitted through certain conduits across geographic space such as the channels of communication, the social system, or a kind of technology diffusion process. Most of those benefits could not be obtained by markets or ensured by contractual arrangements. If personnel contacts are the main source for absorbing, the number of students of a university should have a positive impact on firm location. Thus, the relative importance of tacit knowledge is reflected by the number of students of a university, which serves as a measure for the intense demand for labor and interpersonal communication. Otherwise, the access to students also captures factors like network effects, social contacts and other sources of tacit knowledge. Furthermore, students in Germany are quite immobile (Fabel et al., 2002). This

suggests that the higher the human capital output of a university, the lower the distance between a university and the firm. Apart from the spillover mechanism, there might be at least two other groups of variables influencing the distance between a university and a new knowledge-based firm: location variables and firm characteristics.

Previous studies have shown that firm location decisions are influenced by such factors as the size of a city or region. It is possible that firms locate close to the areas where universities are located for network reasons. A drawback of most studies on the impact of university spillover on firm location is to explain their finding of a negative sign of spillover sources. One possible interpretation is that such knowledge sources—patents, citations, and articles—are not essential to locate close towards a university. However, there is no rational argument for this "push away" effect as expressed by the negative sign. Since our basic assumption is that locating close towards a university is associated with high costs, we also include a measure for these costs. Now, the negative sign could be interpreted in the way that the trade-off between the costs and benefits of locating close to the universities is more influenced by the costs, i.e. the costs of the close location exceed the benefits of spillover effects.

As pointed out by Audretsch and Thurik (2001) among others, the impact of such spillovers may be more important for young firms than for established firms. This is because new firms may rely on external knowledge produced by either other firms or universities (see also Link and Scott, in press; Hall et al., 2003). It has been observed (Scherer, 1991) that small and new firms do not devote a large share of resources to formal R&D. In contrast, larger and more established enterprises are able to generate their own formal R&D, and therefore are less dependent upon external knowledge. This implies that geographic proximity to universities is a source of competitive advantage for young firms, when the competitive advantage is based on intangible assets, such as ideas and the human capital of the employees. This suggests that locational strategy of firm geographic proximity is more important for young firms. Finally, previous research has shown that spillover effects differ between industries in their necessity and capability to absorb spillover effects (Jaffe, 1989; Cohen and Levinthal, 1990; Henderson and Cockburn, 1994).

---

[1] See also Stephan et al. (in press), analyzing the firm's placement of Ph.D. students.

D.B. Audretsch et al. / Research Policy 34 (2005) 1113–1122 1117

4. Data and methodology

4.1. The data

The link between proximity and university spillovers is tested by using a unique dataset of all of knowledge and high-technology German firms that were publicly listed on the *Neuer Markt*, Germany's equivalent of the *NASDAQ*. Between 1997 and 2002, the total number of firms listed in this index was 341. We excluded all firms located outside Germany as well as holding companies. Though, the underlying dataset consists of 281 publicly listed German firms, collected from IPO prospectuses, and publicly available information from on-line data sources including the *Deutsche Boerse AG*. First, this database includes firms from highly innovative industries, like biotechnology, medical devices, life sciences, e-commerce and other high-technology industries, which represent the knowledge-based economy. Secondly, there is strong evidence from the U.S. for a growth effect of clusters influenced by active research universities (Feldman, 2000) and thus we follow this line of research. Finally, this dataset represents the technological change in the German business sector from the predominance of medium sized firms in the production and manufacturing towards the high-technology and service sector.

The university-related data are collected from different sources. Information about the number of students is provided by the Federal Statistical Office. Publication data are hand-collected from the research database ISI (Information Sciences Institutes, see also Warning, 2004).

As we examine the impact of university output on locational proximity to the university, the distance of a new knowledge-based firm to the closest university is applied as endogenous variable (*distance*). This measure is sensible enough to ensure capturing also small differences in firm–university distances that is especially necessary in Germany as universities are much more geographically concentrated compared to the United States. The online database of the *German Automobile Club* (www.adac.de) is used to determine the distance between the firm and the closest university. Firms located within a radius of 1.5 km are classified as belonging in the distance category of 1 km.

Table 1 shows the descriptive statistics for the endogenous variable *distance* as well as for the exogenous variables. The median distance of a firm and a university is 7 km while the mean is more than double as high with 16.75 km. Thus, the variable distance is highly skewed, as shown in graph 1. The 92% percentile shows of the endogenous variable is 50 km and means that the 92% of the shortest distances from a firm to a university are 50 km or even shorter. This quantile is chosen for several reasons. First, we assume that within this circle, the firm is located in the metropolitan area of the university town. Second, we assume that this distance is the maximum distance for employees to travel each day to the respective firm. However, all the universities, which are taken as the nearest university of those firms, are universities located in big cities.

The independent variables are categorized into three main groups. The first group contains spillover mechanism variables for research and human capital. The second group consists of location variables, which contain university location variables as well as

Table 1
Descriptive statistics

	Mean	S.D.	Min	Max	Median
Distance	16.75	23.93	1	177	7
No. of publications in natural sciences	5139.43	4603.16	0	14,176	4069
No. of publications in social sciences	253.86	220.01	0	659	204
No. of students in natural sciences	7304.89	3988.45	0	20,570	7725
No. of students in social sciences	20,321	15,409.63	0	47,112	15,741
Inhabitants of the city of the university	916,796	830,554	76,000	3,410,000	615,000
Hotel price in the university town in Euro	180.81	68.44	55	319	179
No. of universities in the city	1.84	0.960	1	3	1
Inhabitants of firm location	640,442	897,371	1850	3,387,000	190,000
Firm age	10.400	10.025	<1	90	8

firm location variables. And finally, the third group considers firm-specific variables.

To capture the first spillover mechanism research, we include the number of articles published in high quality journals (see Zucker et al., 1998; Audretsch and Stephan, 1996). Since university spillovers are neither restricted to patent inventions[2] nor solely in the natural sciences, we include separate measures for social science research output and natural science output. This enables us also to discriminate between the types of spillover effects. Since knowledge-based industries include services such as media and entertainment, service, or e-commerce, spillovers can also be generated by fields without high patent activities. Research in the social sciences is captured by the number of articles published in journals listed in the Social Science Citation Index (SSCI). The number of publications in the Science Citation Index (SCI) indicates the research activity of universities in the natural sciences. We include the number of listed papers of both indices for each university published from 1997 until 2000.[3]

Table 1 clearly shows that the universities differ in their research activities, both in natural sciences and social sciences. Of course, the number of articles in natural sciences cannot be compared to those in social sciences, as articles in natural science are typically shorter and written by a larger number of co-authors. However, the median university published in this time period 204 articles in the social sciences and 4069 in the natural sciences. In both fields, the mean value exceeds the median value, which suggests that some universities are more research intensive than others.

The second spillover mechanism, "human capital", is captured by the number of students enrolled at each university. Consistent with our approach to the research mechanism, we consider students from the natural sciences and from the social sciences separately to control for the different types of spillover. We calculated the number of students in natural sciences and social sciences by adding the number of students from different disciplines. The natural sciences students' variable contains the study fields biology,

chemistry, physics, mathematics, computing, agriculture, forestry, dietetics, engineering, and medicine. The social science variable consists of students from the fields of languages, cultural studies, law, economics, social science, and arts. For two reasons, all student data are taken from the year 1997. First, those data are not always available for every year and university. Second, the *Neuer Markt* started in 1997 and thus, we take this year as the base year. As shown in Table 1, the number of new graduates in the social sciences is twice as much as those in natural sciences.

The second group of exogenous variables consists of location variables for the university as well as for the firm. The number of inhabitants form the location of the university is taken from the official statistics based on 1997 as proxy for the size of the city where the university is located. In the lack of adequate data for the costs of living at the university location, we include the average price of a basic single room from the most expensive hotel in the city where the university is located. These prices differ significantly across cities with the most expensive in Frankfurt, which is also the most expensive city in Germany as measured by the OECD. The number of universities in the town captures a cluster effect but also a competition effect between the universities. The variables of firm location include the number of inhabitants where the firms is located and a dummy variable that indicates location of the firm in the former western part of Germany.

In the third group of exogenous variables, we control for specific industry effects by including dummy variables for the following industries: software, e-services, e-commerce, computer and hardware, telecommunication, biotechnology, medicine and life science, media and entertainment, and high-technology. Finally, the age of the firm is considered.

4.2. Analysis and methodology

We use OLS regressions to estimate the impact of the spillover mechanisms on the endogenous variable distance, as measured in kilometers first. A closer examination of Fig. 1 shows that the endogenous variable "kilometer" is highly skewed. Thus, we not only use the natural log of the distance variable but also quantile regressions. This semi-parametric technique provides a general class of models in which the conditional quantiles have a linear form. In its

---

[2] For an analysis of university patenting, see Henderson et al. (1998) and Jaffe et al. (1993). For university patenting, see Jensen and Thursby (2001) and Jensen et al. (2003).

[3] The publications in social science and natural science did not vary across the universities during time (see Warning, 2004).

D.B. Audretsch et al. / Research Policy 34 (2005) 1113–1122 1119

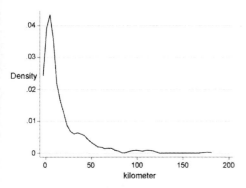

Fig. 1. Kernel density estimation of kilometer (Epanechnikow).

simplest form, the least absolute deviation estimator fits medians to a linear function of covariates. The method of quantile regression is potentially attractive for the same reason that the median or other quantiles are a better measure of location than the mean. Other useful features are the robustness against outliers and that the likelihood estimators are in general more efficient than least square estimators. Besides the technical features, quantile regressions allow that potentially different solutions at distinct quantiles may be interpreted as differences in the response of the dependent variable, namely the distance, to changes in the regressors at various points in the conditional distinction of the dependent variable. Thus, quantile regressions reveal asymmetries in the data, which could not be detected by simple OLS estimations (see Buchinsky, 1998). While the median regression focuses on the median firm, the regression on the 92% percentile focuses on the firms 50 km away from the university.

5. Empirical results: startup proximity to a university

In order to identify the impact of university output on the importance of locational proximity to the university, Table 2 shows the mean, median and the 92%-quantile regression results. Using these different estimations enables us to examine the impact of startups with greater distance from the university (compared to the median and mean).

The first column shows the results from the OLS regression with the natural logarithm of kilometers as the endogenous variable. In this approach, none of the spillover mechanisms enters the regression significantly. Next, we include the absolute number of kilometers. Now, the number of students in the natural science enters the regression significantly. The larger the number of students in the natural sciences, the closer a firm is to a university.

However, the mean distance between a firm and the closest university is about 16 km, while the median distance is only 7 km. To consider this skewed distribution, we apply quantile regressions. The results are shown in column three and four. The third column shows the results from the median regression. As the positive and statistically significant coefficient of the number of publications in the natural sciences suggests, new firms do not have a high propensity to locate within close proximity to universities with a high research output in the natural sciences. In fact, as the research output increases, the distance of the new startup from the university also tends to increase. Thus, there is no statistical evidence suggesting that new firms locate close to research universities in order to access the spillover of knowledge using the research mechanism for the knowledge type represented by the natural sciences.

However, as the negative and statistically significant coefficient of the number of publications in the social sciences indicates, the importance of locating within close geographic proximity to a university may not be invariant to the type of knowledge. This result suggests that knowledge transmitted through published research in the social sciences may, in fact, be less codified and more tacit, leading new firms to locate closer to the university in order to access the knowledge spillover.

The results in the third column of Table 2 also suggest that the magnitude of university output in the form of human capital also affects locational decisions. As the negative and statistically significant coefficient of the number of students in the natural sciences indicates, new firms tend to locate more closely to universities with a large output of students. However, this result does not hold in the social sciences. This may indicate that human capital in the natural sciences is more specific and less general than in the social sciences. The results also indicate that the other location-specific characteristics also impact the locational choice of new firms. The size of the city in which the university is

Table 2
Regressions on the mean, median and the 92%-quantile

Variables	OLS (semi-log)	OLS	Median	0.92-quantile
Spillover mechanism research				
Natural science research	−0.00009 (1.05)	−0.001 (0.10)	0.0012 (3.22)***	−0.0016 (0.26)
Social science research	0.00093 (0.42)	0.0144 (0.39)	−0.0303 (3.80)***	0.1116 (0.69)
Spillover mechanism human capital				
Natural science human capital	−0.00003 (1.46)	−0.0006 (1.95)**	−0.0005 (4.93)***	−0.0002 (0.10)
Social science human capital	0.00001 (0.91)	−0.0007 (0.36)	0.0001 (2.31)**	−0.0011 (0.88)
Location variables				
City size (for university)	0.0080 (0.85)	0.0246 (0.94)	0.0153 (11.01)***	0.0323 (1.45)
Cost of living (for university)	0.0121 (0.64)	−0.0129 (0.47)	−0.00258 (3.58)***	−0.0895 (0.56)
Number of universities in town	0.5340 (3.74)***	1.5741 (0.65)	−2.0271 (2.16)**	−13.822 (0.82)
West location	0.5826 (1.40)	−11.882 (1.87)*	3.8011 (2.31)***	−12.180 (0.91)
City size (for firm)	−0.0080 (5.98)***	−0.0122 (4.34)***	−0.0013 (15.71)***	−0.0365 (2.58)***
Firm characteristics				
Firm age	0.0151 (2.06)**	0.0744 (0.49)	0.0507 (1.37)	−0.3421 (0.64)
Software	−0.0029 (0.03)	0.4810 (0.73)	0.4966 (1.26)	−0.3421 (0.11)
Service	−0.2311 (0.82)	1.2914 (0.28)	−1.1929 (1.16)	9.7641 (0.45)
E-commerce	0.0425 (0.11)	4.5571 (0.51)	1.8528 (1.16)	35.874 (1.12)
Hardware	−0.0984 (0.29)	8.4662 (0.86)	−1.1422 (0.80)	22.321 (0.85)
Telecom	−0.0066 (0.21)	−4.7332 (1.22)	0.7564 (0.50)	−4.315 (0.25)
Biotechnology	0.5687 (1.28)	−7.8921 (1.25)	−5.0633 (3.13)***	−4.4202 (0.12)
Medical devices	−0.9444 (1.56)	−13.445 (1.87)*	−1.0453 (0.55)	2.8956 (0.15)
Media	−0.8593 (3.33)***	−8.293 (2.67)**	−4.0047 (3.24)***	−5.9651 (0.25)
Constant	2.0104 (3.99)***	32.3856 (3.93)***	11.9244 (6.05)***	96.441 (3.33)
R-squared	0.1235	0.1479	0.1603	0.2848

The endogenous variable is the distance from the new firm to the closest university. t-values are in parenthesis. The baseline is firms in the technology sector. The asterisks, *, **, and *** indicate significance at the 10%, 5%, and 1% level, respectively. The number of observations is 281. The variables for city size (for university) and city size (for firm) are multiplied with 1000.

located, the cost of living in which the university is located, and the city size where the firm is located are all found to influence the locational decision of new firms. Since we focus only on academic research, as expressed by the number of articles published in academic journals and the number of students, we restrict our analysis extremely on those two aspects. However, there are several aspects which also influence the strategic choice of founders which are captured by variables like the size of a city or the cost of living.

As column three in Table 2 shows, the results are considerably different when the 92.5%-quantile estimation is used. Neither the spillover mechanisms nor the knowledge types have a statistically significant impact on the location of new firms. This would suggest that the knowledge spillovers are geographically bounded within a small distance from the university. The same holds for the mean regression in column two, where the mean distance is about 16 km. Thus,

we prefer the median regression to capture the effect that half of the firms are located within a small circle about 7 km around a university.

6. Conclusions

Recent studies suggest that regional characteristics have a critical impact on the locational decisions made by new firms. Our findings are consistent with this view, but we also identify an additional locational factor: the presence of a university. New firms in high-technology industries are influenced not only by the traditional regional characteristics, but also by the opportunity to access knowledge generated by universities.

An important finding of this paper, however, is the impact of university output on new firm location is sensitive to both the type of knowledge and mechanism used to access that knowledge. Thus, the role of geographic proximity to access university knowledge is not simple and straightforward, but rather depends on the knowledge type and spillover mechanism.

The emergence of knowledge as a basic resource of competitiveness, along with the propensity for knowledge to remain localized, means that locations have new policy opportunities. Entrepreneurs flourish under supportive public policy regimes. By providing high skilled and well-educated students, cities help entrepreneurs find the necessary human capital, which will, subsequently, help develop new ideas and faster growth. Increasing university spending leads to better educated and trained students, as well as improving research activities and enhancing spillovers. Finally, regional and local initiatives can lower the costs of locating close to universities for entrepreneurs. However, the impact of entrepreneurship policy on entrepreneurship is affected by factors which are not considered in this paper.

Future research may be expected to focus less on uncovering the existence of knowledge spillovers and more on identifying the heterogeneity inherent in both types of knowledge generated by universities, as well as the various mechanisms that firms use to access knowledge spillovers.

Acknowledgments

Financial support by the German Research Foundation (DFG) through the research group #FOR454 "Heterogeneous Labor" at the University of Konstanz and the ZEW, Mannheim, is gratefully acknowledged. We would also like to thank Paula Stephan, Al Link, Don Siegel, Frank T. Rothaermel, Adam Lederer, Dieter Sadowski, the participants of the Technology Transfer Society (T2S) Meeting 2004, and two anonymous referees for their helpful comments. The usual disclaimer applies.

References

Alvarez, S.A., Barney, J.B., 2004. Organizing rent generation and appropriation: toward a theory of the entrepreneurial firm. Journal of Business Venturing 19, 621–635.

Audretsch, D.B., Stephan, P.E., 1996. Company-scientist locational links: the case of biotechnology. American Economic Review 86, 641–652.

Audretsch, D.B., Thurik, R., 2001. What's new about the new economy? Sources of growth in the managed and entrepreneurial economies. Industrial and Corporate Change 10, 267–315.

Bartik, T.J., 1985. Business location decisions in the United States: estimates of the effects of unionization, taxes, and other characteristics of states. Journal of Business and Economic Statistics 3, 14–22.

Baum, J.A.C., Sorenson, O., 2003. Advances in Strategic Management: Geography and Strategy, vol. 20. JAI Press, Greenwich, CT.

Bottazzi, L., Peri, G., 2003. Innovation and spillovers in regions: evidence from European patent data. European Economic Review 47, 687–710.

Buchinsky, M., 1998. Recent advantages in quantile regression models. Journal of Human Resources 33, 88–126.

Carlton, D.W., 1983. The location and employment choices of new firms: an econometric model with discrete and continuous endogenous variables. Review of Economics and Statistics 54, 440–449.

Cohen, W.M., Levinthal, D.A., 1990. Absorptive capacity: a new perspective on learning and innovation. Administrative Science Quarterly 35, 128–152.

Fabel, O., Lehmann, E.E., Warning, S., 2002. Der relative Vorteil deutscher wirtschaftswissenschaftlicher Fachbereiche im Wettbewerb um studentischen Zuspruch. Zeitschrift für betriebswirtschaftliche Forschung 54, 509–526 (with an English summary).

Feldman, M.P., 2000. Location and innovation: the new economic geography of innovation. In: Clark, G., Feldman, M.P., Gertler, M. (Eds.), Oxford Handbook of Economic Geography. Oxford University Press, Oxford.

Hall, B.A., Link, N., Scott, J.T., 2003. Universities as research partners. Review of Economics and Statistics 85, 485–491.

Harhoff, D., 2000. R&D spillovers, technological proximity, and productivity growth—evidence from German panel data. Schmalenbach Business Review 52, 238–260.

Harris, R.G., 2001. The knowledge-based economy: intellectual origins and new economic perspectives. International Journal of Management Review 3, 21–41.

Henderson, R., Jaffe, A., Trajtenberg, M., 1998. Universities as a source of commercial technology: a detailed analysis of university patenting 1965–1988. Review of Economics and Statistics 65, 119–127.

Henderson, R., Cockburn, I., 1994. Measuring competence? Exploring firm effects in pharmaceutical research. Strategic Management Journal 15 (Special Issue), 63–84.

Holmes, T.J., Schmitz, J.A., 1990. A theory of entrepreneurship and its application to the study of business transfer. Journal of Political Economy 98, 265–294.

Jaffe, A.B., 1989. Real effects of academic research. American Economic Review 79, 957–970.

Jaffe, A.B., Trajtenberg, M., Henderson, R., 1993. Geographic localization of knowledge spillovers as evidenced by patent citations. Quarterly Journal of Economics 63, 577–598.

Jensen, R.A., Thursby, M., 2001. Proofs and prototypes for sale: the licensing of university inventions. American Economic Review 91, 240–259.

Jensen, R.A., Thursby, J.G., Thursby, M.C., 2003. Disclosure and licensing of university inventions: 'The Best We Can Do with the S**t We Get to Work With'. International Journal of Industrial Organization 21, 1271–1300.

Jovanovic, B., 1994. Entrepreneurial choice when people differ in their management and labor skills. Small Business Economics 6 (3), 185–192.

Khilstrom, R., Laffont, J.-J., 1979. A general equilibrium entrepreneurial theory of firm formation based on risk aversion. Journal of Political Economy 87, 719–748.

Krugman, P., 1991. Geography and Trade. Leuven University, MIT Press.

Knight, F., 1921. Risk, Uncertainty and Profit. Augustus Kelly, New York.

Kogut, B., Zander, U., 1992. Knowledge of the firm, combinative capabilities, and the replication of technology. Organizational Science 3, 383–397.

Lazear, E.P., 2002. Entrepreneurship. NBER Working Paper No. 9109.

Link, A.N., Scott, J.T., in press. U.S. science parks: the diffusion of an innovation and its effects on the academic mission of universities. Journal of Productivity Analysis.

Marshall, A., 1890. Principles of Economics. MacMillan, London.

Mowery, D.C., Ziedonis, A.A., 2001. The geographic reach of market and non-market channels of technology transfer: comparing citations and licenses of university patents. NBER Working Paper No. 8568.

Reynolds, P.D., Storey, D.J., Westhead, P., 1994. Regional variations in new firm formation—special issue. Regional Studies 28, 343–456.

Saxenian, A., 1994. Regional Advantage: Culture and Competition in Silicon Valley and Rte., vol. 128. Harvard University Press, Cambridge, MA.

Scherer, F.M., 1991. Changing perspectives on the firm size problem. In: Acs, Z.J., Audretsch, D.B. (Eds.), Innovation and Technological Change: An International Comparison. University of Michigan Press, Ann Arbor, pp. 24–38.

Siegel, D.S., Westhead, P., Wright, M., 2003. Assessing the impact of science parls on the research productivity of firms: exploratory evidence from the United Kingdom. International Journal of Industrial Organization 21, 1217–1225.

Sorenson, O., Audia, G., 2000. The social structure of entrepreneurial activity: geographic concentration of footwear production in the U.S. 1940–1989. American Journal of Sociology 106, 324–362.

Spence, M.A., 1984. Cost reduction, competition, and industry performance. Econometrica 52, 101–121.

Stephan, P.E., Sumell, A.J., Black, G.C., Adams, J.D., in press. Public knowledge, private placements: new Ph.D.s as a source of knowledge spillovers. Economic Development Quarterly.

Stuart, T.E., Sorenson, O., 2003. The geography of opportunity: spatial heterogeneity in founding rates and the performance of biotechnology firms. Research Policy 25, 1139–1157.

Varga, A., 2000. Local academic knowledge transfers and the concentration of economic activity. Journal of Regional Science 40, 289–309.

Warning, S., 2004. Performance differences in German higher education. Empirical analysis of strategic groups. Review of Industrial Organization 24, 393–408.

Zucker, L.G., Darby, M.R., Armstrong, J., 1998. Intellectual human capital and the birth of U.S. biotechnology enterprises. American Economic Review 88, 290–306.

[7]

Industrial and Corporate Change, Volume 16, Number 4, pp. 641–655
doi:10.1093/icc/dtm020
Advance Access published June 24, 2007

An empirical analysis of the propensity of academics to engage in informal university technology transfer*

Albert N. Link, Donald S. Siegel and Barry Bozeman

Formal university technology transfer mechanisms, through licensing agreements, research joint ventures, and university-based startups, have attracted considerable attention in the academic literature. Surprisingly, there has been little systematic empirical analysis of the propensity of academics to engage in informal technology transfer. This paper presents empirical evidence on the determinants of three types of informal technology transfer by faculty members: transfer of commercial technology, joint publications with industry scientists, and industrial consulting. We find that male, tenured and research-grant active faculty members are more likely to engage in all three forms of informal technology transfer.

1. Introduction

The enactment of the Bayh-Dole Act in 1980 was followed by a rapid rise in formal commercial knowledge transfers from US universities to firms through such mechanisms as licensing agreements, research joint ventures, and university-based startups.[1] Universities have welcomed this trend because formal technology transfer can potentially generate large sums of revenue, as well as build relations with external stakeholders and enhance economic growth and development in the local region. A concomitant trend has been a burgeoning literature on the managerial and policy implications of such formal technology transfers.

---

*This work was performed as part of the project "Assessing Economic and Social Impacts of Basic Research Sponsored by the Office of Basic Energy Sciences," under contract DE-FG02-96ER45562 and "Assessing R&D Projects' Impacts on Scientific and Technical Human Capital Development" (SBR 98-18229)—Barry Bozeman, P.I.

[1]For a history of the Bayh-Dole Act, see, for example, Stevens (2004); for an overview of public policy implications related to Bayh-Dole, see Mowery et al. (2004) and Link (2006).

Most researchers who assess university technology transfer have examined institutions that have emerged to facilitate commercialization, such as university technology transfer offices (TTOs), industry–university cooperative research centers, science/research parks, and incubators. However, certain research questions are better addressed by focusing directly on agents involved in technology commercialization, such as academic scientists. A smaller literature has emerged in which individual-level behavior relating to formal technology transfer mechanisms is studied. Specifically, several authors have examined the determinants and outcomes of faculty involvement in university technology transfer, such as their propensity to patent, disclose inventions, publish with industry scientists, and establish university-based startups.[2]

While formal technology transfer mechanisms have attracted considerable attention in the academic literature and popular press (e.g. Bozeman, 2000; Siegel and Phan, 2005), there has been little systematic empirical analysis of informal technology transfer mechanisms. We mean by formal technology transfer mechanisms ones that embody or directly result in a legal instrumentality such as, for example, a patent, license or royalty agreement. An informal technology transfer mechanism is one facilitating the flow of technological knowledge through informal communication processes, such as technical assistance, consulting, and collaborative research. While formal technology transfer mechanisms sometimes result ultimately in formal instrumentalities, they often do not and there is not always an expectation that they will. Formal technology transfer is focused on allocation of property rights and obligations, whereas with informal technology transfer, property rights play a secondary role, if any, and obligations are normative rather than legal.

In extensive interviews of faculty members, Siegel *et al.* (2003, 2004) reported a key stylized fact: many faculty members are not disclosing their inventions to their university. Furthermore, these authors also found that even when an invention is publicly disclosed, some firms will contact scientists directly and arrange to work with them through informal technology transfer. Markman *et al.* (2006a,b) recently documented that many technologies are indeed "going out the back door." Taken together, these findings suggest that channels of informal technology transfer may be prevalent and important for university administrators to understand given their objective to formalize such activities.

The purpose of this paper is to present empirical evidence—the first systematic empirical evidence to our knowledge—on the extent of and determinants of informal technology transfer by university faculty. Our empirical analysis is based on information collected through an extensive survey of university scientists and engineers. We identified faculty who were involved in several dimensions

---

[2]See, for example, Louis *et al.* (1989) and Audretsch (2000).

of informal technology transfer activity, and we then correlated the likelihood of such involvement with selected faculty and institutional characteristics.

The remainder of the paper is organized as follows. Section 2 presents a discussion of the extant literature and from that literature we identified factors that are hypothesized to be associated with faculty members engaging in informal technology transfer. Section 3 describes the data set and the econometric models used to test these hypotheses. Section 4 summarizes our empirical findings, and Section 5 offers concluding observations, prefaced by a discussion of the caveats associated with this study.

2. Technology transfer: brief overview of the literature

Before contemplating the determinants of the propensity of faculty members to engage in informal technology transfer, it is useful to consider the goals, norms, standards, and values of academic scientists. A key objective of academic scientists is recognition within the scientific community. This results primarily from scholarly papers published in leading journals; presentations at eminent institutions, conferences, and workshops; and receipt of extramural research grants. Untenured faculty members have a strong incentive to pursue such goals because they are requirements for promotion and tenure at research universities.

It is also important to note that university scientists are also motivated by personal financial gain, as well as the need to secure additional funding for physical and human capital required for additional experimental research and professional advancement. Key resources include laboratory equipment and facilities, graduate assistants, and post-doctoral fellows. The norms, standards, and values of scientists reflect an organizational culture that values creativity, innovation, and especially an individual's contribution to the advancement of knowledge through basic research.

Siegel *et al.* (2003) and Siegel *et al.* (2004) conducted over 100 structured interviews of academic scientists who had interacted with their university TTO. Their qualitative research revealed that many academics perceive, among other things, that there are insufficient rewards for faculty involvement in university technology transfer. Of particular importance for faculty involvement are the terms of the university royalty distribution formula that determines the fraction of the licensing revenue that is allocated to the faculty member who developed the new technology.

Quantitative research has confirmed the importance of the university royalty distribution formula. Using data on 113 US TTOs, Link and Siegel (2005) reported that universities allocating a higher percentage of royalty payments to faculty members are more productive in technology transfer activities. This finding was independently confirmed in Friedman and Silberman (2003) and Lach and Schankerman (2004), each using slightly different data and methodologies.

Non-pecuniary rewards, such as credit towards promotion and tenure, are also relevant factors. Some academic respondents suggested to Link and Siegel (2005) that involvement in technology transfer might be detrimental to their careers. Many faculty expressed intense frustration with the university bureaucracy. Some pointed to concerns about licensing officers: some mentioned the high rate of turnover among licensing officers, which is detrimental towards the establishment of long-term relationships with either the TTO or with firms; and still others mentioned insufficient business and marketing experience within the TTO and the possible need for incentive compensation.

Other authors have explored the role of organizational incentives in university technology transfer from a theoretical standpoint. Jensen *et al.* (2003) modeled the process of faculty disclosure and university licensing through a TTO as a game. The principal is the university administration, while the faculty and the TTO are agents who maximize expected utility. The authors treated the TTO as a dual agent (i.e., an agent of both the faculty and the university). Faculty members must decide whether to disclose the invention to the TTO and at what stage (i.e., whether to disclose at the most embryonic stage or wait until it is a laboratory prototype).

University administration influences the disclosure incentives of the TTO and faculty members by establishing university-wide policies for the shares of licensing income and/or sponsored research. If an invention is disclosed, the TTO decides whether to search for a firm to license the technology and then negotiates the terms of the licensing agreement with the licensee. Quality is incorporated in their model as a determinant of the probability of successful commercialization. According to the authors, the TTO engages in a balancing act in the sense that it can influence the rate of invention disclosures, evaluate the inventions once they are disclosed, and negotiate licensing agreements with firms as the agent of the administration.

Jensen *et al.* (2003) theoretical analysis generates some interesting empirical predictions. For instance, in equilibrium, the probability that a university scientist discloses an invention and the stage at which this happens is related to the pecuniary reward from licensing, as well as faculty quality. The authors tested the empirical implications of the dual agency model based on an extensive survey of the objectives, characteristics, and outcomes of licensing activity at 62 US universities.[3] Their survey results provide empirical support for the hypothesis that the TTO is a dual agent. They also found that faculty quality is positively associated with the rate of invention disclosure at the earliest stage and negatively associated with the share of licensing income allocated to inventors.

Social networks appear to play an important role is important in university-industry technology transfer processes. These networks include academic and

---

[3]See Thursby *et al.* (2001) for an extensive description of this survey.

industry scientists, and perhaps, university administrators, TTO directors, and managers/entrepreneurs (Powell, 1990; Liebeskind *et al.*, 1996). Social networks that allow knowledge transfer appear to work in both directions. Scientists who were interviewed noted that interacting with industry enabled them to conduct better basic research, a finding that has also been documented in biotechnology industries (Zucker and Darby, 1996).

Murray (2004) studied social networks from the perspective of the academic careers of biotechnology scientists and examined, for a small sample of scientists, the relationship between academic careers and their social capital. Murray showed that social capital affected the success of scientist's relationship with firms, as did their human capital. Human capital is often associated with tacit knowledge, and tacit knowledge engenders scientists to firms.[4]

Institutional factors and cultural norms across scientific fields may also influence technology transfer activity. Owen-Smith and Powell (2001, 2003) compared faculty involvement in technology transfer in the life sciences and physical sciences. They reported substantial variation in perceptions across scientific fields on the outcomes of patenting. On the one hand, life scientists appear to be more concerned about the proprietary benefits of patents and using them to obtain leverage with firms. On the other hand, physical scientists patent so that they can have the freedom to publicize their work without fear of losing potentially valuable intellectual property rights, and also to gain leverage with the university. The authors concluded that institutional success in technology transfer depends on faculty attitudes toward the TTO; perceptions about the ease of working with the TTO appear to be an important factor in faculty decisions to patent. They also argued that a crucial first step in the process of technology transfer is for faculty members to disclose inventions, which will require effort on the part of the TTO to elicit disclosures.

Some authors have recently explored the outcomes of research collaborations among industry scientists and university scientists. Adams *et al.* (2005) assessed scientific teams and institutional collaborations, at the level of the individual researcher. The authors analyzed data from 2.4 million scientific papers published by researchers at 110 top US research universities during the 1981–1999 period. These scientific papers accounted for a substantial share of published basic research conducted in the United States during this period. The authors measured team size by the number of authors on a scientific paper. Using this measure they found

---

[4]Nicolaou and Birley (2003) hypothesized that networks with industry, "exoinstitutional research networks," lead to scientist involvement in direct or orthodox spin out formations that do not involve the university. Relatedly, Druilhe and Garnsey (2004) examined longitudinal data from Cambridge University and found that informal relationships with industry were often precursors to a formal spin out that likewise did not involve the university.

that both team size and the rate of collaboration have increased substantially over the 19-year period.

Placement of former graduate students was found to be a key determinant of institutional collaborations, especially collaborations with firms and with foreign scientific institutions. Finally, the evidence suggested that scientific output and influence increase with team size and that influence rises along with institutional collaborations. Because increasing team size implies an increase in the division of labor, these results are in a way suggestive that scientific productivity increases with the scientific division of labor.

Hertzfeld *et al.* (2006) interviewed then surveyed chief intellectual property attorneys at 54 R&D-intensive US firms concerning intellectual property protection mechanisms related to university patents. They found that firms expressed great difficulty in dealing with university TTOs on intellectual property issues, citing the inexperience of the TTO staff, their lack of general business knowledge, and their tendency to inflate the commercial potential of the patent. The authors reported that firms were similarly frustrated and were inclined, when possible, to by-pass the TTO and deal directly with the university scientist or engineer.

Dietz and Bozeman (2005) analyzed the career paths of scientists and engineers working at US university research centers. The authors followed career transitions within the industrial, academic, and governmental sectors and their relation to the publication and patent productivity of these researchers. They hypothesized that among university scientists, inter-sectoral changes in jobs throughout their careers provided access to new social networks and scientific and technical human capital, which resulted in higher productivity. To test this hypothesis, the authors collected and coded the academic vita of each of the 1,200 research scientists and engineers. In addition, patent data were collected from the US Patent and Trademark Office and linked to career data on these researchers.

Dietz and Bozeman (2005) concluded that the career paths of academic scientists and engineers affiliated with university research centers are quite different than those characterized in the standard literature on career transitions of researchers. The wave of center creation activity that began in the early 1980s has resulted in markedly different academic careers and greater ties between universities and industry. At least within the domain of university research centers, there seems to be considerable industrial ties, reflected in changes in careers and other factors, which are associated with different productivity outcomes.

In sum, the extant literature on institutional productivity in licensing, patenting, and entrepreneurial startups and the role of individual scientists in that process suggests that faculty members may have strong incentives to engage in informal technology transfer. In the following sections of this paper, we present systematic empirical evidence on the propensity of faculty members to circumvent the TTO through information technology transfer.

3. Data set and econometric model

Our data on informal technology transfer are derived from the Research Value Mapping Program Survey of Academic Researchers.[5] Survey data were collected from a sample of university scientists and engineers with a Ph.D. at the 150 Carnegie Extensive Doctoral/Research Universities during the time period spring 2004 to spring 2005.[6] The sample of researchers selected to receive the survey was not random but rather proportional to the numbers of academic researchers in the various fields of science and engineering, and it was balanced between randomly selected men and women.[7]

The measures of informal technology transfer considered herein are based on faculty responses to the following three statements in the survey:

During the past 12 months:

(1) I worked directly with industry personnel in an effort to transfer or commercialize technology or applied research.
(2) I co-authored a paper with industry personnel that has been published in a journal or refereed proceedings.
(3) I served as a formal paid consultant to an industrial firm.

To the best of our knowledge, this study represents the first systematic collection of such information from a large cross-section of university scientists and engineers. The three dependent variables in our econometric analysis relate to these alternative mechanisms of informal faculty technology transfer.[8]

From the sampling population of 1514 full-time tenured or tenure-track scientists and engineers, nearly 52% responded that they had some working relationship with industry during the past 12 months; of these faculty, 16% have been involved in the transfer of commercial technology, 15% have co-authored with industry personnel, and 18% have served as formal consultants with industry.

---

[5]This database was assembled under the sponsorship of these agencies within the Research Value Mapping Program at Georgia Tech for the purpose of understanding the teaching, research, and grant experiences of university scientists and engineers and their career trajectories.

[6]See, http://www.carnegiefoundation.org/Classification/index.htm.

[7]The target sample was 200 men and 200 women from each of the 12 National Science Foundation science and technology disciplines: biology, computer science, mathematics, physics, earth and atmospheric science, chemistry, agriculture, chemical engineering, civil engineering, electrical engineering, mechanical engineering, and materials engineering (http://www.nsf.gov/sbe/srs/nsf03310/start.htm). Sampling proportions by gender and field are taken into account in the weighted regressions discussed below; these weights are available from the authors upon request.

[8]Data were collected on the propensity of faculty to patent with industry; but we could not determine conclusively if such patenting activity involved the TTO or not. Thus, patenting activity was not considered in the analysis below.

The empirical model used to quantify the relationship among these measure of informal technology transfer and faculty and institutional characteristics is:

$$ITT = COMMERC, JOINTPUB, \text{ or } CONSULT = f(\mathbf{X}). \qquad (1)$$

where *ITT* represents three dimensions of informal technology transfer: involvement in activity to transfer or commercialize technology (*COMMERC*), involvement in joint publications (*JOINTPUB*), and consulting (*CONSULT*). Independently, Cohen *et al.* (2002) identified such dimensions of information technology transfer. And, with reference to equation (1), $\mathbf{X}$ is a vector of faculty characteristics, including gender (*GENDER*, males = 1; 0 otherwise); faculty tenure (*TENURE*, tenured = 1; 0 otherwise; or years with tenure, *YRSTEN*); preeminence of the faculty member as measured by the percent of time spent on grants-related research (*GRANTRES*); and the scientific or engineering discipline of the faculty member.

This descriptive model is based in part on predictions from the extant literature and in part on the availability of data. Gender is a control variable. The academic status and past research success of each faculty member is proxied by the tenure variables. Although this faculty dimension has not previously been investigated empirically, its inclusion in our model is motivated from the theory of social networks, with emphasis on both the demand side and supply side. While many faculty may be willing to supply their research capabilities to firms, those faculty most credentialed will logically be in greater demand, as Murray's (2004) findings suggest. Also, the confirmation of tenure signals to firms what we refer to as "accumulative advantage." Tenured faculty have had a longer time to develop industry networks as well as skills and a body of accepted research potentially useful to industry. And, tenured faculty may have a stronger inclination to in fact supply their talents to industry. The fact that the tenure hurdle has been vaulted means that such faculty may be more likely to feel the freedom to engage in activities that, while important to them and to their institution, are self-enriching.

Holding tenure constant, faculty who are more grants-research active, as proxied by the percent of time they currently allocated to grants-related research, is yet another measure of the human capital of the scientist. He or she has cleared the hurdle of peer review to receive an extramural research grant and may thus be in greater demand by industry because of their external or third-party confirmation of research excellence. It is an empirical issue whether such faculty will in fact supply their talents in the face of industry demand, all else remaining constant.

Finally, the academic discipline of each faculty member is held constant to control for, among other things, differences in what Klevorick *et al.* (1995) called technological opportunity.

Table 1 Descriptive statistics ($n = 1502$)

Variable	Mean	Standard deviation
COMMERC	0.158	0.365
JOINTPUB	0.146	0.353
CONSULT	0.180	0.385
GENDER	0.481	0.500
TENURE	0.716	0.451
YRSTEN*	15.87	10.89
GRANTRES	0.246	0.164
AGE**	46.31	10.37
Biology	0.079	0.270
Computer Science	0.087	0.281
Mathematics	0.066	0.248
Physics	0.093	0.290
Earth and Atmospheric Science	0.105	0.307
Chemistry	0.085	0.278
Agriculture	0.080	0.271
Chemical Engineering	0.075	0.264
Civil Engineering	0.104	0.305
Electrical Engineering	0.076	0.265
Mechanical Engineering	0.091	0.288
Materials Engineering	0.060	0.237

Note: A number of faculty members were deleted from the population of 1514 because data were not reported on years with tenure or on age.

*$n = 1462$.

**$n = 1485$.

4. Empirical results

Descriptive statistics on all of these variables are presented in Table 1. While the stratified sample is evenly split between men and women, there appears to be a high, but representative, proportion of tenured faculty members—nearly 72% of the respondents are tenured, with an average of being tenured for 16 years. The average faculty member in our sample is currently spending a little more than 24% of his or her work time on research grants.

Table 2 presents econometric results from alternative specifications of equation (1). Specifications related to the results in columns (1), (5), and (9) include the dichotomous tenure variable, *TENURE*, while those in columns (2), (6), and (10) quantify tenure in terms of years with tenure, *YRSTEN*. Paralleling these specifications are others that also control for the age of the faculty member, *AGE*.

Table 2 Probit estimates from equation (1) (standard errors in parentheses)

Independent variable	Dependent variable											
	COMMERC				JOINTPUB				CONSULT			
	(1)	(2)	(3)	(4)	(5)	(6)	(7)	(8)	(9)	(10)	(11)	(12)
GENDER	0.262* (0.08)	0.226** (0.09)	0.274* (0.09)	0.246* (0.09)	0.141*** (0.08)	0.102 (0.09)	0.098 (0.09)	0.084 (0.09)	0.391* (0.08)	0.320* (0.09)	0.379* (0.86)	0.335* (0.09)
TENURE	0.266* (0.10)	—	0.291* (0.11)	—	0.264* (0.10)	—	0.221** (0.11)	—	0.387* (0.10)	—	0.375* (0.11)	—
YRSTEN	—	0.087** (0.03)	—	0.225* (0.07)	—	0.081** (0.03)	—	0.089 (0.07)	—	0.108* (0.03)	—	0.188* (0.07)
GRANTRES	0.848* (0.23)	0.854* (0.23)	0.846* (0.23)	0.836* (0.23)	0.798* (0.22)	0.828* (0.23)	0.804* (0.23)	0.813* (0.23)	0.438** (0.20)	0.509** (0.21)	0.520** (0.21)	0.575** (0.21)
AGE	—	—	-0.0009 (0.005)	-0.201** (0.01)	—	—	-0.004 (0.005)	-0.001 (0.009)	—	—	-0.002 (0.005)	-0.012 (0.01)
Intercept	-2.363* (0.17)	-2.521* (0.21)	-2.356* (0.26)	-2.098* (0.29)	-2.219* (0.16)	-2.345* (0.26)	-2.379* (0.26)	-2.293* (0.28)	-2.091* (0.15)	-2.241* (0.19)	-2.227* (0.25)	-2.033* (0.27)
Log Likelihood	-575.9	-555.1	-569.5	-549.7	-571.9	-553.2	-565.5	-547.4	-641.8	-623.1	-633.1	-613.7
Pseudo R²	0.110	0.101	0.114	0.115	0.164	0.164	0.164	0.162	0.185	0.185	0.185	0.184
n	1502	1462	1485	1462	1502	1462	1485	1462	1502	1462	1485	1462

Notes: Discipline effects are held constant; these results along with other descriptive statistics by discipline, are available from the authors. Probit results are weighted by discipline sampling proportions.

*Significant at 0.01 level; **significant at 0.05 level; ***significant at 0.10 level.

AGE is included as an independent variable in an effort to segment the impact of tenure, per se, as a signal about faculty quality, and time, per se, as a necessary condition for being able to develop industrial relationships. As noted below, however, the *AGE* is generally not statistically significant.

The Probit estimates reported in Table 2 suggest that male faculty members are more likely than female faculty members to engage in informal commercial knowledge transfer and consulting. Recent research (e.g., Corley and Gaughan, 2005) from this same data set suggests that these gender findings may be attenuated by institutional setting. Women who are affiliated with interdisciplinary university research centers have commercial activity profiles that more closely resemble male center affiliates than females affiliated only with traditional academic departments. It is also likely the case that gender findings are explained in part by disciplinary selection effects, which we do control for in the model. Women represent a smaller portion of those disciplines and fields most active in technology transfer.

Not surprisingly, tenured faculty members are more likely than untenured faculty members to engage in all three forms of informal technology transfer. Years with tenure also has a positive impact especially on the transfer of commercial technology and on publications.

Finally, we find that faculty members who currently allocate a relatively higher percentage of their time to grants-related research are more likely to engage in all forms of informal technology transfer. Companion research using the same data as herein suggests that this is especially the case for grants and contracts from industry (Bozeman and Gaughan, 2006).

5. Concluding observations

Our empirical findings should be interpreted with caution for three reasons. The first concern is possible response bias to the survey, although we weighted responses to mirror the population of scientists and engineers. Another concern is that we have simple, dichotomous measures of informal technology transfer. The latter may be problematic because such measures do not account for the extent of such activity or for the nature and characteristics of the technology that is transferred. In addition, our data do not allow us to control for the possibility that informal technology transfer, as we have measured it, in the current time period can develop into formal technology transfer in subsequent time periods. As well, our data do not allow us to explore the possibility of a complementary relationship among the three measures of information technology transfer—contemporaneously complementary or complementary over time.

And, there could be a two-stage process, or perhaps a simultaneous process, underlying our statistical analysis. The first stage might consist of the decision by the faculty member to establish a relationship with a private company; the second stage, or perhaps the simultaneous stage, might consist of the decision by the faculty member to actually engage in informal technology transfer activities. We also note that our econometric analysis does not control for the quality of the TTO, namely the competence of those in the office or the efficiency with which the office operates.

These caveats and data shortcomings aside, the results in Table 2 are the first such results and should be especially useful to university administrators. A clear finding is that tenured faculty members and those who are actively involved in research grants are more likely to engage in informal technology transfer than non-tenured faculty members. One interpretation of this result is that industry is simply more interested in interacting with more successful research faculty, a finding that is consistent with the "star scientist" phenomenon in the biotechnology industry by Zucker and Darby (1996, 2001). It is also possible that the incidence of such informal technology transfer might be a signal that technologies are going "out of the back door" and hence the university is not realizing sufficient revenue from its intellectual property portfolio. Another interpretation is that university incentives need to be properly aimed towards keeping tenured faculty members involved in formal technology transfer activities.

The results relating to research grants might imply that there is tension between grants-active faculty and university incentives to participate in university formal technology transfer activities. Generally, extramural research grants, or at least successful ones, propose research toward the basic end of the research spectrum whereas formal university technology transfer activities, or at least successful ones, are often applied in nature.[9] Such an applied focus for research may not resonate well with many faculty members.

Hall *et al.* (2003: 491) conclude from their analysis of university-with-industry joint research activities that university faculty " . . . are included (invited by industry) in those research projects [where they] could provide research insight that is anticipatory of future research problems and [where they could] be an ombudsman anticipating and communicating to all parties the complexity of the research undertaken. Thus, one finds [university faculty] purposively involved in projects that are characterized as problematic with regard to the use of basic knowledge." As a result, informal technology transfer is more likely to occur.

Universities establish formal technology transfer mechanisms and institutions (e.g., research/science parks and incubators) to ensure that commercialization efforts are managed through the university and that financial returns are internalized. In general, the university might want to encourage its more accomplished faculty members to participate in such internal infrastructures.

If our interpretation is correct, universities might rethink aspects of their technology transfer policies and procedures. Many universities are focusing their

---

[9]This said, it is of course the case that in some disciplines, such as biology, the distinction between basic research and applied research is blurred.

faculty hiring efforts on academics who have secured large research grants, which can raise its ranking and generates immediate overhead for the institution. Our results imply that this hiring strategy could lead to unintended or unanticipated results, given that such faculty members may ultimately become more involved in aspects of informal technology transfer activity outside of the university's formal infrastructure.

Instead, it seems desirable for universities to focus their efforts on changing incentive structures, so that faculty members are more likely to participate in technology transfer through their institutional roles as university faculty members rather than only as consultants (though in some instances the two roles can be complementary). From the standpoint of faculty incentives, universities could consider shifting the royalty distribution formula in favor of faculty members. This will elicit more invention disclosures and participation in formal university technology transfer. It also seems prudent for universities that place a high priority on formal technology transfer to place a higher value on patenting, licensing, and start-up formation in promotion and tenure decisions.

Acknowledgements

The research reported here was supported under grants to Georgia Tech from the Department of Energy and the National Science Foundation. This paper has benefited from the comments and suggestions of Mike Wright, Andy Lockett, and two anonymous referees.

Addresses for correspondence

Albert N. Link, Department of Economics, University of North Carolina at Greensboro, Greensboro, NC 27412, USA. e-mail: al_link@uncg.edu
Donald S. Siegel, Department of Management and Marketing, A. Gary Anderson Graduate School of Management, University of California at Riverside, Anderson Hall, Riverside, CA 92521, USA. e-mail: donald.siegel@ucr.edu
Barry Bozeman, Department of Public Administration and Policy, University of Georgia, Athens, GA 30602, USA. e-mail: bbozeman@uga.edu

References

Adams, J., G. Black, R. Clemmons and P. Stephan (2005), 'Scientific teams and institutional collaborations: evidence from U.S. universities, 1981–1999,' *Research Policy*, **34**(3), 259–286.

Audretsch, D. B. (2000), *Is University Entrepreneurship Different?* Indiana University: Mimeo.

Bozeman, B. (2000), 'Technology transfer and public policy: a review of research and theory,' *Research Policy*, **29**, 627–655.

654   A. N. Link *et al.*

Bozeman, B. and G. Gaughan (2006), 'Impacts of Grants and Contracts on Academic Researchers' Interactions with Industry,' Georgia Tech Working Paper, Research Value Mapping Program, Atlanta, GA.

Cohen, W. M., R. R. Nelson and J. P. Walsh (2002), 'Links and impacts: the influence of public research on industrial R&D,' *Management Science*, **48**, 1–23.

Corley, E. and M. Gaughan (2005), 'Scientists' participation in university research centers: what are the gender differences?,' *Journal of Technology Transfer*, **30**, 371–381.

Dietz, J. S. and B. Bozeman (2005), 'Academic careers, patents, and productivity: industry experience as scientific and technical human capital,' *Research Policy*, **34**(3), 349–368.

Druilhe, C. and E. Garnsey (2004), 'Do academic spin-outs differ and does it matter?,' *Journal of Technology Transfer*, **29**, 269–285.

Friedman, J. and J. Silberman (2003), 'University technology transfer: do incentives, management, and location matter?,' *Journal of Technology Transfer*, **28**, 81–85.

Hall, B. H., A. N. Link and J. T. Scott (2003), 'Universities as research partners,' *Review of Economics and Statistics*, **85**, 485–491.

Hertzfeld, H. R., A. N. Link and N. S. Vonortas (2006), 'Intellectual property protection mechanisms in research joint ventures,' *Research Policy*, **35**, 825–838.

Jensen, R., J. G. Thursby and M. C. Thursby (2003), 'The disclosure and licensing of university inventions: the best we can do with the S**t we get to work with,' *International Journal of Industrial Organization*, **21**, 1271–1300.

Klevorkck, A. K., R. C. Levin, R. R. Nelson and S. G. Winter (1995), 'On the sources and significance of interindustry differences in technological opportunities,' *Research Policy*, **24**, 185–205.

Lach, S. and M. Schankerman (2004), 'Royalty sharing and technology licensing in universities,' *Journal of the European Economic Association*, **2**, 252–264.

Liebeskind, J., A. Oliver, L. G. Zucker and M. Brewer (1996), 'Social networks, learning, and flexibility: sourcing scientific knowledge in new biotechnology firms,' *Organization Science*, **7**, 428–443.

Link, A. N. (2006), *Public/Private Partnerships: Innovation Strategies and Public Policy Alternatives.* Springer: New York.

Link, A. N. and D. S. Siegel (2005), 'Generating science-based growth: an econometric analysis of the impact of organizational incentives on university–industry technology transfer,' *European Journal of Finance*, **11**, 169–182.

Louis, K. S., D. Blumenthal, M. E. Gluck and M. A. Stoto (1989), 'Entrepreneurs in academe: an exploration of behaviors among life scientists,' *Administrative Science Quarterly*, **34**, 110–131.

Markman, G. D., P. T. Gianiodis and P. Phan (2006a), *Sidestepping the Ivory Tower: Rent Appropriations through Bypassing of U.S. Universities.* Mimeo.

Markman, G. D., P. T. Gianiodis and P. Phan (2006b), 'An agency theoretic study of the relationship between knowledge agents and university technology transfer offices,' Rensselaer Polytechnic Working Paper, Troy, NY.

Mowery, D. C., R. R. Nelson, B. N. Sampat and A. A. Ziedonis (2004), Ivory Tower and Industrial Innovation: University-Industry Technology Transfer Before and After the Bayh-Dole Act. Stanford University Press: Palo Alto, CA.

Murray, F. (2004), 'The role of academic inventors in entrepreneurial firms: sharing the laboratory life,' *Research Policy*, **33**, 643–659.

Nicolaou, N. and S. Birley (2003), 'Academic networks in a trichotomous categorisation of university spinouts,' *Journal of Business Venturing*, **18**, 333–359.

Owen-Smith, J. and W. W. Powell (2001), 'To patent or not: faculty decisions and institutional success at technology transfer,' *Journal of Technology Transfer*, **26**, 99–114.

Owen-Smith, J. and W. W. Powell (2003), 'The expanding role of university patenting in the life sciences: assessing the importance of experience and connectivity,' *Research Policy*, **32**, 1695–1711.

Powell, W. W. (1990), 'Neither market nor hierarchy: network forms of organization,' *Research in Organizational Behavior*, **12**, 295–336.

Siegel, D. S. and P. Phan (2005), 'Analyzing the effectiveness of university technology transfer: implications for entrepreneurship education,' in G. Liebcap (ed.), *Advances in the Study of Entrepreneurship, Innovation, and Economic Growth*. Elsevier Science/JAI Press: Amsterdam, pp. 1–38.

Siegel, D. S., D. Waldman and A. N. Link (2003), 'Assessing the impact of organizational practices on the productivity of university technology transfer offices: an exploratory study,' *Research Policy*, **32**, 27–48.

Siegel, D. S., D. Waldman, L. Atwater and A. N. Link (2004), 'Toward a model of the effective transfer of scientific knowledge from academicians to practitioners: qualitative evidence from the commercialization of university technologies,' *Journal of Engineering and Technology Management*, **21**, 115–142.

Stevens, A. J. (2004), 'The enactment of Bayh-Dole,' *Journal of Technology Transfer*, **29**, 93–99.

Thursby, J. G., R. Jensen and M. C. Thursby (2001), 'Objectives, characteristics and outcomes of university licensing: a survey of major U.S. universities,' *Journal of Technology Transfer*, **26**, 59–72.

Zucker, L. G. and M. R. Darby (1996), 'Star scientists and institutional transformation: patterns of invention and innovation in the formation of the biotechnology industry,' *Proceedings of the National Academy of Sciences*, **93**, 709–716.

Zucker, L. G. and M. R. Darby (2001), 'Capturing technological opportunity via Japan's star scientists: evidence from Japanese firms' biotech patents and products,' *Journal of Technology Transfer*, **26**, 37–58.

[8]

J Technol Transf (2010) 35:585–596
DOI 10.1007/s10961-010-9176-5

The university technology transfer revolution in Saudi Arabia

Ahmed Alshumaimri · Taylor Aldridge · David B. Audretsch

Published online: 28 May 2010

Abstract This paper explains why and how a technology transfer revolution is taking place in Saudi Arabia to meet the mandate that Saudi Arabia become globally competitive as a knowledge-based innovative economy. The paper explains and identifies the new policies and institutions that have been introduced and developed to facilitate technology transfer and knowledge spillovers from the universities for commercialization and ultimately innovative activity and economic growth. The paper finds that a technology transfer revolution in Saudi Arabia is taking place, with the goal of leapfrogging from the factor-based stage of economic development to the innovation-based stage of economic development, while bypassing the intermediary efficiency-based stage of economic development.

Keywords University technology transfer · Science Park · Saudi Arabia · Innovation · Patents · Entrepreneurship · Economic development

JEL Classification L26 · L38 · O31 · O32 · M13 · O12

1 Introduction

Saudi Arabia has experienced rapid and impressive economic growth in the last decades on the basis of its production of crude oil. The wealth of oil resources has been a double edge sword. On the one hand, it has endowed the country with one of the most valuable natural

A. Alshumaimri · D. B. Audretsch
King Saud University, Riyadh, Saudi Arabia

T. Aldridge
Max Planck Institute of Economics, Jena, Germany

D. B. Audretsch (✉)
Indiana University, Bloomington, IN, USA
e-mail: daudrets@indiana.edu

D. B. Audretsch
WHU Otto Beisheim School of Management, Vallendar, Germany

 Springer

resources in the global economy. On the other hand, this has enabled the country to avoid developing a knowledge-based economy along with the concomitant institutions and policies. Thus, there has been no tradition of the institutions and mechanisms that are the cornerstone of a successful knowledge economy—technology transfer and knowledge spillovers.

However, as we show in the subsequent section of this paper, the sustainability of a natural resource driven economy has been challenged. This has led to the explicit mandate that Saudi Arabia shift from a resource-driven economy to a knowledge-based innovative economy.

The purpose of this paper is to explain how a technology transfer revolution is taking place in Saudi Arabia to meet the mandate that Saudi Arabia become globally competitive as a knowledge-based innovative economy. In the second section of this paper, why natural resource production is not sustainable is explained. In addition, the role of technology transfer and knowledge spillovers and the key contribution of instruments such as science parks is explained. The third section of the paper explains and identifies the new policies and institutions that have been introduced and developed to facilitate technology transfer and knowledge spillovers from the universities for commercialization and ultimately innovative activity and economic growth. In the fourth section a summary and conclusions are provided. In particular, we conclude that a technology transfer revolution in Saudi Arabia is taking place, with the goal of leapfrogging from the factor-based stage of economic development to the innovation-based stage of economic development, while bypassing the intermediary efficiency-based stage of economic development.

2 When the oil runs dry—the strategic role of knowledge

Saudi Arabia is the largest oil producer in the world, with a daily output of 11 million barrels per day in 2008. It also has the largest amount of proven oil reserves in the world, which are estimated at 267 billion barrels, including 2.5 billion barrels in the Saudi-Kuwaiti neutral zone. Saudi Arabia accounts for 36 percent of oil reserves located in the mid-east (Simmons 2005 a, b). Estimates place around one-fifth of the world's conventional oil reserves within Saudi Arabian borders.

However, there are a number of reasons to suspect that oil production in Saudi Arabia has peaked and may be forced to decline in the future. While there are a large number of oil fields, 60 percent of oil production comes from a single oil field, the Ghawar field, and 90 percent of oil production in Saudi Arabia comes from five fields. Simmons (2005 a, b), in *Twighlight in the Desert*, predicts the inevitable decline of oil production in Saudi Arabia. The inevitable decline of Saudi Arabian oil production was confirmed in a massive collection of over 200 technical studies by the Society of Petroleum Engineers (Simmons 2005 a, b).

It has been estimated that, given the demographics of Saudi Arabia, with a large share of young people accounting for the population, around nine million jobs must be created to ensure full employment. However, oil production will not come close to creating that number of jobs. Thus, in the Eighth Development Plan (2005–2009) of the Kingdom of Saudi Arabia, it was concluded that, "revenue from oil resources, which are non-renewable by nature, should best be invested in renewable assets that would contribute to diversifying the economic base and achieving sustainable development. It is, therefore, essential for non-oil public revenues to be enhanced, so that oil revenues may be gradually transformed into productive assets and effective human capital (Ministry of Economy and Planning 2004, p. 52)".

 Springer

In response to the inevitable decline and perhaps demise of the natural resource based economy, the Ninth Development Plan (2010–2014) of the Kingdom of Saudi Arabia has an explicit mandate to develop a globally competitive knowledge economy. In particular, this involves establishing a world class science and technology sector so that innovative activity would emerge as a driving engine of economic growth for Saudi Arabia. The Ninth Development Plan of the Kingdom sets 13 goals (Ministry of Economy and Planning 2010). Four out of the thirteen goals clearly concentrate on the drivers of a knowledge-based economy—developing sectors of small and medium-sized enterprises to increase their contribution to the gross domestic product, diversification of the economy to enhance economic competitiveness, achieving sustainable economic and social development through the acceleration of the pace of economic and social welfare, and moving towards a knowledge-based economy.

As was already established in the previous Development Plan (Ministry of Economy and Planning 2004), "The Eighth Development Plan marks a new phase in the development process of the Kingdom. As key factors for increased output and productivity, and for further science and technology system and of informatics, on support and promotion of scientific research, and on the drive for a knowledge-based economy".

In particular, "Industries that could contribute effectively to moving towards a knowledge-based economy. These are technology-and-capital intensive industries, capable of advancing several other industries, in addition to creating competitive advantages, which are increasingly more important than comparative advantages internationally. Most important among such industries are information technology (particularly software) and capital-goods industries. Small and medium size enterprises which play an important role in diversification of the economic base and provision of employment opportunities".

The Plan envisages increased investment in scientific and technological education and development of technical and research manpower, with particular emphasis on redirecting scientific and technological education towards supporting the innovative capabilities of Saudi youth and producing capable cadres of scientists, researchers and educationalists who would play a major role in the development of local technologies. Also envisaged are measures to amend science and technology strategies, in an effort to improve efficiency and effectiveness of research institutions and enhance their technology transfer role, in addition to increasing collaboration between research-and-development institutions and industrial institutions. Moreover, funding of research and development will be increased to support local capabilities in appropriate basic technologies, such as advanced materials, biotechnology, electronics and information technology. In addition, support will be given to "centers of excellence" in universities and research centers, which will be encouraged to support innovative capabilities and ensure a better match between acquired skills and knowledge and demand. Furthermore, establishment of science parks in universities and research centers will be encouraged, as will be joint funding and joint research programs by industry and public sector institutions".

Thus, the Ninth Development Plan of the Kingdom of Saudi Arabia reiterates the new policy approach mandated in the Eighth Development Plan (Ministry of Economy and Planning 2004):

- Gradual systematic indigenization of advanced strategic technologies to promote productivity and competitiveness in a global economy.
- Upgrading of science and technology research capabilities by investing in existing research centers and creating new research centers.

 Springer

- Promotion of technology transfer within the various constituents and participants in the science and technology system, as well as through imports.
- Improving the awareness of science and technology in the overall society, and enhancing the creative class and human capital involved in science and technology.
- Investing in the creation of technology parks and business incubators.
- Increasing the investment in science, technology and innovative activity, along with an increased diversification of sources of funding.
- Developing the requisite institutions facilitating the regulation and governance of the national system of science, technology and innovation.

Thus, a key element of the shift in Saudi Arabian policy approach involves a new role for promoting the technology transfer spillover of knowledge from the universities. There are numerous examples (Wonglimpiyarat 2010; Aldridge and Audretsch 2010; Jackson and Audretsch 2004; Vaidyanathan 2008; Sofoulie and Vonortas 2007) and precedents guiding the new policy approach, and in particular, the priority for creating science parks at the universities to facilitate knowledge spillovers in Saudi Arabia. For example, Link (1995, 2002) attributes both the formation of the Research Triangle Park in North Carolina, as well as the growth of the entire Research Triangle region, linking Chapel Hill to Raleigh and Durham, to committed and enlightened leadership. As Link (2002, p. 1) describes, "At a luncheon at the Carolina Hotel in Raleigh on September 25, 1956, North Carolina's Governor Luther H. Hodges and Robert M. Hanes, president of Wachovia Bank and Trust Company, announced to 45 prominent business leaders in the state that the Research Triangle Committee, Inc., had been established. While most in attendance knew about the Triangle, at least in the most general of terms, this luncheon signaled to these men, and in fact, to the citizenry of North Carolina, that it was time for the leadership of the state and universities to step forward and begin to build a foundation for the future economic growth of North Carolina".

Saxenian (1994, pp. 96–97) undertook a detailed study comparing Silicon Valley and Route 128 around Boston. After documenting that the knowledge factors, in terms of human capital, R&D, and university research, are roughly comparable between the two regions, she then shows that the economic performance exhibited by Silicon Valley has been vastly superior to that of Route 128. She attributes the superior economic performance of Silicon Valley to the rich networks in linkages that are prevalent in the Silicon Valley region but less so around Boston, "It is not simply the concentration of skilled labor, suppliers and information that distinguish the region. A variety of regional institutions—including Stanford University, several trade associations and local business organizations, and a myriad of specialized consulting, market research, public relations and venture capital firms—provide technical, financial, and networking services which the region's enterprises often cannot afford individually. These networks defy sectoral barriers: individuals move easily from semiconductor to disk drive firms or from computer to network makers. They move from established firms to startups (or vice versa) and even to market research or consulting firms, and from consulting firms back into startups. And they continue to meet at trade shows, industry conferences, and the scores of seminars, talks, and social activities organized by local business organizations and trade associations. In these forums, relationships are easily formed and maintained, technical and market information is exchanged, business contacts are established, and new enterprises are conceived. This decentralized and fluid environment also promotes the diffusion of intangible capabilities and understandings". Saxenian claims further (pp. 97–98) that even the language and vocabulary used by technical specialists can be specific to the region, where "a distinct language has evolved in the region and certain technical terms used by semiconductor production engineers in Silicon Valley would not even be understood by their counterparts in Boston's Route 128".

As Link (2002, p. 43) points out, the success of the Research Triangle Park has been attributed by a former governor of North Carolina, Governor Hunt, to the interactions and linkages among key people, "The secret of the Park's success is the relationships between those people who teach, those people who do research, and the public and the private sector and those of us in government".

Similarly, the founder and CEO of eSilicon, a Silicon Valley semiconductor startup, Jack Harding, explains the link between the linkages afforded in Silicon Valley and the ensuing superior economic performance, "There are durable reasons why we lead the country. Silicon Valley, as a hotbed for entrepreneurial success, combines: The most experienced concentration of risk capital in the world; (2) a vast, deep relationship with its region's higher-education institutions, whose leaders understand and participate in our innovation model, and (3) friendly local government infrastructure that understands it must excel in support of Silicon Valley's unique and thriving climate for innovation.

Further, as ground zero for this architecture for innovation, we attract a diverse, sophisticated and motivated workforce from around the world. Here at eSilicon, a small company of about 100 people, we have nearly 20 nationalities represented—clearly not a sign that Silicon Valley is fading. There's a technical and cultural integration here that results in better business practices, better products and a better understanding of how to market these products on a global basis. I'd suspect that there are few, if any, other communities where everyone, from the CEO to the bench engineer, understands and is singularly motivated by the innovation model: how it works, where its risks lie and what its rewards are (cited in Audretsch 2009)".

However, there is also evidence that even having a world class university and spillover mechanisms, such as science parks and incubators, may not suffice to guarantee technology transfer and knowledge spillovers from the university. For example, in a thorough and influential study of *Building High-Tech Clusters: Silicon Valley and Beyond*, Timothy Bresnahan and Alfonso Gambardella (2002) assemble a world class team of scholars to address how high tech clusters emerged in contexts as disparate of the Silicon Wadi in Israel, India, Ireland, Cambridge, U.K., Sweden, and the Hsinchu region of Taiwan. The statistical and econometric empirical evidence finding no significant link between policy and the emergence of high technology clusters echoes the insight of Gordon Moore, founder of Intel, who warns about leaping to public policy prescriptions, "The potential disaster lies in the fact that these static, descriptive efforts culminate in policy recommendations and analytical tomes that resemble recipes or magic potions, such as: Combine liberal amounts of technology, entrepreneurs, capital, and sunshine. Add one (1) University. Stir vigorously" (Moore and Davis 2002, p. 9).

In fact, after weighing the volume of evidence assembled from the various country studies, Bresnahan and Gambardella (2002, p. 5) conclude, "Our research design took seriously the proposition that government policy leading and directing cluster formation might be an important part of the cluster formation story, although we ultimately reject that proposition".

Similarly, Lerner (2009), in *Boulevard of Broken Dreams: Why Public Efforts to Boost Entrepreneurship and Venture Capital Have Failed*, paints a dismal picture of public policy attempts to spur economic performance. On the other hand, studies such as Florida (2002) highlight the policies implemented by Austin, Texas that transformed the city from a sleepy town to a technological powerhouse. In particular, the investments in the University of Texas served as a magnet attracting talent to the region.

 Springer

Similarly, Link (1995, 2002) attributes the remarkable turnaround of the Research Triangle region connecting three North Carolina cities—Raleigh, Durham, and Chapel Hill –to the success in leveraging the three main universities associated with these universities—University of North Carolina, North Carolina State University and Duke University—in attracting both large corporations and small startup companies to locate in the region. Link (2002) identifies more than 1,000 technology-based startup companies in the Research Triangle region that were founded since 1970, many of which are directly traceable to either Triangle Park companies (spinoffs) or else the universities. As Link (2002, p. 37) points out, "These startups not only provide immediate employment opportunities for North Carolinians but also have demonstrated the potential to influence the state's economic growth in the future as they grow and possibly act as magnets for related organizations to move into the area.

The goals of the Research Triangle Park were and remain (Link 2002):

1. Attract industrial research laboratories and facilities to North Carolina,
2. Increase opportunities of citizens of North Carolina for employment, and
3. Increase the per capita income of the citizens of the state.

Link (2002, p. 117) argues and provides statistical evidence that the Research Triangle Park has had a major impact on growth, economic development and incomes in the region by quoting Jim Robinson, then president of the Research Triangle Foundation, "As Research Triangle Park enters the twentieth-century it will be as arguably the best known and most successful university-related research park in the United States, and perhaps the world. The Park is at the center of one of the most dynamic economic regions in the country and is, by many accounts, the engine behind the region's exuberant growth, growth which has resulted in straining the infrastructure's ability to provide adequate transportation facilities and public school capacities and (in) increasing the region's cost of living. As the Park moves towards its final build-out, the primary challenge it faces is to be catalytic in finding solutions to the problems an inadequate infrastructure poses. At the same time, it must continue its mission of helping to create quality jobs for North Carolina residents including the graduates of the universities".

In fact, the empirical evidence shows that the Research Triangle Park has fundamentally changed the region, and in particular, vastly improved the economic performance of the region. Link and Scott (2003) document the growth in the number of research companies in the Research Triangle Park, increasing from none in 1958 to fifty in the mid-1980s, to over one hundred in 1997. At the same time, employment soared from zero in 1958 to over 40,000 in 1997. Lugar (2001) attributes to Research Triangle Park the direct and indirect generation of one-quarter of all jobs in the region between 1979 and 1990, and the shifting of the nature of those jobs towards high-value-added knowledge activities. The industries range from software development to pharmaceuticals and biotechnology. As Gray observes, "the vision has yielded greater benefits than anyone probably could have imagined. Today, Research Triangle Park is the hard-thumping heart of this success story in North Carolina into one of the nation's most prominent technology centers (cited in Audretsch 2009).

Another example of a city which was transformed by promoting technology transfer and knowledge spillovers from the university is San Diego. In 1992 San Diego suffered from widespread unemployment and stagnant growth, as a result of massive layoffs and downsizing triggered by the closing of the U.S. Navy's San Diego bases and research facilities. Mary Walshok, a professor at the University of California-San Diego started the

 Springer

CONNECT program, which will provide entrepreneurs and startups in member regions access to global capital providers and financial markets, research opportunities, corporate partners, and new customer channels. International corporations, universities, and research institutions will have a powerful new resource to link with emerging companies for partnership and collaboration. Shared best practices and resources, improved assessment of innovation capacity, and strengthened university/industry interaction will bring the benefits of globalization to the region (cited in Audretsch 2009). In its now world-famous pioneering program, CONNECT San Diego, public policy succeeded in changing the region's identity, as well as its source of competitiveness.

Walshok and Lee (forthcoming), attribute the transformation of San Diego not just to the factors of knowledge, in the form of research at the universities and human capital, or the organization of those factors in San Diego. Rather, according to Walshok and Lee (forthcoming, p. 3), "Without the new institutional mechanisms that were created in the past two decades to encourage technology commercialization, nurture and support local enterprise creation, new high-tech based industry clusters would never have taken root in San Diego and flourished".

3 The new technology transfer approach

Given the limitations of the traditional technology transfer regime in facilitating knowledge spillovers and technology transfer, a new approach had to be forged in order to address the goals mandated in the eight Development Plan of the Kingdom of Saudi Arabia. In March 2010 the Saudi Cabinet approved licenses for the first three university companies in the kingdom. Riyadh Techno Valley (Wadi Al-Riyadh Technology Co) in King Saud University, Wadi Jeddah in King Abdulaziz University, and Wadi Al-Dhahran in King Fahad University.

One example of the new technology transfer approach of Saudi Arabia is provided by the development of the technology park at one of the most important universities in the country, King Saud University. The Riyadh Techno Valley (RTV) project was initiated at the King Saud University in order to accelerate and promote knowledge spillovers from the large and rapidly growing in knowledge investments at the university for commercialization and innovative activity, which in turn, should spur economic growth and job creation.

The vision of the Riyadh Techno Valley Park is to provide "leadership in research, development and technology transfer" (RTV KSU 2010, p. 5) In order to realize that vision, the mission of RTV is "To provide a stimulating and attractive environment for research and development, which will contribute to achieving sustainable development and enhance competitiveness of the national economy based on knowledge" (RTV KSU 2010, p. 5). The Riyadh Techno Valley Park has the explicit goals of (1) developing human resources to excel in research and development (2) contributing to the development of a sustainable economy, and (3) facilitating an environment that is conducive to research and development.

To accomplish the mission of the Riyadh Techno Valley Park, seven stated main objectives must be met:

1. Develop a viable system of technology transfer,
2. Promote cooperative activities between the research activities at the universities with counterparts both locally and globally,

3. Create an environment that attracts investment from both Saudi Arabia as well as abroad to facilitate the creation of specialized R&D companies,
4. Attract and develop the creative class and innovative workers, both from within and beyond the Kingdom,
5. Generate high quality human capital and scientific capabilities in students in order to meet the corresponding demand from private industry,
6. Facilitate high wage employment opportunities in the emerging knowledge economy,
7. Provide revenues for the university to facilitate financial stability.

Just as the development of Research Triangle Park (RTP) in North Carolina was based on leveraging key knowledge assets in the region, Riyadh Techno Valley Park is also based on leveraging key knowledge assets in Saudi Arabia. In particular, the King Saud University provides a world class university offering research and higher education. Studies have found that the effectiveness of knowledge spillovers and technology transfer depends on the geographic proximity between the knowledge source, in this case, King Saudi, and the private and non-profit organization benefitting from the knowledge spillovers. Because King Saud University is located in the capital of Saudi Arabia, Riyadh, its location is conducive to knowledge spillovers and technology transfers.

While the research profile of King Saud University is broad, and spans more than 186 specialties, over 4,500 faculty members (80 percent with degrees with degrees from the top twenty universities in the world), an infrastructure valued over 70 billion Saudi Riyals ($18.7 billion), certain priority technological areas, such as nontechnology, will benefit from the high research profile already present at King Saud University (RTV KSU 2010). The King Abdullah Institute for Nanotechnology provides a strong platform for both research and commercialization. Similarly, the state-of-the art Prince Salman Entrepreneurship Institute is conducive to research, innovative activity and commercialization.

Given the research strengths and research profile of King Saud University, along with the mandate posed by the Strategic Plans of the Kingdom, three areas of research and technology provide the focal points of Riyadh Techno Valley Park (RTV KSU 2010, p. 19). These are:

*   Chemical technology and materials
*   Biological, agricultural and environmental technologies
*   Information and communication technologies

In the area of chemical technology and materials, there are four specific priority sub-areas—petrochemicals technology, chemical technology, material technology and energy and alternative energy technologies. In the area of biological, agricultural and environmental technologies, there are three important sub-areas—pharmaceuticals technologies, environmental technologies, and food science and agriculture technologies. In the area of information and communications technologies, there are three important sub-areas—information technology, communications technology, and information security technology.

While Research Triangle Park (RTP) in North Carolina can be considered to be a pioneering effort, or a first generation research park, Riyadh Techno Valley Park can be viewed as a fourth generation science park, in that it has short-term goals as well as longer-term goals. The short-term goals include (RTV KSU 2010):

1. Attract anchor companies to the Valley
2. Obtain stable and sustainable financial support
3. Keeping in contact with local and international research institutes
4. Acquire intellectual property of high value

 Springer

5. Create an attractive eco system in the valley
6. Establish international alliances
7. Optimize the use of smart outsourcing

Longer term goals are considered to involve strategies for sustainability (RTV KSU 2010):

1. Establish a technology incubator
2. Establish an entrepreneurship program
3. Attract venture capital
4. Encourage support from angel funds
5. Market patents in a professional and commercial manor
6. Build a solid base of highly skilled and competent human resources
7. Create a knowledge-based community.

Research (Feldman and Audretsch 1999) has shown that geographic proximity among firms working on similar technologies based on the same areas of basic research exhibit the highest performance. measured in terms of innovative activity. The Riyadh Techno Valley is designed to take advantage of such spatially constrained knowledge spillovers and consists of five zones. The first is the Biotechnology Valley, which contains the leading companies in research and development in the fields of pharmacology, environment technology, and food science.

The second zone is the Chemical Technology and materials Valley, and contains the leading companies in research and development in the fields of petrochemical materials, chemical materials, and energy. The third zone is the Informatics Technologies and Communications Valley, and consists of the leading companies in research and development in the areas of information and communications technology and information security.

The fourth Zone is the Scientific Village, which contains residential units and recreational facilities. The purpose of this zone is to provide a high quality standard of living for employees of the science park, as well as accommodations to visitors to The Riyadh Techno Valley Park. The fifth zone is the Central Core, which includes the incubators and the Centre for Entrepreneurs, the Office of Support Services of Operations Research and Intellectual Property, as well as laboratory space to serve the local market, along with governmental and semi-governmental centers for research and development.

To facilitate technology transfer and knowledge spillovers from King Saud University, or what is referred to as the "RTV Eco System", a new legal framework for managing intellectual property had to be developed that was commensurate with the goals and mission of Riyadh Techno Valley Park. A Public Private Partnership (PPP) was established to managed and operate Riyadh Techno Valley Park, which consists of a Board of Directors supervising a professional team of executive managers.

In order to serve as a conduit of technology transfer and knowledge spillovers, an appropriate intellectual property regime had to be put in place. The Intellectual Property Program of King Saud University was initiated with the explicit mission of protecting the rights of the intellectual property of affiliates of King Saud University. Such intellectual property ranges from patented inventions, to licensed technology, and to copyrights. The Intellectual Property Program facilitates the registering of patents by University affiliates and identifies opportunities for licenses and other modes of technology transfer that yield revenues for the University. The mission of the intellectual Property Program is (Ministry of Higher Education 2010).

1. Facilitate patent applications by University researchers
2. Evaluates and identifies potential patent opportunities from the research undertaken at the university
3. Evaluates and identifies licensing technology developed at the University. The decision whether to pursue a license is based on a licensing and marketing strategy, "taking into consideration technological and marketing risks, and seeking interested firms and individuals within firms wanting to adopt the technology and advertize it" (Ministry of Higher Education 2010, p. 3)
4. To make revenues accruing from licensed technologies applicable to scientific research at the department in which the inventor works, which will obtain a major part of the financial rights to the intellectual property developed in the academic department
5. To assist the inventor in finding commercialization opportunities.

In addition, the Intellectual Property Program is assigned the responsibility of protecting the copyrights associated with publications by researchers and scientists at King Saud University.

Under the Intellectual Property Program of King Saud University, 10–15 percent of the revenue accruing from licensed technology remains with the Program, which is intended to cover registration, administrative costs, and legal expenses. The remaining rights are distributed as (Ministry of Higher Education 2010):

1. The inventor receives one-half of the residual financial rights
2. The department where the inventor is affiliated receives one-quarter of the residual remaining financial rights
3. The college where the inventor resides receives one-quarter of the residual remaining financial rights.

The Riyadh Techno Valley Park is designed to evolve through several stages of development. The first stage aims at creating and enhancing the abilities and capabilities of the knowledge workers at King Saud University, which includes professors, researchers and students. In addition, private industrial and research companies should be provided access to and integrated into research activities at King Saud University and at the Riyadh Techno Valley Park. As the Park evolves, it is expected that later stages will focus on enhancing the skills and research and development capabilities of the community, which in turn will help transform the entire region into an entrepreneurial knowledge cluster.

4 Conclusions

Sala-Marin in the 2009–2010 edition of the *Global Competitiveness Report*, suggests that there are three distinct stages of economic development. The first stage is factor-driven economic development. The second stage is efficiency driven economic development. The third stage is innovation driven economic development. Saudi Arabia has been characterized by this first stage, with the main factor underlying economic growth and development natural resources, and in particular, oil.

A new and bold policy approach to Saudi Arabia aims to leapfrog the stages of economic development from the first stage, which involves dependency on natural resources, to the third stages, which requires the development of a sustainable knowledge-based economy to generate innovative activity. The second stage of economic development, which is based on efficiency of production, is to be surpassed by this new policy approach.

 Springer

This paper has identified the key policy strategy to leapfrogging from a natural resource dependent economy to a knowledge-based innovative economy. This involves not just the massive and substantial investments in creating knowledge resources, which in particular, involves investing in the research and educational capabilities of the universities. It also involves creating and investing in key institutions to transfer the technology created at universities and facilitate the spillover of knowledge created at the universities for commercialization and ultimately innovative activity and economic growth. One key technology transfer and knowledge spillover mechanism that has been created is the Riyadh Techno Valley Park. Subsequent research will need to address the actual impact of this new technology transfer revolution taking place in Saudi Arabia.

References

Aldridge, T., & Audretsch, D. (2010). Does policy influence the commercialization route? Evidence from National Institutes of Health Funded Scientists. *Research Policy, 39*, 583–588.

Audretsch, D. B. (2009). The entrepreneurial society. *Journal of Technology Transfer, 34*(3), 245–254.

Bresnahan, T., & Gambardella, A. (2002). Old-economy inputs for new-economy outcomes: What have we learned?". In T. Bresnahan & A. Gambardella (Eds.), *Building high-tech clusters: Silicon Valley and beyond* (pp. 351–358). New York: Cambridge University Press.

Feldman, M. P., & Audretsch, D. B. (1999). Innovation in cities: Science-based diversity, specialization and localized monopoly. *European Economic Review, 43*, 409–429.

Florida, R. (2002). *The rise of the creative class*. New York: Basic Books.

Jackson, S., & Audretsch, D. B. (2004). The Indiana university advanced research and technology institute: A case study. *Journal of Technology Transfer, 29*, 119–124.

Lerner, J. (2009). *Boulevard of broken dreams: Why public efforts to boost entrepreneurship and venture capital have failed*. Princeton: Princeton University Press.

Link, A. N. (1995). *A Generosity of spirit: The early history of the research triangle park*. Research Triangle Park: The Research Triangle Park Foundation of North Carolina.

Link, A. N. (2002). *From seed to harvest: The growth of the research triangle park*. Research Triangle Park: Research Triangle Park Foundation of North Carolina.

Link, A., & Scott, J. (2003). The growth of research Triangle Park. *Small Business Economics, 20*, 167–175.

Lugar, M. (2001). The research triangle experience. In C. Wessner (Ed.), *Industry-laboratory partnerships: A review of the sandia science and technology park initiative* (pp. 35–38). Washington, DC: National Academy Press.

Ministry of Economy and Planning, Kingdom Of Saudi Arabia. (2004). "The Eighth Development Plan" (1425/1430) A. H., downloaded at http://www.mep.gov.sa/index.jsp?event=ArticleView&Article. ObjectID=3.

Ministry of Economy and Planning, Kingdom Of Saudi Arabia. (2010). The ninth development plan.

Ministry of Higher Education, King Saud University, Kingdom of Saudi Arabia. (2010). *Intellectual Property Program at KSU*. Riyadh: King Saud University.

Moore, G., & Davis, K. (2002). Learning the Silicon Valley way. In T. Bresnahan & A. Gambardella (Eds.), *Building high-tech clusters: Silicon Valley and beyond* (pp. 7–39). New York: Cambridge University Press.

RTV DSU (Riyadh Techno Valley at King Saud University). (2010). *Riyadh Techno Valley*. Riyadh: King Saud University.

Sala-i-Martin, X. (2009). *Global competitiveness report*. Geneva: World Economic Forum.

Saxenian, A. (1994). *Regional advantage: Culture and competition in Silicon Valley and Route 128*. Cambridge, MA: Harvard University Press.

Simmons, M. (2005a). *Twilight in the desert: The coming Saudi oil shock and the world economy*. New York: Wiley.

Simmons, M. (2005b). *Twilight in the desert: The coming Saudi oil shock and the world economy*. New York: Wiley.

Sofoulie, E., & Vonortas, N. S. (2007). S & T parks and business incubators in middle-sized countries: The case of Greece. *Journal of Technology Transfer, 32*, 525–544.

Vaidyanathan, G. (2008). Technology parks in a developing country: The case of India. *Journal of Technology Transfer, 33*, 285–299.

Walshok, M. L. & Lee, C. W. B. forthcoming. The partnership between entrepreneurial science and entrepreneurial business: A case study of the integrated development of UCSD and San Diego's high-tech economy. In R. O'Shea & T. J. Allen (Eds.), *Building technology transfer within research universities: An entrepreneurial approach.*

Wonglimpiyarat, J. (2010). Commercialization strategies of technology: Lessons from Silicon Valley. *Journal of Technology Transfer, 35*, 225–236.

 Springer

PART III

COMPLEMENTARY NATURE OF UNIVERSITY-BASED RESEARCH

Firm Size, University Based Research, and the Returns to R&D

Albert N. Link
John Rees

ABSTRACT. This paper compares university-based research relationships between small and large firms as an explanation for the difference in innovative activity across firm sizes. We test the hypothesis that there are diseconomies of scale in producing innovations in large firms due to the inherent bureaucratization process which inhibits both innovative activity as well as the speed with which new inventions move through the corporate system towards the market. By utilizing university-based research relationships, small firms are able to avoid bureaucratic inefficiencies.

I. Introduction

Over the past decade scholars have studied the role of small-sized firms in the innovation process. A number of important conclusions have come forth as a result of these inquiries.[1] First, small firms are more innovative (in terms of the number of product innovations) relative to their size than large firms. Second, product innovations coming from small firms appear to be more significant than those coming from large firms. Surprisingly, no studies to date have sought to explain, or even speculate, why small firms have this innovation-related advantage.[2]

This paper compares university-based research relationships between small and large firms in an effort to identify one factor that might explain this noted difference in innovativeness. Our hypothesis is that innovation-based diseconomies of scale exist in large firms owning to the fact that bureaucratization in the innovation decision making

Final version accepted on August 22, 1989

Department of Economics
Department of Geography
University of North Carolina at Greensboro
Greensboro, NC 27412, U.S.A.

process inhibits not only inventiveness but also slows the pace at which new inventions move through the corporate system toward market. Small firms who utilize university-based research relationships and are as a result more efficient in their internal R&D, partially avoid such problems.

This paper is outlined as follows. In Section II, the data that form the basis for our empirical investigations are described. In Section III, we provide an overview of firms' involvement in university-based research relationships. The empirical analysis in Section IV demonstrates that small firms are able to leverage their internal R&D activity through their research relationships with universities to a greater extent than large firms and, thus, enjoy a higher return on their research investments.

II. Description of the data

A. The sample of firms

In 1986/87 we assembled a data set related to firms' involvement with university-based research programs. Based on preliminary interviews with directors from both university and state research centers, several broad industry groups were identified to be the major 'users' of such external research relationships. These industry groups included computing equipment, machine tools, and aircraft and components. From these broad industry groups, a population of 1046 firms was identified from the 1986 DUNS file of the Dun and Bradstreet Corporation. After an initial mail survey to vice presidents of production/engineering, and follow-up telephone resurveys, complete information (defined below) was obtained on 209 firms.[3]

When surveyed, these firms were asked to

classify themselves into one industry category based on their primary line of business. From their classification, these firms could be placed into five major SIC industry groups within the U.S. manufacturing sector: metalworking machinery (SIC 354), office and computing machinery (SIC 357), electronic components and accessories (SIC 367), aircraft and parts (SIC 372), and engineering and scientific instruments (SIC 381). The distribution of firms across these five industry groups is shown in Table I. Table II presents the distribution of these sample firms by size category. Along with the number of firms in each size category, the average number of employees per firms is also reported in that table.

TABLE I
Distribution of sample firms by industry

Industry	No. Firms
SIC 354	15
SIC 357	69
SIC 367	82
SIC 372	19
SIC 381	24
	209

TABLE II
Distribution of sample firms by size category

No. Employees	No. Firms	Avg. No. Employees
< 100	40	31
100 to 249	83	118
250 to 499	19	328
500 to 999	17	653
1000 to 9999	22	2,930
> 10,000	28	76,556

B. *Innovation-related characteristics of the firms in the sample*

Although there are many ways to characterize the innovativeness of a firm, one dimension relates to self-financed R&D activity. The sample firms were classified as R&D-active or not based on two separate criteria: R&D expenditures and R&D personnel. *A priori*, there was no reason to believe that these two indices would be perfectly corre-

lated. For example, a firm that relies heavily on contracted research may not have an R&D budget proportional to its R&D staff. Likewise, especially in smaller firms, the R&D budget may be so insignificant both in absolute and relative terms that the category 'R&D personnel' is not meaningful. Or, the accounting system may not be refined sufficiently to separate R&D expenditures from other investments even when personnel are classified as related to R&D. Nevertheless, 93 percent of the firms in this sample expended funds on R&D in 1986 and 88 percent of all firms had at least one individual classified under the heading of R&D personnel. Table III shows the percentage

TABLE III
Percentage of sample firms involved in R&D by size category

No. Employees	$ Percentage	Emp. Percentage
< 100	88%	83%
100 to 249	93	90
250 to 499	95	95
500 to 999	100	100
1000 to 9999	100	95
> 10,000	93	68

of sample firms involved in R&D using each criterion. With the exception of firms with more than 10,000 employees, there is a marked similarity between the percentage of firms with an R&D budget and those with classified R&D personnel. In this largest category, 93 percent of the firms reported an R&D budget but only 68 percent reported having R&D personnel. Perhaps, and the data do not permit an investigation of this point, these largest firms rely most heavily on contracted research which is paid internally and conducted externally. For the entire sample of firms, the correlation coefficient between total R&D expenditures and total R&D personnel is 0.65 (significant at the 0.01 level or better).

Table IV presents the percentage of sales devoted to R&D activity by size category for all firms in the sample. It appears that small firms devote a greater percentage of their sales to R&D than do large firms. While the percentage differences do not seem to be significant between the middle size categories, they are distinct between the categories of firms with less than 100 em-

TABLE IV
Percentage of sales devoted to R&D by size category

No. Employees	Percentage
< 100	13.3%
100 to 249	10.4
250 to 499	12.2
500 to 999	12.3
1000 to 9999	10.5
> 10,000	5.0

ployees and with more than 10,000 employees. For all firms in the sample, the average percent of sales allocated toward R&D is 10.6 percent.

A similar pattern across size categories for all firms in the sample is shown in Table V. There, the percentage of total personnel involved in R&D decreases from 16.1 percent for firms with fewer than 100 employees to 7.9 percent for firms with more than 10,000 employees. The variation between the middle categories is again not striking.

TABLE V
Percentage of total personnel involved in R&D by size category

No. Employees	Percentage
< 100	16.1%
100 to 249	12.1
250 to 499	15.1
500 to 999	11.4
1000 to 9999	11.9
> 10,000	7.9

III. Overview of firms' university-based research relationships

Sixty-nine percent of the sample firms were involved with at least one university-based research program in 1986. As shown in Table VI, the degree of university involvement appears to increase with firm size. Whereas just over 50 percent of the smallest firms (less than 250 employees) were active in at least one research relationship with a university in 1986, about 90 percent of the firms with more than 1,000 employees were so involved.

TABLE VI
Involvement with university-based research programs by size category

No. Employees	% Firms
< 100	59%
100 to 249	51
250 to 499	74
500 to 999	94
1000 to 9999	86
> 10,000	100

Information on three specific categories of involvement with a university-based research program was collected: faculty used as technical consultants (Consultants), contracted research projects (Contracts), and graduate students used as research assistants (Research Assts.). If a sample firm participated in at least one of these dimensions, then it was classified in Table VI as involved in a university-based research program. The percentage of firms active in each of these three types of activities is shown in Table VII by size category. In general, firms in the larger size categories make greater use of university faculty as technical consultants; however, in all three cases the percentage of firms with more than 10,000 employees who are involved in any dimension is greater than for any of the other size categories.

The existing literature on industry-university research relationships suggests that these types of relationships are fostered by firms for two major reasons: it is a mechanism to reduce research costs and a method to identify potential productive employees. To investigate this issue further, each firm was asked to indicate which of the following

TABLE VII
Involvement with university-based research programs by type of activity and by size category

No. Employees	Consultants	Contracts	Research Assts.
< 100	41%	15%	47%
100 to 249	44	22	38
250 to 499	67	44	72
500 to 999	76	29	59
1000 to 9999	77	54	64
> 10,000	96	96	82

were incentives (expected results from the relationship) to their participating in a university-based research relationship: 'problem solving in production processes' (Pbl. Sol.), 'product development' (Prd. Dev.) , 'use of university computing facilities' (Compt.), 'use of other university facilities' (Facil.), and 'gaining access to students as future employees' (Emplmt.). The percentage of firms noting each of these as incentives is shown in Table VIII by size category.

With the exception of firms in the smallest two size categories, fewer than 100 employees and 100 to 249 employees, the potential for solving production process problems appears to be an important reason for firms to forge research relationships with universities. The importance of this potential as an incentive for such collaboration does not vary much by size category beyond firms with 250 or more employees. Over 60 percent of the firms in the sample view product development as an important incentive for engaging in a research relationship with a university. The use of university relationships as a vehicle to gain access to computing facilities appears to be primarily a small-firm (more than 500 employees) phenomenon. It may be the case that large firms have the in-house computer capabilities to conduct the requisite research operations. Access to other university facilities as an incentive for engaging in a university-based research relationship is important to some firms, but it does not seem to be systematically related to the size of these firms. In accordance with anecdotal information, gaining access to students as future employees is a significant incentive for firms of all sizes to pursue university-based research relationships.

The last column in Table VIII reports firms' responses to a question regarding the importance of 'federal tax incentives as a motivation for engaging in collaborative research' with a university. While responses vary over size categories, only in the largest size category, firms with more than 10,000 employees, did more than 50 percent of the firms respond affirmatively.

Three response categories were used to determine firms' overall success with their university research relationships. The lion's share of the firms were satisfied with their collaborative research experience, as reported in Table IX.[4]

This overview of the primary data suggests several preliminary patterns of firm behavior. One, firms in all size categories were engaged in university research relationships to use, in general, faculty as technical consultants; and firms in the larger size categories do this to a greater degree than firms in the smaller size categories (Table VII). This collaboration tends to be oriented primarily toward product development and secondarily toward problem solving in areas related to production (Table VIII). Two, in addition to research expertise, firms in all size categories viewed access to students as future employees as a significant incentive for engaging in a university-based research relationship (Table VIII).

IV. The empirical analysis

This section presents the results of two empirical investigations into aspects of firms' participation in university-based research activity. In Part A, the trend noted in Table VI that firms in the larger size categories were more active in university-based

TABLE VIII
Incentives to engage in university research relationships by size category

No. Employees	Pbl. Sol.	Prd. Dev.	Compt.	Facil.	Emplmt.	Tax
< 100	3%	61%	5%	23%	55%	24%
100 to 249	19	69	18	19	65	16
250 to 499	57	71	29	57	79	40
500 to 999	37	63	6	19	69	29
1000 to 9999	42	47	5	16	84	11
> 10,000	63	77	13	62	93	54

TABLE IX

Firm's overall success in university research relationships by size category

No. Employees	"Very Satisfied"	"Somewhat Satisfied"	"Not Satisfied"
<100	29%	64%	7%
100 to 249	38	62	0
250 to 499	71	29	0
500 to 999	44	56	0
1000 to 9999	46	54	0
>10,000	25	75	0

research relationships than firms in the smaller size categories is investigated statistically. The specific question considered is: Is the probability of involvement with a university-based research program related to firm size? In Part B, the impact of external research relationships on the rate of return to firms' internal R&D is examined. Does the rate of return to R&D vary by firm size? Does the rate of return to R&D vary according to research participation with a university?

A. *The propensity to engage in external research relationships*

An inspection of the descriptive information in Table VI suggests that the propensity to engage in a university-based research relationships is related to firm size. The percentage of firms active with a university-based research program increases with category size.

To test formally for the influence of size on the propensity to engage in an external research relationship, a probit model was estimated. The independent variables in this model were firm size (SIZE) measured in terms of firm sales ($millions), industry concentration (CR),[5] and a binary variable equalling 1 if the firm was involved in basic research and 0 if it was not (BASRES).

The probit results, with asymptotic t-statistics in parentheses, are:

$F^{-1}(P) = 0.114 + 0.016$ SIZE $- 0.004$ CR $+ 0.19$ BASRES
(0.31)   (2.94)   (−0.44)   (0.63)

$-2 \times$ log of the likelihood function = 185.92

where $P = F(\alpha + \beta_0$ SIZE $+ \beta_1$ CR $+ \beta_2$

BASRES) $= F(z)$ for F being the cumulative probability function. These regression results complement the pattern of activity shown in Table VI. The probability of participating in a university-based research program does increase with firm size.[6] The estimated coefficient on SIZE is significant at the 0.01 level or better. Industry concentration and involvement in a basic research program have no explanatory power in this specification.

B. *Firm size, university-based research relationships, and the returns to R&D*

A framework frequently used by researchers in economics for estimating the returns to R&D reduces to the following regression model:[7]

$$\text{TFPG} = \alpha + \beta\,(\text{RD}/Q) + \varepsilon$$

where TFPG represents total factor productivity growth, (RD/Q) is the ratio of R&D spending to firm sales, and β is the estimated rate of return to R&D which could be interpreted as an index of R&D efficiency.

To estimate this model, data were needed for the calculation of total factor productivity over a defined period. Sufficient data for these calculations were not available for all firms in the sample. TFPG over the period 1982 to 1987 could be calculated for only 158 R&D-active firms of the 209 firms in the sample. The 51 firms deleted from the analysis were mostly small firms with fewer than 100 employees. Overall, the rate of return to the 158 firms in this subsample was 26.1 percent. This result is reported in Table X.

Several versions of the basic model were estimated. First, to test for differences between the rate of return to R&D in large versus small firms, a second regressor was included in the above equation. Its equalled a binary variable interacted with the (RD/Q) term where the binary variable was given the value 1 for firms with less than 500 employees and 0 otherwise. The estimated least-squares coefficient on this term was not statistically different from zero, implying that there was no statistical difference between the returns in the two size groups.[8] This result is also reported in Table X.

Second, a similar specification was estimated to account for possible differences in the rate of

TABLE X
Estimated rates of return to R&D expenditures

Category	Estimated Rate of Return
Subsample of 158 firms	26.1%
Large firms	26.0%
Small firms	26.1%
Firms involved in university research	34.5%
Firms not involved in university research	13.2%
Large firms	
Involved in university research	29.7%
Not involved in university research	14.1%
Small firms	
Involved in university research	44.0%
Not involved in university research	13.9%

return to firms engaged in and not engaged in a university-based research relationships. For this, the binary variable equalled 1 if the firm was so engaged and 0 otherwise. As reported in Table X, the estimated returns to R&D in firms involved in university-based research relationships are more than twice those of firms that are not — 34.5 percent versus 13.2 percent.[9]

Finally, segmenting both by size and by university involvment by including two regressors in the original specification (one with a size dummy and the other with an university-based research dummy), the returns to R&D in small, university-based research-active firms was found to be quite large. As reported in Table X, the estimated rate of return to R&D in this group of firms was 44.0 percent compared to (1) 29.7 percent in large university-based research-active firms, (2) 14.1 percent in large non-university-based research-active firms, (3) 13.9 percent in small non-university-based research-active firms. Small firms appear to be able to transfer knowledge gained from their unviersity research association most effectively, compared to large firms, to increase the returns to their internal R&D activities.

V. Conclusions

While the results presented in this paper by no means explain fully why small firms have an innovation-related advantage over large firms,

they do point out one interesting difference between an aspect of large and small firm research behavior. Although large firms are more active in university-based research *per se*, small firms appear to be able to utilize their university-based associations to leverage their internal R&D to a greater degree than large firms.

The analysis presented here did not take into account many of the other important factors associated with R&D efficiency, and so the results presented in Table X should be interpreted with caution. Still, the findings are noteworthy enough to encourage other investigators to investigate in more detail the ways in which firms internalize external technical information.

Acknowledgement

This paper was prepared for the Conference on Innovation and Technological Change: An International Comparison, organized by the Wissenschaftszentrum Berlin für Sozialforschung, Berlin, August 10—11, 1989. Funding for this research came from the U.S. Small Business Administration under contract SBA-89-989.

Notes

[1] Much of this research is summarized in U.S. Small Business Administration (1986) and in Link and Bozeman (1987).
[2] Relatedly, Acs and Audretsch (1987a, 1987b, 1988) show that the market environment most conducive for innovation is similar for both large and small firms. Also, they show that industry structure influences large firms' ability to innovate relative to small firms' ability to innovate, other things remaining equal.
[3] Whenever possible reported survey information (e.g., sales data) was verified against published data (e.g., Form 10-K data) to insure response reliability. When explainable differences occurred (e.g., a survey respondent reporting sales in $ millions rather than $ thousands) the primary data were corrected.
[4] There is not sufficient variation between the three response categories to conduct a more detailed investigation of interfirm differences in success with university-based research.
[5] $0 < CR < 100$. These data came from Weiss and Pascoe (1986).
[6] A non-linear size variable was included in separate regressions, but the associated coefficient was not significant. As well, two other independent variables were considered. An index of foreign competition was included in a separate regression. This variable, based on data from the International Trade Commission and the Bureau of Industrial Economics, was constructed as the ratio of industry (four-digit) imports

divided by the value of industry shipments plus imports less exports (Link and Bauer, 1989). It exhibited no statistical influence on the estimated probability. And, a vector of three-digit SIC industry dummies was included in the various versions of the model. As a group, these dummies were not significantly different from zero and thus were deleted. Similar results were obtained when SIZE was measured in terms of employees.

[7] This model is fully explained in Griliches (1979). See Link (1987) for a review of the empirical literature. Using cross-sectional firm data from the U.S. manufacturing sector, the estimated rate of return to internal R&D is in the neighborhood of 20 percent.

[8] Link's (1980) analysis of the rate of return to R&D among firms in the chemicals industry found that the return increased with firm size to a modest threshold level, and then remained constant.

[9] This finding may not be inconsistent with the findings of others that the returns to basic research are greater than for other categories of R&D spending. Generally, research conducted at universities is toward the basic end of the R&D spectrum; however, the underlying data (see Tables VII and VIII) do not allow us to separate clearly this form of research relationship. This finding also corresponds favorably with that of Link and Bauer (1989). They report, based on a sample of 92 manufacturing firms, the rate of return to R&D in firms involved in cooperative research programs with other firms is nearly three time that of firms not so involved — 37.7 percent versus 12.9 percent.

References

Acs, Z. J. and D. B. Audretsch, 1987a, 'Innovation in Large and Small Firms', *Economics Letters* 23(1), 109—112.

Acs, Z. J. and D. B. 1987b, 'Innovation, Market Structure, and Firm Size', *Review of Economics and Statistics* 69(4), 567—574.

Acs, Z. J. and D. B. Audretsch, 1988, 'Innovation in Large and Small Firms: An Empirical Analysis', *American Economic Review* 78(4), 678—690.

Griliches, Z., 1979, 'Issues in Assessing the Contribution of Research and Development to Productivity Growth', *Bell Journal of Economics* 10, 92—116.

Link, A. N., 1980, 'Firm Size and Efficient Entrepreneurial Activity: A Reformulation of the Schumpeter Hypothesis', *Journal of Political Economy* 88, 771—782.

Link, A. N., 1987, *Technological Change and Productivity Growth*, London: Harwood Academic Publishers.

Link, A. N. and L. L. Bauer, 1989, *Cooperative Research in U.S. Manufacturing*, Lexington, Mass.: Lexington Books.

Link, A. N. and B. Bozeman, 1987, 'Firm Size and Innovative Activity: A Further Examination,' final report to the Office of Advocacy, U.S. Small Business Administration.

U.S. Small Business Administration, Office of Advocacy, 1986, *Innovation in Small Firms*, Washington, D.C.

Weiss, L. W. and C. A. Pascoe, 1986, *Adjusted Concentration Ratios in Manufacturing, 1972 and 1977*, Washington, D.C.

[10]

Real Effects of Academic Research: Comment

By Zoltan J. Acs, David B. Audretsch, and Maryann P. Feldman*

A fundamental issue which remains unresolved in the economics of technology is the identification and measurement of R&D spillovers, or the extent to which a firm is able to exploit economically the investment in R&D made by another company. In a 1989 paper in this *Review*, Adam Jaffe extended his pathbreaking 1986 study measuring the total R&D "pool" available for spillovers to identify the contribution of spillovers from university research to "commercial innovation" (Jaffe, 1989 p. 957). Jaffe's findings were the first to identify the extent to which university research spills over into the generation of inventions and innovations by private firms.

To measure technological change, Jaffe relies upon the number of patented inventions registered at the U.S. patent office, which he argues is "a proxy for new economically useful knowledge" (Jaffe, 1989 p. 958). In order to relate the response of this measure to R&D spillovers from universities, Jaffe modifies the "knowledge production function" introduced by Zvi Griliches (1979) for two inputs:

$$(1) \quad \log(P_{ik}) = \beta_{1k} \log(I_{ik}) + \beta_{2k} \log(U_{ik})$$
$$+ \beta_{3k} [\log(U_{ik}) \times \log(C_{ik})]$$
$$+ e_{ik}$$

where P is number of patented inventions, I represents the private corporate expenditures on R&D, U represents the research expenditures undertaken at universities, C is a measure of the geographic coincidence

*Acs: Department of Economics and Finance, University of Baltimore, Baltimore, MD; Audretsch: Wissenschaftszentrum Berlin für Sozialforschung, Berlin, Germany; Feldman: Carnegie Mellon University and Goucher College. We thank two referees for their helpful comments and suggestions. All errors and omissions remain our responsibility.

of university and corporate research, and e represents stochastic disturbance. The unit of observation is at the level of the state, i, and what Jaffe terms the "technological area," or the industrial sector, k. In addition, Jaffe includes the state population (Pop_{ik}) in his estimating equation in order to control for the size differential across the geographic units of observation.

Jaffe's (1989) statistical results provide evidence that corporate patent activity responds positively to commercial spillovers from university research. Not only does patent activity increase in the presence of high private corporate expenditures on R&D, but also as a result of research expenditures undertaken by universities within the state. The results concerning the role of geographic proximity in spillovers from university research are clouded, however, by the lack of evidence that geographic proximity *within the state* matters as well. According to Jaffe (1989 p. 968), "There is only weak evidence that spillovers are facilitated by geographic coincidence of universities and research labs within the state."

While Jaffe's (1989) model is constructed to identify the contribution of university research to generating "new economically useful knowledge" (p. 958), F. M. Scherer (1983), Edwin Mansfield (1984), and Griliches (1990) have all warned that measuring the number of patented inventions is not the equivalent of a direct measure of innovative output. For example, Ariel Pakes and Griliches (1980 p. 378) argued that "patents are a flawed measure (of innovative output); particularly since not all new innovations are patented and since patents differ greatly in their economic impact." In addressing the question "Patents as indicators of what?" Griliches (1990 p. 1669) concludes that "Ideally, we might hope that patent statistics would provide a measure of the (innovative) output.... The reality, however, is very far from it. The dream of

TABLE 1—COMPARISON AMONG PATENT, UNIVERSITY RESEARCH, AND INNOVATION MEASURES

Measure	Mean	Standard deviation	Minimum	Maximum	Number of innovations yielded per unit of input
University research expenditures (millions of dollars)	98.8	144.0	12.0	710.4	1.3
Drugs	28.5	35.3	2.2	142.3	3.3
Chemicals	5.7	9.7	0.5	46.7	1.9
Electronics	21.0	49.2	0.3	239.0	2.8
Mechanical	12.7	25.6	0.9	126.1	3.5
Corporate patents	879.4	975.7	39.0	3,230.0	0.148
Drugs	71.7	99.4	1.0	418.0	0.132
Chemicals	201.2	249.0	6.0	908.0	0.054
Electronics	225.0	295.3	7.0	1,142.0	0.263
Mechanical	300.8	319.9	20.0	993.0	0.146
Innovations	130.1	206.4	4.0	974.0	—
Drugs	9.5	16.0	0.0	75.0	—
Chemicals	10.9	17.7	0.0	80.0	—
Electronics	59.2	100.5	1.0	475.0	—
Mechanical	44.5	79.7	0.0	416.0	—

Notes: All dollar figures are millions of 1972 dollars. Data on university research funds by state are available for the four broad technical areas of drugs and medical technology; chemicals; electronics, optics and nuclear technology; and mechanical arts. These groups, along with the data for university research expenditures and corporate patents, are from Jaffe (1989).

getting hold of an output indicator of inventive activity is one of the strong motivating forces for economic research in this area."

The use of patent counts to identify the effect of spillovers from university research might be expected to be particularly sensitive to what Scherer (1983 p. 108) has termed the "propensity to patent." Just as Albert N. Link and John Rees (1990) found that small new entrepreneurial firms tend to benefit more than their established larger counterparts from university research spillovers, Griliches (1990) and Scherer (1983) both concluded that the propensity to patent does not appear to be invariant across a wide range of firm sizes.

A different and more direct measure of innovative output was introduced in Acs and Audretsch (1987), where the measure of innovative activity is the number of innovations recorded in 1982 by the U.S. Small Business Administration from the leading technology, engineering, and trade journals in each manufacturing industry. A detailed description and analysis of the data can be found in Acs and Audretsch (1988, 1990).

Because each innovation was recorded subsequent to its introduction in the market, the resulting data base provides a more direct measure of innovative activity than do patent counts. That is, the innovation data base includes inventions that were not patented but were ultimately introduced into the market and excludes inventions that were patented but never proved to be economically viable enough to appear in the market.

The extent to which university-research spillovers serve as a catalyst for private-corporation innovative activity can be identified by using the direct measure of innovative activity in the model introduced by Jaffe in equation (1). This enables a direct comparison of the influence of university R&D spillovers on innovation with the results that Jaffe reported using the patent measure.

Table 1 compares the mean measures of university research expenditures and corporate patents for all 29 states used by Jaffe with the mean number of innovations per state. It should be noted that, while Jaffe's university-research and patent measures are

TABLE 2—A COMPARISON BETWEEN REGRESSION RESULTS USING JAFFE'S PATENT MEASURE AND
THE INNOVATION MEASURE

Independent variable	All areas		Electronics		Mechanical arts	
	Patents (i)	Innovations (ii)	Patents (iii)	Innovations (iv)	Patents (v)	Innovations (vi)
$Log(I_i)$	0.668 (8.919)	0.428 (4.653)	0.631 (5.517)	0.268 (1.370)	0.643 (6.712)	0.649 (4.720)
$Log(U_{ik})$	0.241 (3.650)	0.431 (6.024)	0.265 (2.598)	0.520 (2.977)	0.059 (0.490)	0.329 (1.999)
$Log(U_{ik}) \times Log(C_i)$	0.020 (0.244)	0.173 (1.914)	.063 (0.531)	0.272 (1.331)	−0.046 (−0.406)	0.224 (1.436)
$Log(Pop_i)$	0.159 (1.297)	−0.072 (−1.287)	0.076 (1.263)	0.076 (0.742)	0.177 (3.767)	−0.143 (−2.051)
$\hat{S}$:	0.444	0.451	0.203	0.348	0.181	0.247
R^2:	0.959	0.902	0.992	0.951	0.994	0.974
N:	145	125	29	29	27	27

Note: Numbers in parentheses are *t* statistics.

based upon an eight-year sample (1972–1977, 1979, and 1981), the innovation measure is based upon a single year, 1982. Both the number of innovations per university research dollar (millions) and the number of innovations per patent vary considerably across the four industrial sectors included in Jaffe's sample. The number of innovations yielded per dollar of university research is apparently highest in the mechanical industries and lowest in the chemical industries. As in Acs and Audretsch (1988), the amount of innovative activity yielded per patent is highest in the electronics sector and lowest in chemicals.

While Jaffe (1989) was able to pool the different years across each state observation in estimating the production function for patented inventions, this is not possible using the innovation measure, due to data constraints. Thus, it is important first to establish that Jaffe's (1989) results do not differ greatly from estimates for a single year. This is done in equation (i) of Table 2, where Jaffe's (1989) patent measure for 1981 is used in the same estimating equation found in his table 4B, based on all (technological) areas. All of the data sources and a detailed description of the data and measures can be found in Jaffe (1989). Using the patent measure for a single year yields

virtually identical results to those based on the pooled estimation reported in Jaffe's article. That is, both private corporate expenditures on R&D and expenditures by universities on research are found to exert a positive and significant influence on patent activity. Similarly, both the geographic coincidence effect and the population variables have positive coefficients. The estimated coefficient of 0.668 for $log(I_i)$ in equation (i) of Table 2 is remarkably close to the coefficient of 0.713 estimated by Jaffe using the pooled sample. We conclude that using a single estimation year does not greatly alter the results obtained by Jaffe (1989) using several years to measure the extent of patent activity.

The number of 1982 innovations is substituted for the number of registered patents as the dependent variable in equation (ii) of Table 2, which estimates the impact of spillovers on all technological areas combined.[1] There are two important differences that emerge when the innovation measure is used instead of the patent measure. First, the elasticity of $log(U_{ik})$ almost doubles,

[1]The sample sizes differ between the patent and innovation estimations because the observations with the value of zero had to be omitted.

from 0.241 when the patent measure is used in equation (i) to 0.431 when the innovation measure is used in equation (ii). That is, the impact of university spillovers is apparently greater on innovations than on patented inventions. Second, the impact of the geographic coincidence effect also is much greater on innovation activity than on patents, suggesting that spillovers from geographic proximity may be more important than Jaffe (1989) concluded.

Jaffe (1989) also estimated knowledge-production functions for what he calls specific technical areas.[2] Equations (iii) and (iv) in Table 2 compare the estimations based on the patent and innovation measures for the electronics area, and equations (v) and (vi) compare the estimations based on the two measures for the mechanical-arts area. The patent and innovation measures yield somewhat different results. For the electronics area, expenditures on R&D by private corporations are found to have a positive and significant influence on patents but not on innovative activity. By contrast, in the mechanical-arts area, both patent and innovative activity respond positively to private R&D spending. This may reflect the difference in what Sidney G. Winter (1984) termed the "technological regime" between the electronics and mechanical-arts areas. That is, under the "entrepreneurial regime," the underlying technological information required to produce an innovation is more likely to come from basic research and from outside of the industry. By contrast, under the "routinized regime," an innovation is more likely to result from technological information from an R&D laboratory within the industry. Since the electronics area more closely corresponds to Winter's notion of the entrepreneurial regime, while the mechanical-arts area more closely resembles the routinized regime, it is not surprising that company R&D expenditures are relatively less important and university expenditures on research are relatively more impor-

tant in producing innovations in electronics but not in the mechanical arts. Further, as Mansfield (1984 p. 462) noted, innovations may have a particular tendency not to result from patented inventions in industries such as electronics: "The value and cost of individual patents vary enormously within and across industries.... Many inventions are not patented. And in some industries, like electronics, there is considerable speculation that the patent system is being bypassed to a greater extent than in the past."

Substitution of the direct measure of innovative activity for the patent measure in the knowledge-production function generally strengthens Jaffe's (1989) arguments and reinforces his findings. Most importantly, use of the innovation data provides even greater support than was found by Jaffe: as he predicted, spillovers are facilitated by the geographic coincidence of universities and research labs within the state. In addition, there is at least some evidence that, because the patent and innovation measures capture different aspects of the process of technological change, results for specific sectors may be, at least to some extent, influenced by the technological regime. Thus, we find that the importance of university spillovers relative to private-company R&D spending is considerably greater in the electronics sector when the direct measure of innovative activity is substituted for the patent measure.

REFERENCES

Acs, Zoltan J. and Audretsch, David B., "Innovation, Market Structure and Firm Size," *Review of Economics and Statistics,* November 1987, *69,* 567–75.

_____ **and** _____, "Innovation in Large and Small Firms: An Empirical Analysis," *American Economic Review,* September 1988, *78,* 678–90.

_____ **and** _____, *Innovation and Small Firms,* Cambridge, MA: MIT Press, 1990.

Griliches, Zvi, "Issues in Assessing the Contribution of R&D to Productivity Growth," *Bell Journal of Economics,* Spring 1979, *10,* 92–116.

_____, "Patent Statistics as Economic In-

---

[2] The technological areas are based on a technological classification and not on an industrial classification. For further explanation see appendix A in Jaffe (1989).

dicators: A Survey," *Journal of Economic Literature*, December 1990, *28*, 1661–1707.

Jaffe, Adam B., "Technological Opportunity and Spillovers of R&D: Evidence from Firms' Patents, Profits, and Market Value," *American Economic Review*, December 1986, *76*, 984–1001.

_____, "Real Effects of Academic Research," *American Economic Review*, December 1989, *79*, 957–70.

Link, Albert N. and Rees, John, "Firm Size, University Based Research, and the Returns to R&D," *Small Business Economics*, March 1990, *2*, 25–32.

Mansfield, Edwin, "Comment on Using Linked Patent and R&D Data to Measure Interindustry Technology Flows," in Zvi Griliches, ed., R&D, *Patents, and Productivity*, Chicago: University of Chicago Press, 1984, pp. 462–4.

Pakes, Ariel and Griliches, Zvi, "Patents and R&D at the Firm Level: A First Report," *Economics Letters*, 1980, *5* (4), 377–81.

Scherer, F. M., "The Propensity to Patent," *International Journal of Industrial Organization*, March 1983, *1*, 107–28.

Winter, Sidney G., "Schumpeterian Competition in Alternative Technological Regimes," *Journal of Economic Behavior and Organization*, September-December 1984, *5*, 287–320.

[11]

Company-Scientist Locational Links:
The Case of Biotechnology

By DAVID B. AUDRETSCH AND PAULA E. STEPHAN*

The emergence of a recent literature (re)-discovering the importance of economic geography[1] might seem paradoxical in a world increasingly dominated by E-mail, faxes, and electronic communications superhighways. Why should geographic proximity matter when technology has advanced in a manner that has drastically reduced the cost of transmitting information across geographic space? This paper explores why geography matters more in certain economic relationships than in others by focusing on the locational incidence of contacts between firms in the biotechnology industry and university-based scientists affiliated with these firms. In particular, we suggest that the specific role played by the scientist shapes the importance of geographic proximity in the firm-scientist link.

* Audretsch: Wissenschaftszentrum Berlin für Sozialforschung and the Centre for Economic Policy Research (CEPR), Reichpietschufer 50, D-10785 Berlin, Germany; Stephan: Department of Economics and Policy Research Center, Georgia State University, Atlanta, GA 30303. This paper was started while Paula Stephan was a visiting professor at the Wissenschaftszentrum Berlin für Sozialforschung. We would like to acknowledge financial support from the North Atlantic Treaty Organization (NATO) under grant number CRG.940792, the College of Business Administration, Georgia State University, and the Policy Research Center of Georgia State University. Richard Hawkins, Meghan Crimmins, Anne Gilbert and Janet Keene coded the data. Steve Everhart provided computer assistance. Earlier versions of this paper were presented at the 1995 meetings of the American Economics Association in Washington, DC; the May 1995 Conference on R&D, Innovation, and Productivity at the Institute for Fiscal Studies in London; the September 1995 annual conference of the European Association for Research in Industrial Economics (EARIE) at Juan-Les-Pins, France; and an October 1995 seminar at INSEAD, Fontainebleau, France. We are also grateful to the suggestions and comments of James Adams, Maryann P. Feldman, Mary Beth Walker and an anonymous referee of this journal. Any remaining errors or omissions are our responsibility.
[1] See for examples Paul Krugman (1991a, b), Robert E. Lucas (1993), Paul Romer (1990), and Audretsch and Maryann P. Feldman (1996).

We shed light on two questions concerning biotechnology companies and the university-based scientists associated with the companies:

1) To what extent are the links between university scientists and biotechnology companies geographically bounded?
2) Is the spatial dimension of geographic links between biotechnology firms and scientists shaped by the role and characteristics of the scientist?

We are able to answer these questions by linking the location of the biotechnology firm with the location of the university-based scientists affiliated with the firm. Thus, while Krugman (1991a) may be correct in pointing out that no "paper trail" exists to facilitate measuring and tracking networks, in this paper we develop a trail of geographic linkages between scientists and firms in biotechnology.

The method used to identify and measure linkages between scientists and biotechnology firms is described in Section I. In particular, we employ a new data base, which includes virtually the entire population of biotechnology firms that prepared an initial public offering (IPO) in the early 1990's, to examine the extent to which the firms and the university-based scientists involved with the firms are located within the same region. In Section II we provide a theory suggesting that the relationship between the locations of a biotechnology firm and a university scientist will be shaped by the potential economic knowledge residing in that scientist and the role that she or he plays in working with the firm. In Section III a probit analysis is undertaken to link the likelihood that a scientist is located in the same region as the biotechnology firm with which she or he is involved to characteristics specific to the scientist and to the role played with the biotechnology firm. Finally, a summary and conclusions are presented.

642   THE AMERICAN ECONOMIC REVIEW   JUNE 1996

I. Measuring Links Between Scientists and Firms

Biotechnology is a new industry that is knowledge based and predominantly composed of new small firms having close ties with university-based scientists. The relative small scale of most biotechnology firms is arguably attributable to the diseconomies of scale inherent in the "bureaucratic process which inhibits both innovative activity and the speed with which new inventions move through the corporate system towards the market" (Albert N. Link and John Rees, 1990 p. 25). Lynne G. Zucker et al. (1994 p. 1) provide considerable evidence suggesting that the timing and location of new biotechnology firms is "primarily explained by the presence at a particular time and place of scientists who are actively contributing to the basic science." More specifically, they find that biotechnology firms are likely to be found in close geographic proximity to where scientists who have published articles on gene sequencing are located. Their work, however, does not explore the geographic linkages among scientists at these institutions and biotech firms. That is, while Zucker et al. show that a region such as the San Francisco Bay Area, which produces a disproportionate amount of research in biotechnology, is home to a disproportionate number of biotech firms, their work sheds virtually no light upon the extent to which biotech firms, once located in the region, establish networks with university-based scientists located in the area. The implicit assumption, of course, is that the networks are overwhelmingly local. Their research design, however, lacks a paper trail linking firms and scientists, and thus can neither affirm nor deny the assumption. Furthermore, they do not explore the variety of roles that university scientists play with biotech firms, but instead focus exclusively on the role of knowledge transfer.[2]

The uniqueness of our approach is that it allows us to determine the actual geographic location of the firm as well as the geographic location of the university-based scientists affiliated with the firm. We are also able to make inferences about the role the scientist plays with the firm since we are able to identify the title they hold with the firm as well as whether the scientist was a founder of the firm. We do this by collecting data from the prospectuses of biotechnology companies that prepared an initial public offering in the United States during the period March 1990 to November 1992. All told, 54 firms affiliated with 445 university-based scientists meet this criterion.[3] By carefully reading these prospectuses, we determine the names of university-based scientists affiliated with each firm, the role they play in the firm, and the name and location of their home institution. Universities and firms are then grouped into regions which are generally larger than a single city but considerably smaller than a state. Certain areas, for example, metropolitan New York, cross several state lines. A straightforward way to examine our data is to determine the percentage of university-based scientists affiliated with the firm that are from universities in the same region as the firm. This is done in the Data Appendix.

Four major conclusions can be drawn from Table A1. First, firms are geographically concentrated in three primary regions (the San Francisco Bay Area, San Diego and Boston), two secondary regions (Philadelphia and New York), and a number of smaller clusters.[4] Second, the degree to which regions rely upon local scientific talent varies substantially. For example, the Boston area firms draw nearly one-half of their scientists from universities located within the region. By contrast, firms located in the San Diego area draw only about one-quarter of their scientists from universities in the region. Third, the degree to which firms rely upon local scientists varies significantly across individual firms. Eighty percent of the scientists employed by Anergen are located in

---

[2] See also Zucker et al. (1995).

[3] The study includes several firms for which the initial public offering was prepared but postponed at the last minute.

[4] Although these data are drawn from a two and one-half year time period, the geographic distribution of the 54 firms in our sample is virtually identical to the entire population of biotechnology firms in the United States. Ernst and Young identify three primary regions, two secondary regions, several other regions with at least 20 companies, and a host of smaller clusters (G. Steven Burrill and Kenneth B. Lee, 1992).

TABLE 1—LOCATION OF SCIENTISTS BY REGION OF UNIVERSITY

	Contacts	Unique firms	Contacts in region	Percentage in region
San Francisco Bay Area	66	28	44	66.7
Stanford University	37	17	24	64.9
University of California, San Francisco	26	14	17	65.4
San Diego, CA	27	13	21	77.8
Scripps College	7	5	5	71.4
University of California, San Diego	16	10	14	87.5
Boston, MA	69	26	41	59.4
Harvard University	43	21	24	55.8
Massachusetts Institute of Technology	15	9	7	46.7
Philadelphia, PA	17	14	8	47.1
University of Pennsylvania	9	8	3	33.3
New York, NY	36	22	9	25.0
Albert Einstein College of Medicine	7	6	1	14.3
Columbia University	11	8	3	27.3
Rockefeller	11	7	4	36.4
Maryland	11	9	1	9.1
Johns Hopkins University	5	4	0	0.0
Seattle, WA	6	5	2	33.3
University of Washington	6	5	2	33.3
Boulder, CO	3	3	1	33.3
Kansas	0	0	0	0.0
Research Triangle, NC	8	8	2	25.0
Los Angeles, CA	13	9	0	0.0
California Institute of Tech	7	5	0	0.0
Dallas, TX	9	5	1	11.1
University of Texas, South Western Medical Center	5	3	0	0.0
Houston, TX	22	9	8	36.4
University of Texas, Anderson Center	11	3	7	63.6
Baylor College of Medicine	7	6	0	0.0
East	37	25	0	0.0
Penn State University	6	5	0	0.0
Pittsburgh University	5	5	0	0.0
Yale University	8	7	0	0.0
Foreign Countries	33	21	0	0.0
Midwest	39	21	0	0.0
Michigan	13	10	0	0.0
South	24	15	0	0.0
Alabama, Birmingham	6	4	0	0.0
West	25	19	0	0.0
University of California, Davis	5	4	0	0.0
Total	**445**		**138**	

the San Francisco Bay Area. By contrast, only one of Genta's 19 university-based scientists is located in the same geographic area as the company. The final conclusion to be drawn from Table A1 is that the propensity to draw upon local networks appears unrelated to firm density. For example, the region with the most firms, the San Francisco Bay Area, does not have the greatest propensity to rely upon local-based scientific networks.

Table 1 explores geographic linkages between universities and firms. Eighteen educational regions are defined and within each region institutions with at least five scientific contacts to biotechnology firms are listed. The Table also gives the number of scientist-firm contacts that exist by region and institution as well as the number of firms involved in these contacts. Six important points should be emphasized from Table 1. First, although universities in the San Francisco Bay Area and the Boston-Cambridge Area together supply approximately 30 percent of the scientists, the supply of talent is much less regionally concentrated than are the firms. Second, three institutions are major producers of contacts: Harvard, with 43; Stanford, with 37; and the University of California at San Francisco (UCSF), with 26. Third, universities that are major producers send talent to a large number of firms. Harvard scientists had contact with 40 percent of the firms in our sample; Stanford and UCSF scientists each had contact with over 25 percent of the firms.

Fourth, *commuting patterns* vary by region. For example, two thirds of the university-based scientists in the San Francisco Bay Area work with biotechnology firms located in the Bay Area. By contrast, one fourth of the scientists located in the New York area work with firms in their area. Fifth, commuting patterns also vary considerably according to institutional affiliation. For example, only one in eight of the scientists at the University of California at San Diego (UCSD) commute while six out of seven scientists at the Albert Einstein College of Medicine are affiliated with firms outside the region. Finally, Table 1 indicates the existence of regions in the United States rich in scientific talent but not in biotechnology firms. For example, although 13 of the university-based scientists are located at the University of Michigan, there were no new public offerings filed by biotechnology firms located in the Ann Arbor/ Detroit area during our two and one-half year window of observation.

In Table 2 firms are classified into 13 regions and universities into 18 geographic areas. The final row at the bottom indicates the number of scientists drawn from the 18 distinct university regions and is identical to the summary statistics found in Table 1. The column at the extreme right of the last group indicates the number of university-based sci-

entists affiliated with biotechnology companies from the 13 distinct regions and is identical to the summary entries of Table A1.

The virtue of Table 2 is that it reflects the regional location of biotech talent as well as commuting patterns of university-based scientists. For the 13 regions in which there are both firms and universities, the entries on the diagonal represent the number of university-based scientists involved with firms located within that region. Off-diagonal row entries in Table 2 report the regional source of imported talent.

Table 2 invites two conclusions. First, geographic proximity does not play an important role for most company-scientist location links. Only 138 of the 445 observations lie on the diagonal. Yet, a Chi-square test implies that the null hypothesis of factor independence can be rejected at better than the 0.001 level. Linkages may not be overwhelmingly local but neither are they random. Second, distance does not appear to affect commuting patterns. For example, the hypothesis that scientists are just as likely to make a 2500 mile trip as a 250 mile trip cannot be rejected at the 10-percent level of significance.

II. The Role of University-Based Scientists

The results from the previous section clearly show that in some cases the geographic link between a biotechnology company and a university scientist occurs within the same region, while in other cases geographic proximity does not matter. Here we hypothesize that the locational incidence of contacts between firms and university-scientists is shaped by the particular role played by the scientist with the firm. When university-based scientists are actively involved in knowledge transfer, their knowledge is more easily tapped if the firm is located in the same region as the scientist. But when the scientist plays other roles geographic proximity is considerably less important. Balanced against the benefits of local proximity to the scientist is proximity to other firms and research organizations and also to better inputs. The fewer firms there are in a region, holding all else constant, the less likely the firm would be to locate near scientists in that region with which it has contacts. Also relevant would be unobserved features of the firm,

TABLE 2—GEOGRAPHIC DISTRIBUTION OF FIRM-UNIVERSITY LINKS

	Region of University					
	SF Bay	Los Angeles	San Diego	Boulder	Kansas	Boston
Region of Firm:						
SF Bay	44	9	2	1	0	13
Los Angeles	1	0	0	0	0	0
San Diego	5	1	21	0	0	3
Boulder	1	0	0	1	0	1
Kansas	1	0	0	0	0	0
Boston	4	3	3	1	0	41
Maryland	1	0	0	0	0	1
RTI	0	0	0	0	0	0
New York	5	0	0	0	0	6
Philadelphia	0	0	1	0	0	4
Dallas	0	0	0	0	0	0
Houston	1	0	0	0	0	0
Seattle	3	0	0	0	0	0
Total	66	13	27	3	0	69

	Region of University					
	Maryland	RTI	New York	Philadelphia	Dallas	Houston
Region of Firm:						
SF Bay	2	3	11	2	3	1
Los Angeles	0	0	0	0	0	0
San Diego	2	0	5	4	1	5
Boulder	0	1	0	0	0	0
Kansas	0	0	0	0	0	0
Boston	4	1	6	2	0	0
Maryland	1	0	2	0	0	3
RTI	0	2	0	0	0	0
New York	1	1	9	1	4	1
Philadelphia	1	0	3	8	0	1
Dallas	0	0	0	0	1	3
Houston	0	0	0	0	0	8
Seattle	0	0	0	0	0	0
Total	11	8	36	17	9	22

	Region of University						
	Seattle	East	Foreign	Midwest	South	West	Total
Region of Firm:							
SF Bay	2	9	11	12	10	10	145
Los Angeles	0	2	1	3	1	1	9
San Diego	1	5	9	7	3	5	77
Boulder	0	0	0	0	0	0	4
Kansas	0	0	1	2	1	1	6
Boston	0	3	4	7	3	3	85
Maryland	1	3	0	0	1	0	13
RTI	0	1	0	1	1	1	6
New York	0	3	5	1	1	1	39
Philadelphia	0	8	0	2	1	2	31
Dallas	0	1	1	2	2	0	10
Houston	0	2	1	0	0	1	13
Seattle	2	0	0	2	0	0	7
Total	6	37	33	39	24	25	445

such as where the main participants in the firm that are not university scientists reside.

University-based scientists provide three key functions to biotech firms: they facilitate knowledge transfer from university laboratories to the firm; they signal the quality of the firm's research to both capital and resource markets; and they help chart the scientific direction of the company. The knowledge transfer function of university-based scientists has received the most attention (Gary P. Pisano et al., 1988; Zucker et al., 1994; Zucker et al., 1995; and Henry Etzkowitz, 1983). It occurs, for example, whenever a university-based scientist founds a firm for the explicit purpose of developing knowledge created in the scientist's lab or when a university-based scientist is extensively involved in the research agenda of the firm. It is not the only way that knowledge moves from university labs and companies. Companies can also learn about the research occurring in university labs through social contacts between employees and university scientists and by sending employees to participate in workshops and seminars at the university (Zucker et al., 1995).

In addition to providing knowledge to newly formed biotechnology companies, university-based scientists also signal the quality of the firm to the scientific and financial communities. An effective way to recruit young scientists is to have a scientific advisory board (SAB) composed of the leaders in the field. According to George B. Rathmann, former president and CEO of Amgen, some of the young scientists that Amgen recruited would not have come "without the knowledge that an outstanding scientific advisory board took Amgen seriously" (Burill, 1987 p. 77). University-based scientists can also serve as *bait* to the investment community. In the early stages of development, biotechnology firms miss no opportunity to signal the abilities of their scientists as well as the science they are undertaking. It is not uncommon for prospectuses to read like proposals to the National Institutes of Health, both in terms of the projects they describe and the accomplishments of the scientists. Stephan (1994) has shown that the proceeds raised from an initial public offering as well as the "day one" value of the firm is positively and significantly related to the reputation of the university-based scientist affiliated with the firm.

University-based scientists also help chart the scientific direction of the company. Most biotech companies go public long before they have a flagship product ready for clinical tests. Some go public in the earliest stages of development.[5] Having few employees, and working in what has proved to be an exceptionally risky environment with regard to product effectiveness, firms seek guidance from the scientific community.[6]

The tacit nature of knowledge in biotechnology (Pisano et al., 1988) suggests that knowledge transfer between university-based scientists and biotechnology firms is facilitated by face to face contact and thus geographic proximity. On the other hand, the geographic proximity of all major researchers in a particular subfield is unlikely given the opportunity cost universities face in buying into a single research agenda. The broad-based nature of the knowledge used in biotechnology (Luigi Orsenigo, 1989) also suggests that knowledge links may not be exclusively local.

Scientists whose primary function is to signal the quality of the company are less likely to be local than are scientists who provide essential knowledge to the company. Their quality signal is produced by lending prestige to a venture they have presumably reviewed, a task that can be accomplished with credibility from a distance. The only reason that university-based scientists fulfilling the role of signal bearer might be geographically linked with the company is that the company may find it useful to locate near talent on the assumption that it makes scientific stars that much more willing to be involved. A similar line of reasoning can be made concerning the geographic proximity of scientists whose primary function is to chart the scientific course of the company.

It is, of course, difficult to know the exact functions the university-based scientist fulfills and many scientists undoubtedly fulfill multi-

---

[5] This was particularly true in the early 1990's when companies, sensing an open financial "window," rushed to go public in fear that the window would close and they would find themselves without the resources needed for product development.

[6] Such guidance is also often required by the financial backers and underwriters. Recent examples of product failure in biotechnology underscores the risky nature of the industry (Jim Shrine, 1994).

TABLE 3—ROLE OF SCIENTIST

	Founder	SAB	SAB chair	Majorstock
Nonlocal	16	249	7	20
$n = 307$	(42.1)	(68.2)	(33.3)	(50.0)
Local	22	116	14	20
$n = 138$	(57.9)	(31.8)	(66.7)	(50.0)
Total	38	365	21	40
χ^2	14.04[a]	0.56	13.10[a]	7.41[b]

Note: Percentages of the total are given in parentheses.
[a] Significant at 0.000 or better.
[b] Significant at 0.02 or better.

ple functions. The title the scientists holds at the firm, however, gives some insight into the function performed, and the genesis of the firm also allows for inference. In particular, we expect university-based founders to be a source of knowledge transfer. Presumably scientists start new biotechnology companies because their knowledge is not transferable to other firms for the expected economic value of the knowledge.[7] If this were not the case, there would be no incentive to start a new and independent company. Chairs of scientific advisory boards arguably also play a key role in knowledge transfer. Members of SABs, on the other hand, provide ballast to the masthead and help chart the course of the company. They can also facilitate knowledge transfer by providing the firm, at minimal cost, a full roster of key players doing research in the area.[8]

Table 3 explores the hypothesis that the role played by the scientist in the firm relates to the probability that the linkage is local. Consistent with the above discussion concerning knowledge transfer, we find, using a Chi-square test, that scientific founders are significantly more likely to have a local linkage than are non-

[7] Kenneth Arrow (1962), Oliver E. Williamson (1975), and Audretsch (1995) have argued that when new economic knowledge cannot be easily transferred to established firms, perhaps due to organization factors, the holder of such knowledge must start a new firm in order to appropriate the potential economic value of the knowledge.

[8] Members of scientific advisory boards usually receive compensation in the neighborhood of $10,000 per year. In addition, they are often granted options which prove in some cases to be quite valuable (Stephan and Stephen Everhart, 1996).

founders. We also find that the university scientists who are chairs of scientific advisory boards are significantly more likely to have a local linkage than are nonchairs.[9] One cannot, however, conclude that chairs and founders who (presumably) provide a source of knowledge do so exclusively for firms in close geographic proximity to where they work. Over 40 percent of the university-based founders establish firms outside of the region of their university; a third of the chairs of SABs are not in the same geographic region as the firm. This is consistent with the idea that while tacit knowledge requires face to face interaction, such interaction does not require that the scientist and the firm be permanently located in the same area.

The table also indicates that the 40 scientists who have sufficient equity holdings in the company (Majorstock) to require disclosure at the time of the initial public offering are more likely to have local ties than those scientists who are not major stockholders. This relates not only to the fact that major stockholders are often founders.[10] It is also consistent with the hypothesis that monitoring is facilitated through geographic proximity. Once again, however, the ties are far from exclusively local. The table also shows that we cannot reject the hypothesis that networks of the 365 SAB members are any more local than networks of other scientists in the data base, as indicated by the Chi-square value of 0.56.

III. Probit Analysis

While suggestive, the results from Table 3 examine geographic linkages only in terms of the role played by the university-based scientist in the firm. No attempt is made to control for personal characteristics of the scientists. Yet, the willingness of a scientist to be involved, as well as the attractiveness of a scientist to a company, undoubtedly influences the extent to which linkages between firms and scientists are geographically bounded. In order

[9] Twenty-two of the 54 firms designate the chair of the SAB in the prospectus. In all but two instances the chair is employed by a university. In another instance the SAB has co-chairs, both of whom work at a university.

[10] Fifty percent of the major stockholders are founders.

to examine these relations, we estimate a probit model of the probability that a scientist is located in the same region as the biotechnology firm with which she or he is involved. The probit model permits us to determine how various factors affect the likelihood of being part of a local network as opposed to a nonlocal network. Individual characteristics introduced into the analysis include age, citation history, and Nobel status.[11] Before presenting the results, we discuss the variables and link them to the main hypotheses introduced above. In interpreting the results, it is important to remember that the data do not permit us to examine *who* on university faculties is involved with a biotechnology firm. By definition, *everyone* in our sample is involved. Rather, the analysis focuses upon the geographic dimension of the link between university-based scientists and biotechnology companies — that is, under what circumstances this link occurs within the same geographic space and under which circumstances the scientist and the firm are located in different regions.

A necessary condition for participation is that the firm is aware of the capabilities of the scientist. The dispersion of such information is clearly shaped by the geographic breadth of the scientist's network (contacts). Scientists with limited networks are more likely to be constrained to participate within a local rather than a nonlocal sphere. This suggests that, other things equal, a younger person is more likely to be involved with a local firm than with a nonlocal firm. The expected sign is not only based on factors affecting the size of networks. Life-cycle models of the allocation of time by scientists (David Levy, 1988; and Sharon G. Levin and Stephan, 1991) suggest that in the early stages of their lives scientists invest in human capital in order to build a reputation, while in the later stages of their career scientists trade or *cash in* their reputation for economic return. That is, early in their careers, scientists invest in the creation of knowledge in order to establish a reputation reflecting the scientific value of that new knowledge; with maturity, scientists cash in by seeking ways to

appropriate the economic value of that new knowledge. Thus, we expect older scientists to accept multiple offers of firm involvement. By contrast, younger scientists who have a higher opportunity cost of travel are expected to focus contacts within their own geographic region.

Age is not the only factor shaping the geographic extent of a scientist's network. Scientists who publish are much more likely to be known outside their local network than are nonpublishers. This is especially true if the publications are heavily cited, indicating that the scientific community has a high regard for the work (Robert Merton, 1957; Jonathan R. Cole and Stephen Cole, 1973; and Eugene Garfield, 1979). Thus, just as the involvement of older scientists is likely to be nonlocal in nature, the involvement of scientists with many citations is also likely to be nonlocal. An analogous argument suggests that Nobel laureates are more likely to have nonlocal than local ties.

A major qualification, however, relating to what we call *drawing power*, must be made to the above line of reasoning. Scientists become involved with start-up firms when venture capitalists find the scientist and science she or he is doing sufficiently attractive to warrant financing. Thus, mature scientists with strong reputations have the drawing power to attract firms to locate near them. For example, venture capital and other components of a start-up team for a new biotechnology company will be attracted to locations near scientists with extraordinary reputations to increase the probability that a contact can be established. Whether this drawing power effect outweighs the more general reputation effect is an empirical question.

A different type of qualification is that the higher the density of firms in the region in which any given scientist is located, the greater is the extent of opportunities for her or him within that region. To control for this effect, we include the density of biotechnology firms in the region, measured by the share of the 54 firms located in the scientist's geographic region. The probit model also controls for the role played by the scientist in the biotechnology firm by including a dummy variable defined to be 0 if the scientist founded the firm or chairs the SAB and 0 if she or he did not.

---

[11] Nine of the 445 scientists are Nobel prize recipients and have 10 contacts with biotechnology firms.

The probit regression is estimated for the 312 scientists for whom there is information identifying both their age and citation history. The results are reported in Table 4.[12] The dependent variable is equal to 1 if the link between the scientist and firm is local, and 0 if it is nonlocal. In addition to presenting the probit coefficients and asymptotic standard errors, Table 4 also presents the marginal effect that a one unit change in an independent variable has on the probability of commuting.[13]

The results are striking. The negative and statistically significant coefficient of the age variable suggests that, ceteris paribus, older scientists, are more likely than younger scientists to have contacts with biotechnology firms located outside of the regions of their universities. The marginal effect of an additional year is to increase the probability of a scientist commuting by 0.6 percent; of a decade is 6.0 percent. As expected, the specific role played by the scientist in the biotechnology firm also shapes the geographic dimension of the contact. Those scientists serving as founders of biotechnology firms have a significantly higher propensity to be located in the same region as the firm than those who are not founders. According to the marginal effect, a shift in status from nonfounder to founder increases the likelihood of a contact being local by more than 20 percent. The combined impact (equation (2)) of serving as a founder *or* chair of a SAB is slightly larger.

Having been awarded a Nobel prize significantly increases the propensity for the scientist to engage in local contacts with biotechnology firms.[14] This may reflect the willingness of venture capitalists and other key members of new biotechnology start-ups to locate close to a Nobel prize recipient, and suggests that for scientific stars drawing power overwhelms general reputational effects. On the other hand, there is no evidence that the citation history of a scientist influences the propensity of a scientist to engage in local versus nonlocal contacts.[15] This presumably reflects the offsetting effects of reputation and drawing power discussed in Section II.

One of the concerns in the probit model is that the majority of scientist-firm contacts are concentrated in just two sections of the country: California, which spans the three areas of the San Francisco Bay Area, Los Angeles and San Diego, and the North East, which includes the three areas of Boston, Philadelphia and New York. Because of the proximity of opportunities in neighboring areas, after controlling for density we would expect scientists in the North East and California to have a higher propensity to commute than scientists located in alternative regions of the country. In order to test this hypothesis, we include two dummy variables, the first taking on a value of 1 for scientists located in California, and the other taking on a value of 1 for scientists located in the North East. The results suggest a type of asymmetry between west coast and east coast scientific networks. The positive and statistically significant coefficient on the North East dummy variable implies that despite the large number of opportunities in neighboring areas, scientists located in the North East tend to be insular in their propensity to engage in contacts with firms located in their specific area. By contrast, the coefficient on the California dummy variable, which cannot be considered statistically significant, suggests that proximity of opportunity does not affect commuting patterns for California scientists.

IV. Conclusions

A key finding of this paper is that while a substantial number of university-based scientists participate in networks that are

---

[12] Thirty-one scientists working for three firms are excluded because citation histories were not collected for scientists working for these firms. Of the remaining 414 scientists we found birth dates (and citation histories) for 312, yielding a sample retention rate of 75 percent.

[13] For the continuous variables the marginal effect is evaluated at the mean of the explanatory variable. For the dummy variables the marginal effect reflects the difference between having the characteristic versus not having the characteristic.

[14] The dummy variable for the Nobel prize indicates receipt of the prize since 1970. One scientist received the prize in 1958. The inclusion of this scientist reduces the statistical significance of the coefficient of the Nobel prize dummy variable to being statistically significant at the 10-percent level of significance, for a two-tailed test.

[15] The citation history measure is not statistically significant regardless of the specification by which it is included in the probit equation.

TABLE 4—PROBIT RESULTS FOR PROBABILITY OF SCIENTIST-FIRM CONTACT BEING LOCAL[a]

	(1)	Marginal effect[b]	(2)	Marginal effect[b]	(3)	Marginal effect[b]	(4)	Marginal effect[b]
Constant	-0.45 (0.47)	—	-0.42 (0.47)	—	-0.59 (0.48)	—	-0.56 (0.48)	—
Age	-0.018^* (0.008)	-0.006	-0.019^* (0.008)	-0.006	-0.022^* (0.009)	-0.007	-0.023^{**} (0.009)	-0.008
Citations	0.74×10^{-4} (0.56×10^{-3})	0.25×10^{-4}	0.32×10^{-4} (0.56×10^{-3})	0.10×10^{-4}	0.79×10^{-4} (0.59×10^{-3})	0.25×10^{-4}	0.12×10^{-3} (0.58×10^{-3})	0.40×10^{-4}
Nobel prize	1.13^* (0.49)	0.427	1.14^* (0.50)	0.430	1.12^* (0.50)	0.420	1.12^* (0.49)	0.420
Founder	0.62^* (0.27)	0.233	—	—	0.67^* (0.27)	0.240	—	—
Founder/chair	—	—	0.65^{**} (0.25)	0.242	—	—	0.68^{**} (0.25)	0.250
Firm density[c]	7.39^{**} (0.31)	0.250	7.36^{**} (0.82)	0.248	6.25^{**} (1.37)	0.198	6.15^{**} (1.37)	0.209
California	—	—	—	—	0.38 (0.38)	0.13	0.41 (0.38)	0.14
North East	—	—	—	—	0.87^{**} (0.28)	0.30	0.87^{**} (0.28)	0.30
Log-Likelihood	-142.02		-141.27		-134.72		-134.07	
Sample size	312		312		312		312	

[a] Asymptotic standard errors are listed in parentheses.
[b] See the text for how the marginal effect is computed.
[c] The marginal effect is calculated for a 0.10 change in firm density.
* Statistically significant at the 95-percent level of confidence, two-tailed test.
** Statistically significant at the 99-percent level of confidence, two-tailed test.

geographically bounded, approximately 70 percent of the links between biotechnology companies and the university-based scientists are nonlocal. We conclude that while proximity matters in establishing formal ties between university-based scientists and companies, its influence is anything but overwhelming.

The results clearly suggest that the importance of proximity is shaped by the role played by the scientist. Proximity matters more in the case of founders than for members of scientific advisory boards. It also matters more for chairs of SABs. This presumably reflects the qualitative difference in the services provided by the scientist. In addition, characteristics specific to the scientist shape the geographic dimension of the scientist-firm contact. The status of being a *star,* as reflected by receipt of a Nobel prize, for example, reduces the need to commute outside of the region in which the scientist is located. Apparently, other key components comprising a biotechnology start-up, such as venture capital and managerial competence, may be willing to locate within close proximity to such stars. In addition, we find that older scientists, other things being equal, are more likely to have links with biotechnology firms that are not geographically bounded. This apparently reflects both the desire of mature scientists to cash in and the geographic breadth of their networks.

Our findings also suggest that the links between scientists and companies involve a multiplicity of dimensions, only one of which is knowledge transfer, and that the importance of local proximity varies considerably across these dimensions. The results also suggest that even in the case of knowledge transfer, scientists and firms are often geographically separated. For example, 40 percent of the university-based founders of biotech firms in the data base are affiliated with firms outside their region. Does this mean that the proponents of the new growth economics may have overemphasized the importance that geography plays? Not necessarily, if one recalls that much of this work stresses the informality of knowledge spillovers while our work focuses on relationships that have been intentionally formed to capitalize on the scientist's knowledge. In both the informal and formal case, the marginal cost of transmitting new economic knowledge, particularly tacit knowledge, across geographic space is nontrivial. This means, as the studies by Audretsch and Feldman (1996) and Adam B. Jaffe et al. (1993) imply, that geographic proximity matters when knowledge spillovers are *informal*. But an important conclusion of this paper is that when knowledge is transmitted through *formal* ties between researchers and firms, geographic proximity is not necessary, since face to face contact does not occur by chance but instead is carefully planned.

Finally, it is important to realize that while geographic proximity between university scientists and firms is valuable, other factors that are related to agglomeration, such as the location of other firms and research organizations, play an important role in mediating the geographic proximity of firms and their affiliated university scientists. These broader types of spillovers have not been examined in this paper. Perhaps future research should shift away from asking *if* geography plays a role to exploring in more depth *how* the role of geography varies by function as well as by characteristics of the region.

APPENDIX TABLE A1—LOCATION OF BIOTECH FIRMS BY REGION

	University-based scientists	Scientists from within region			University-based scientists	Scientists from within region	
		Number	Percent			Number	Percent
San Francisco Bay Area, CA				*Philadelphia, PA*			
Anergen	5	4	80.0	Affinity Biotech	5	1	20.0
Applied Immune Sciences	8	1	12.5	Cephalon	5	1	20.0
Biocircutis	4	2	50.0	DNX	5	2	40.0
Biotime	6	2	33.3	Magainin Pharmaceuticals	6	2	33.3
Cell Genesis	16	2	12.5	Medarex	6	0	0.0
COR Therapeutics	15	5	33.3	Zynaxis	4	2	50.0
Cygnus	5	1	20.0	Total	31	8	25.8
Genelabs Technologies	13	6	46.2				
Genpharm	15	0	0.0	*New York, NY*			
Gilead Sciences	7	1	14.3	Alteon	6	4	66.6
Neurex	22	6	27.3	Biomatrix	6	1	16.7
Oclassen Pharmaceuticals	7	1	14.3	Biospecifics Technologies	5	2	40.0
Protein Design Labs	7	4	57.1	Medicis	9	0	0.0
Sciclone	8	7	87.5	Regeneron Pharmaceuticals	13	2	15.4
Systemix	7	2	28.9	Total	39	9	23.0
Total	145	44	30.3				
				Maryland			
San Diego, CA				Genetic Therapy	7	0	0.0
Amylin	10	3	30.0	Univax Biologics	6	1	16.7
Corvas	9	3	33.3	Total	13	1	7.7
Cytel	9	1	33.3				
Genta	19	1	5.2	*Seattle, WA*			
Idec Pharmaceuticals	2	1	50.0	Cell Pro	7	2	28.6
Immune Response	7	2	28.6				
Ligand Pharmaceuticals	7	4	57.1	*Boulder, CO*			
Protein Polymer Technologie	7	1	14.3	Somatogen	4	1	25.0
Vical	7	3	42.3				
Total	77	21	27.2	*Kansas*			
				Deprenyl	6	0	0.0
Boston, MA							
Alpha-Beta Technology	7	7	100.0	*Research Triangle, NC*			
Cambridge Neuroscience	10	4	40.0	Sphinx Pharmaceuticals	6	2	33.3
Creative Biomolecules	11	4	36.4				
Cytotherapeutics	14	4	28.6	*Los Angeles, CA*			
Epigen	8	2	25.0	Watson Pharmaceuticals	9	0	0.0
Immulogie	11	5	45.5				
Matritech	8	3	37.5	*Dallas, TX*			
Sepracor	7	3	42.8	Carntech	10	1	10.0
Seragen	3	3	100.0				
Vertex Pharmaceuticals	6	6	100.0	*Houston, TX*			
Total	85	41	48.2	Argus Pharmaceuticals	13	8	61.5
				Total	**445**	**138**	**31.0**

REFERENCES

Arrow, Kenneth. "Economic Welfare and the Allocation of Resources for Invention," in Richard R. Nelson, ed., *The rate and direction of inventive activity.* Princeton, NJ: Princeton University Press, 1962, pp. 609–26.

Audretsch, David B. *Innovation and industry evolution.* Cambridge, MA: MIT Press, 1995.

Audretsch, David B. and Feldman, Maryann P. "R&D Spillovers and the Geography of Innovation and Production." *American Economic Review,* June 1996, *86*(3), pp. 630–40.

Burrill, G. Steven. *Biotech 88: Into the marketplace.* San Francisco: Arthur Young High Technology Group, 1987.

Burrill, G. Steven and Lee, Kenneth B., Jr. *Biotech 93: Accelerating commercialization.* San Francisco: Ernst & Young, 1992.

Cole, Jonathan R. and Cole, Stephen. *Social stratification in science.* Chicago: University of Chicago Press, 1973.

Etzkowitz, Henry. "Entrepreneurial Scientists and Entrepreneurial Universities in American Academic Science." *Minerva,* 1983, *21*(2), pp. 198–233.

Garfield, Eugene. *Citation indexing: Its theory and application in science, technology and humanities.* New York: Wiley, 1979.

Jaffe, Adam B.; Trajtenberg, Manuel and Henderson, Rebecca. "Geographic Localization of Knowledge Spillovers as Evidenced by Patent Citations." *Quarterly Journal of Economics,* August 1993, *63*(3), pp. 577–98.

Krugman, Paul. "Increasing Returns and Economic Geography." *Journal of Political Economy,* June 1991a, *99*(3), pp. 483–99.

_____. *Geography and trade.* Cambridge, MA: MIT Press, 1991b.

Levin, Sharon G. and Stephan, Paula E. "Research Productivity over the Life Cycle: Evidence for Academic Scientists." *American Economic Review,* March 1991, *81*(4), pp. 114–32.

Levy, David. "The Market for Fame and Fortune." *History of Political Economy,* Winter 1988, *20*(4), pp. 615–25.

Link, Albert N. and Rees, John. "Firm Size, University Based Research, and the Returns to

R&D." *Small Business Economics,* 1990, *2*(1), pp. 25–32.

Lucas, Robert E., Jr. "Making a Miracle." *Econometrica,* March 1993, *61*(2), pp. 251–72.

Merton, Robert. "Priorities in Scientific Discovery: A Chapter in the Sociology of Science." *American Sociological Review,* December 1957, *22*(6), pp. 635–59.

Orsenigo, Luigi. *The emergence of biotechnology: Institutions and markets in industrial innovation.* New York: St Martins Press, 1989.

Pisano, Gary P.; Shan, Wiejnian and Teece, David. "Joint Ventures and Collaboration in the Biotechnology Industry," in David Mowery, ed., *International collaborative ventures in U.S. manufacturing.* Cambridge, MA: Ballinger Publishers, 1988, pp. 183–222.

Romer, Paul. "Endogenous Technological Change." *Journal of Political Economy,* October 1990, *98*(5) Part 2, pp. S71–102.

Shrine, Jim. "Telios Offers to Buy Back Shares from Offering." *Bioworld Today,* October 1994, *10,* p. 1.

Stephan, Paula E. "Differences in the Post-Entry Value of Biotech Firms: The Role of Human Capital." Presented at the Conference on the Post-Entry Performance of Firms," hosted by the Bank of Portugal, Lisbon, May 22–28, 1994.

Stephan, Paula E. and Everhart, Stephen. "The Changing Rewards to Science: The Case of Biotechnology." *Small Business Economics,* forthcoming 1996, *8.*

Stephan, Paula E. and Levin, Sharon G. *Striking the mother lode in science.* New York: Oxford University Press, 1992.

Williamson, Oliver E. *Markets and hierarchies: Antitrust analysis and implications.* New York: Free Press, 1975.

Zucker, Lynne G.; Darby, Michael R. and Armstrong, Jeff. "Intellectual Capital and the Firm: The Technology of Geographically Localized Knowledge Spillovers." National Bureau of Economic Research (Cambridge, MA) Working Paper No. 4946, 1995.

Zucker, Lynne G.; Darby, Michael R. and Brewer, Marilynn B. "Intellectual Capital and the Birth of U.S. Biotechnology Enterprises." National Bureau of Economic Research (Cambridge, MA) Working Paper No. 4653, 1994.

[12]

Small Bus Econ (2013) 41:797–817
DOI 10.1007/s11187-013-9507-7

Knowledge spillovers, collective entrepreneurship, and economic growth: the role of universities

Dennis Patrick Leyden · Albert N. Link

Accepted: 15 September 2013 / Published online: 15 October 2013
© Springer Science+Business Media New York 2013

Abstract To improve our understanding of the role that universities play in facilitating the transmission of knowledge to private-sector business enterprises so as to generate economic growth, this article builds on the Knowledge Spillover Theory of Entrepreneurship to develop a formal model of university-with-business enterprise collaborative research partnerships in which the outcome is both mutually desirable and feasible. This model shows that if a university seeks to act as a complement to private-sector collaborative R&D so that it will be attractive to both incumbent firms and startup entrepreneurs, it needs to structure its program so that business enterprise revenues increase and business enterprise R&D costs rise by a smaller proportion than revenues increase, if they rise at all (and a fall would be better). Such a structure is consistent with both business enterprise and university interests, but is only likely to be feasible if the university is subsidized to cover the cost of such public-private collaborative research partnerships. In the absence of such support, the university will have to cover its costs through a fee charged to participating business enterprises and that will result in the university being seen as a substitute rather than a complement to private-sector collaborative R&D, and thus the university will be seen as an unattractive partner for many business enterprises.

Keywords Collective entrepreneurship · Knowledge spillovers · University collaboration

JEL Classifications D73 · L26 · O31

1 Introduction

Endogenous growth models have long recognized the connection between knowledge spillovers and growth. However, as Acs et al. (2009) and Braunerhjelm et al. (2010) note in their Knowledge Spillover Theory of Entrepreneurship (KSTE), such spillovers do not generate growth of their own accord. Rather, such spillovers must be transmitted through entrepreneurial actions. Thus, economic growth requires a balance between research and entrepreneurial activity (Michelacci 2003) that is actuated by a matching process similar to that observed in labor markets (Pissarides 1990).[1]

D. P. Leyden · A. N. Link (✉)
Department of Economics, University of North Carolina at Greensboro, Greensboro, NC 27412, USA
e-mail: anlink@uncg.edu

D. P. Leyden
e-mail: dpleyden@uncg.edu

---

[1] Thus, the debate over whether entrepreneurship is essentially a process of creation or discovery (Alvarez and Barney 2007) misses the point. As Michelacci (2003) and Acs et al. (2009) argue, creation of knowledge by researchers and existing firms and the discovery of such knowledge by entrepreneurs are both required.

This article investigates the role that a university plays in determining that balance through such arrangements as research joint ventures, consortia, and research parks.[2] Empirical evidence, both anecdotal (Babbage 2011) and more formally derived (Audretsch and Lehmann 2005; Tassey 2008; Link and Welsh 2013), suggests that universities may play a significant role in the process by which knowledge is transformed into economic knowledge and that this process takes place at a local or regional level.[3] And, certainly in the USA, industry/university relationships, either formal as a research joint venture[4] or informal as a member of a consortium or a resident of a university research park,[5] have been increasing since the early 1980s. This trend is likely a result of both a university response to incentives established through, for example, the Bayh-Dole Act of 1980 and a response by industry to the productivity slowdown during the late 1970s and the realization that technology life cycles are shortening.[6]

Nearly a decade ago, Hall et al. (2000, 2003) wrote that little is known about the types of roles that universities play in general in such research partnerships or about the economic consequences associated

with those roles, and little has changed since then.[7] What research there is on the topic of universities as research partners focuses solely on industry motivations or on university motivations for engaging in an industry/university research relationship, but not on how the two sides interact. We know that industry has many motivations for partnering with universities, only one of which is to gain first access to complementary research activity and research results,[8] and that universities' motivation is to relieve administration-based financial pressures by incentivizing faculty to engage in applied commercial research with industry.[9] To our knowledge, no previous studies have attempted to formalize, mathematically, the relationship between the two parties.[10]

Intriguingly, however, the KSTE (see, for example, Audretsch and Lehmann 2005) characterization of business enterprises firms or startup entrepreneurs suggests that how firms interact with universities may be at least in part dependent on whether the business enterprise is a firm or an entrepreneur.

---

[2] We abstract from the important impact that universities have through their role in educating and graduating students.

[3] Åstebro and Bazzazian (2011), in their wide-ranging review of the empirical literature on the impact of universities on local entrepreneurship and economic development, rightly sound a cautionary note on our ability to make definitive claims about the causal impact of universities on economic development.

[4] See Link and Scott (2005).

[5] See Link and Scott (2007), Layson et al. (2008), Leyden et al. (2008), and Åstebro and Bazzazian (2011) for discussions of university research parks.

[6] The Council on Competitiveness (1996, pp. 3–4) recently noted and emphasized this trend in the USA: "[P]articipants in the U.S. R&D enterprise will have to continue experimenting with different types of partnerships to respond to the economic constraints, competitive pressures and technological demands that are forcing adjustments across the board....[and in response] industry is increasingly relying on partnerships with universities ...." Relatedly, Link (1996) showed that university participation in formal research joint ventures (RJVs) has increased steadily since the mid-1980s, Cohen et al. (1997) documented that the number of industry/university R&D centers increased by more than 60 % during the 1980s, and a recent survey of US science faculty by Morgan (1998) revealed that many desire even more partnership relationships with industry. Mowery and Teece (1996, p. 111) contend that such growth in strategic alliances in R&D is indicative of a "broad restructuring of the U.S. national R&D system."

[7] Hall's (2004) subsequent emphasis on industry/university research partnerships in the US is on intellectual property. See also the role of intellectual property protection mechanisms (Hertzfeldet al. 2006).

[8] Cohen et al. (1997) provide a selective review of this literature, emphasizing the studies that have documented that university research enhances firms' sales, R&D productivity, and patenting activity. See Blumenthal et al. (1986), Jaffe (1989), Adams (1990), Berman (1990), Feller (1990), Mansfield (1991, 1992), Van de Ven (1993), Bonaccorsi and Piccaluga (1994), Klevorick et al. (1994), Winter (1995), Zucker et al. (1994), Henderson et al. (1995), Mansfield and Lee (1996), Zeckhauser (1996), Campbell (1997), Baldwin and Link (1998), Lee (2000) and Lööf and Broström (2008). Cockburn and Henderson (1997) show that it was important for innovative pharmaceutical firms to maintain ties to universities. Hall et al. (2000, 2003) suggest that perhaps such research ties with universities increase the "absorptive capacity," in the sense of Cohen and Levinthal (1989, 1990), of the innovative firms. This literature is reviewed by Audretsch et al. (2012).

[9] See Berman (1990), Feller (1990), Henderson et al. (1995), Zeckhauser (1996), and Siegel et al. (1999).

[10] GUIRR (2006, p. 8) point out that "Institutional practices and national resources should focus on fostering appropriate long-term partnerships between universities and industry." While we do not offer recommendations about such partnerships in this article, we do acknowledge the importance of the timing of such relationships and their longevity. However, our model (below) is static and does not taking timing into account. Clearly, that is an area for future research.

There is thus a need for a broader framework that jointly accounts for the motivations of both universities and the two types of business enterprises when assessing the benefits and costs to collaboration and predicting the situations under which collaboration will be mutually beneficial. Absent this broader framework, responses to naïve policy prescriptions might be costly and unproductive. Acs et al. (2009, p. 28), for example, note the "need to explain where [entrepreneurial] opportunities come from, [and] how intra-temporal knowledge spillovers occur," and the State Science and Technology Institute (SSTI) recently proclaimed (2008, p. 13):

> Innovation, in and of itself, will not necessarily translate into economic activity. Rather, it is the application of that technology and its introduction into the marketplace that results in economic growth. Having a strong R&D base is necessary but not sufficient to grow a technology-based economy. *An effective means of moving technology into the commercial marketplace is to encourage relationships between the researchers who are making the discoveries and the entrepreneurs and companies that have the ability to commercialize them* [emphasis added].

As we demonstrate in this article, it is only under a specific set of cost and profit conditions based on the interplay of university and business enterprise behaviors, which we refer to as collective entrepreneurship, that university-with-business enterprise partnerships are beneficial to both parties and therefore likely to occur.[11,12]

The remainder of this article is outlined as follows. In Sect. 2 we examine the decision by private-sector business enterprises (that is, both KSTE firms and entrepreneurs)[13] to collaborate with other private-sector business enterprises. In that decision-making process, business enterprises have to balance the increased potential for revenues that comes with greater collaboration with both the decreased ability to appropriate those potential revenues and the increased cost of engaging in R&D that also come with greater collaboration. Then, in Sect. 3, we turn to the possibility that a business enterprise could engage in collaborative R&D with a university, and if it does, whether it will view the university as a complement to private-sector collaborative R&D, in which case it will increase that activity, or as a substitute, in which case it will reduce that private-sector collaborative activity. With Sect. 3 as background, Sect. 4 examines the policy alternatives for the university and the implications of its choices for the level and type of collaborative R&D that occurs as a result and the dependency of that choice on its own motivations and constraints. Being an initial theoretical exploration of what we refer to as collective entrepreneurship, we have relied on a number of simplifying assumptions, such as only focusing on cost and profit conditions. As we note below, we are aware of these modeling simplifications, and we expect that others will build upon our effort to address them in future analyses. Section 5 considers the normative implications of the model. Finally, Sect. 6 concludes the article with a brief summary and discussion of the implications of this work for future research.

2 Private-sector collaboration

Consider a geographic region in which N heterogeneous profit-maximizing, private-sector business enterprises engage in R&D in collaboration with other business enterprises and use the results of that R&D to

---

[11] Leyden and Link (2013) discuss collective entrepreneurship in the context of the management of places. Therein they hypothesize that the strategic management of places is functionally related to the collective positive entrepreneurial effort of individuals, each exercising his/her perception and action at different time based on their personal preferences, expertise, and estimation of the best steps forward. Collectively, they engage in what might be called a process of social sequential learning that moves a place forward for the common weal.

[12] We thank an anonymous referee for pointing out that in a knowledge spillover perspective costs and profits are certainly important, as are other intermediary inputs and long-term strategies (for example, those that affect regional R&D culture and economic knowledge) that may or may not be captured in a static model that focused on costs and profits. We fully agree with this point, and we are hopeful that our initial theoretical effort toward collective entrepreneurship will provide a

Footnote 12 continued
foundation for later extensions in the literature to account for these subtleties.

[13] For an interesting antecedent to the KSTE distinction between firms and entrepreneurs, see Hébert and Link's (2009) discussion of Adam Smith's and Jeremy Bentham's contrasting views of the entrepreneur.

produce and sell product. Assume that each business enterprise in the region seeks to maximize its profit π associated with R&D,[14] and, following the KSTE, let the impact of that R&D be the result of the business enterprise's status as an incumbent firm or startup entrepreneur, its ability σ to efficiently transform knowledge into economic (that is, commercially viable) knowledge, and the synergies it experiences that are associated with interacting with some n number of other business enterprises ($n < N$) in the region.

The revenue r associated with conducting such R&D will depend on the amount of the R&D, on its ability σ to transform the results of that R&D into economic knowledge, and on the degree to which the business enterprise can appropriate the value of the economic knowledge that it generates. Let p represent the potential revenue that could be earned by the firm were it not subject to competition from any other business enterprise in the region, and assume that p is an increasing function of σ (which lies between 0 and 1) and an increasing, concave function of n[15]:

$$p = p(\sigma, n) \ni \frac{dp}{d\sigma} > 0, \quad \frac{dp}{dn} > 0, \quad \frac{d^2 p}{dn^2} < 0 \qquad (1)$$

p is an increasing function of σ because a higher σ indicates that the enterprise has generated a greater level of economically usable knowledge.[16] p is an increasing function of n because of the economies of technological scope that come from interacting with a larger number of business enterprises and a concave function of n because the business enterprise faces downward sloping demand curves in its product markets that results in revenues rising at a diminishing rate as the number of firms it collaborates with, and hence the research output of the business enterprise, increases.

The actual revenue r that a firm can earn is typically less than its potential revenue p because the business enterprise is unlikely to be able to appropriate the full amount of p in the marketplace. While a number of factors affect the ability of a business enterprise to appropriate p, an increase in n will in general reduce the ability of the business enterprise to appropriate p because (1) an increase in n increases the probability that among the business enterprise's collaborators will be some of the business enterprises with which it competes, and (2) an increase in n reduces the time it takes before the knowledge spreads to non-collaborating, competitor business enterprises that are located in the region.[17] Thus, letting a be the proportion of p that the business enterprise can actually appropriate, we can describe the determination of a as:

$$a = a(n) \ni 0 < a < 1, \quad \frac{da}{dn} < 0, \quad \text{and} \quad \frac{d^2 a}{dn^2} > 0. \qquad (2)$$

Hence, the actual revenues r of the business enterprise can be defined as:

$$r = r(\sigma, n) = a(n) \cdot p(\sigma, n). \qquad (3)$$

Finally, there are the costs c that the business enterprise incurs when it engages in R&D. We assume that such costs increase at an increasing rate with n for two reasons. First, with an increase in n, we would expect to see an increase in the scale of R&D activity. While there may be some scale economies at first, ultimately, diminishing returns are likely to be present. Second, as n increases, so will the likelihood that some of those n partners may attempt to manipulate the activities of the group for their own private benefit or even to free ride, and that will drive up the business enterprise's cost of maintaining and monitoring its partnerships in order to protect itself against such activities. Thus:

---

[14] For expository reasons, we reduce the dynamic, uncertain problem of maximizing expected profits to a static, deterministic one. See Knight's (1921) classic work on risk and uncertainty for a justification of this approach.

[15] The assumption that potential revenue (and later appropriability and costs) is a function of n is a simplifying assumption intended to proxy for the complex matching process by which business enterprises identify and partner with other business enterprises in ways that are to the mutual advantage to those business enterprises.

[16] Economically usable knowledge includes the results of the entrepreneurial discovery process that may result in novel applications of technology and forms of output.

---

[17] Anand and Khanna (1996) argue that the inability to fully appropriate the value of an innovation is due to the presence of weak property rights that arise because of an inability to specify the context and boundaries of knowledge in a manner that makes violation of those property rights verifiable. Cohen (1994) notes that this inability to fully appropriate the value of the research may, if severe enough, lead to incentive problems in engaging in efficient private-sector collaboration, that is, collaboration that results in more research than would be generated in the absence of the collaboration.

$$c = c(n) \ni \frac{dc}{dn} > 0, \quad \frac{d^2c}{dn^2} > 0. \tag{4}$$

The profits of the business enterprise will therefore be the difference between the actual revenue r associated with the appropriable amount of the business enterprise's research and the cost c of that business enterprise engaging in the R&D process:

$$\pi = \pi(\sigma, n) = r(\sigma, n) - c(n). \tag{5}$$

The optimal number n^* of collaborators for the business enterprise will then be that number of business enterprises that sets marginal profits to zero:

$$\frac{\partial \pi(\sigma, n^*)}{\partial n} = \frac{\partial r(\sigma, n^*)}{\partial n} - \frac{dc(n^*)}{dn} = 0 \tag{6}$$

such that:

$$\pi^* = \pi(\sigma, n^*) \geq 0 \tag{7}$$

Note that the business enterprise's marginal revenue, $\frac{\partial r(\sigma, n^*)}{\partial n}$, is the result of changes in both potential revenue $p(\sigma, n)$ and the level of appropriability $a(n)$:

$$\frac{\partial r(\sigma, n^*)}{\partial n} = \frac{da(n^*)}{dn} \cdot p(\sigma, n^*) + a(n^*) \cdot \frac{\partial p(\sigma, n^*)}{\partial n},$$
$$\tag{8}$$

and the business enterprise's marginal cost is $\frac{dc(n^*)}{dn}$. Figure 1 illustrates the partnership problem for a given business enterprise with a given σ. In the top diagram, the problem is illustrated in terms of total values with the profit-maximizing number of R&D partners n^* being where total profits are greatest. Total profits $\pi(\sigma, n)$ are maximized where the slopes of the revenue curve $r(\sigma, n)$ and the cost curve $c(n)$ are the same. In the bottom diagram, the same problem is illustrated in terms of marginal values. Thus, the profit-maximizing number of R&D partners n^* is located where the marginal revenue (mr) intersects the marginal cost (mc) curve, and the greater σ is, *ceteris paribus*, the greater will be n^*.

The logic of this problem is the same for all business enterprises. However, as the KSTE notes, there is a significant difference between incumbent firms and startup entrepreneurs, and this difference results in incumbent firms generally preferring a higher number of R&D partners than will startup entrepreneurs. Incumbent firms engage in R&D to generate marginal improvements in knowledge that they can exploit; startup entrepreneurs are typically

individuals who only recently exited from an incumbent firm and whose focus is on the exploitation of the total knowledge set that they have taken from incumbent firms. Collaborative R&D among business enterprises focuses on marginal increases in knowledge that is not likely to significantly change the total store of knowledge. As a result, incumbent firms are more likely to have the institutional infrastructure and the volume of trade to exploit such marginal increases in knowledge, while startup entrepreneurs are not. Moreover, startup entrepreneurs are more likely to perceive the loss of appropriation associated with having R&D partners to be a greater threat than will incumbent firms both because the entrepreneurs are more susceptible to such risks and because they are unlikely to have the infrastructure and negotiating leverage to protect themselves from such loss of appropriation. Thus, despite the fact that startup entrepreneurs generally have greater σ than incumbent firms, they will have lower revenue functions $r(\sigma, n)$ that decline more quickly as the number of R&D partners increases. Hence, their marginal revenue curves will be lower, and they will prefer a smaller number of private-sector R&D partners.

3 Business enterprise demand for university collaboration

For the private-sector business enterprise, whether incumbent firm or startup entrepreneur, the decision to collaborate with a university ultimately depends on whether profits are higher or lower as a result of that collaboration. However, whether the business enterprise collaborates, and if so whether it views such collaboration as a substitute or a complement for private-sector collaboration, will depend not only on whether profits increase, but also on the relative change in the business enterprise's R&D costs and revenues that come about as a result of collaborating with a university.

3.1 Which business enterprises will collaborate with the university?

A university as a research partner can affect a business enterprise's profits in three ways: It can (1) increase the business enterprise's economies of technological scope, (2) reduce the business enterprise's ability to

Fig. 1 Private-sector business enterprise collaboration

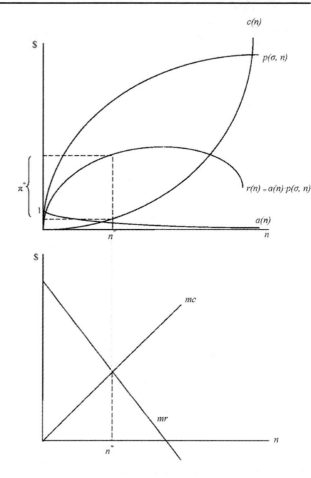

appropriate potential revenues, and (3) change the business enterprise's cost of engaging in R&D.

Collaboration with a university creates economies of technological scope. At a minimum, the university may be thought of as simply another collaborating business enterprise in the region. Thus, the university, like any business enterprise, creates the possibility of more interactions and more access to research capital and other knowledge spillovers, and this, in turn, gives the business enterprise in general the opportunity to increase its revenue stream. Interestingly, however, the startup entrepreneur in this regard will view the university as a somewhat safer partner to the extent the university is perceived as less of a competitive threat.

But of course, the university is more than just another collaborating business enterprise; it also embodies unique human and technical capital that might not be available in the private sector or, if available, for which the acquisition cost might be higher.[18] The university makes such unique capital available to the business enterprises with which it collaborates, thereby increasing for those business

---

[18] There are, of course, markets for human and technical capital, but the nature of R&D in a business enterprise is likely to be more focused on the development side and therefore more applied and proprietary, while the nature of R&D in a university is likely to be more focused on the research side.

 Springer

enterprises the research synergies that come from being able to explore a broader spectrum of research issues and from being able to view research questions from a different perspective. Particularly for startup entrepreneurs whose stock of human and especially physical capital is likely to be low compared to incumbent firms, this benefit is potentially of great significance. The university also may act as a facilitator of (potential or additional) synergies among the business enterprises themselves. By providing physical facilities for collaborations (e.g., meetings) and joint research, by sponsoring seminars, conferences, workshops, receptions, and by generally acting as matchmaker and objective chaperone, the university can thereby increase the quality of interactions among those business enterprises.[19] But as noted in the previous section, while this may be of benefit to startup entrepreneurs, particularly if it provides those enterprises with a safer environment in which to develop trust with other private-sector enterprises, it nonetheless also contains the potential risk of an increased loss of appropriation. On the whole, then, the university affords business enterprises with some ability to earn greater revenue from both their direct interaction with the university and the increased value of their collaboration with other business enterprises. In terms of our model, these effects increase the marginal value of potential revenue, $\frac{\partial p(\sigma, n)}{\partial n}$, for each participating business enterprise. Assume, then, that potential revenue $p(\sigma, n)$ and its marginal value $\frac{\partial p(\sigma, n)}{\partial n}$ both change by the parameter $\omega \geq 1$ (shown below) as a result of these economies of technological scope.

The presence of the university also reduces the ability of collaborating business enterprises to appropriate the output of their shared research for private gain. The reward structure for researchers in a university is primarily based on publications (Link 1996). As a result, there will be limited interest on the part of university researchers to collaborate with business enterprises if they cannot use such collaboration to generate publications. Moreover, because university missions typically include providing general benefits to society in the form of increased knowledge, they tend to focus more on basic research than do business enterprises, and the commercial value

of basic research is by its nature more difficult to appropriate. For these reasons, the presence of the university reduces the ability of business enterprises to appropriate the increased potential revenue that those business enterprises get from collaborating with the university and with other business enterprises. In terms of our model, these effects decrease the marginal degree of appropriability, $\frac{da(n)}{dn}$, for each participating business enterprise. Assume, then, that the degree of appropriability $a(n)$ and its marginal value $\frac{da(n)}{dn}$ both change by the parameter $\alpha \leq 1$ as a result of these effects. As suggested above, this is more likely to be a significant issue for the startup entrepreneur.

Finally, collaboration with a university will affect a business enterprise's cost of undertaking R&D, although the direction of change is not clear. On the one hand, the presence of the university might be expected to reduce the business enterprise's R&D costs because (1) the university may not require full compensation for the R&D production costs it incurs as a collaborator owing to the infrastructural nature of university research, (2) the university in its role as an "honest broker" can reduce various monitoring and transaction costs incurred by the business enterprises with whom it collaborates and thereby reduce the chance of the R&D process being manipulated to the benefit of a subset of collaborating business enterprises, and (3) the university may cover the cost of interactions among business enterprises by providing physical facilities for meetings and joint research as well as sponsoring seminars, conferences, workshops, and receptions. On the other hand, a business enterprise's R&D cost may rise as a result of collaborating with the university because of the additional costs associated with university requirements (including a possible fee) or with added lobbying and reporting costs associated with participating in a bureaucratic or political process.[20] Assume, then, that as a result of these factors, the business enterprise's R&D costs $c(n)$ and its marginal value $\frac{dc(n)}{dn}$ both change by the

---

[19] Bozeman et al. (2008) and Leyden et al. (2008) demonstrate this point.

[20] See Baldwin and Link (1998) and Leyden and Link (1999) for empirical analyses based on the latter two effects—a reduction in appropriability and a (reduction) in business enterprise research costs. Clearly, we are only focusing on university-industry factors that affect costs and profits. We acknowledge, as urged by an anonymous referee, that there are other important rationales to consider. He/she is correct, but their inclusion is beyond the scope of our model.

parameter $\kappa > 0$ (shown below). Because of the smaller typical size of a startup entrepreneur, these factors, whether positive or negative, are likely to weigh more heavily with the entrepreneur.

Given the above changes associated with university collaboration, the profits to the collaborating business enterprise in interacting with a university can be represented by:

$$\pi^U = \pi^U(\sigma, n) = \alpha \cdot a(n) \cdot \omega \cdot p(\sigma, n) - \kappa$$
$$\cdot c(n) \ni 0 < \alpha \leq 1, \quad \omega \geq 1, \quad \text{and} \quad \kappa > 0. \tag{9}$$

The optimal number n^{U*} of collaborators for the business enterprise will then be that number of business enterprises that sets marginal profits to zero:

$$\frac{\partial \pi^U(\sigma, n^{U*})}{\partial n} = \frac{\partial r^U(\sigma, n^{U*})}{\partial n} - \frac{dc^U(n^{U*})}{dn} = 0, \tag{10}$$

where the business enterprise's marginal revenue $\frac{\partial r^U(\sigma,n)}{\partial n}$ is $\alpha\omega$ times the business enterprise's marginal revenue in the absence of university collaboration (see Eq. (8)):

$$\frac{\partial r^U(\sigma, n^{U*})}{\partial n} = \alpha\omega \cdot \frac{\partial r(\sigma, n^{U*})}{\partial n} \tag{11}$$

and the business enterprise's marginal R&D cost $\frac{dc^U(n^{U*})}{dn}$ is κ times the business enterprise's marginal R&D cost in the absence of university collaboration:

$$\frac{dc^U(n^{U*})}{dn} = \kappa \cdot \frac{dc(n^{U*})}{dn} \tag{12}$$

The question of whether a business enterprise chooses to collaborate with the university hinges on whether its profits in the absence of the university π^* are greater or less than the business enterprise's profits with the university π^{U*}. Using Eqs. (5) and (9), that condition can be describe as:

$$\pi^{U*} \gtrless \pi^* \quad \text{if} \quad (\delta_r \alpha\omega - 1) \cdot a(n^*) \cdot p(\sigma, n^*) \gtrless (\delta_c \kappa - 1)$$
$$\cdot c(n^*) \tag{13}$$

where δ_r indicates the ratio of revenue in the absence of university collaboration with n^{U*} versus the revenue associated with the number of collaborators n^* in the absence of university collaboration, and δ_c indicates the same ratio with respect to the business enterprise's costs:

$$\delta_r = \frac{a(n^{U*}) \cdot p(\sigma, n^{U*})}{a(n^*) \cdot p(\sigma, n^*)} > 0 \tag{14}$$

$$\delta_c = \frac{c(n^{U*})}{c(n^*)} > 0 \tag{15}$$

The values of δ_r and δ_c indicate the impact on revenues and costs of the business enterprise choosing to change the number of private-sector collaborators as a result of the collaboration with the university. If $n^{U*} > n^*$, then $\delta_r > \delta_c > 1$. If $n^{U*} < n^*$, then $\delta_c < \delta_r < 1$. And if $n^{U*} = n^*$, then $\delta_r = \delta_c = 1$.

To determine which business enterprises will choose to collaborate with the university, consider the four ways (summarized in Fig. 2) in which the business enterprise's R&D costs and revenues can change as a result of such collaboration:[21]

Case 1—revenues and R&D costs both rise Revenues and R&D costs will both rise if $\delta_r \alpha\omega > 1$ and $\delta_c \kappa > 1$. Because of that, we can rewrite Eq. (13) as:

$$\pi^{U*} \gtrless \pi^* \quad \text{if} \quad \frac{a(n^*) \cdot p(\sigma, n^*)}{c(n^*)} \gtrless \frac{\delta_c \kappa - 1}{\delta_r \alpha\omega - 1}, \tag{16}$$

and note that the final ratio is the elasticity of the business enterprise's R&D costs with respect to revenues associated with collaborating with the university:[22]

$$E_{c,r} = \frac{\delta_c \kappa - 1}{\delta_r \alpha\omega - 1} \tag{17}$$

Because the firm's revenue-cost ratio $\frac{a(n^*) \cdot p(\sigma,n^*)}{c(n^*)} \geq 1$, all business enterprises will choose to collaborate with

---

[21] The ensuing discussion assumes that α, ω, and κ are not functions of n. This assumption is made for the sake of model clarity. However, we recognize that these parameters may indeed vary to some degree with the number of private-sector collaborators. One possibility that is plausible and consistent with the conclusions of this article is that the loss in appropriability associated with the presence of a university is smaller for incumbent firms (i.e., those that have a larger number of private-sector collaborators) than for startup entrepreneurs (i.e., those that have a smaller number of private-sector collaborators) so that $\partial\alpha/\partial n > 0$. Likewise, the cost savings associated with collaborating with the university is relatively greater for startup entrepreneurs than for incumbent firms (i.e., $\partial\kappa/\partial n < 0$). Of course, the issue is an empirical one and deserving of future work.

[22] This is an arc elasticity with the base equal to the level of revenues and costs associated with the absence of university collaboration.

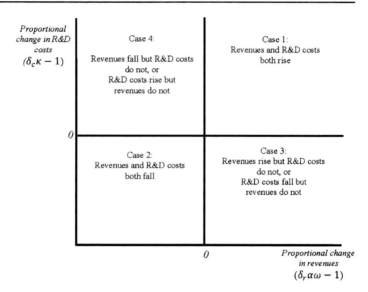

Fig. 2 Effect of university collaboration on revenues and R&D costs

the university if $E_{c,r} < 1$, that is, if the proportional increase in revenues exceeds the proportional increase in R&D costs. However, if $E_{c,r} \geq 1$, the decision to collaborate with the university will depend on whether the business enterprise's revenue-cost ratio $\frac{a(n^*) \cdot p(\sigma,n^*)}{c(n^*)}$ exceeds $E_{c,r}$. The convexity assumptions of our model imply that the revenue-cost ratio is a declining function of n. Hence, if n is sufficiently small, the revenue-cost ratio will be greater than $E_{c,r}$, and the business enterprise will choose to collaborate with the university; if n is sufficiently large, the revenue-cost ratio will be less than $E_{c,r}$, and the business enterprise will choose not to collaborate with the university. Thus, startup entrepreneurs, who are relatively inactive in collaborating with other business enterprises, are more likely to find university collaboration attractive in this case than will incumbent firms. Figure 3 illustrates this conclusion with $\widehat{n^*}$ indicating the level of n^* at which a business enterprise would be indifferent between collaborating and not collaborating with the university.

Case 2—revenues and R&D costs both fall Because revenues and R&D costs will both fall if $\delta_r \alpha \omega < 1$ and $\delta_c \kappa < 1$, we can rewrite equation (13) as (note the reversal of the inequality sign in the conditional inequality due to $\delta_r \alpha \omega - 1$ being negative):

$$\pi^{U*} \gtrless \pi^* \quad \text{if} \quad \frac{a(n^*) \cdot p(\sigma,n^*)}{c(n^*)} \lesseqgtr \frac{\delta_c \kappa - 1}{\delta_r \alpha \omega - 1} \quad (18)$$

Because the business enterprise's revenue-cost ratio $\frac{a(n^*) \cdot p(\sigma,n^*)}{c(n^*)} \geq 1$, no business enterprise will choose to collaborate with the university if $E_{c,r} < 1$, that is, if the proportional fall in revenues exceeds the proportional fall in R&D costs. However, if $E_{c,r} \geq 1$, the decision to collaborate with the university will depend on whether the business enterprise's revenue-cost ratio $\frac{a(n^*) \cdot p(\sigma,n^*)}{c(n^*)}$ exceeds $E_{c,r}$. Because revenue-cost ratio is a declining function of n, if n is sufficiently small, the revenue-cost ratio will be greater than $E_{c,r}$, and the business enterprise will choose not to collaborate with the university. Likewise, if n is sufficiently large, the revenue-cost ratio will be less than $E_{c,r}$, and the business enterprise will choose to collaborate with the university. Thus, incumbent firms, which are relatively active in collaborating with other business enterprises, are more likely to find university collaboration attractive in this case than will startup entrepreneurs.

Figure 4 illustrates this conclusion with $\widehat{n^*}$ indicating the level of n^* at which a business enterprise would be indifferent between collaborating and not collaborating with the university.

Fig. 3 R&D collaboration with the university when revenues rise proportionately less than R&D costs rise

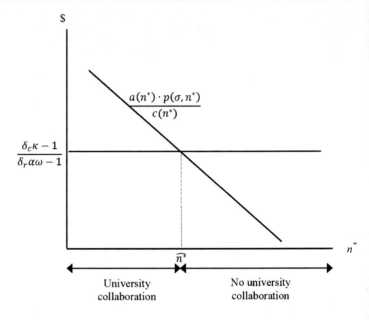

Fig. 4 R&D collaboration with the university when revenues fall proportionately less than R&D costs fall

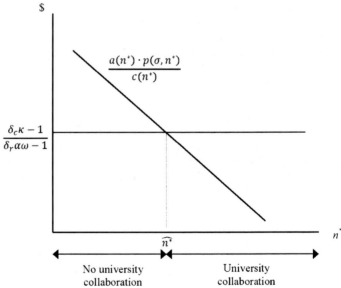

Case 3—revenues rise but R&D costs do not, or R&D costs fall but revenues do not   Revenues and R&D costs will change in opposite directions with revenues

rising but R&D costs not rising (or with R&D costs falling but revenues not falling) if $\delta_r \alpha \omega \geq 1$, $\delta_c \kappa \leq 1$, and one of these conditions holds as a strict inequality.

 Springer

If the first inequality holds as a strict inequality, the effect of increased economies of scope will outweigh the effect of a loss in appropriability. As a result, revenues will rise, and all business enterprises regardless of the degree to which they collaborate with other firms will choose to collaborate with the university. Similarly, if the second inequality holds as a strict inequality, then R&D costs will fall, revenues will not, and all business enterprises will choose to collaborate with the university.

Case 4—Revenues fall but R&D costs do not, or R&D costs rise but revenues do not   The final possible case is that revenues fall but R&D costs do not (or R&D costs rise but revenues do not), which will occur if $\delta_r \alpha \omega \leq 1$, $\delta_c \kappa \geq 1$, and one of these conditions holds as a strict inequality. If the first inequality holds as a strict inequality, the effect of a loss in appropriability will outweigh the effect of increased economies of scope. As a result, revenues will fall, R&D costs will at best stay the same, and hence no business enterprise regardless of the degree to which they collaborate with other business enterprises will choose to collaborate with the university. Similarly, if the second inequality holds as a strict inequality, then R&D costs will rise, revenues at best will stay the same, and once again no business enterprise will choose to collaborate with the university.

Summarizing these four cases, then, no business enterprise will collaborate with the university if its revenues fall and R&D costs rise, or if its revenues fall but its R&D costs fall by a smaller proportion. If revenues and R&D costs rise, but R&D costs rise by a greater proportion, only business enterprises that have relatively few private-sector collaborators (particularly startup entrepreneurs) will choose to engage in university collaboration. And if R&D costs fall but revenues fall by a smaller proportion, only business enterprises that have a relatively large number of private-sector collaborators (particularly incumbent firms) will choose to engage in university collaboration. Finally, if revenues increase and R&D costs decrease, all business enterprises will choose to collaborate with the university. Figure 5 provides a summary of these results.

3.2 Is university collaboration a complement or substitute for private-sector business enterprise collaboration?

The presumed purpose of universities engaging in R&D with private-sector business enterprises is not simply to assist those firms with current R&D projects but to increase the level of collaborative R&D among private-sector business enterprises more generally so as to create a more active R&D culture in the regional economy that results in greater regional economic growth through the appropriation and transformation of knowledge into economic knowledge. Thus, the presumed purpose of universities is to increase the efficiency with which business enterprises convert knowledge to economic knowledge.

An important question, therefore, is whether the firms that choose to engage in collaborate R&D with the university treat that collaboration as a substitute or as a complement to private-sector collaborative R&D. In terms of our model, this question turns on whether the firms that engage in collaborative R&D with the university increase or decrease as a result the number of private-sector R&D partners, that is, whether n^{U*} is greater or smaller than n^*.

To answer that question, recall the first-order conditions [Eq. (10)] for the business enterprise that collaborates with the university. That first-order condition states that the business enterprise's marginal revenue with n^{U*} private-sector R&D partners should be equal to the business enterprise's marginal R&D cost associated with n^{U*}. Using Eqs. (11) and (12), we can express this requirement as:

$$\alpha\sigma \cdot \frac{\partial r(\sigma, n^{U*})}{\partial n} = \kappa \frac{dc(n^{U*})}{dn} \qquad (19)$$

To understand the implications of Eq. (19), recall the first-order conditions [Eq. (6)] for private-sector business enterprise collaboration:

$$\frac{\partial r(\sigma, n^*)}{\partial n} = \frac{dc(n^*)}{dn} \qquad (20)$$

If as a result of university collaboration the business enterprise's marginal revenue and marginal R&D cost functions change by the same proportion (that is, if $\alpha\omega = \kappa$), then Eq. (20) tells us that Eq. (19) will be satisfied with $n^{U*} = n^*$. However, if the marginal revenue function rises by a greater proportion than the marginal R&D cost function or falls by a smaller proportion (that is, $\alpha\omega > \kappa$), Eq. (19) requires a lower value for $\frac{\partial r(\sigma, n^*)}{\partial n}$ and/or a higher value for $\frac{dc(n^{U*})}{dn}$, and given the concavity of the revenue function and the convexity of the R&D cost function, this will occur with a value of n^{U*} that is greater than n^*. Finally, if

162   *Universities and the Entrepreneurial Ecosystem*

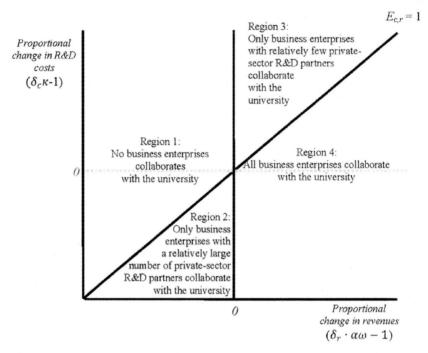

Fig. 5 Which business enterprises collaborate with university?

the marginal revenue function rises by a smaller proportion as the R&D cost function or falls by a greater proportion (that is, $\kappa > \alpha\omega$), then Eq. (19) requires that $n^{U*} < n^*$. Thus, university collaboration can be either a substitute or a complement to private-sector collaboration, depending on whether the revenues of the business enterprise change proportionally more or less than does that same business enterprise's R&D costs. Figures 6, 7, and 8 illustrate the dynamics that generate these outcomes, and Fig. 9 summarizes these results in the same *change in revenues × change in R&D costs* policy space that we used to summarize whether a firm will choose to collaborate with the university.[23]

3.3 Overall results

Figure 10 provides an overall summary of the results of the behavior of business enterprises that are offered the opportunity to collaborate with the university. The incentive to collaborate with the university depends on how R&D costs and revenues change:

- If collaboration with the university results in revenues rising and R&D costs falling, revenues rising proportionately more than R&D costs rise, or revenues falling proportionately less than R&D costs fall, then business enterprises that are relatively more active in private-sector R&D collaborative activity (particularly incumbent firms) will choose to collaborate with the university.
- If collaboration with the university results in higher revenues, then firms that are relatively less active in private-sector R&D collaborative activity (particularly startup entrepreneurs) will choose to collaborate with the university.

---

[23] Because $n^{U*} = n^*$ when $\alpha\sigma = \kappa$, and because the degree to which n^{U*} differs from n^* is a positive, continuous function of the degree to which $\alpha\sigma$ differs from κ, we can illustrate these results in the same *change in revenue × change in R&D costs* policy space used to summarize the conditions under which a business enterprise will choose to collaborate with the university.

 Springer

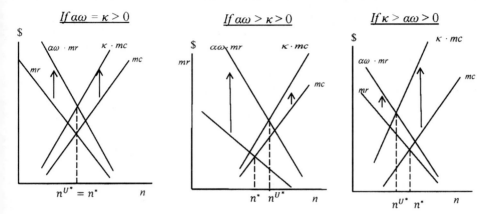

Fig. 6 Changes in the ideal number of private-sector R&D partners when university collaboration results in a rise in marginal revenue and marginal R&D cost

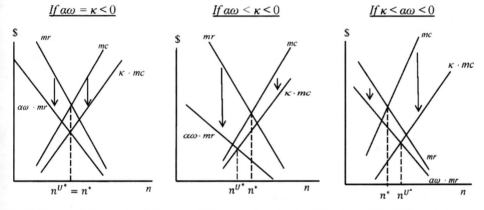

Fig. 7 Changes in the ideal number of private-sector R&D partners when university collaboration results in a fall in marginal revenue and marginal R&D cost

For those business enterprises that choose to collaborate with the university, whether those business enterprises treat the university as a substitute or complement to private-sector collaboration will depend on the relative change in R&D costs versus revenues:

• If R&D costs rise proportionally more than revenues rise, university collaboration will be a substitute for private-sector R&D collaboration and the number of private-sector R&D collaborators will fall.

• If revenues rise and R&D costs fall, or rise proportionately more than R&D costs rise, or fall proportionately less than R&D costs do, university collaboration will be a complement for private-sector R&D collaboration and the number of private-sector R&D collaborators will rise.

4 University supply of collaboration

The degree to which business enterprises collaborate with the university and the effect of that collaboration

Fig. 8 Changes in the ideal number of private-sector R&D partners when university collaboration results in marginal revenue and marginal R&D cost changing in opposite directions

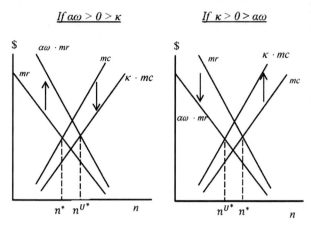

on the level of private-sector collaboration will depend not just on the business enterprises but on the choices that the university makes regarding the collaborative R&D program it establishes. And those choices depend in turn on the objectives of the university, the cost of delivering that program, and how that program is paid for.

4.1 The university's cost function

Consider first the R&D cost function for the university. As noted above, the university increases the profits of a collaborating business enterprise by providing some combination of enhanced economies of technological scope and possible reduced costs that is sufficient to overcome any loss in appropriability and possible increased costs. If we assume that the cost of providing enhanced economies of technological scope rises at an increasing rate, and that the cost of providing reduced R&D costs to a collaborating business enterprise rises in the same manner, then the university's cost function can be characterized as:

$$c_U = c_U(\omega, \kappa) \ni \frac{\partial c_U}{\partial \sigma} > 0, \quad \frac{\partial^2 c_U}{\partial \sigma^2} > 0, \quad \frac{\partial c_U}{\partial \kappa} < 0,$$
$$\frac{\partial^2 c_U}{\partial \kappa^2} > 0 \tag{21}$$

such that:

$$c_U(1, 1) = 0. \tag{22}$$

Note that implicit in Eqs. (21) and (22) is the assumption that the level of diminished appropriability, that is, the value of α, is exogenous at some value $\alpha_0 < 1$ and imposes no cost on the university. We will examine this assumption later.

The university's policy options implied by this university cost function can be described using a set of iso-cost curves, beginning with the iso-cost curve associated with a minimal program characterized by Eq. (22), that is, a program of no net cost to the university and in which there are no enhanced economies of scope and no change in the R&D cost function for participating business enterprises. That program is illustrated in Fig. 11 by the point A and is associated with the iso-cost curve B_0.[24] Note that because of the convexity of the university's cost function c_U, this zero-cost iso-cost line will cross the $\delta_r \alpha \omega - 1 = 0$ line at some point D where $\delta_c \kappa - 1 > 0$. Whether it comes in contact with the $n^{U*} = n^*$ line (where $\alpha \ \omega = \kappa$) is an empirical question. If it does, it will be at a value of $\omega > \frac{1}{\alpha_0}$

---

[24] Technically, point A lies in Region 1 below the $\delta_c \kappa - 1 = 0$ line because $\alpha_0 \omega < \kappa$ (recall that ω and κ equal 1 and α_0 is less than 1), which implies $n^{U*} < n^*$ (see the discussion following Eq. (20)), and $n^{U*} < n^*$ implies that $\delta_c \kappa - 1 < 0$ (see the discussion following Eq. 15). Intuitively, point A lies in Region 1 below the $\delta_c \kappa - 1 = 0$ line because the increased loss of appropriability ($\alpha_0 < 1$) results (given no compensating gains in terms of a lower cost function or increase prospects for revenue) in participating firms reducing their level of collaboration with other business enterprises, and that results in a fall in costs and a (proportionately greater) fall in revenues.

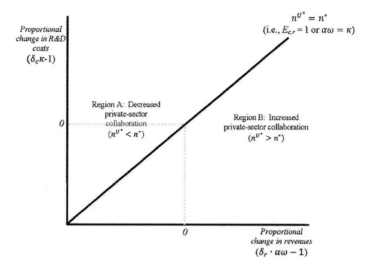

Fig. 9 Effects of university R&D collaboration on private-sector R&D collaboration

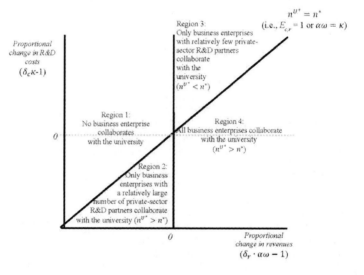

Fig. 10 Business enterprise demand for university collaboration-summary

and a value of $\kappa > 1$, thus requiring (in a loose sense) that the cost to the university of increasing the firm's economies of scope rises more slowly than does the cost to the university of reducing the firm's R&D cost function. Figure 11 is drawn assuming that this latter condition is not the case.

The iso-cost curve for a university program that reduces a participating business enterprise's R&D cost function (that is, $\kappa < 1$) and/or increases expected revenue (that is, $\omega > 1$) will lie to the southeast of the iso-cost curve B_0. Thus, the iso-budget curves B_1 and B_2 in Fig. 11 represent programs that result in positive

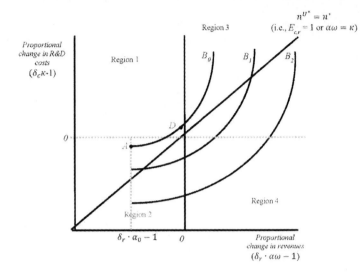

Fig. 11 University supply of collaboration

net costs to the university with the cost associated with B_2 being greater than the cost associated with B_1.

4.2 The university's objective

What option the university chooses will depend on the university's objective and what funding arrangements exist. Coates and Humphreys (2002) and Coates et al. (2004) argue that university motivations are bureaucratic with the essential question being whether they are slack-maximizing (which is akin to profit-maximizing) versus budget maximizing.

If universities are slack-maximizing, they would prefer programs to the northwest of the iso-cost curve B_0 in Fig. 11, that is, programs located in Region 3 that involve firms that are relatively inactive in private-sector collaborative R&D with other business enterprises. In such a case, while the program would enhance the revenue potential for participating business enterprises, it also would essentially charge participating business enterprises a price (that is, κ would be >1). While some business enterprises would choose to participate in such a program, because the program lies in Region 3, it would be limited to business enterprises that have relatively few private-sector R&D partners (particularly startup entrepreneurs), and those business enterprises that would participate would treat the program as a substitute for

private-sector collaboration and therefore reduce the number of their private-sector R&D collaborators.[25]

By contrast, if universities are budget-maximizing, they would prefer programs to the southeast of the iso-cost curve B_0, that is, programs located in Region 2 (where business enterprises that are already relatively active participants in private-sector collaborative R&D (particularly incumbent firms) would choose to participate) or in Region 4 (where a wide variety of business enterprises, both incumbent firms and startup entrepreneurs, would choose to participate). In either case, the university in this case would act as a complement to private-sector collaborative R&D.

As Coates and Humphreys (2002) and Coates et al. (2004) demonstrate, one can distinguish a slack-maximizing bureaucrat from a budget-maximizing bureaucrat by its reaction to grants. In the case of a slack-maximizing bureaucrat, a lump-sum grant would not alter its behavior, while in the case of a

---

[25] If the iso-budget line B_0 were to cross the $\alpha\sigma = \kappa$ line, the university could design a balanced-budget program or even positive-profit program that lies in the upper part of Region 4 in Fig. 11. This would still result in a program that essentially charges a fee to participate ($\kappa > 1$), though all business enterprises would find the program attractive. Those that participated would have an incentive to increase the number of private-sector partners. However, because the program would be in the upper part of Region 4, this latter incentive would be weak.

budget-maximizing bureaucrat, such a grant would result in an expansion of its program. Although more formal empirical analysis is required, it is our experience that universities typically expand their programs when provided with lump-sum grants, thus implying that the budget-maximizing model is the more accurate one.[26]

Of course, the ability of a budget-maximizing university to offer a program on a iso-cost curve such as B_1 or B_2, and thereby stimulate increased private-sector collaborative R&D among a wide array of business enterprises, will depend on the university's ability to garner grants: the larger the grant, the greater ability to offer a program that stimulates private-sector collaborative R&D.[27] And that ultimately depends on the interests of sponsors, governmental or otherwise.,[28,29]

---

[26] See Wyckoff (1990) for a simple comparative static analysis of budget maximization versus slack maximization.

[27] Our analysis assumes that the university program exists in isolation. However, we recognize that university objectives are likely more complex with multiple objectives and the possibility for fungibility in the funding of multiple programs. Åstebro and Bazzazian (2011), for example, note the potential conflict between university efforts to support local startups and university desire for licensing revenue, and Ehrenberg, Rees, and Brewer (1993) provide evidence of universities using revenues from one program to subsidize others. To the extent universities treat the revenues of various programs as fungible, a research program with somewhat higher costs (on the iso-cost curve B_1 for example) might be possible without a grant. Initial work on a more sophistical model of university objectives suggests that the relative salience to the university of its various programs determines the degree to which funding in one program is used to subsidize others.

[28] Breton and Wintrobe (1982) take a more expansive view of bureaucracy by focusing broadly on policy decisions rather than technical production decisions. The Niskanen literature, which derives from Niskanen (1971) and within which our work fits, focuses on policy as well. However, that focus is primarily from a quantitative perspective (such as the quantity to produce) and not from a qualitative one, such as what should be produced and what the qualities of that output should be. From the perspective of this article, Breton and Wintrobe's work is potentially of greater value for understanding the design of a research program, that is, whether it focuses on the goals of increasing revenues and reducing costs that are identified in this article and what mix (that is where on the iso-cost curve) the program would operate.

[29] Business enterprise support for universities, to the extent it is motivated by profit considerations, is subsumed within the structure of this article's model. However, as an anonymous referee rightly points out, business support for universities may also be motivated by more uncertain, dynamic, and longer term

Finally, before turning to normative issues, consider the role that α plays. The value of α may in part be exogenously determined by the academic culture within which the program operates. But to the extent that α can be controlled, an α that is closer to one (that is, one in which there is less loss of appropriability) will mean that a lower subsidy is required to make a program viable and potentially make the program more attractive to a wider range of business enterprises.[30] Thus, in Fig. 11, a higher α would shift all the iso-cost curves to the right (though the B_0 iso-budget line would still cross the $\delta_r \alpha \sigma - 1 = 0$ line at some point where $\delta_c \kappa - 1 > 0$), thereby reducing the grant that the university would have to receive in order to be attractive to business enterprises and to act as a complement for private-sector R&D collaboration.[31] However, there may be limits to the ability to increase α due to constraints imposed by the university's academic culture and to interactions between α and ω. Indeed, to the extent that increased economies of technological scope can only come about through increased sharing, this would result in the iso-cost curves being steeper. And this would result in it being more costly to attract firms to the program for any given ω and κ, and thereby make it more difficult for the university to serve as a complement to private-

---

Footnote 29 continued
considerations such as the development and maintenance of relationships, access to future graduates, etc. Such motivations are clearly worthy of inquiry but are beyond the scope of this article.

[30] Åstebro and Bazzazian (2011) in their discussion of university entrepreneurial activity suggest that while there are tensions within universities regarding the balance between traditional academic and entrepreneurial interests, the culture of some universities has adapted to entrepreneurial interests.

[31] Baldwin and Link (1998) provide empirical evidence that research joint ventures with universities tend to be larger than those that do not involve universities and argue that the reason for this is that business enterprises in a large research joint venture (because they already have a large number of research partners) incur relatively little additional loss of appropriability if they also collaborate with a university. Leyden and Link (1999) provide similar evidence and argument for research joint ventures involving governmental labs. In terms of the model in this article, this suggests that university programs may empirically tend to be located in Region 2 and that α may be a positive function of the total number private-sector business enterprises (which in Region 2 would primarily be incumbent firms) that choose to collaborate with the university. See Cohn et al. (1989) for more general evidence of economies of scope in universities.

814   D. P. Leyden, A. N. Link

sector R&D collaboration rather than as a substitute for such activity.

5 Normative considerations

It is well known that in general the lack of complete appropriability results in business enterprises engaging in an inefficiently low level of R&D. Likewise, a well-established finding in the bureaucracy literature is that budget-maximizing bureaucrats typically overproduce. Together these observations suggest that the two inefficient behaviors would to some extent counteract each other so that the participation of universities in the collaborative R&D process might result in an improvement in the overall efficiency in the level of R&D reminiscent (this time in a public context) of Smith's invisible hand.

The creative destruction literature provides some reason to believe that this argument may be true.[32] Of particular interest is work by Aghion and Howitt (1992) and Howitt and Aghion (1998), which argues that creative destruction is likely to result in an inefficiently low level of innovation due to a lack of appropriability, intertemporal spillovers, and business-stealing effects, but that R&D subsidies can counteract such inefficiencies, particularly those that target capital and thereby avoid the agency problems associated with direct R&D subsidies.[33] Within the context of this article, this argument suggests that

university programs properly structured to avoid agency problems would indeed improve efficiency.

6 Conclusions

To improve our understanding of the role that universities play in facilitating the transmission of knowledge to private-sector business enterprises and its conversions to economic, that is, commercially viable, knowledge so as to generate economic growth, this article developed a formal model of university-with-business enterprise collaborative research partnerships in which the outcome was both mutually desirable and feasible, and concluded that if a university seeks to act as a complement to private-sector collaborative R&D, it needs to structure its program so that business enterprise revenues increase and business enterprise R&D costs rise by a smaller proportion than revenues increase, if they rise at all (and a fall would be better). Such a structure is consistent with both business enterprise and university interests, but is only likely to be feasible if the university is subsidized. In the absence of such support, the university will have to cover its costs through a fee charged to participating business enterprises, and this will result in the university being seen as a substitute rather than a complement to private-sector collaborative R&D and thus as an unattractive partner for many business enterprises.

A number of additional issues concerning university collaborative research programs remain. Perhaps most important is the need to explore the mechanism by which firms choose collaborative research partners. As suggested by an anonymous referee, two options are possible here. The first option would be to formally model the partnering process using Pissarides's (1990) work on matching in labor markets. The second option would be to characterize business enterprises by overlapping knowledge bases with the choice of partners being the result of a tension between a desire for greater knowledge spillovers between partners (which would argue for less overlap) and a desire for reduced coordination costs between partners (which would argue for greater overlap). With either approach, the university would then be characterized by its own (perhaps unique) characteristics, and the implications of this for business enterprise partnering choice explored.

---

[32] The creative destruction literature traces its origins to Schumpeter (1934). For a discussion of Schumpeter's work on entrepreneurship, the context within which it was developed, and how it compares to other theories of entrepreneurship, see Hébert and Link (2009).

[33] See also Segerstrom and Zolnierek (1999) for an alternative approach. There are two extensions of the Aghion and Hewitt argument worth noting. First, Morales (2003) extends that argument to the realm of financial capital, arguing that subsidies to financial capital are also growth enhancing, though this time because of improved monitoring. Second, Thesmar and Thoenig (2000) argue that recent decades (if not the past century) have seen an increase in product market volatility and creative destruction that has led to a shift away from fixed capital and unskilled labor and toward skilled labor, that is, higher levels of human capital. Such an argument suggests that universities, beyond their value in creating skilled workers, may provide an important role in acting as matchmaker between skilled workers and firms in the regional economy. See Audretsch et al. (2012) for empirical evidence of this connection with respect to the use of graduate students.

A second issue concerns the market environment of business enterprises. This article assumes that individual business enterprises act in isolation when deciding whether to participate in university programs. However, as Åstebro and Bazzazian (2011) argue, local and regional conditions almost surely play a role in the effectiveness of university efforts. To the extent that is true, the success of university collaborative research programs may depend on understanding that role.

Finally, several issues remain concerning the university's funding process. Given the current political pressure to reduce governmental deficits in both the USA and Europe, there is reason to believe that external public funding is not likely to be forthcoming in the near future. The question is whether this conclusion is unique to current circumstances or is a more general phenomenon connected to macroeconomic fluctuations. In the absence of Keynesian fiscal policies (which seems to be increasingly the case), governments are most likely to support university collaborative research programs at the peak of a macroeconomic expansion and least likely to support such programs at the bottom of a contraction, thus giving rise to a dynamic funding problem for universities. Moreover, as shown in this article, business enterprises are attracted to university collaborative research programs to the degree those programs increase expected revenues and reduce expected R&D costs for the business enterprise. But it is also true that interest rates (which provide the foundation for calculating present values) typically rise as the macroeconomy expands and fall as the economy contracts.[34] Thus, for a given university collaborative research program, and because future revenues associated with collaborative research are likely to be more distant than future R&D costs, business enterprises would likely be least interested in collaborating with universities at the height of an expansion and most interested in collaborating in the depth of a contraction. This then would result in business enterprise behavior exacerbating the problem of fluctuating support for university collaborative research programs. To the extent this argument is correct (more research would be useful in this regard), universities that wish to offer collaborative research programs face

a complicated dynamic funding and participation problem.[35] Of course, one possible solution to the external funding problem is for universities to look internally for funds. As noted above in footnote 25, universities are complex organizations with a large number of programs and multiple objectives. The issue arises, therefore, whether that complexity affects the choices universities make with regard to collaborative research program design and support. If the boundaries between various university programs are impermeable, there may be little effect of such complexity on the design and funding of collaborative research programs. But to the extent there are synergies between university programs and fungibility in the funding of those programs, it may be that universities may be able to direct support to collaborative research programs internally and therefore may not need to depend on external funding as much.

Acknowledgments This article was presented at the Workshop on Academic Policy and the Knowledge Spillover Theory of Entrepreneurship, sponsored by the Competence Center for Global Business Management and the CisAlpino Institute for Comparative Studies in Europe, and held 20–21 August 2012 at the University of Augsburg, Augsburg, Germany. Special thanks to Zoltan Acs, Maksim Belitski, David B. Audretsch, Christopher Hayter, Marcel Hülsbeck, Mirjam Knockaert, Erik E. Lehmann, and two anonymous referees for their helpful comments and suggestions.

References

Acs, Z. J., Braunerhjelm, P., Audretsch, D. B., & Carlsson, B. (2009). The knowledge spillover theory of entrepreneurship. *Small Business Economics, 32*(1), 15–30.

Adams, J. D. (1990). Fundamental stocks of knowledge and productivity growth. *Journal of Political Economy, 98*(4), 673–702.

Aghion, P., & Howitt, P. (1992). A model of growth through creative destruction. *Econometrica, 60*(2), 323–351.

Alexopoulos, M. (2011). Read all about it!! What happens following a technology shock? *American Economic Review, 101*(4), 1144–1179.

Alvarez, S. A., & Barney, J. B. (2007). Discovery and creation: Alternative theories of entrepreneurial action. *Strategic Entrepreneurship Journal, 1*(1–2), 11–26.

Anand, B. N., & Khanna, T. (1996). *Intellectual property rights and contract structure (Working Paper #3, Working Paper Series H)*. New Haven: Yale School of Management.

Åstebro, T. B., & Bazzazian, N. (2011). Universities, entrepreneurship and local economic development. In

---

[34] A classic description of this pattern can be found in Fisher (1932).

[35] For evidence of other links between R&D and macroeconomic fluctuations, see Alexopoulos (2011).

M. Fritsch (Ed.), *Handbook of Research on Entrepreneurship and Regional Development.* New York: Edward Elgar.

Audretsch, D. B., & Lehmann, E. E. (2005). Does the knowledge spillover theory of entrepreneurship hold for regions? *Research Policy, 34*(8), 1191–1202.

Audretsch, D. B., Leyden, D. P., & Link, A. N. (2012). Universities as research partners in publicly supported entrepreneurial firms. *Economics of Innovation and New Technology, 21*(5–6), 529–545. doi:10.1080/10438599. 2012.656523.

Babbage. (2011). MIT and the art of innovation. *The Economist.* Retrieved from http://www.economist.com/blogs/babba ge/2011/01/mit_and_art_innovation.

Baldwin, W. L., & Link, A. N. (1998). Universities as research joint venture partners: Does size of venture matter? *International Journal of Technology Management, 15*(8), 895–913.

Berman, E. M. (1990). The economic impact of industry-funded university R&D. *Research Policy, 19*(4), 349–355.

Blumenthal, D., Gluck, M., Lewis, K. S., Stoto, M. A., & Wise, D. (1986). University-industry research relationships in biotechnology: Implications for the university. *Science, 232*(4756), 1361–1366.

Bonaccorsi, A., & Piccaluga, A. (1994). A theoretical framework for the evaluation of university-industry relationships. *R&D Management, 24*(3), 229–247.

Bozeman, B., Hardin, J., & Link, A. N. (2008). Barriers to the diffusion of nanotechnology. *Economics of Innovation and New Technology, 17*(7–8), 751–753.

Braunerhjelm, P., Acs, Z. J., Audretsch, D. B., & Carlsson, B. (2010). The missing link: Knowledge diffusion and entrepreneurship in endogenous growth. *Small Business Economics, 34*(2), 105–125.

Breton, A., & Wintrobe, R. (1982). *The logic of bureaucratic conduct: an economic analysis of competition, exchange, and efficiency in private and public organizations.* New York: Cambridge University Press.

Campbell, T. I. D. (1997). Public policy for the 21st century: Addressing potential conflicts in university-industry collaboration. *The Review of Higher Education, 20*(4), 357–379.

Coates, D., & Humphreys, B. R. (2002). The supply of university enrollments: University administrators as utility maximizing bureaucrats. *Public Choice, 110*(3–4), 365–392.

Coates, D., Humphreys, D. R., & Vachris, M. A. (2004). More evidence that university administrators are utility maximizing bureaucrats. *Economics of Governance, 5*(1), 77–101.

Cockburn, I., Henderson, R. (1997). *Public-private interaction and the productivity of pharmaceutical research* (NBER Working Paper 6018).

Cohen, L. (1994). When can government subsidize research joint ventures? Politics, economics, and limits to technology policy. *American Economic Review, 84*(2), 159–163.

Cohen, W. M., & Levinthal, D. A. (1989). Innovation and learning: The two faces of R&D. *The Economic Journal, 99*(397), 569–596.

Cohen, W. M., & Levinthal, D. A. (1990). The implications of spillovers for R&D and technology advance. In

V. K. Smith & A. N. Link (Eds.), *Advances in applied micro-economics.* Greenwich, CT: JAI Press.

Cohen, W. M., Florida, R., Randazzese, L., & Walsh, J. (1997). Industry and the academy: Uneasy partners in the cause of technological advance. In R. Noll (Ed.), *Challenge to the university.* Washington, DC: Brookings Institution Press.

Cohn, E., Rhine, S. L., & Santos, M. C. (1989). Institutions of higher education as multi-product firms: Economies of scale and scope. *Review of Economics and Statistics, 71*(2), 284–290.

Council on Competitiveness. (1996). *Endless frontiers, limited resources: U.S. R&D policy for competitiveness.* Washington, DC: Council on Competitiveness.

Ehrenberg, R. G., Rees, D. I., & Brewer, D. J. (1993). How would universities respond to increased federal support for graduate students? In C. Clotfelter & M. Rothschild (Eds.), *Studies of supply and demand in higher education* (pp. 183–210). Chicago: University of Chicago Press.

Feller, I. (1990). Universities as engines of R&D-based economic growth: They think they can. *Research Policy, 19*(4), 335–348.

Fisher, I. (1932). *Booms and depressions: Some first principles.* New York: Adelphi.

Government-University-Industry Research Roundtable (GUIRR. (2006). *Guiding principles for university-industry endeavors.* Washington, DC: National Academy Press.

Hall, B. H. (2004). University-industry research partnerships in the United States. In J.-P. Contzen, D. Gibson, & M. V. Heitor (Eds.), *Rethinking science systems and innovation policies.* West Lafayette, IN: Purdue University Press.

Hall, B. H., Link, A. N., Scott, J. T. (2000). *Universities as research partners* (NBER Working Paper 7643).

Hall, B. H., Link, A. N., & Scott, J. T. (2003). Universities as research partners. *Review of Economics and Statistics, 85*(2), 485–491.

Hébert, R. F., & Link, A. N. (2009). *A history of entrepreneurship.* New York: Routledge.

Henderson, R., Jaffe, A. B., Trajtenberg, M. (1995). *Universities as a source of commercial technology: A detailed analysis of university patenting 1965-1988* (NBER Working Paper No. 5068).

Hertzfeld, H. R., Link, A. N., & Vonortas, N. S. (2006). Intellectual property protection mechanisms in research partnerships. *Research Policy, 35*(6), 825–838.

Howitt, P., & Aghion, Philippe. (1998). Capital accumulation and innovation as complementary factors in long-run growth. *Journal of Economic Growth, 3*(2), 111–130.

Jaffe, A. (1989). Real effects of academic research. *American Economic Review, 79*(5), 957–978.

Klevorick, A. K., Levin, R. C., Nelson, R. R., & Winter, S. G. (1995). On the sources and significance of interindustry differences in technological opportunities. *Research Policy, 24*(2), 185–205.

Knight, F. H. (1921). *Risk, uncertainty, and profit.* Boston, MA: Houghton Mifflin.

Layson, S. K., Leyden, D. P., & Neufeld, J. R. (2008). To admit or not to admit: The question of research park size. *Economics of Innovation and New Technology, 17*(7/8), 691–699.

Lee, Y. S. (2000). The sustainability of university-industry research collaboration: An empirical assessment. *Journal of Technology Transfer, 25*(2), 111–133.

Leyden, D. P., & Link, A. N. (1999). Federal laboratories as research partners. *International Journal of Industrial Organization, 17*(4), 575–592.

Leyden, D. P., & Link, A. N. (2013). Collective entrepreneurship: The strategic management of Research Triangle Park. In D. P. Audretsch & M. L. Walshok (Eds.), *Creating competitiveness: Entrepreneurship and innovation policies for growth* (pp. 176–185). MA: Northampton.

Leyden, D. P., Link, A. N., & Siegel, D. S. (2008). A theoretical and empirical analysis of the decision to locate on a university research park". *IEEE Transactions on Engineering Management, 55*(1), 23–28.

Link, A. N. (1996). Research joint ventures: Patterns from *Federal Register* filings. *Review of Industrial Organization, 11*(5), 617–628.

Link, A. N., & Scott, J. T. (2005). Universities as partners in U.S. research joint ventures. *Research Policy, 34*(3), 385–393.

Link, A. N., & Scott, J. T. (2007). The economics of university research parks. *Oxford Review of Economic Policy, 23*(4), 661–674.

Link, A. N., & Welsh, D. H. B. (2013). From laboratory to market: On the propensity of young inventors to form a new business. *Small Business Economics, 40*(1), 1–7.

Lööf, H., & Broström, A. (2008). Does knowledge diffusion between university and industry increase innovativeness? *Journal of Technology Transfer, 33*(1), 73–90.

Mansfield, E. (1991). Academic research and industrial innovation. *Research Policy, 20*(1), 1–12.

Mansfield, E. (1992). Academic research and industrial innovation: A further note. *Research Policy, 21*(3), 295–296.

Mansfield, E., & Lee, J.-Y. (1996). The modern university: Contributor to industrial innovation and recipient of industrial R&D support. *Research Policy, 25*(7), 1047–1058.

Michelacci, C. (2003). Low returns to R&D due to the lack of entrepreneurial skills. *Economic Journal, 113*(484), 207–225.

Morales, M. F. (2003). Financial intermediation in a model of growth through creative destruction. *Macroeconomic Dynamics, 7*(3), 363–393.

Morgan, R. P. (1998). University research contributions to industry: The faculty view. In P. D. Blair & R. A. Frosch (Eds.), *Trends in Industrial Innovation: Industry*

Perspectives & Policy Implications. Research Triangle Park, NC: Sigma Xi, The Scientific Research Society.

Mowery, D. C., Teece, D. J. (1996). Strategic alliances and industrial research. In R. S. Rosenbloom, W. J. Spencer (Eds.), *Engines of innovation: U.S. industrial research at the end of an era.* Boston: Harvard Business School Publishing.

Niskanen, W. A. (1971). *Bureaucracy and Representative Government.* Chicago: Aldine-Atherton.

Pissarides, C. A. (1990). *Equilibrium unemployment theory.* Oxford: Basil Blackwell.

Schumpeter, J. A. (1934). *The theory of economic development* (R. Opie, Trans.). Cambridge: Harvard University Press (Original work published 1912).

Segerstrom, P. S., & Zolnierek, J. M. (1999). The R&D incentives of industry leaders. *International Economic Review, 40*(3), 745–766.

Siegel, D., Waldman, D., Link, A. N. (1999). *Assessing the impact of organizational practices on the productivity of university technology transfer offices: An exploratory study* (NBER Working Paper No. 7256).

State Science and Technology Institute (SSTI). (2008). *A resource guide for technology-based economic development.* Washington, DC: Economic Development Administration.

Tassey, G. (2008). Globalization of technology-based growth: The policy imperative. *Journal of Technology Transfer, 33*(6), 560–578.

Thesmar, D., & Thoenig, M. (2000). Creative destruction and firm organization choice. *Quarterly Journal of Economics, 115*(4), 1201–1237.

Van de Ven, A. H. (1993). A community perspective on the emergence of innovations. *Journal of Engineering and Technology Management, 10*(1–2), 23–51.

Wyckoff, P. G. (1990). The simple analytics of slack-maximizing bureaucracy. *Public Choice, 67*(1), 35–47.

Zeckhauser, R. (1996). The challenge of contracting for technological information. *Proceedings of the National Academy of Science, 93*(23), 12743–12748.

Zucker, L. G., Darby, M., Armstrong, J. (1994). *Intellectual capital and the firm: The technology of geographically localized knowledge spillovers* (NBER Working Paper 4946).

PART IV

UNIVERSITIES AS RESEARCH PARTNERS

[13]

UNIVERSITIES AS RESEARCH PARTNERS

Bronwyn H. Hall, Albert N. Link, and John T. Scott*

Abstract—Universities are a key institution in the U.S. innovation system, and an important aspect of their involvement is the role they play in public-private partnerships. This note offers insights into the performance of industry-university research partnerships, using a survey of precommercial research projects funded by the Advanced Technology Program. Although results must be interpreted cautiously because of the small size of the sample, the study finds that projects with university involvement tend to be in areas involving new science and therefore experience more difficulty and delay, yet are more likely not to be aborted prematurely. Our interpretation is that universities are contributing to basic research awareness and insight among the partners in ATP-funded projects.

Received for publication April 21, 2000. Revision accepted for publication January 7, 2002.

* University of California at Berkeley and NBER, University of North Carolina at Greensboro, and Dartmouth College, respectively.

We are grateful for comments on earlier versions from William L. Baldwin, Adam Jaffe, Don Siegel, participants at the ASSA 2000 meetings in Boston and the Wake Forest University economics workshop, and an anonymous referee. Also, we appreciate the suggestions and guidance of Rosalie Ruegg and Jeanne Powell, both of the Advanced Technology Program, during the data collection stage.

I. Introduction

MANY OBSERVERS have emphasized the importance of research partnerships for U.S. innovative capacity (Council on Competitiveness, 1996, pp. 3–4). Indeed, industry-university research relationships appear to have strengthened over the past few decades. University participation in formal research joint ventures (RJVs) has increased steadily since the mid-1980s (Link, 1996), and the number of industry-university R&D centers increased by more than 60% during the 1980s. Cohen et al. (1997) and a recent survey of U.S. science faculty revealed

The Review of Economics and Statistics, May 2003, 85(2): 485–491

TABLE 1.—DISTRIBUTION OF ATP-FUNDED PROJECTS BY TYPE OF UNIVERSITY INVOLVEMENT

Type of University Involvement (Dummy)	Number of Projects	Filtered Projects	Sample Projects	Sampling Probability	Number Responding
Joint venture:	118	81	36	44.4%	29
No university involvement (*jv*)	47	31	9	29.0%	8
Universities involved as subcontractors (*jvs*)	42	28	9	32.1%	8
Universities involved as research partners (*jvu*)	16	11	9	81.8%	8
Universities involved as both partner and sub. (*jvus*)	13	11	9	81.8%	5
Single applicant:	234	111	18	16.2%	18
No university involvement (*s*)	106	45	9	20.0%	9
Universities involved as a subcontractor (*ss*)	128	66	9	13.6%	9
Total	352	192	54	28.1%	47

Filtered projects are projects that have been active one year or more and are still active in the beginning of 1998.
Sampled projects were selected from the filtered project universe to ensure an equal number in each category.

that many universities desire even more partnerships with industry (Morgan, 1998). Yet, surprisingly, very little is known about the types of roles that universities play in such research partnerships or about the economic consequences associated with those roles. Our investigation is a first effort—an exploratory inquiry—to provide empirical information about universities as research partners.

Previous research falls broadly into examinations either of industry motivations or of university motivations for engaging in an industry-university research relationship. That research has not investigated the economic effects of university participation as thoroughly as the motivations for it. Hall, Link, and Scott (2000) review the literature and document its identification of two broad *industry motivations* for industry-university RJVs. The first is access to complementary research activity and research results; the second is access to key university personnel. The literature shows *university motivations* to be largely financially based. This note reports on the results of a small survey of such partnerships that focuses on their performance rather than the reasons underlying their formation.

II.   An Analysis of the Data

A.   Identifying an Appropriate Database

Given the potentially heterogeneous research role for universities, we developed and analyzed project-level data from the Advanced Technology Program (ATP), established within the National Institute of Standards and Technology (NIST) through the Omnibus Trade and Competitiveness Act of 1988. The ATP combines public funds with private investments to create and apply generic technology needed to commercialize new technology rapidly; it received its first appropriation from Congress in FY 1990.

ATP projects will not give a complete picture of industry-university R&D interaction. These projects are likely to have high social value and high risk, involve largely generic rather than largely proprietary technology, and be at such an early stage in development that the technology is not easily appropriable. Nonetheless, describing universities' roles in RJVs spawned by the ATP provides long-overdue insights into universities as research partners with industry.

Hall, Link, and Scott (2000) describe the population of ATP projects in terms of the numbers of awards since the program began, status of the projects (active, completed, or terminated), organizational types (single participants or RJVs), funding characteristics (mean total funding and the proportions from public and private sources), project durations, technology areas, and university involvement by technology area. We refer

herein to some of the population characteristics, but the complete overview provides important additional detail.

In addition to classifying each project into a unique technology area, ATP classifies each project by lead participant. Each lead participant is placed in one of four ATP-defined type-size categories, including not-for-profit organizations.[1] Among the for-profit organizations, a small organization is defined as one with fewer than 500 employees; a large one is defined as a *Fortune* 500 or equivalent organization (a moving definition, requiring $2.6 billion in annual revenue at the time of our analysis). All others are medium. More than one-half of the lead participants are small.

B.   Selecting a Sample of ATP-Funded Projects

We selected our sample of projects from the population of 352 projects funded by ATP from April 1991, when its first awards were made, through the start of our study in October 1997, using a series of filters, some under our control and others not. The first filter was that 21 projects terminated early (analyzed below) and were therefore unavailable for sampling. The second filter was that each project must be active and have been active for at least one year, to help ensure the respondent's use of a research project history when responding to the survey. These two filters reduced the population of 352 projects to 192. The 192 projects were then grouped by the six types of university involvement, listed in table 1 (column 3).[2] From each of the categories, a sample of nine projects was selected (column 4), with attention given to technology areas, sizes of lead participants, lengths of time the projects had been active, and total proposed research budgets of the projects. Also reported in table 1 are the sampling probabilities by type of university involvement.[3] This process of random stratified sampling yielded 54 projects.

Separate and distinct survey instruments were designed to obtain information about the nine projects selected in each of the six

---

[1] Nonprofit lead partners are not classified with respect to size, nor do we have revenue for these partners. This fact has two implications: (1) all of the size effects we measure are for for-profit lead partners, and (2) it is essential to include the nonprofit dummy when we include size in the regression in order to avoid misleading conclusions.
[2] In an industry-university relationship, either the university is a sub-contractor, or it is a research partner, which means that it is a formal member of the joint venture.
[3] Variability in these probabilities reflects that the sample size is constant at 9 and that the size of the population of appropriate projects to sample, by category type, varies (column 3).

TABLE 2.—DETERMINANTS OF THE PROBABILITY OF EARLY TERMINATION

Variable	(1) Coefficient (s.e.)	(2) Coefficient (s.e.)	(3) Coefficient (s.e.)
D (university involvement)	−0.434 (0.258)*	−0.537 (0.269)**	−0.478 (0.249)*
ATP share of funding	−1.783 (0.943)*	−1.472 (0.957)	−1.374 (0.899)
Time trend	−0.112 (0.082)	−0.112 (0.084)	−0.079 (0.075)
Small lead participant	−0.716 (0.317)**	−0.818 (0.326)**	−0.914 (0.302)***
Large lead participant	−0.929 (0.348)***	−0.943 (0.351)***	−0.848 (0.335)***
Nonprofit lead participant	−0.401 (0.466)	−0.337 (0.467)	−0.516 (0.419)
Chi-squared for 3 size vars. (prob.)	8.47 (0.037)**	9.47 (0.024)**	10.50 (0.015)**
Information technology	0.025 (0.338)	−0.074 (0.347)	
Electronics	−0.488 (0.465)	−0.478 (0.389)	
Biotechnology	−0.533 (0.455)	−0.510 (0.569)	
Chemicals, energy, and environ.	−0.039 (0.387)	−0.022 (0.457)	
Chi-squared for 4 tech. vars. (prob.)	2.90 (0.575)	2.16 (0.675)	
Intercept	0.738 (0.655)	0.662 (0.664)	0.285 (0.569)
Number of observations	313	312	351
Log likelihood	−67.33	−64.42	−67.89
Scaled *R²*	0.126	0.133	0.115
Chi-squared (d.f.)	19.38 (10)	19.75 (10)	17.67 (6)

Probit estimates: dependent variable = 1 if project terminated early.
Column (1) includes the full sample excluding projects in other manufacturing (none of which were terminated).
Columns (2) and (3) delete a single observation for a project that was terminated prior to starting.
The excluded category is a project in materials with no university participation and where the lead participant is of medium size.
Coefficient significance levels are denoted by * (10%), ** (5%), and *** (1%).
The scaled *R²* is a measure of goodness of fit relative to a model with only a constant term, computed as a nonlinear transformation of the LR test for zero slopes (see Estrella, 1998).

categories of university involvement.[4] Table 1 (column 6) shows the number of surveys received.[5] With 7 nonrespondents, our sample for analysis is 47.[6]

By ATP guidelines, universities cannot be lead partners. RJVs where the lead partner is a not-for-profit organization do have an affinity for inviting universities to be research partners. Yet the sample distinguishes such cases from RJVs with a university partner yet no not-for-profit lead partner. Thus, the effects of nonprofit lead partners and the effects of universities on RJV performance can be distinguished in our sample: there are 10 RJVs with a university and a nonprofit lead partner, 8 with a university but no nonprofit lead partner, 1 with a nonprofit lead partner but no university, 17 with no university and no nonprofit partner, 9 non-RJV projects with a university subcontractor, and 9 non-RJV projects with no university subcontractor. In sum, our sample has no nonprofits (as the main participant apart from a university) in the non-RJV observations, and nonuniversity nonprofits are mainly involved in RJVs with universities. However, the two—universities and nonprofit lead partners—are not the same thing (note the number of RJVs with universities without a nonprofit lead partner), and sometimes in our exploratory analyses of performance, coefficients for both universities and for nonprofit lead partners are identified.

[4] Copies of the survey instruments are available upon request from the authors.
[5] Because there are multiple dimensions of ATP-funded projects, we do not claim that our sample of 47 respondents is representative of the filtered population or of the whole population in all dimensions. We offer our sample as one sample to consider, and possibly to generalize about, given the stated filtering and selection process. More detailed information about the representativeness of the sample by other characteristics of ATP-funded projects is available from the authors.
[6] We are aware of the limitations of the self-reported data that will be analyzed below. Although our survey instruments were pretested, the possibility that our primary data reflect the personal attitudes of the respondents as well as objective characterizations of their projects is still present. This study is one of the first of its kind in attempting to quantify the role of universities in research partnerships. Efforts to generalize from our findings should be made with the utmost caution.

C. Analysis of Terminated Projects in the Population

We investigated the reasons for the early termination of 21 projects among the population of 352. These reasons ranged from the financial health of the participant(s) to lack of research success in the early part of the project. We estimated a probit model of termination probability conditional on ATP's share of funding, involvement of a university, type of project, size of the lead participant, and technology area.[7] A time variable denoting the year in which each project was initially funded was also included.

The probit estimates from alternative specifications are reported in table 2. Our particular interest is the nature of the relationship between university involvement and termination. The results imply that the projects with university involvement as either a research partner or subcontractor have a lower probability of early termination. Also, the probability of early termination decreases as ATP's share of funding increases, although the effect is barely significant, and only for the specification used to simulate the predicted probabilities shown in table 3. The termination rate does not vary across technology area,[8] but projects where the lead partner is of medium size are more likely to terminate early than the others.

The upper portion of table 3 presents the calculated probabilities for a project terminating early, by size of lead participant. For this example (information technology projects begun in 1991), the calculated probability of early termination is lower for each size category when a university is involved in the project. Similarly (lower portion of table 3), the calculated probability of early termination is lower for each discrete level of ATP's share of funding when a university is

[7] To be precise, we estimated the following model: Pr(project *i* terminates early) = $F(X_i, \beta)$, where F is the cumulative normal probability function, X_i is a vector of variables that characterizes project *i*, and β is the conformable vector of coefficients.
[8] This conclusion needs to be qualified slightly: because no projects in other manufacturing terminated early, these projects could not be included in the models estimated in the first two columns of table 2 (where we use technology dummies). Clearly, projects in this technology area have a lower early termination rate than projects in the other technology areas.

TABLE 3.—SIMULATION OF PROBABILITY OF TERMINATION: ATP INFORMATION
TECHNOLOGY PROJECTS BEGUN IN 1991

	University Involved	No University Involved
Size of lead participant (50% ATP share):		
Small	0.036	0.094
Medium	0.189	0.344
Large	0.042	0.106
Not-for-profit	0.081	0.179
ATP share of funding (medium lead part.):		
0%	0.423	0.612
25%	0.296	0.477
50%	0.189	0.344
75%	0.111	0.228
100%	0.059	0.138

This simulation is based on specification (1) in table 2.

involved in the project.[9] In the population of ATP projects, university involvement is clearly associated with a lower probability of early termination.[10]

D.   Estimating the Probability of Response to the Sample Survey

Only two of the six categories of university involvement listed in table 1 (column 6) had a 100% response rate. Contacts in joint ventures were less likely to respond, with the least responsive category being joint ventures with universities as both partners and subcontractors—only five of nine surveys were returned. We examined the probability of survey response using a probit model. When we include all of the right-side variables, nothing is very significant. The only variable that is even marginally informative is the dummy for joint ventures with universities as both partner and subcontractor (*jvus*), arguably the most complex arrangement contractually. Other factors held constant, joint ventures with universities as research partners and as subcontractors have a lower probability of response.

In the results presented below, we test and correct for response bias simply by including the *jvus* dummy in our estimations.[11] The implication of this strategy will be that we cannot identify the direct effects

---
[9] Similar relationships, available from the authors, exist across other research technology areas.

[10] The information in table 2 is used to calculate a hazard rate for the probability that a project does not terminate early for use in the subsequent statistical analyses of a sample of ATP-funded projects to control for possible sample selection bias. To anticipate the use of this variable in later survey-question equations, it is important to note that its inclusion in an ordered probit is not really econometrically correct if it actually enters. That is, if the probability distribution in the termination equation and the distribution in the survey question equation are dependent, then the appropriate method is to specify a full maximum likelihood model for the two random variables and estimate jointly [such a model is outlined in Hall, Link, and Scott (2000)]. In fact, we found that the termination hazard and the sample response hazard never entered significantly, and that joint maximum likelihood estimates did not differ significantly from our single-equation estimates, which implies that sample selection is unlikely to produce significant bias in our estimates. However, our sample size is small, so the power of all these tests is low.

[11] As with our analysis of the probability of early termination, the results from the response probit model could be used to calculate a survey hazard rate for the statistical analyses that follow. However, in practice, the only variable that predicted response or nonresponse in a simple probit model was *jvus*. We therefore used a simpler and more robust method to correct for response bias, by including the *jvus* dummy directly in our estimated model. Unlike the use of a hazard rate, this correction does not require normality of the response probability equation to be valid. For a single-

on performance of being a joint venture with a university participating as a partner and as a subcontractor separately from the effect of such a joint venture on the probability of survey response.

III.   Role of Universities in ATP-Funded Projects

We ask three general questions about the roles of universities as research partners:

1. What roles do universities play in research partnerships in general?
2. Do universities enhance the research efficiency of research partnerships?
3. Do universities affect the development and commercialization of industry technology?

A.   Role Played by Universities in ATP-Funded Projects

What research role do universities play in ATP-funded projects? At one level, the answer to this question comes from the organizational or administrative role that universities have in various projects. In a joint venture, the research role of a university is either as a research partner in the joint venture or as a subcontractor to the joint venture. In single-applicant projects, by definition, the research role of a university is only as a subcontractor.[12]

At a second level, we explored the role played by universities by asking each contact person to indicate, using a seven-point Likert scale, the extent to which the research project experienced difficulties acquiring and assimilating basic knowledge necessary for the project's progress. Strong agreement that such difficulties had been experienced was indicated with a 7, the responses ranging downward to 1 to indicate strong disagreement. Ordered probit models were estimated to explain interproject differences in responses about the difficulties. Held constant in these models are several characteristics of the project as determined from ATP information and from survey responses.

The estimates are in table 4. In column 1 we include the hazard rate for nontermination (the conditional probability density that the project will go forward to completion) and the proxy for the survey response hazard (*jvus*) in the model. Neither of these enters into the equation significantly, implying that selection bias is unlikely to be a problem for our estimates.[13]

We have five observations about the estimates in table 4:

---
dummy-variable predictor, of course, the two approaches for converting any response bias would be equivalent if normality held.

[12] Related to this organizational or administrative research role that universities have is another level at which to answer the first research question. Four of the six groups of contact persons for the survey were asked why the university subcontractors on this project were selected. For joint ventures where a university is only involved as a subcontractor and for single participants where the university is only involved as a subcontractor, the most frequent response was that the subcontractor was selected to gain access to eminent researchers. Joint ventures in which the university is only involved as a research partner reported that the university was most commonly invited to participate because of previous research interactions with other members of the joint venture. And, finally, the dominant response when universities are involved in a joint venture as research partners and as subcontractors (*jvus*) was that each was selected because of their overall research reputation.

[13] For completeness, we have estimated the full model for sample selection (an ordered probit equation plus an equation for the probability that the survey was returned), and the selection into the sample does not appear to be important for our results (Hall, Link, and Scott, 2000).

TABLE 4.—DETERMINANTS OF DIFFICULTY ACQUIRING BASIC KNOWLEDGE

Variable	(1) Ordered Probit Coefficient (s.e.)	(2) Ordered Probit Coefficient (s.e.)
Log of total project budget	−0.76 (0.36)**	−0.68 (0.30)**
ATP share (fraction)	−0.92 (3.00)	
D (university participant)	1.16 (0.61)*	1.12 (0.49)**
D (no prior experience)	1.16 (0.50)**	1.12 (0.48)**
log(revenue of lead part., $1,000)	0.12 (0.07)*	0.12 (0.06)**
Nonprofit lead part.	1.98 (1.22)	2.15 (1.09)**
Information technology	0.03 (0.64)	0.04 (0.57)
Manufacturing	−1.17 (0.94)	−1.24 (0.92)
Electronics	3.03 (1.07)***	3.03 (1.08)***
Biotechnology	0.07 (0.62)	0.06 (0.61)
Chemicals, energy, and environ.	−0.97 (0.84)	−0.92 (0.82)
Chi-squared for 5 tech. vars.		
(prob.)	12.7 (0.027)**	12.8 (0.025)**
Nontermination hazard	−0.34 (1.00)	
jvus	−0.29 (0.75)	
Number of observations	47	47
Pseudo R^2	0.216	0.209
Chi-squared (*p*-value)ᵃ	24.16 (0.030)	23.40 (0.009)

ᵃ This *chi*-squared is for the joint test that all coefficients except the intercept are zero. The categories have been collapsed from seven to five, using the groupings (1&2), 3, 4, 5, (6&7). The excluded category is a project in materials with no university participant. Coefficient significance levels are denoted by * (10%), ** (5%), and *** (1%).

1. Respondents with a university participant (as a research partner or as a subcontractor) systematically agreed that the project had experienced difficulties acquiring and assimilating basic knowledge necessary for progress toward completion. Joint-venture projects are larger than others, which tends to lower difficulty in general but raise it if a partner is a university. That is probably also consistent with such projects being more difficult or closer to new science than are others, so that the university partner was chosen in anticipation of the difficulties. Or the university's presence may create a greater awareness that such difficulties exist.
2. Prior experience working with a university as a research partner or as a subcontractor is a significant factor in decreasing the difficulty of acquiring and assimilating basic knowledge.
3. Acquisition and assimilation difficulties with basic knowledge decrease slightly as overall project size increases.
4. Projects in the electronics area have substantially more difficulty in acquiring and assimilating basic knowledge than do projects in other technology areas.
5. Projects with larger for-profit lead partners or nonprofit lead partners have experienced difficulties acquiring and assimilating basic knowledge.

B. Research Efficiencies from Universities in ATP-Funded Projects

Are there systematic differences in the research efficiency of ATP-funded projects that have universities involved and those that do not? We addressed this question of research efficiency by asking each contact person to respond to a series of five statements. The first three of these statements investigate unexpected research problems encountered relative to expectations when the project began. Had the number of problems encountered been more than, less than, or about the same as what had been anticipated at the project's outset? The three types of research problems investigated are conceptual problems, equipment-related problems, and personnel problems.

TABLE 5.—DETERMINANTS OF THE PROBLEMS IN THE PROJECT: ORDERED PROBIT ESTIMATES

Variable	Personnel-Related Coefficient (s.e.)
Log of total project budget	−0.04 (0.34)
D (university participant)	0.89 (0.54)*
log(revenue of lead part., $1,000)	0.15 (0.08)*
Nonprofit lead partner	−0.57 (1.27)
Information technology	1.26 (0.77)
Manufacturing	1.30 (1.09)
Electronics	1.84 (1.26)
Biotechnology	1.53 (0.86)*
Chemicals, energy, and environ.	1.61 (0.93)*
Chi-squared for 5 tech. vars. (prob.)	4.61 (0.465)
Number of observations	44
Pseudo R^2	0.244
Chi-squared (*p*-value)ᵃ	14.51 (0.105)

ᵃ This *chi*-squared is for the joint test that all coefficients except the intercept are zero. The excluded category is a project in materials with no university participant. Coefficient significance levels are denoted by * (10%), ** (5%), and *** (1%).

To evaluate the responses to the first three statements, ordered probit models were estimated. Held constant in these models are several characteristics of the project as determined from ATP information and from survey responses.[14] In the specifications for conceptual problems and for equipment problems, none of the individual variables was significant in explaining the existence of unexpected conceptual or equipment-related research problems, apart from the perhaps obvious fact that problems with research about information technology were not equipment-related. Because only a few projects had fewer problems of any type than expected, we experimented with collapsing the responses from the original three categories (the number of problems encountered was more than, less than, or about the same as what had been anticipated at the project's outset) into two categories. Even when reestimated in this form in probit models, essentially no identifiable individual variable effects explained the existence of unexpected research problems. The presence of unexpected problems is perhaps random or a complex result of many factors that we cannot disentangle—truly unexpected given the information available to the firm (and to us).

Table 5 shows the specification for personnel problems, and the estimates suggest that the presence of unexpected personnel-related problems is associated somewhat with the technology field. Lead-partner size is a marginally significant explanatory variable in explaining the presence of unexpected personnel problems; projects with nonprofit lead partners are less likely to experience this kind of problem, although the effect is not significant. Joint ventures with university partners are both more likely to have personnel-related problems and, as we saw above, also less likely to respond to the survey, so we cannot disentangle these two effects.

The fourth and fifth statements addressed aspects of research efficiency related to the productive use of complementary research resources. The first of these asks for the approximate percentage of the project's research time that, in retrospect, had been unproductive. The

---

[14] Ordered probit models that allowed for sample selection were also estimated, but proved to be very difficult to identify because of the small sample. Therefore we rely mainly on the ad hoc correction terms discussed above; hence the effect for university participation cannot be disentangled from the selection effect.

TABLE 6.—PERCENTAGE OF UNPRODUCTIVE RESEARCH TIME AND COST:
ORDERED PROBIT ESTIMATES

	Dependent Variable[a]:	
Variable	(1) Research Time Coefficient (s.e.)	(2) Research Cost Coefficient (s.e.)
D (university participant)	0.41 (0.39)	0.98 (0.41)**
Log (revenue of lead part., $1,000)	−0.16 (0.06)***	−0.14 (0.06)**
Nonprofit lead participant	−1.35 (0.83)	−1.08 (0.83)
Information Technology	−1.07 (0.50)**	−0.77 (0.51)
Manufacturing	−1.73 (0.73)**	−1.73 (0.74)**
Electronics	2.19 (0.98)**	2.87 (0.99)***
Biotechnology	−0.21 (0.53)	−1.26 (0.57)**
Chemicals, energy, and environ.	1.31 (0.62)**	0.93 (0.62)
Chi-squared for 5 tech. vars. (prob.)	20.8 (0.001)***	19.7 (0.001)***
No. of observations	42	42
Pseudo R²	0.162	0.172
Chi-squared (p-value)[b]	24.86 (0.002)	23.95 (0.002)

[a] The dependent variable takes on the values 0%, 5%, 10%, 15%, 20%, 25%, 30%.
[b] This chi-squared is for the joint test that all coefficients except the intercept are zero.
The excluded category is a project in materials.
Coefficient significance levels are denoted by * (10%), ** (5%), and *** (1%).

second asks for the approximate percentage of the project's financial resources that, in retrospect, had been unproductive. These two statements are analyzed together because of the high correlation between responses. Of 42 contact persons, 22 responded to both questions with the same percentage.

Table 6 uses an ordered probit model to evaluate the responses across the categories of approximate percentage response.[15] Although we originally included all variables in the estimation, only the size of the lead partner and the technology variables were significant, and table 6 presents the model with just those effects and the effects of a university participant or a nonprofit lead participant. Unproductive time and cost is associated most with electronics projects and associated least with information technology and manufacturing projects. Projects with university participants are more likely to report unproductive costs.

Comparing further the estimates in the two columns of table 6, projects in electronics have the largest share of time and money that is unproductively used, whereas projects in manufacturing have the least. Unproductive research time and money in electronics may be related to projects in this field also having difficulty acquiring and assimilating the basic research they need. Biotechnology projects have relatively little unproductive research expenditure, although somewhat more unproductive research time. Larger (profit-making) lead partners are better at making productive use of research time and expenditure, or at least they perceive that to be the case.

C. Accelerated Development and Commercialization of Technology from Universities in ATP-Funded Projects

Are there systematic differences in the ability of ATP-funded projects to accelerate the development and commercialization of technology when universities are involved in the project and when they are not? We addressed this question by asking each contact person to provide a seven-point Likert-scale (7 denoting strong agreement and 1 denoting strong disagreement) response to two statements.

---

[15] Note that this survey statement addresses realized unproductive research time and not expected unproductive research time. The same is true for the unproductive use of financial resources.

TABLE 7.—PERFORMANCE DETERMINANTS: ORDERED PROBIT ESTIMATES

	Dependent Variable:	
Variable	(1) New applications of technology developed[a] Coefficient (s.e.)	(2) Commercialized sooner than expected Coefficient (s.e.)
Log of total project budget		−0.95 (0.26)***
ATP share (fraction)	2.97 (1.68)*	
D (university participant)	0.02 (0.34)	−0.78 (0.37)**
D (no prior experience)		−0.98 (0.44)**
Small lead participant		−1.52 (0.57)***
Large lead participant		−1.96 (0.65)***
Nonprofit lead participant		0.39 (0.65)
Chi-squared for size vars. (prob.)		15.04 (0.002)***
Information technology		1.08 (0.43)**
Manufacturing		
Electronics		
Biotechnology		
Chemicals, energy, and environ.		1.13 (0.65)*
Materials		1.69 (0.52)**
Chi-squared for tech. vars. (prob.)		12.49 (0.006)***
No. of observations	47	47
Pseudo R²	0.024	0.167
Chi-squared (p-value)[b]	3.29 (0.193)	28.05 (0.001)

[a] The dependent variable takes on only six values, because one of the cells (y = 3) is empty.
[b] This chi-squared is for the joint test that all coefficients except the intercept are 0.
The excluded category in column 2 is a project where the lead participant is of medium size.
Coefficient significance levels are denoted by * (10%), ** (5%), and *** (1%).

The first statement posed to the lead participant assessed whether potential new applications of the technology being developed had been recognized over the course of the project. Ordered probit estimates for this question were for the most part insignificant; column 1 of table 7 shows a minimal specification of the model. It may be that the generation of new applications from a project in process cannot be attributed to any particular individual project characteristics and is essentially unpredictable regardless of the technology area. The results do however suggest that projects with a larger ATP share are more likely to develop unanticipated applications for the technology. Perhaps a larger ATP share brings greater resources for ATP monitoring or imparts to the research performers a greater leveraging effect to search for or to recognize new applications of the technology. University participation shows no effect on the generation of new technology applications.

The second statement assessed whether the lead participant—at the stage of the research reached at the time of the survey—believed that the technology would be developed and commercialized sooner than expected when the project began. The ordered probit estimates are shown in column 2 of table 7. A number of variables are significant, leading to five interesting conclusions:

1. Projects involving universities as partners are less likely to develop and commercialize technology sooner than expected, perhaps reflecting that universities are involved in more dif-

ficult projects to begin with, namely projects with a lower probability of early completion.

2. Large projects and/or projects with large lead participants are less likely to expect to develop and commercialize their technology sooner than expected than are projects with non-profit or medium-size lead participants. Perhaps such larger projects reveal a whole new set of research insights. To the extent that larger research budgets are associated with research projects that can stretch the frontiers of knowledge then less time will be devoted toward looking for early-on commercialization opportunities of the technology.

3. Projects with a small lead participant are less likely to expect to develop and commercialize technology sooner than expected. Recall that this group is very small firms, and this may reflect resource constraints they face in development when the project budget does not cover the full cost of making the technology commercially viable.

4. Lack of experience with a university partner reduces the expectation of early commercialization, as does university involvement, perhaps because of lack of market pressure and focus on the particular project by the university participant, or perhaps simply because some adjustment costs are included as the participants learn to work with a university.

5. Projects in information technology, chemicals, energy, environment, and materials are significantly more likely to commercialize earlier than expected than are projects in manufacturing, electronics, and biotechnology.

IV. Concluding Observations

The focus of this survey-based study of ATP-funded research projects is on universities as research partners.[16] Our analyses of the survey data allow us to set forth in this concluding section a consistent and illuminating story about their research role. Nonetheless, all of the results from the descriptive analyses and qualitative choice models presented should be interpreted cautiously, given the need for theoretical foundation, understanding of causality, and increased sample size. Given the caveats, we conclude the paper by emphasizing two themes that are consistent with our data.

A. Universities Create Research Awareness in ATP-Funded Projects

Our first conclusion is that universities create research awareness among the research partners in the ATP-funded projects studied. The qualitative models estimated suggest that projects with university involvement, either as a research partner or as a subcontractor, are (1) experiencing difficulties acquiring and assimilating basic knowledge for the project's progress (table 4), and (2) also not anticipating being able to develop and commercialize technology sooner than expected when the project began (table 7).

---

[16] We set out to develop understanding of universities as research partners, designing our survey instruments to gather information pertinent to that understanding. Now that we have the results, as the referee for our note has observed, we have several findings about the importance of the characteristics of the RJV's lead partner. In that light, and at the suggestion of the referee, we gathered additional data about the lead partners beyond the characteristics used in our original statistical analyses and reported here. The additional information did not add to the explanatory power of our models. We believe that our small sample makes impractical the idea of pursuing in the present paper the importance of detailed characteristics—beyond size and profit versus nonprofit organization—of both the lead partner and all of the other partners to a RJV. We do believe the pursuit is an important one for future research.

At one level, these two findings could be interpreted to mean that university involvement is creating research problems acquiring and assimilating basic knowledge and commercializing technology rapidly. We eschew that interpretation, because projects with university involvement are less likely to terminate early than are projects without university involvement (table 2). We conclude, albeit cautiously, that university involvement is creating a greater awareness of research problems.

We offer a possible interpretation of the research role of a university.[17] Universities are included (invited by industry) in those research projects that involve what we have called "new" science. Industrial research participants perceive that the university could provide research insight that is anticipatory of future research problems and that it could be an ombudsman anticipating and communicating to all parties the complexity of the research being undertaken. Thus, one finds universities purposively involved in projects that are characterized as problematic with regard to the use of basic knowledge. Because of the type of project into which a university is likely to be invited as a research partner, the research will not move faster than expected toward a commercial application of the resulting technology. Universities are more likely to partner in new technological fields where R&D is closer to science, and such fields can be more uncertain and difficult.

B. Research Funding Influences the Scope of the Research

We infer from the findings that projects with larger research budgets undertake research of broader scope, as opposed to researching narrower projects in greater detail. Projects with larger budgets are less likely to commercialize their technology ahead of schedule (table 7). That is not inconsistent with such projects attempting to foster newer frontiers of research. It is, however, also true that projects with larger budgets have fewer problems acquiring and assimilating basic knowledge (table 4). Thus, if the larger budgeted projects are broader, the scope and breadth may address new applications (new generic technology across many industries, for example) rather than fundamental research.

We do not speculate as to the extent to which our findings can be generalized either to other projects that are partially publicly funded, or to private sector joint ventures with and without university research interactions. As more research is conducted on this topic, the wider applicability of our observations will be tested.

REFERENCES

Cohen, Wesley M., Richard Florida, Lucien Randazzese, and John Walsh, "Industry and the Academy: Uneasy Partners in the Cause of Technological Advance," in R. Noll (Ed.), *Challenge to the University* (Washington: Brookings Institution Press, 1997).

Council on Competitiveness, *Endless Frontiers, Limited Resources: U.S. R&D Policy for Competitiveness* (Washington: Council on Competitiveness, 1996).

Estrella, Arturo, "A New Measure of Fit for Equations with Dichotomous Dependent Variables," *Journal of Business and Economic Statistics* (April 1998), 198–205.

Hall, Bronwyn H., Albert N. Link, and John T. Scott, "Universities as Research Partners," NBER working paper no. 7643 (April 2000).

Link, Albert N., "Research Joint Ventures: Patterns from Federal Register Filings," *Review of Industrial Organization* 11 (1996), 617–628.

Morgan, Robert P., "University Research Contributions to Industry: The Faculty View" (pp. 163–170), in Peter D. Blair and Robert A. Frosch (Eds.), *Trends in Industrial Innovation: Industry Perspectives & Policy Implications*, (Research Triangle Park: Sigma Xi, 1998).

---

[17] Absent baseline information about the technical difficulty of the projects or their closeness to new science other than the technology field, this interpretation is offered cautiously.

[14]

Economics of Innovation and New Technology
Vol. 21, Nos. 5–6, September 2012, 529–545

Universities as research partners in publicly supported entrepreneurial firms[†]

David B. Audretsch[a], Dennis P. Leyden[b] and Albert N. Link[b]*

[a]*Institute for Development Strategies, Indiana University, Bloomington, IN, USA;* [b]*Department of Economics, University of North Carolina at Greensboro, Greensboro, NC, USA*

(*Received 8 September 2011; final version received 23 December 2011*)

Partnerships between universities and industrial firms can play a key role in enhancing competitiveness because they provide a conduit for the spillover of knowledge from the academic organization where knowledge is created to the firm where it is transformed into innovative activity. We set forth in this paper a model of industry/university participation, and we test the model empirically, using research project data on entrepreneurial firms that were funded through the US Department of Energy's Small Business Innovation Research (SBIR) program. We find that larger firms are more likely to be involved in a research partnership with a university, in general, as are firms with founders who have an academic background. We find the latter result holds across disaggregated types of university partnerships, as well. We find no empirical evidence that the size of the SBIR award influences the likelihood of a research partnership.

Keywords: research partnership; innovative behavior; entrepreneurship; industry/university relationship

JEL Classification: O31; L24; O32; O34; L26

1. Introduction

The issue of competitiveness has emerged as one of the great policy concerns confronting the USA. The inability of the country to be competitive in traditional manufacturing industries as well as emerging high technology industries has been linked to higher rates of unemployment and lower rates of economic growth.[1] A key issue in enhancing American competitiveness is to generate more innovative activity from investments in science and technology. Partnerships between universities and industrial firms can play a key role because they provide a conduit for the spillover of knowledge from the academic organization where knowledge is created to the firm where it is transformed into innovative activity, which ultimately enhances the competitiveness of the firm, industry, and country.[2]

---

*Corresponding author. Email: anlink@uncg.edu
[†]This paper was prepared for presentation at the Workshop on Academic Entrepreneurship and Economic Competitiveness, Basque Institute of Competitiveness, San Sebastian, Spain, 8–9 September 2011.

ISSN 1043-8599 print/ISSN 1476-8364 online
http://dx.doi.org/10.1080/10438599.2012.656523
http://www.tandfonline.com

The Council on Competitiveness (1996, 3–4) emphasized more than a decade and a half ago the importance of industry/university relationships in the USA:

> [P]articipants in the U.S. R&D enterprise will have to continue experimenting with different types of partnerships to respond to the economic constraints, competitive pressures and technological demands that are forcing adjustments across the board. … [and in response] industry is increasingly relying on partnerships with universities …

A number of academic studies support this claim as well.[3] For example, Link (1996) showed that university participation in formal research joint ventures (RJVs) has increased steadily since the mid-1980s, Cohen et al. (1998) documented that the number of industry/university R&D centers increased by more than 60% during the 1980s, and a related survey of US science faculty by Morgan (1998) revealed that many desire even more partnership relationships with industry. Mowery and Teece (1996, 111) argue that such growth in strategic alliances in R&D is indicative of a 'broad restructuring of the US national R&D system'. The findings of these studies are consistent with the view that partnerships between industry and universities are conducive to knowledge spillovers that promote innovative activity and ultimately enhance competitiveness.

According to Hall, Link, and Scott (2000, 2003), little is known about the types of roles that universities play in such research partnerships or about the economic consequences associated with those roles.[4] What research there is on the topic of universities as research partners falls broadly into either examinations of *industry motivations* or *university motivations* for engaging in an industry/university research relationship.[5]

Hall, Link, and Scott (2000, 2003) noted that the literature has identified two broad *industry motivations* for engaging in an industry/university research relationship. The first is access to complementary research activity and research results.[6] Rosenberg and Nelson (1994, 340) emphasized: 'What university research most often does today is to stimulate and enhance the power of R&D done in industry, as contrasted with providing a substitute for it'. Pavitt (1998), based on his review of this literature, was more specific in this regard. He concluded that academic research augments the capacity of businesses to solve complex problems. The second industry motivation is access to key university personnel.[7] A third motivation might be that through a university relationship, the firm can expand its boundaries while at the same time eliminating market transactions for research services. Following Coase (1937, 388), it might be the case that university-based research services are an example of the 'entrepreneur-co-ordinator' who, through the partnership, is able to direct research without the complications of a market with exchange transactions.

University motivations for partnering with industry seem to be financially based. Administration-based financial pressures for faculty to engage in applied commercial research with industry are growing.[8] Zeckhauser (1996, 12746), for example, was subtle when he referred to the supposed importance of industry-supported research to universities as he describes how such relationships might develop: 'Information gifts [to industry] may be a part of [a university's] commercial courtship ritual'. Along those same lines, Cohen et al. (1997, 177) argued that:[9] 'University administrators appear to be interested chiefly in the revenue generated by relationships with industry'. They are also of the opinion that faculty, who are fundamental to making such relationships work: '… desire support, *per se*, because it contributes to their personal incomes [and] eminence … primarily through foundation research that provides the building blocks for other research and therefore tends to be widely cited'.

However, several drawbacks to university involvement with industry have been identified, such as the diversion of faculty time and effort from teaching, the conflict between industrial trade secrecy and traditional academic openness, and the distorting effect of industry funding on the university budget allocation process (in particular, the tension induced when the distribution of resources is vastly unequal across departments and schools).

Empirical research related to universities as research partners, as recently summarized by Link and Wessner (2011), does so by drawing on the industrial organization paradigm developed by Bain (1949). Defining 'conduct' as partnering with a university and 'structure' as those firms or universities or environmental characteristics that bring about partnering, then the structure → conduct literature can be summarized as follows. Partnering (i.e. conduct) is more likely in the following independent situations (i.e. structure): the firm is engaged in exploratory internal R&D (Bercovitz and Feldman 2007); the firm is mature and large (Fontana, Geuna, and Matt 2006; Stuart, Ozdemir, and Ding 2007); there is a lack of intellectual property issues between the firm and the university (Hall 2004; Hall, Link, and Scott 2001); and university faculty are male, with tenure, and are part of a university research center (Link, Siegel, and Bozeman 2007; Boardman and Corley 2008). Defining performance in terms of the economic consequences of partnering with a university, then the conduct → performance literature can be summarized as follows: there will be two-way flows of knowledge through publication and conferences, and through the formation of RJVs (Cohen, Nelson, and Walsh 2002; Link 2005; Link and Scott 2005; Hertzfeld, Link, and Vonortas 2006); firm R&D will be more successful (Link and Rees 1990; Hall, Link, and Scott 2000, 2003; Kodama 2008); and university research parks – literally a university-based manifestation – will grow as will attendant industries (Link and Scott 2007; Bozeman, Hardin, and Link 2008).

The remainder of this paper is outlined as follows. In Section 2, we set forth a model of industry/university participation. In Section 3, we test this model by developing a reduced form equation of the probability that a firm will partner with a university on a specific research project. Our data for this empirical test comes from projects funded by the US Department of Energy's (DOE's) Small Business Innovation Research (SBIR) program. Finally, in Section 4, we conclude the paper with summary remarks.

2. Model of the industry/university participation

When firms initiate a research partnership with a university, or when a university initiates a research partnership with a firm, each is acting entrepreneurially as it systematically and purposely attempts to identify, or explore, and capture a new source of supply – knowledge. For the firm, this new source of supply is knowledge that the university has (or can generate), but that the firm cannot acquire easily (i.e. at low cost) on its own; for the university, this new source of supply is finances that the firm has, but that the university cannot easily (i.e. at low cost) acquire on its own. Each uses, or exploits, systematically and purposely this new source of supply to create jointly, among other things, a new method of production, be it a good or service/ intellectual output. That new method of production can lead to a new market or organization of industry.[10]

The degree to which a firm will engage with a university in an innovation process is a two-step decision process in which the firm first decides whether to establish a relationship, and second what level of involvement it will have assuming it has already decided to establish a relationship.

Consider the second decision first. The value of working with a university is twofold. It increases the probability that the innovation process will be successful, and it increases the value of any innovation that might result. Letting the level of involvement with the university be represented by Q, where Q might be thought of empirically as R&D inputs, the probability that the innovation process results in a marketable product can be represented by the concave function $p(Q)$ and the revenues (net of production costs) associated with the production and sale of the resulting innovation can be represented by the concave function $R(q)$ where q indicates the quality/marketability of the innovation.[11] The quality q of the innovation is itself assumed to be a concave function $q(Q)$ of the level Q of involvement with the university. Thus, expected net revenues from the production and sale of the resulting innovation will be:

$$R^e = p(Q) \cdot R(q(Q)), \tag{1}$$

and expected marginal net revenues associated with the production and sale of the innovation will be

$$\mathrm{MR}^e = p'(Q) \cdot R(q(Q)) + p(Q) \cdot R'(q(Q)) \cdot q'(Q). \tag{2}$$

There are, of course, costs to engaging in the R&D process itself, both in terms of the physical and intellectual effort required as well as in terms of the costs of raising the funds to be able to make such effort.[12] Assuming that these costs include both fixed and variable components, we can represent the cost function by the function:

$$c = c(Q) \quad \ni \quad c(0) > 0, c'(Q) > 0, \text{ and } c''(Q) > 0. \tag{3}$$

The optimal level of university involvement, assuming the firm wishes to maximize the expected profits from engaging in an R&D process, will be some Q^* that maximizes the expected profits associated with the R&D process:

$$\pi^e(Q) = p(Q) \cdot R(q(Q)) - c(Q), \tag{4}$$

that is, Q^* will be that level of Q that equates expected marginal revenue, MR^e, to the marginal cost, MC, of the R&D process:

$$p'(Q) \cdot R(q(Q)) + p(Q) \cdot R'(q(Q)) \cdot q'(Q) = c'(Q). \tag{5}$$

Figure 1 provides a graphical illustration of the determination of the optimal level of involvement with the university.

Of course, the above analysis is based on the assumption that the firm in fact chooses to work with the university. Unlike the decision as to how large Q should be, the decision whether to engage with the university is a discrete one in which the firm chooses from among three possibilities: partner with a university, perform the R&D in-house, or not engage in R&D. Following Coase's (1937) analysis on the boundaries of a firm, the decision to partner with a university requires that the expected profits associated with that partnership, $\pi^e(Q^*)$, be at least as great as the expected profits associated with performing the R&D in-house, $\pi^e_{\text{in-house}}$. Thus, a necessary condition for partnering with a university is that:

$$\pi^e(Q^*) \geq \max\{\pi^e_{\text{in-house}}, 0\}. \tag{6}$$

The level of expected profits associated with a university partnership, $\pi^e(Q^*)$, will depend on the nature of the partnership. To better understand the factors that will affect the value of a university partnership, note that those expected profits can be defined as the area between

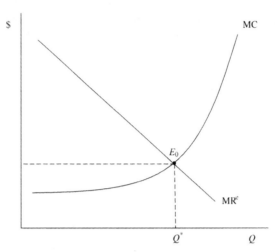

Figure 1.   Determining the level of involvement with a university.

the MR^e curve and the MC curve in Figure 1 (minus, of course, the fixed costs associated with the R&D process), that is

$$\pi^e(Q) = \int (p'(Q) \cdot R(q(Q)) + p(Q) \cdot R'(q(Q)) \cdot q'(Q) - c'(Q)) \cdot dQ - c(0). \quad (7)$$

Thus, the level of these profits will depend on the degree to which the following factors are part of a university partnership:[13]

- *University provision of human and/or physical capital that the firm otherwise would not have access to.* To the extent, this is true, the partnership will relax a resource constraint of the firm, thus resulting in the MC curve being further to the right (and perhaps vertically lower) that it would be otherwise. This results in a higher level of engagement, Q^*, a higher level of expected profits, $\pi^e(Q^*)$, and therefore a greater probability that a university partnership will meet the necessary condition described in Equation (6).
- *The presence of the partnership reduces the cost of raising capital to fund the R&D process.* This cost in large part will be determined by the degree to which the firm can fund the R&D project internally versus externally, by the perceived riskiness of the R&D process by financial markets, and by the perceived market value of the resulting innovation. A lower cost of raising capital will mean that the MC curve is vertically lower. To the extent that this occurs, the level of engagement Q^* with the university will be higher, the level of expected profits $\pi^e(Q^*)$ will be greater, and therefore there will be a greater probability that a university partnership will meet the necessary condition described in Equation (6).
- *Engagement with the university results in a transfer of knowledge (such as an increase in the absorptive capacity of the firm) and/or skills to the firm.* To the extent this is present in university partnership, the MR^e curve and/or the MC curve will be further to the right than they otherwise would be. This results in a greater level of engagement Q^* with the university, an increase in expected profits $\pi^e(Q^*)$, and therefore a greater

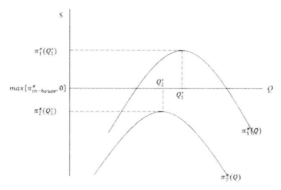

Figure 2.   The decision to engage with a university.

probability that a university partnership will meet the necessary condition described in Equation (6).

- *University partnership results in a reduced ability by the firm to appropriate the benefits of the R&D process.* Such a characteristic of a university partnership may be due to the more open research environment that universities operate in. To the extent this factor is present, the MR^e curve would be further to the left than it otherwise would be. That results in a lower level of engagement Q^*, lower expected profits $\pi^e(Q^*)$, and therefore a diminished likelihood that the necessary condition in Equation (6) is met.

Figure 2 summarizes this choice problem by illustrating two cases, the first of which (defined by the expected profit function $\pi_1^e(Q)$) is associated with the firm deciding to engage with the university, the second of which (defined by the expected profit function $\pi_2^e(Q)$) results in the firm deciding not to engage with the university.

Finally, note that these results are based on the assumption that the firm seeks to maximize the profits associated with the R&D process. However, experiments by Fehr, Herz, and Wilkening (2010) based on a theoretical principal-agent model by Aghion and Tirole (1997) find that principals tend to value control in the decision-making process independent of the level of profit and therefore are willing to pay a premium (in the form of foregone profits) to preserve that control. In the context of this paper, this suggests that firms may insist on a higher, strictly positive threshold of profitability before deciding to partner with a university. To the extent this is true, the condition for partnering with a university would become:

$$\pi^e(Q^*) \geq \max\{\pi_{\text{in-house}}^e, 0\} + \rho, \tag{6'}$$

where ρ represents the value that firm places on maintaining control of the R&D process rather than delegating its authority to a university. As Fehr, Herz, and Wilkening (2010) note, the likelihood that the principal will delegate authority to an agent will increase, the greater the principal perceives that its interests coincide with the interests of the agent or the more the agent has expertise/knowledge that the principal does not have. In the context of this paper, that suggests that the presence of specialized university knowledge and/or a greater comfort level on the part of the firm with engaging with a university, the smaller will be ρ, and therefore the greater the likelihood that the firm decides to partner with the university.

3. Statistical analysis

3.1. *Empirical model*

Our empirical model focuses on identifying those factors that play a role in the discrete choice problem of whether to partner with a university. We define our empirical model to be

$$\text{Univ} = f(\mathbf{X}, \mathbf{Z}),\tag{8}$$

where Univ is a dichotomous representation of whether a firm partners with a university on a particular research project, $\mathbf{X}$ is a vector of project characteristics, and $\mathbf{Z}$ is a vector of firm characteristics. Following the theoretical discussion above, we seek variables for $\mathbf{X}$ and $\mathbf{Z}$ that are associated with changes in the firm's expected marginal revenue, its marginal cost, and/or its expectation that its interests coincide with those of a university.

3.2. *SBIR database*

The SBIR program was created in 1982 under the US Small Business Innovation Development Act of 1982 with the following stated objectives: to stimulate technological innovation, to use small business to meet Federal research and development needs, to foster and encourage participation by minority and disadvantaged persons in technological innovation, and to increase private sector commercialization of innovations derived from Federal research and development (R&D).[14] The 1992 reauthorization of the program broadened the above objectives to emphasize the participation of woman owned and controlled businesses.

Each government agency with an extramural research budget is required to set aside a portion (currently equal to 2.5%) of that budget to award to small (500 or fewer employees) US businesses (at least 51% owned by US citizens or lawfully admitted permanent resident aliens) in response to requests for proposals on defined topics. The structure of the SBIR program is defined by three phases: Phase I has awards to assist businesses as they assess the feasibility of an idea's scientific and commercial potential in response to the funding agency's objectives; currently these are 6-month awards for up to $100,000. Phase II has awards to assist businesses further their research with an expectation that the resulting technology will be commercialized; currently these are two-year awards for up to $1,000,000. There are no agency awards in Phase III; it is the period of time when the funded businesses are to move their technology from the laboratory into the market place. The business is expected to find private-sector funding (e.g. from venture capitalists) during this period.

Eleven agencies currently participate in the SBIR program, with the Department of Defense (DoD) accounting for nearly 58% of all awards, followed by Health and Human Services' National Institutes of Health (NIH) with about 19%, and DOE with about 6% (along with the National Aeronautics and Space administration and the National Science Foundation with similar percentages). Currently, about $2 billion is allocated per year to Phase I and Phase II awards, with nearly 98% account for the contribution by these five agencies.

As part of the SBIR program's reauthorization in 2000, the US Congress charged the National Research Council (NRC) within the National Academies to make recommendations for improvements in the program. Among those evaluatory activities that the NRC undertook was an extensive and balanced survey in 2005 based on a population of 11,214 projects completed from Phase II awards during the 1992–2001 time period. DOE Phase II projects in this database are studied herein.

Although not the largest agency participating in the SBIR program, there are some compelling reasons for focusing on DOE for this study. First, businesses that are funded

Table 1.   Descriptive statistics on the NRC survey of DOE Phase II awards, 1992–2001.

Data reduction	Number of Phase II projects
Completed Phase II projects	808
Phase II survey sample size	439
Phase II random survey sample size[a]	436
Response to the random survey (percent)	154 (35.3%)
Projects uses herein based on responses to all survey questions	92

[a] The NRC surveyed a number of non-randomly chosen projects ($n = 3$) so as to be able to emphasize pre-selected success examples (National Research Council 2008).

through DoD and are successful in completing Phase II have a captive audience for much of their resulting technology, namely DoD (Nelson 1982; Link and Scott 2009). In 2005, the year of the NRC survey, nearly 40% of the technology developed by businesses through DoD Phase II awards was sold to that agency. Thus, the behavior of those businesses, especially their behavior toward partnering with universities is not guided entirely by market pressures. Second, NIH is comprised of 27 research institutes and centers, but there is a great amount of heterogeneity among Phase II award recipients because of heterogeneity of the Institute's focus (Link and Ruhm 2009). In our opinion, businesses funded by Phase II awards from DOE are more likely to have market-based incentives for creating new technologies and commercializing them, and thus relying strategically on universities as a source of technical knowledge and technology (National Research Council 2008). See Table 1 for descriptive statistics on the DOE sample of Phase II awards.

3.3.   Specification of the model

The variables used to estimate versions of Equation (8) are defined in Table 2, and descriptive statistics are presented in Table 3.

We consider seven dependent variables in the estimation of Equation (8), although our focal dependent variable is Univ (Table 2). This variable measures dichotomously whether an SBIR award-recipient firm partnered with a university in any manner while executing its funded Phase II research project. In our sample of 92 funded and completed Phase II projects (Table 1), nearly 35% had a university relationship (Table 3).

The remaining six non-mutually independent university variables measure dichotomously the type of university relationship and allow us indirectly to obtain a fuller indication of the motivations for partnering with a university, particularly with regard to whether universities provide specialized inputs that are not readily or otherwise available to the firm.[15] Most commonly (Table 3), firms are involved with a university through the use of graduate students ($Univ_{GA}$); nearly 22% of the Phase II research projects employed graduate students. The less frequent relationships are when the Phase II research relies on a technology developed at the university by a participant in the Phase II project – this occurs only about 5% of the time – or a technology licensed from the university – this occurs about 2% of the time.

The dependent variables reflect the propensity for the university to be involved in SBIR Phase II research projects in a variety of ways. Alvarez, Barney, and Young (2010), Eckhardt and Shane (2010), and Sarasvathy et al. (2010) stress the roles that the recognition of entrepreneurial opportunity plays in the decision by individuals to undertake entrepreneurial activity. There are three categories of available variables that influence either the existence of

Table 2.   Definition of variables.

Variable	Definition
Dependent variable	
Univ	= 1 if in executing the Phase II research project there was involvement by a university
Univ$_{Faculty}$	= 1 if faculty member(s) or adjunct member(s) worked on the Phase II research project as a consultant
Univ$_{GA}$	= 1 if graduate student(s) worked on the Phase II research project
Univ$_{Equpt}$	= 1 if university facilities and/or equipment were used on the Phase II research project
Univ$_{Sub}$	= 1 if a university was a subcontractor on the Phase II research project
Univ$_{License}$	= 1 if the technology for the Phase II project was licensed from a university
Univ$_{Develop}$	= 1 if the technology for the Phase II project was developed at a university by a participant in the Phase II research project
Independent project variable	
Award	Phase II award amount ($1000)
FemalePI	= 1 if the PI on the Phase II project was a female
Software	= 1 if the actual/expected commercialized output is software
Hardware	= 1 if the actual/expected commercialized output is hardware
ProcessTech	= 1 if the actual/expected commercialized output is a process technology
ServiceCapab	= 1 if the actual/expected commercialized output is service capability
Tool	= 1 if the actual/expected commercialized output is a research tool
EducMat	= 1 if the actual/expected commercialized output is educational material
Other	= 1 if the actual/expected commercialized output is other than listed above
Independent firm variable	
Bus	= 1 if a founder of the firm has a business background
Acad	= 1 if a founder of the firm has an academic background
Emp	Employment in the firm at the time of the Phase II award
FemaleOwn	= 1 if the firm is owned by a female

Table 3.   Descriptive statistics on the variables ($n = 92$).

Variable	Mean	Std. Dev.	Range
Dependent variable			
Univ	0.348	0.479	0/1
Univ$_{Faculty}$	0.185	0.390	0/1
Univ$_{GA}$	0.217	0.415	0/1
Univ$_{Equpt}$	0.120	0.326	0/1
Univ$_{Sub}$	0.130	0.339	0/1
Univ$_{License}$	0.022	0.147	0/1
Univ$_{Develop}$	0.054	0.228	0/1
Independent project variable			
Award	688.60	96.96	387.29–750.00
FemalePI			
Software	0.217	0.415	0/1
Hardware	0.565	0.498	0/1
ProcessTech	0.337	0.475	0/1
ServiceCapab	0.207	0.407	0/1
Tool	0.130	0.339	0/1
EducMat	0.043	0.205	0/1
Other	0.076	0.267	0/1
Independent firm variable			
Bus	0.446	0.450	0/1
Acad	0.587	0.495	0/1
Emp	23.84	38.69	0–200
FemaleOwn	0.043	0.205	0/1

entrepreneurial opportunities or the ability of the firms to recognize that such entrepreneurial opportunities are associated with university–firm partnerships.

The first category of independent variables reflects characteristics specific to SBIR Phase II award project. Regarding project characteristics, the level of Phase II funding (Award) will affect the firm's decision to partner in two ways. First, the greater the level of Phase II funding the greater will be the firm's access to human and/or physical capital. Second, the greater the level of Phase II funding, the lower the cost of raising capital to fund the R&D process will be. The difficulty in predicting the result of these effects is that they argue for increased profits for the firm whether it partners with the university or not. Thus, in terms of Figure 2, both the $\pi^e(Q)$ curve and the $\pi^e_{\text{in-house}}$ line will shift up, and thus the likelihood of partnering with the university could increase or decrease, depending on the relative degree to which $\pi^e(Q)$ and $\pi^e_{\text{in-house}}$ line increase. It should be noted, however, that if the firm chooses to partner with the university, the larger the level of Phase II funding, the greater will be the level of involvement with the university Q^* due to the large level of funding shifting the firm's marginal cost curve down and to the right.

A second independent variable indicates whether the PI on the Phase II project is female. The relative propensity of females to engage in entrepreneurial activity, and the recentness of that activity, has been extensively documented (Acs and Audretsch 2010). Thus, we would expect a negative coefficient between female principle investigators (FemalePI), and possibly female owners (FemaleOwn) – a firm variable discussed below – and the dependent variables.[16] However, to the extent to which women entrepreneurs are less protective of the ability to control (Fehr, Herz, and Wilkening 2010), the likelihood of partnering with a university could increase.

The second category of project-specific independent variables reflects the relevant technology. Entrepreneurial opportunities are not assumed to be homogeneous across different technologies. Rather, Scherer (1983) observed that the propensity to innovate any given technology is, in fact, influenced by the commercial opportunities associated with that technology. Differences in entrepreneurial opportunities across technologies are accounted for by using a series of dichotomous variables, reflecting whether the funded research has or is expected to generate commercialized output that is software, hardware, or a process technology. Similarly, entrepreneurial opportunities may vary across the expected/actual commercialized outputs of service capabilities, research tools, educational material, and other outputs, so dichotomous variables are included. These controls are of particular interest for the potential light that they shed on financial market views of the riskiness and profitability of one line of research versus another. If, for example, financial markets view more tangible innovations (software, hardware, and research tools) as less risky and/or more profitable than intangible innovations (process technology, service capabilities, and educational products), we would expect the former group to be associated with a higher likelihood of university partnering.

The third category of independent variables reflects characteristics specific to the firm, and in particular, to its owner. These variables indicate the ability of the firm to identify and act on entrepreneurial opportunities. A growing literature has identified the background and career trajectory of the founder as having a large influence on firm strategy and performance. The ability of the firm to recognize and act on entrepreneurial opportunities is enhanced when the founder has a business background. Similarly, a founder with an academic background might be expected to increase the propensity for the firm to partner with the university because the ability of the founder and firm to identify entrepreneurial opportunities emanating from research undertaken at the university is presumably higher. Link and Ruhm (2011) have argued that the background of an entrepreneur influences his/her firm's behavior. Background establishes blueprints that tend to become a stable element of the structure of the firm, and the structure of the firm guides its strategy, including partnering or not with a university. Viewed in the light of Fehr, Herz, and Wilkening (2010), a possible explanation as to why such entrepreneurial background is important is that it is connected to the degree to which the entrepreneur values control and on the degree to which the entrepreneur sees his/her interests as similar to that of a university. In the SBIR database, this dimension of the entrepreneur is quantified in terms of having either a business background (Bus) or an academic background (Acad),[17] with a business background perhaps indicating a stronger desire for control and an academic background perhaps indicating a closer perceived alignment between the entrepreneur and a university. Additionally, a business background might be associated with the perception that the enterprise is less risky. To the extent these conjectures are true, a business background would have an ambiguous effect on the likelihood of partnering with a university, while an academic background would be associated with a greater likelihood of partnering with a university.

Regarding other firm characteristics, we control for firm size by the level of employment (Emp) at the time of the Phase II award. On the one hand, larger firms may be less likely to partner with a university, holding constant the scope of the Phase II project, because they have a breadth of internal resources to draw upon to meet any uncertainties associated with the research. On the other hand, larger firms may be more likely to partner with a university, *ceteris paribus*, if associated with its size is specialization of its employees. Moreover, to the extent that a larger firm is viewed as a less risky venture, that too would result in the level of employment being positively associated with the likelihood of university partnering.

3.4.   Econometric findings

The probit results from the estimation of Equation (8) are in Table 4.[18] With respect to our focal dependent variable, Univ, the results in column (8) show that larger firms, measured in terms of number of employees at the time of the Phase II award (Emp) are more likely to be involved with a university. This finding is not inconsistent with our prior findings that larger firms have less fungible human capital or view that larger firms may be considered less risky. There is no statistical evidence that this size relationship is nonlinear. The results also show that entrepreneurs with an academic background (Acad) are, as conjectured, more likely to partner with a university than those with some other background.

We find no evidence that either the size of the SBIR award (Award) or gender (FemalePI or FemaleOwn) influence the likelihood of a research partnership, although our theoretical arguments were not conclusive for such a relationship. The exception (columns (4) and (5)) is that female-owned firms are more likely to enter a university research relationship to gain access to technical capital (i.e. equipment) or research capital (i.e. subcontract). This finding, although not predicted from our theoretical arguments might reflect the still infant research nature of firms owned by female entrepreneurs.

Finally, we find that the expected outputs of software, hardware, and research tools are positively associated with greater university partnering, while the expected outputs of service capability and education products have a negative association. This is not inconsistent with financial markets perceptions of the value of these different lines of research.

In our opinion, the most striking finding when the nature of the university partnership is disaggregated (columns (2)–(7)) is that the background of the entrepreneur is statistically significant in every specification. In particular, having an academic background is significantly and positively correlated with every dimension of the relationship (except that the positive coefficient in the graduate student equation in column (3) is not significant),

Table 4.   Probit regression results (n = 92) (std. errors).

Variables	(1) Univ	(2) Univ_Faculty	(3) Univ_GA	(4) Univ_Equpt	(5) Univ_Sub	(6) Univ_License	(7) Univ_Develop
Award	−0.001 (0.002)	−0.0008 (0.002)	0.002 (0.002)	−0.002 (0.002)	−0.003 (0.002)***	−0.004 (0.060)	−0.004 (0.004)
FemalePI	0.192 (0.715)	—	−0.085 (0.716)	—	0.196 (0.862)	—	0.962 (0.847)
Software	1.376 (0.532)*	0.551 (0.482)	0.646 (0.475)*****	0.042 (0.581)	0.762 (0.517)***	—	0.389 (0.790)
Hardware	0.602 (0.412)****	0.522 (0.438)	0.603 (0.391)****	0.341 (0.447)	0.389 (0.469)	—	−0.039 (0.646)
ProcessTech	0.412 (0.341)	0.047 (0.368)	0.417 (0.347)	0.065 (0.457)	0.364 (0.450)	—	0.131 (0.652)
ServiceCapab	−0.115 (0.413)	−0.452 (0.473)	−0.109 (0.433)	−0.204 (0.610)	0.296 (0.523)	—	0.815 (0.730)
Tool	0.858 (0.435)**	0.573 (0.441)	0.292 (0.470)	0.813 (0.497)	0.940 (0.451)**	7.374 (1.269)*	—
EducMat	−1.378 (0.937)****	—	—	—	—	—	—
Other	0.209 (0.674)	0.120 (0.759)	—	—	—	—	0.774 (0.868)
Emp	0.007 (0.004)***	0.005 (0.005)	0.004 (0.004)	0.008 (0.005)****	0.009 (0.005)***		0.003 (0.007)
Bus	−0.118 (0.309)	−0.223 (0.339)	0.460 (0.319)****	0.691 (0.413)***	−0.098 (0.413)	−0.075 (1.142)	—
Acad	0.749 (0.342)**	0.219 (0.011)**	0.250 (0.351)	0.853 (0.489)****	0.532 (0.348)****	10.841 (1.269)*	5.744 (1.230)*
FemaleOwn	0.576 (0.800)	0.706 (0.767)	0.438 (0.723)	1.092 (0.770)*****	1.236 (0.815)****	—	—
Intercept	−0.920 (1.178)	−1.004 (1.218)	−3.234 (1.434)**	−1.040 (1.430)	−0.220 (1.318)	−18.011 (14.19)	−4.680 (1.23)*
Log Likelihood	−50.45	−41.81	−43.76	−28.41	−31.74	−3.53	−13.92
Pseudo R^2	0.283	0.231	0.187	0.302	0.329	0.635	0.559

Note: Variables that predict perfectly are omitted and noted by '—'.
*Significant at 0.01-level or better.
**Significant at 0.05-level.
***Significant at 0.10-level.
****Significant at 0.15-level.
*****Significant at 0.20-level.

thus suggesting a general willingness to exploit a variety of relationships with a university that finds its origins in a perception by the entrepreneur that his/her interests and the interests of the university are similar. For entrepreneurs with a business background, however, that flexibility is not present except for the use of graduate students and university equipment (columns (3) and (4)), thus suggesting less of a perceived alignment between the entrepreneur's interests and a university's interests and a greater premium placed on control.

4.   Discussion of the findings and conclusions

One of the major economic challenges confronting the USA is a lack of competitiveness in many industries. Policies to enhance US competitiveness, particularly in knowledge-based industries focus on increasing the spillover of knowledge from universities to the private sector. However, to actualize such knowledge spillovers, public policy needs to identify and promote conduits of knowledge spillovers from the university to private firms.

This paper has focused on a particular conduit of knowledge spillovers, namely partnerships between firms awarded a Phase II SBIR grant and universities. The propensity for an SBIR Phase II Award firm to partner with a university is linked to three types of factors – those involving the underlying technology, those involving the anticipated outputs, and those involving the firm and in particular the background of the founder. The empirical evidence provided in this paper suggests that all three of these factors influence the propensity of the firms to partner with a university. The likelihood of a firm entering into a partnership with a university is apparently greater for certain technologies, such as software and hardware, than for other technologies, such as process technologies.

Similarly, the likelihood of a firm–university partnership existing is greater for certain anticipated outputs than for others. If the anticipated output is a research tool, the likelihood of the firm partnering with a university is greater. However, other anticipated outcomes, such as the commercialized output being a service capability, are not statistically linked to the existence of a university–firm partnership.

The background of the founder of the firm is also linked to the likelihood of a firm–university partnership existing. If the founder has an academic background, there is a greater likelihood of the firm partnering with a university. Still, those founders with a business background do exhibit a greater propensity to partner with the university in more limited and specific ways, such as having a graduate student working on the Phase II research project, or using university facilities.

Taken together, the results from the analyses presented in this paper suggest that partnerships between firms and a university may flourish as entrepreneurs from the universities become more prevalent. It may be that facilitating entrepreneurship from university scientists and researchers not only has a direct benefit in terms of increased entrepreneurial activity, but also may enhance the subsequent spillovers of knowledge from the university to private firms, ultimately fuelling innovation, growth, and competitiveness.

Notes

1. Link and Tassey (1987) were among the first to emphasize this trend from an economic policy perspective.
2. See Hagedoorn, Link, and Vonortas (2000) for review of the literature on research partnerships.
3. An earlier version of this literature review is in Link and Wessner (2011).
4. Hall's (2004) subsequent emphasis on industry/university research partnerships in the USA is on intellectual property. See also the role of intellectual property protection mechanisms in research partnerships, as discussed by Hertzfeld, Link, and Vonortas (2006).

5. Schacht (2009) provides an excellent review of public policies to promote industry/university relationships. Her starting point is (p. 4): 'The promotion of cooperative efforts among academia and industry is aimed at increasing the potential for the commercialization of technology'. To wit, legislation in the USA to promote such partnerships traces at least to public policy responses to the productivity slowdown in the early and late 1970s. Specifically, such initiatives included the Bayh–Dole Act of 1980 (P.L. 96-517), Economic Recovery Tax Act of 1981 (P.L. 97-34), and the Tax Reform Act of 1986 (P.L. 99-514).

6. Cohen et al. (1998) provide a selective review of this literature, emphasizing the studies that have documented that university research enhances firms' sales, R&D productivity, and patenting activity. See, Blumenthal et al. (1986); Jaffe (1989); Adams (1990); Berman (1990); Feller (1990); Mansfield (1991, 1992); Van de Ven (1993); Bonaccorsi and Piccaluga (1994); Klevorick et al. (1994); Zucker, Darby, and Armstrong (1994); Henderson, Jaffe, and Trajtenberg (1995); Mansfield and Lee (1996); Zeckhauser (1996); Campbell (1997); and Baldwin and Link (1998). Cockburn and Henderson (1997) show that it was important for innovative pharmaceutical firms to maintain ties to universities. Hall, Link, and Scott (2000, 2003) suggest that perhaps such research ties with universities increase the 'absorptive capacity', in the sense of Cohen and Leventhal (1990), of innovative firms.

7. See Leyden and Link (1992) and Burnham (1997). Link (1995) documented that one reason for the growth of Research Triangle Park in North Carolina was the desire of industrial research firms to locate near the triangle universities (University of North Carolina in Chapel Hill, North Carolina State University in Raleigh, and Duke University in Durham).

8. See Berman (1990), Feller (1990), and Henderson, Jaffe, and Trajtenberg (1995), and Siegel, Waldman, and Link (1999, 2003).

9. Siegel, Waldman, and Link (1999, 2003) document that university administrators consider licensing and royalty revenues from industry as an important output from university technology transfer offices.

10. Bercovitz and Feldman (2007), building on the conceptual advances of Pisano (1991) and Chesbrough (2003), refer to exploration and exploitation in the context of upstream university research alliances.

11. By concave, we mean that that first derivative of the function is positive and the second derivative is negative.

12. David, Hall, and Toole (2000) provide an insightful description of the R&D process from an investment perspective.

13. David, Hall, and Toole (2000) provide a more complete treatment of the variety of factors that affect the level of R&D activity.

14. For a more detailed discussion of the economic role of the SBIR program, see National Research Council (2008) and Link and Scott (2010).

15. These six types of involvement are defined by the availability of data from the NRC survey and not by our perception of importance.

16. The gender of the Phase II research project's PI (FemalePI) and the gender of the firm's owner (FemaleOwn) are also considered because of the SBIR program's emphasis on woman entrepreneurs.

17. Subsumed in the intercept are those entrepreneurs whose background is other than business or academics.

18. To test empirically for selection bias, we estimated the probability of response to the NRC survey as a function of the age of the project and the number of employees in the firm at the time of the survey (2005). We conjecture that older award recipients would be less likely to respond to the survey because of a loss of institutional memory, and the larger the firm the more likely it would respond because of available resources, *ceteris paribus*. While this was statistically the case, we could not reject the null hypothesis that the model of response and the model of university partnership are independent from one another (i.e. the correlation of the errors in the two models is not significantly different from zero).

References

Acs, Z., and D.B. Audretsch. 2010. *Handbook of entrepreneurship research.* New York: Springer.

Adams, J.D. 1990. Fundamental stocks of knowledge and productivity growth. *Journal of Political Economy* 98: 673–702.

Aghion, P., and J. Tirole. 1997. Formal and real authority in organizations. *Journal of Political Economy* 105: 1–29.

Alvarez, S.A., J.B. Barney, and S.L. Young. 2010. Debates in entrepreneurship: Opportunity formation and implications for the field of entrepreneurship. In *Handbook of entrepreneurship research*, ed. Z.J. Acs and D.B. Audretsch, 23–46. New York: Springer.

Bain, J.S. 1949. Price and production policies. In *A survey of contemporary economics*, ed. H.S. Ellis, 129–73. Philadelphia, PA: The Blakiston Company.

Baldwin, W.L., and A.N. Link. 1998. Universities as research joint venture partners: Does size of venture matter? *International Journal of Technology Management* 15: 895–913.

Bercovitz, J.E.L., and M.P. Feldman. 2007. Fishing upstream: Firm innovation strategy and university research alliances. *Research Policy* 36: 930–48.

Berman, E.M. 1990. The economic impact of industry-funded university R&D. *Research Policy* 19: 349–55.

Blumenthal, D., M.E. Gluck, K.S. Lewis, M.A. Stoto, and D. Wise. 1986. University industry research relationships in biotechnology: Implications for the university. *Science* 232: 1361–6.

Boardman, P.C., and E.A. Corley. 2008. University research centers and the composition of research collaborations. *Research Policy* 37: 900–13.

Bonaccorsi, A., and A. Piccaluga. 1994. A theoretical framework for the evaluation of university–industry relationships. *R&D Management* 24: 229–47.

Bozeman, B., J. Hardin, and A.N. Link. 2008. Barriers to the diffusion of nanotechnology. *Economics of Innovation and New Technology* 17: 751–3.

Burnham, J.B. 1997. Evaluating industry/university research linkages. *Research-Technology Management* 40: 52–5.

Campbell, T.I.D. 1997. Public policy for the 21st century: Addressing potential conflicts in university–industry collaboration. *The Review of Higher Education* 20: 357–79.

Chesbrough, H. 2003. *Open innovation: The new imperative for creating and profiting from technology*. Boston: Harvard Business School Publishing.

Coase, R.H. 1937. The nature of the firm. *Economica* 4: 386–405.

Cockburn, I., and R. Henderson. 1997. Public–private interaction and the productivity of pharmaceutical research. NBER working paper 6018, National Bureau of Economic Research, Cambridge MA. http://www.nber.org/papers/w6018.pdf.

Cohen, W.M., R. Florida, L. Randazzese, and J. Walsh. 1998. Industry and the academy: Uneasy partners in the cause of technological advance. In *Challenges to research university*, ed. R. Noll, 171–200. Washington, DC: Brookings Institution Press.

Cohen, W.M., and D.A. Leventhal. 1990. The implications of spillovers for R&D and technology advance. In *Advanced in applied micro-economics*, ed. A.N. Link and V.K. Smith, 29–46. Greenwich, CT: JAI Press.

Cohen, W.M., R.R. Nelson, and J.P. Walsh. 2002. Links and impacts: The influence of public research on industrial R&D. *Management Science* 48: 1–23.

Council on Competitiveness. 1996. *Endless frontiers, limited resources: US R&D policy for competitiveness*. Washington, DC: Council on Competitiveness.

David, P.A., B.H. Hall, and A.A. Toole. 2000. Is public R&D a complement or a substitute for private R&D? A review of the econometric evidence. *Research Policy* 29: 497–529.

Eckhardt, J.T., and S. Shane. 2010. An update to the individual-opportunity nexus. In *Handbook of entrepreneurship research*, ed. Z.J. Acs and D.B. Audretsch, 47–76. New York: Springer.

Fehr, E., H. Herz, and T. Wilkening. 2010. The lure of authority: Motivation and incentive effects of power. Working paper, Department of Economics, University of Zurich.

Feller, I. 1990. Universities as engines of R&D-based economic growth: They think they can. *Research Policy* 19: 349–55.

Fontana, R., A. Geuna, and M. Matt. 2006. Factors affecting university–industry R&D projects: The importance of searching, screening and signaling. *Research Policy* 35: 309–23.

Hagedoorn, J., A.N. Link, and N.S. Vonortas. 2000. Research partnerships. *Research Policy* 29: 567–86.

Hall, B.H. 2004. University–industry research partnerships in the United States. In *Rethinking science systems and innovation policies*, ed. J.P. Contzen, D. Gibson, and M.V. Heitor, 1–31. West Lafayette, IN: Purdue University Press.

Hall, B.H., A.N. Link, and J.T. Scott. 2000. Universities as research partners. NBER working paper 7643, National Bureau of Economic Research, Cambridge MA. http://www.nber.org/papers/w7643.pdf.

Hall, B.H., A.N. Link, and J.T. Scott. 2001. Barriers inhibiting industry from partnering with universities: Evidence from the Advanced Technology Program. *Journal of Technology Transfer* 26: 87–98.

Hall, B.H., A.N. Link, and J.T. Scott. 2003. Universities as research partners. *Review of Economics and Statistics* 85: 485–91.

Henderson, R., A.B. Jaffe, and M. Trajtenberg. 1995. Universities as a source of commercial technology: A detailed analysis of university patenting 1965–1988. NBER working paper no. 5068, National Bureau of Economic Research, Cambridge MA. http://www.nber.org/papers/w5068.pdf.

Hertzfeld, H.R., A.N. Link, and N.S. Vonortas. 2006. Intellectual property protection mechanisms in research partnerships. *Research Policy* 35: 825–38.

Jaffe, A.B. 1989. Real effects of academic research. *American Economic Review* 79: 957–78.

Klevorick, A.K., R.C. Levin, R.R. Nelson, and S.G. Winter. 1994. On the sources and significance of interindustry differences in technological opportunities. *Research Policy* 24: 195–206.

Kodama, T. 2008. The role of intermediation and absorptive capacity in facilitating university–industry linkages: An empirical study of TAMA in Japan. *Research Policy* 37: 1224–40.

Leyden, D.P., and A.N. Link. 1992. *Government's role in innovation*. Norwell, MA: Kluwer Academic Publishers.

Link, A.N. 1995. *A generosity of spirit: The early history of Research Triangle Park*. Chapel Hill, NC: University of North Carolina Press for the Research Triangle Park Foundation.

Link, A.N. 1996. Research joint ventures: Patterns from *Federal Register* filings. *Review of Industrial Organization* 11: 617–28.

Link, A.N. 2005. Research joint ventures in the United States: A descriptive analysis. In *Essays in honor of Edwin Mansfield: The economics of R&D, innovation, and technological change*, ed. A.N. Link and F.M. Scherer, 187–95. Norwell, MA: Springer.

Link, A.N., and J. Rees. 1990. Firm size, university based research, and the returns to R&D. *Small Business Economics* 2: 25–31.

Link, A.N., and C.J. Ruhm. 2009. Bringing science to market: Commercializing from NIH SBIR awards. *Economics of Innovation and New Technology* 18: 381–402.

Link, A.N., and C.J. Ruhm. 2011. Public knowledge, private knowledge: The intellectual capital of the entrepreneur. *Small Business Economics* 36: 1–14.

Link, A.N., and J.T. Scott. 2005. Universities as partners in US research joint ventures. *Research Policy* 34: 385–93.

Link, A.N., and J.T. Scott. 2007. The economics of university research parks. *Oxford Review of Economic Policy* 23: 661–74.

Link, A.N., and J.T. Scott. 2009. Private investor participation and commercialization rates for government-sponsored research and development: Would a prediction market improve the performance of the SBIR program? *Economica* 76: 264–81.

Link, A.N., and J.T. Scott. 2010. Government as entrepreneur: Evaluating the commercialization success of SBIR projects. *Research Policy* 39: 589–601.

Link, A.N., D.S. Siegel, and B. Bozeman. 2007. An empirical analysis of the propensity of academics to engage in informal technology transfer. *Industrial and Corporate Change* 16: 641–55.

Link, A.N., and G. Tassey. 1987. *Strategies for technology-based competition: Meeting the new global challenge*. Lexington, MA: D.C. Heath.

Link, A.N., and C.W. Wessner. 2011. Universities as research partners: Entrepreneurial explorations and exploitations. In *Handbook of research in innovation and entrepreneurship*, ed. D.B. Audretsch, 290–9. London: Edward Elgar.

Mansfield, E. 1991. Academic research and industrial innovation. *Research Policy* 20: 1–12.

Mansfield, E. 1992. Academic research and industrial innovation: A further note. *Research Policy* 21: 295–6.

Mansfield, E., and J. Lee. 1996. The modern university: Contributor to industrial innovation and recipient of industrial R&D support. *Research Policy* 25: 1047–58.

Morgan, R.P. 1998. University research contributions to industry: The faculty view. In *Trends in industrial innovation: Industry perspectives & policy implications*, ed. P.D. Blair and R.A. Frosch, 98–116. Research Triangle Park, NC: Sigma Xi, The Scientific Research Society.

Mowery, D.C., and D.J. Teece. 1996. Strategic alliances and industrial research. In *Engines of innovation: US industrial research at the end of an era*, ed. R.S. Rosenbloom and W.J. Spencer, 111–30. Boston: Harvard Business School Publishing.

National Research Council. 2008. *An assessment of small business innovation research program at the Department of Energy*, ed. C.W. Wessner. Washington, DC: National Academics Press.

Nelson, R.R. 1982. Government stimulus of technological progress: Lessons from American history. In *Government and technical progress*, ed. R.R. Nelson, 451–82. New York: Pergamon.

Pavitt, K. 1998. The social shaping of the national science base. *Research Policy* 27: 793–805.

Pisano, G. 1991. The governance of innovation: Vertical integration and collaborative arrangements in the biotechnology industry. *Research Policy* 20: 237–49.

Rosenberg, N., and R.R. Nelson. 1994. American universities and technical advance in industry. *Research Policy* 23: 323–48.

Sarasvathy, S.D., N. Dew, S.R. Velamuri, and S. Venkataramanin. 2010. Three views of entrepreneurial opportunity. In *Handbook of entrepreneurship research*, ed. Z.J. Acs and D.B. Audretsch, 77–98. New York: Springer.

Schacht, W. 2009. *Industrial competitiveness and technological advancement: Debate over government policy*. Washington, DC: Congressional Research Service, US Congress.

Scherer, F.M. 1983. The propensity to patent. *International Journal of Industrial Organization* 1: 107–28.

Siegel, D.S., D. Waldman, and A.N. Link. 1999. Assessing the impact of organizational practices on the productivity of university technology transfer offices: An exploratory study. NBER working paper no. 7256, National Bureau of Economic Research, Cambridge MA. http://www.nber.org/papers/w7256.pdf.

Siegel, D.S., D. Waldman, and A.N. Link. 2003. Assessing the impact of organizational practices on the productivity of university technology transfer offices: An exploratory study. *Research Policy* 32: 27–48.

Stuart, T.E., S.Z. Ozdemir, and W.W. Ding. 2007. Vertical alliance networks: The case of university-biotechnology-pharmaceutical alliance chains. *Research Policy* 36: 477–98.

Van de Ven, A.H. 1993. A community perspective on the emergence of innovations. *Journal of Engineering Technology Management* 10: 23–51.

Zeckhauser, R. 1996. The challenge of contracting for technological information. *Proceedings of the National Academy of Science* 93: 12743–8.

Zucker, L.G., M. Darby, and J. Armstrong. 1994. Intellectual capital and the firm: The technology of geographically localized knowledge spillovers. NBER working paper no. 4946, National Bureau of Economic Research, Cambridge MA. http://www.nber.org/papers/w4946.pdf.

[15]

Research Policy 43 (2014) 1697–1706

Contents lists available at ScienceDirect

Research Policy

journal homepage: www.elsevier.com/locate/respol

A new industry creation and originality: Insight from the funding sources of university patents

Marco Guerzoni [a,*], T. Taylor Aldridge [b], David B. Audretsch [c], Sameeksha Desai [c]

[a] Department of Economics and Statistics "Cognetti de Martiis", University of Turin and CRIOS, Bocconi University, Italy
[b] Leibniz Institute for Regional Development and Structural Planning, Germany
[c] School of Public and Environmental Affairs, Indiana University, USA

ARTICLE INFO

Article history:
Received 4 June 2012
Received in revised form 3 October 2013
Accepted 25 April 2014
Available online 2 August 2014

Keywords:
University–industry relations
Academic patenting
Originality
Research funding

ABSTRACT

Scientific breakthroughs coming from universities can contribute to the emergence of new industries, such as in the case of biotechnology. Obviously, not all research conducted in universities leads to a radical change from existing technological trajectories. Patents and patent dynamics have long been recognized as critical in understanding the emergence of new technologies and industries. Specifically, patent citations provide insight into the originality of a discovery that has received patent protection. Yet while a large body of literature addresses the impact of patent originality on various firm performance measures, we address the question of what conditions drive patent originality in the process of knowledge creation within the university. Using data on patented cancer research, we examine how research context – as reflected by the funding source for each scientist – is associated with patent originality. We find that when university scientists are partly funded by their own university, they have a higher propensity to generate more original patents. By contrast, university scientists funded either by industry or other non-university organizations have a lower propensity to generate more original patents. The significance of our findings in the cancer research setting call for further research on this question in other research fields.

© 2014 Elsevier B.V. All rights reserved.

1. Introduction

The university has long been recognized as an important factor in driving innovation. The development of biotechnology in the 1970s represents a case of an emergent industry where the commercialization of new knowledge from a university played a key role. In the case of biotechnology, the underlying knowledge was developed by Herbert Boyer of the University of California at San Francisco and Stanley Cohen at Stanford University. Their laboratory experiments provided a compelling demonstration of the vast potential for DNA recombinant engineering to revolutionize not just agricultural products, but also medicinal and pharmaceutical products.

The discovery itself is not the full story. It took more than scientific breakthroughs from universities to launch biotechnology.

* Corresponding author at: Department of Economics and Statistics "Cognetti de Martiis", University of Torino, Lungo Dora Siena 100 A, 10153 Torino, Italy.
E-mail addresses: marco.guerzoni@unito.it (M. Guerzoni), aaldridge@irs-net.de (T. Taylor Aldridge), daudrets@indiana.edu (D.B. Audretsch), desai@indiana.edu (S. Desai).

http://dx.doi.org/10.1016/j.respol.2014.07.009
0048-7333/© 2014 Elsevier B.V. All rights reserved.

For example, how can the incentives for innovators to engage in high-risk, potentially ground-breaking research be reconciled with commercialization and protection of their hard work and investment? Patent protection of key intellectual property provided a platform for commercialization of the underlying science and its transformation into new biotechnology products. The originality of their patents reflects the extent to which the underlying intellectual property, developed by Boyer and Cohen, was a radical departure from the extant technological trajectories. An important methodology for measuring the originality of a patent was introduced by Henderson et al. (1998) and refined by Jaffe et al. (2005). Patent originality has been used to study a broad range of measures reflecting firm performance, such as growth and survival (Cohen et al., 2002; Jaffe et al., 2005). However, while patent originality has been used extensively to explain firm performance, there has been little research on the factors associated with patent originality itself.

The purpose of this paper is to shed light on this underexamined question and explicitly study the conditions under which some patents are more original than others. We surmise that the relationship between university funding and patent originality could have two possible sources. First, because the type and source of funding could be linked with specific deliverables and expectations, the

1698   *M. Guerzoni et al. / Research Policy 43 (2014) 1697–1706*

nature of funding could direct the process of invention toward more or less original results. Second, it could be that ideas have an a priori potential to produce originality, and it is the scientist who decides to use university funding for more radical ideas. In both cases, we highlight the importance of university funding in the generation of original knowledge, which is the ultimate trigger for the generation of new industries. However, in the context of our study, the first explanation could be more likely: We examine patents resulting from cancer research. These patents are assumed to have both a positive perceived market value and to have qualified for funding. It is reasonable to expect that the scientist looked for any funding possible to pursue her ideas, allowing us to study variance in funding sources. We hypothesize that university-funded researchers are associated with more original patents, whereas industry-funded and other non-university funded researchers are associated with less original patents. We find, indeed, that university funding is associated with greater patent originality. Our findings indicate that heterogeneity in the source of research funding is an important consideration when examining patent outcomes.

In the next section, we discuss the relevant literature and develop hypotheses linking patent originality to the funding context in which the intellectual property was created, drawing upon research on technology trajectories and emergent technologies initiated by Nelson and Winter (1982) and Dosi (1982). In the third and fourth sections, we empirically test our hypotheses using a database linking patents held by university cancer scientists with their funding sources. We summarize and present our conclusions in the last section of the paper.

2. Literature and hypothesis

2.1. Originality and emerging technologies

Schumpeter (1942) argued that creative destruction from innovation was critical to rendering existing products obsolete, fueling economic advancement and generating welfare gains. Related to this, qualitative technical change (Solow, 1967) and labor productivity (Arrow, 1962) have been argued as central to achieving economic growth. An important question concerns the innovation process itself, such as drivers of its rate and direction. Dosi (1982) and Nelson and Winter (1982) provided a compelling theoretical framework considering technology as knowledge, which includes not only knowledge codified in blueprints, manuals, publications, and patents but knowledge of a tacit nature, including know-how and organizational capabilities. Tacit knowledge (e.g. related to technical know-how or non-standard production) is costly to transfer, and transferability is limited by its embeddedness in individuals, teams and organizations. Moreover, if technology is perceived as knowledge embedded in individuals and organizations, its rate and direction are also driven by individual cognitive processes. In this view, Dosi (1982) introduced the concept of technological paradigm and trajectory. Technological paradigm defines the set of common heuristic, institutionalized ideas in a specific technological field and shared views about the future development of an artifact; technological trajectories include the selective and cumulative nature of technological progress within a paradigm (Dosi, 1988). This approach to the economics of innovation suggests that the search process in discovery does not freely explore all the space of technological opportunities, but is focused on a specific path which builds on past knowledge and which is difficult to change.

The path-dependency of technological progress is not per se a problem for a techno-economic system. For instance, many benefits can be derived from continuous progress along a technological trajectory, such as a higher level of predictability of research

output, faster learning economies due to simplification and routinization of the process, scale economies, and easier production of complementary assets and components' interfaces. Over time, standardized knowledge on a technological trajectory allows for efficient routinization of innovation processes by creating order and consequently, reducing uncertainty. However, over time, path-dependency could lead to costs in the form of missed opportunities. New possibilities could arise along a different trajectory, or in times of revolutionary science, as part of a new scientific or technological paradigm. In these cases, cognitive and economic barriers due to path-dependency could hinder responsiveness of the system toward the new path. Even more, they could distort researcher assessment and introduce myopic behavior and status quo bias in the exploitation of technological opportunities (David, 1985). In this situation, an economic system could benefit from the production of original knowledge. Original knowledge is a potential source of new ideas, which can open new sectors and industries relying upon knowledge outside the existing technological path. This line of reasoning is inspired by work suggesting that new paths require new markets, but also new technological knowledge (Malerba et al., 2007). Thus, technological progress as described by Dosi (1982, 1988) can come out of a system with the ability to generate a certain degree of original knowledge to avoid severe technological lock-ins.

Firms incentives to pursue research outside of existing technological trajectories are, however, limited. As noted by Nelson (1959) and Arrow (1962), basic knowledge cannot always be used directly by the firm introducing it. Moreover, in this view, technology is simple information with the nature of a quasi-public good, reproducible at zero marginal cost, and is non-rival and non-excludable (at least without the intervention of some institutions). Agrawal and Henderson (2002) posited that systematic underfunding of basic inventions results from a strong association of applied inventions with commercial success and inappropriability of the results from basic inventions. The returns to investment in basic research are thus not fully appropriable by the innovator, and in equilibrium, this could lead to underinvestment with respect to a social optimum. Firms also have little incentive to invest in original knowledge because of the uncertainty linked with it. In an attempt to integrate theory on investment behavior with theory on searching capabilities, Henderson (1993) focused on sources of resistance to change. Martin and Scott (2000) discussed the lack of incentives for firms to invest in original and general knowledge, proposing a taxonomy which includes factors ranging from limited appropriability and uncertainty to lack of competencies.

The lack of incentives for firms to invest in original and general research has broadly been the rationale since World War II for public funding of university research. Combined with the traditional role of universities in reproducing existing knowledge (Martin, 2003), policymakers financed universities to pursue research for its own sake (Geuna, 2001). Research taking place in universities has been shown to play a key role in technological and other advancements. University research activities have been linked to product innovation and process innovation (Mansfield, 1991) and productivity growth in private industry (Adams, 1990). Some industries have seen important improvements related to university research, such as drug (Toole and Czarnitzki, 2007) and pharmaceutical innovation contributing to lower hospital cost and increased life expectancy (see Lichtenberg, 2001, 2007). Other industries, such as biotechnology in the United States, have been shaped in large part by university research (see Czarnitzki et al., 2011; Zucker and Darby, 1997).

However, since the early 1980s, a shift in the rationale and nature of research funding has occurred in universities in both the United States and in Europe. Geuna (1998) argued this was partly due to greater student enrolment in universities and the rise in expectations for social returns from society. These two events

M. Guerzoni et al. / Research Policy 43 (2014) 1697–1706 1699

introduced an irreconcilable dichotomy between the traditional task of curiosity-driven research on one hand, and research driven by societal need on the other hand (Geuna, 2001). This friction led to the institutionalization of new academic functions, such as "pursuing knowledge and its application for the creation of wealth" and "to serve the specific training and more general research supports needs of the knowledge-based economy at local, regional, and national levels" (Geuna, 2001: p. 617). These changes in the rationale for the existence and nature of knowledge creation within the university occurred with a radical transformation in funding patterns of university research.

The extent to which institutional setting creates incentives for the university to generate wealth and cooperate with firms is driven by many factors and depends on national legislation. These factors include the introduction of arrangements for publicly funded institutions to retain intellectual property of an innovation, and competitive mechanisms for resource allocation. The Bayh–Dole Act of 1980 is a classic example of the first type of institutional change: It paved the way for universities in the United States to maintain ownership and to patent intellectual property resulting from federally funded research, with provisions to share license revenues with the scientist/inventor (see Thursby et al., 2009). Professor privilege – professor retaining ownership of inventions – has been a key difference between the United States and Europe, with faculty in Europe often providing patent rights to their research sponsors (see Geuna and Nesta, 2006; Crespi and Geuna, 2006; Thursby et al., 2009). Recent changes in some European countries to institute legislation similar to Bayh–Dole have been occurring, such as the removal of professor's privilege in Germany in 2002 (see Czarnitzki et al., 2011; Kilger and Bartenbach, 2002; Geuna and Nesta, 2006). The Bayh–Dole Act remains the policy example of standard, and its impact on university patents in the United States has been analyzed extensively (see Mowery et al., 2001; Sampat et al., 2003; Mowery and Ziedonis, 2000, 2002).

While the Bayh–Dole Act supported university ownership of innovations, several studies (Thursby and Thursby, 2011; Audretsch and Aldridge, 2006; Markman et al., 2008) found evidence of patent assignments outside universities. Thursby and Thursby (2011) found that 29% of patents in a sample across universities were assigned to firms; Audretsch and Aldridge (2006) report 30% assignment of at least one patent to firms among scientists funded by the National Cancer Institute. In a study of more than 50 universities, Markman et al. (2008) reported a similar trend of 33% of patents assigned externally. Noting that some empirical studies assume patents assigned outside universities result from circumventing university technology transfer offices (Audretsch and Aldridge, 2006; Markman et al., 2008), Thursby et al. (2009) asked if patents assigned outside universities are in fact legitimately assigned. They considered that patents could be assigned in four types: University assignment, firm assignment where the inventor is a principal, firm assignment where the inventor is not a principal, and unassignment (ownership not by inventor). They found that firm-assigned patents are more incremental than university-assigned patents, and that firm assignment of patents results largely from consulting and not university-conducted research. Additionally, Thursby et al. (2009) found that a higher inventor share increases the chances of university assignment of a patent versus firm assignment in which the inventor is a principal, but has no effect on other types of patent assignment.

A second type of institutional change was discussed by Gulbrandsen and Smeby (2005), who found evidence that professors involved in research with the private sector perceive themselves as more applied than others. Reduced public funding availability in Europe (Geuna and Nesta, 2006) and competitiveness among universities for public funds has created incentives for private and nonprofit funding partnerships. Czarnitzki et al. (2007)

found differences in scientific performance based on funding source among German professors: Patents in partnership with nonprofits enhance performance whereas corporate patents negatively affect scientific performance. Geuna and Nesta (2006) showed an effect of a growing number of patents after the shift of university funding, but this was heterogeneous across sectors.

Assuming that a core role of university research is to overcome knowledge path dependency, we consider it worth assessing how the production of original research is changing within the university. Specifically, because various types of rationale coexist within a university, we investigate the relationship between the type of funding for research and the originality of knowledge produced.

2.2. Originality and the university

Many studies have examined the overall number of university patents resulting from funding changes or policy changes. However, counting total patents does not provide the full story (see Marco, 2006). The technological importance of an invention (Trajtenberg, 1990; Henderson et al., 1998) is the basis for a subgroup of studies on the quality of patents. Understanding the determinants of patent quality can yield important implications for ongoing policy design, particularly as more countries around the world are adopting Bayh–Dole types of legislation. However, evidence on patent quality is mixed. Typically, when data are available, it is still difficult to disaggregate by funding source. For instance, Henderson et al. (1998) show a decrease in the quality of university patents between 1965 and 1988 at the aggregate level. They used a measure of quality as the dependent variable, which is a non-normalized measure of total citations. Their key finding was that relative importance and generality of university patents declined, despite an overall increase in university patents, and this was attributed mainly to growth in the number of low-quality patents. Mowery et al. (2001) found weak evidence of a decrease in university patent quality, which disappeared if the analysis considered experience of the expert. Mowery and Ziedonis (2002) studied patent trends in three universities in the United States (University of California, Stanford University and Columbia University) before and after the passing of Bayh–Dole. Using citations during the 6 years after issue to measure patent importance, they found no decline in importance or generality of patents issued after 1980 at University of California and Stanford University; they find overall that the effects of Bayh–Dole could be "as important as any effects of the act on the internal research culture" of the universities (Mowery and Ziedonis, 2002: p. 399). These works consider universities to be homogenous producers of knowledge and compare their performance before and after the major policy shift of Bayh–Dole. In contrast, we consider heterogeneity *within* the university process of knowledge production. Both publicly-funded and privately co-funded applied research coexist within the university. Thus, in order to assess the importance of changing context on university innovative behavior, we should consider the role of various funding sources. Our study is also different from most previous research in our treatment of patents. While most of the studies mentioned above look at the quality of the patent, we rather look at its originality since we are interested in the analysis of knowledge which is not aligned with the dominant paradigm and can thus be the trigger for new industries.

Following Trajtenberg et al. (1997), we consider originality as the extent to which an idea is a synthesis of divergent knowledge. The capability of recombining components of existing knowledge in a new way connects to the Schumpeterian definition of innovation, which opens new markets and new industries (Schumpeter, 1942: p. 80) Trajtenberg et al. (1997) correctly highlighted that originality is thus a backward-looking type of the knowledge which an invention built upon. For this reason they suggested using the

1700   *M. Guerzoni et al. / Research Policy 43 (2014) 1697–1706*

heterogeneity of a patent's backward citations, measured by the Herfindahl index and calculated as the concentration of citations over 3 digit patent classes. Trajtenberg et al. (1997) were the first to suggest that originality measured in this way might differ between academic and corporate ownership of patents, although they did not find evidence for that. Hall et al. (2001) discussed a possible upward bias of this measure due to the underlying count structure of patent data. Indeed, if a patent had zero citations in a specific patent class, this class was dropped from the analysis. Thus, we make use of a modified version of the index (described in detail when we discuss our variables). It is worth noting that this measure differs from generality, since generality consists of the count of forward citations: That is, generality is forward-looking and measures the success or diffusion of an idea. On the contrary, it could also be the case that the attempt to create original knowledge might fail and only in some cases might lead to the generation of new markets and new industries.

We identify university research which is financed directly by the university, federal projects issued through tender, or funded by the private sector. We are thus able to observe how the primary source of an investment matters.

2.3. Hypotheses

We now turn to our hypotheses. In the previous section, we suggested that university research is a key instrument for maintaining some resource allocation toward the exploration of new areas in technological space. Mitigating the risk of lock-in of the cumulative and selective nature of the discovery process is a related concern, with implications for policy-makers inside and outside universities. As pointed out earlier, recent changes in the funding rationale of academic research could have modified incentives schemes (for more see Geuna and Nesta, 2006; Czarnitzki et al., 2011) and thus, innovative activities coming from the university.

Previous research showed that originality, a measured based on patent citation counts, may be mildly decreasing over time. However, this is not always supported (Mowery and Ziedonis, 2002) or not conclusive and becomes non-significant when other controls are added (see Mowery et al., 2001; Aldridge and Audretsch, 2011).

We argue that whether a patent is (or is not) assigned to a university may not be the only appropriate way to understand how changed incentives affect the originality of research (see Marco, 2006, for a discussion of patent counts). As suggested in a robust body of research, there is a crucial difference in research activity in academia and in the private sector. Indeed, since the work of Merton (1973), the underlying justification of this difference consists of the various contexts of research a researcher faces (e.g., in terms of deliverables and expectations from the scientist). For this reason, since the work by Merton (1973) the characteristics of a patent have been controlled for its origin, whether from academia or from industry.

However, if the changing rationale institutional environment led to greater overlap between these academia and private sector (Geuna, 1998, 2001), we might find a coexistence of several incentives and expectations within the university. We might assume that the divide between academia and industry is not clear-cut and the two different contexts coexist even within the university. In order to disentangle the two, we argue that for each academic patent, it is worth examining the funding source of its specific project. Indeed, within universities various types of funding schemes coexist, e.g., public, private, profit or non-profit. We consider three main sources of possible funding private sector, government, and university. The aim of this paper is to disentangle the different sources of funding and not to investigate university governance of funds or internal financial allocation matters. For this reason, we consider all possible university grants in one category. The type of funding could

reflect different rationales and to some extent proxy the research context in which a project is being carried out. This information could help explain the variation in originality across patents.

In line with the research we discussed earlier on the effect of the Bayh–Dole act, we consider that when the context of a funding source is linked with the university, the curiosity driven rationale could be likely to push the scientist to recombine knowledge in a more original way. Indeed, "curiosity-driven research is 'research that is performed without thought of application, and its goal is simply to understand nature" (Strandburg 2005, p. 8)". Incentives behind such research do not maximize any social optimum, but the personal one of the *homo scientificus* pursuing her own interest. Curiosity could also facilitate serendipitous events such as an accidental discovery in science (Roberts and Royston, 1989).

On the contrary, private research has been considered since Arrow (1962) and Nelson (1959) as more focused on applied research, since in this context approbiability is notably higher. An exception was discussed by Cohen and Levinthal (1989), which showed that private companies might pursue not directly applicable R&D. However, although involved in basic research, their aim is always to develop competencies to tap university knowledge and develop products for existing sectors (Cohen and Levinthal, 1989).

A third source of funding is government (Geuna, 2001). For instance, the website www.grant.gov lists all possible federal grants for the United States: Grants for "Science and Technology and other Research and Development" and for "Health" account in 2013 for more than one third of total grants (1530). Other important categories are "Education" and "Income Security and Social Services".[1] Government grants are policy tools which address societal needs as they emerge as priorities in the political arena. For this reason, it is not surprising that the most important categories are those related to the welfare state. One perspective on the policy process is that policy-makers have a short-term view rather than a long-term view, which would include devoting resources for exploration (which only eventually and at the cost of many failures will end in net welfare gain). Since the work of Lipset and Rokkan (1967), many studies describe this policy process as leading to path-dependency (Collier and Collier, 1991; Ertman, 1996; Hacker, 1998).

We surmise that the nature behind various types of funding might influence the research activity leading to a patent (see e.g., Baker, 2008; Goldfarb and Henrekson, 2003; Geuna, 2001; Gulbrandsen and Smeby, 2005; Geuna and Nesta, 2006). Based on the above discussion, we propose the following hypotheses. First, we expect a patent funded by the university to be associated with patents which are more original:

Hypothesis 1. University-funded projects are associated with greater patent originality.

Second, we could expect the opposite for privately funded research: If firms have few incentives to perform basic and original research because of lack of appropriability and inherent uncertainty, we can expect that they also fund patents which are less original in nature:

Hypothesis 2. Privately-funded projects (with no university funding) are associated with lower patent originality.

Third, we consider government funding. Although university funding can sometimes originate in government funds, we consider the university context different because the funds do not directly come from the government. Rather, we consider government funding which is direct and based on calls for applications. This distinction is crucial because government projects are usually oriented toward existing societal needs (Geuna, 2001) and thus,

---

[1] Data reported as for 10.09.2013 in http://www.grants.gov/web/grants/home.html

M. Guerzoni et al. / Research Policy 43 (2014) 1697–1706   1701

could be expected to reinforce path-dependence of mainstream science and technology, and not necessarily push for original research.

Hypothesis 3. Government-funded projects (with no university funding) are associated with lower patent originality.

The aim of our paper is to not to provide a model of the innovation process but rather, to provide a fresh look at a key component of this process – patents – which we hope can contribute to the development of future research. We provide empirical nuance to the ongoing research and policy debates about university patents.[2]

3. Data and empirical strategy

3.1. Data

We combine two datasets in order to test our hypotheses. The first one, used widely in the literature, is the NBER United States Patent Citations Data File. Second, we collected via a survey information on scientists awarded a National Cancer Institute (NCI) grant in the years 1998–2004. As explained in Audretsch and Aldridge (2006), which utilizes the same dataset, records of the name of the scientist in the NCI dataset and name of the patent assignee were matched when the following criteria were fulfilled:

- A positive match of the first, middle and last name. We include cases where the middle name was absent in either one of the databases.
- We match observations over the time period 1998–2004, which corresponds to the initial year in which observations were available from the NCI database (1998–2002) and the final year in which patents were recorded in the patent database (1975–2004). Since patent applications may take up to two years to be issued, 2003 and 2004 United States Patent and Trademark Office (USPTO) records were included in our query.
- Location: We excluded patents by patentees not residing within an approximate radius of 60 miles from the university.
- Patents which did not fall within the traditional categories of biotechnology were identified and evaluated. For this reason, patents such as "Bread Alfalfa Enhancer"were rejected as a non-NCI scientist patent.

Based on these matched criteria, we identify a subset of 65 distinct patentees[3] between 1998 and 2004 with a total of 167 patents. The matching allowed us to study both the patent and the patentee. We discuss the creation of our variables next.

3.2. Variables

The dependent variable in our study is patent originality. Following Trajtenberg et al. (1997), we estimate the originality of each patent in the dataset. This is calculated as an index score measuring each patent's prior patent citations. As suggested in Trajtenberg et al. (1997) originality of patent i can be measured as:

$$Originality_i = 1 - \sum_j^n H_{ij} \tag{1}$$

where H_{ij} denotes the normalized Herfindahl of the citations over the n technological patent classes of a patent belonging to the technological class j. Hall et al. (2001) highlights a possible bias in the index since, in general, the concentration index will be biased upward when N is small. For this reason, we use the unbiased originality index as proposed by Hall et al. (2001), which corrects the normalized Herfindahl:

$$Originality_i = \frac{N}{N-1} \left(1 - \sum_j^{n_i} H_{ij} \right) \tag{2}$$

If N is small this index reduces the bias; if N is large, it tends asymptotically to originality in Eq. (1).

In order to test if the originality of a patent is at least partially explained by its funding source, we use information provided by patentees. They were asked whether they had any source of research funding from university, industry or government. We created a dummy variable which takes the value of one if a scientist received a total amount of $750,000 of funding from any of three independent sources: university, private sector, government.[4] We can thus also introduce three dummy variables which are each assigned a value of one if a scientist has been funded by the identified source. These categories are not mutually exclusive. Table 1 shows the number of occurrence for multiple sources of funding; the majority of the projects have one source of funding and 10% of them. In the following analysis we are not able to isolate the effect by looking at those projects with one source only without reducing to much the number of observations and also the hypotheses and conclusion are consequently derived. Fig. 1 shows average originality of patents for groups of scientists who received funding from at least one of the three sources. University-funded projects seem to be associated with slightly more original patents, but the complexity of the process leading to patents calls for several additional control variables.

We first measure the total NCI grant funding, a primary source of government funding for the period 2000–2004. We also take into account the legal and economic status of the source of the funding. We thus identify if the funding organization has profit or non-profit status.

Table 1
Frequency of co-occurrence funding sources.

No of funding sources	Cases	Percentage
1	91	66.4
2	19	13.8
3	12	8.7
4	15	10.9

---

[2] The big picture by Henderson et al. (1998) that academic research has declined in quality over time has already been mitigated by other studies looking at finer levels of disaggregation. Moreover, academic patent quality depends on factors including sector, university and technology transfer offices (Mowery et al., 2001; Mowery and Ziedonis, 2002). Our study furthers previous contributions of Henderson et al. (1998) by examining originality, which appropriately grasps the fundamental mission of universities.

[3] The 65 patenting scientists were "Googled" to obtain e-mail and telephone information. The records could generally be found by typing their full name, university and the word "oncology". The ensuing patentee e-mail accounts and telephone numbers were then collected and registered in the scientist database.

[4] In order for any significant sort of research endeavors to occur in oncology, we assumed a minimum threshold of $750,000 of funding from the three independent sources. The primary reason is simply that oncology research is a relatively costly endeavor. For example, the average NCI grant award over the same period of time was $2,578,126. In order to conduct any sort of basic research it was assumed, therefore, that $750,000 be a prerequisite floor for any sort of investigative research over the six-year period. The second reason why this number was chosen was due to informative conversations held with select NCI scientists prior to distributing the survey. After several questions pertaining to research and their respective funding needs, it was decided that $750,000 be a minimum requirement for any sort of meaningful funded research.

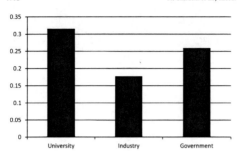

Fig. 1. Originality and source of funding.

Following Aldridge and Audretsch (2011), to control for individual characteristics, we include variables for both individual talent and industry linkage. Individual talent is operationalized by measuring average citations per publication in ISI, reported for each scientist from 2000 to 2004. Despite some obvious limitations (see Lindsey, 1989) the use of citations to grasp research quality of a scientist is a widespread measure since the seminal work of Garfield (1979). Scientist–industry linkages are operationalized using three variables selected to reflect scientist connections to industry. This variable should capture an unobservable tendency of the scientist to be closer to industry and, thus, ceteris paribus, her ability to obtain private funds. The first measure is board membership, a binary variable reflecting scientist participation on a board of directors or scientific advisory board. A second measure is industry co-publications, counted as the number of ISI publications an NCI scientist shared with a private industry employee who had an address field of "co", "corp","inc", "ltd", "llc" and/or "coltd". The third measure of social capital is industry-research lab co-publications, counted as the number of ISI publications an NCI scientist shared with a private industry employee who had an address field of "reslab".

Based on Levin and Stephan (1991), and following Aldridge and Audretsch (2011), we control for scientist age and gender. Scientist age is calculated from the year the scientist was born. Gender is reported as a dummy variable, where a male scientist is assigned a value of one and a female is assigned a value of zero.

We also control for a scientist's institutional context in two ways. First, we include a variable for public institution because of the different nature of private and public intelltual property ownership. The second variable identifies if the scientist's university was a recognized NCI Comprehensive Center. This variable controls for any potential agglomerating effects of knowledge specialization at the scientist's university.

Moreover, originality could be correlated with the quality of the patent, so we control for age of the university technology transfer office (TTO). For example, an older TTO may have more experience and knowledge in a patent application and therefore identify less backward patent citations in its application. A second variable is number of prior patents. Using Stuart and Sorenson (2003) we control for the number of patents issued to the scientist prior to 2000. We also control for the type of patent issued using the NBER two digit patent classification code. This allows us to control for if the scientist was issued a patent in a sub-field, such as drugs or medical instruments. Our variables are described in Tables 2 and 3 and descriptive statistics are presented in Table 4.

Table 2
Dependent variable.

Dependent variable	Description
Originality	An index score measuring how radical each patent was by measuring the patent's prior patent citations

3.3. Empirical strategy

We test our hypotheses on funding source as a determinant of a patent's originality (O). We suggest a model where variation in patent originality is explained by its source of funding (S) and by other covariates which could affect variance of the dependent variable as well. Specifically, we consider three groups of controls. The first is a group of demographic characteristics (D) of the inventor, such as gender or age. The second captures some unobservable quality of the scientist linked with her human capital, her linkage with the industry and the quality of her institution (T). The third is a group of controls consisting of industry dummies and taking into account different research patterns across industries (I). We estimate the following model:

$$O = S\beta + D\gamma + T\delta + I\theta + \varepsilon \tag{3}$$

where O is the vector of n observations of patent originality, S is a $n \times p - 1$ matrix, where p is the number of dummies variables indicating sources of funding, and D, T, and I are the matrix of observations for each control group. ε is the vector of error terms. Although we control for various factors, heteroskedasticty cannot be excluded. Indeed, consistent with cross-sectional microeconomic studies, we should acknowledge that behavioral inclinations of each individual can vary in relation to the phenomenon we want to explain. For this reason, we use a robust estimation of the variance matrix.

Endogeneity is a concern. Although our interest is in observing an association between type of funding rather than a direct causality, estimating our model will require us to reasonably assume that our analysis does not suffer from omitted variables and reverse causality. With respect to omitted variables: In the previous section we discussed the controls which have been suggested in the literature; our controls not only capture individual characteristics but also the nature of knowledge through our sector dummies.

Excluding reverse causality is generally not possible in the complex process of knowledge production. Indeed, it could be that the originality of an idea could drive the choice of a funding source. However, we argue this is not the case in our study, specifically of patented cancer research. Scientists in this area are pursuing research with a high potential market value and a likely market application. It is reasonable to expect that this qualifies each innovation for any kind of source and it is likely that the type of funding depends on other factors, such as the career stage of the scientist, funding availability, prestige of the institutions, colleagues, deadline of calls, personal contact with funders, possibility of clinical trials, and so on. In other words, it is reasonable to assume a scientist working in cancer research with a valuable idea does not spend time considering abstract concepts of originality in identifying potential funding sources.

Moreover, the originality of an idea is not necessarily embedded only in the idea but could also be a function of the discovery process. In an early phase, when a scientist applies for funding, the idea could still be "in progress" and will develop the extent of its originality during the process, after funds have been granted. In this sense "ante hoc, propter hoc" is not necessarily a logical fallacy. The most important caveat about the results holds in this particular case and results should be interpreted bearing this in mind.

Table 3
Description of independent variables.

Independent variables	Description
University funding	Binary variable, for scientists indicating that they received at least $750,000 of funding from a university source, University funding = 1
Nonprofit funding	Binary variable, for scientists indicating that they received at least $750,000 of funding from a university source, Nonprofit funding = 1
Industry funding	Binary variable, for scientists indicating that they received at least $750,000 of funding from a for-profit source, Private funding = 1
Government funding	Binary variable, for scientists indicating that they received at least $750,000 of funding from a governmental source, Government funding = 1
NCI grant	Total amount of NCI funding received by a scientist from 2000 to 2004
Avgcipub	The average citation per publication in ISI from 2000 to 2004
Industry Co-Pub	The number of ISI publications a NCI scientist shared with a private industry employee who had an address field of; co, corp, inc, ltd, llc, and or coltd
Industry ResLab Co-Pub	The number of ISI publications a NCI scientist shared with a private industry employee who had an address field of; reslab
OnBoardDirect	Binary variable, for scientists indicating that they sat on either a board of directors or science advisory board, Board = 1
Scientist age	The year the scientist was born
Male	Binary variable, where a male = 1
TTOFoundYear	Year when the scientist's university TTO was founded
Public institution	Binary variable, for a scientist who was affiliated to a public university, Public Institution = 1
NciComcenter	Binary variable, for a scientist whose institution is recognized by NCI as a comprehensive center for cancer research, NCI Center = 1
Prior patents	Count, the number of issued patents a scientist had, 1975–1998
Two digit NBER patent sub category code	
PCResins	Two digit patent subcategory in the patent field of Chemicals
PCBio Tech	Two digit patent subcategory in the patent field of Drugs and Medical
PCMiscel. Chem	Two digit patent subcategory in the patent field of Chemical
PCComputer Hard/Software	Two digit patent subcategory in the patent field of Computers and Communications
PCSurgery and Med Inst	Two digit patent subcategory in the patent field of Drugs and Medical
PCOrganic Componds	Two digit patent subcategory in the patent field of Chemical
PCDrugs	Two digit patent subcategory in the patent field of Drugs and Medical

Table 4
Means and standard deviations.

Variable	Obs.	Mean	Std. dev.	Min	Max
Patent originality	167	0.327	0.289	0	0.826
University funding	167	0.156	0.364	0	1
Nonprofit funding	167	0.168	0.375	0	1
Industry funding	167	0.329	0.471	0	1
Government funding	167	0.365	0.483	0	1
NCI grant	167	2,578,126	1,612,474	1,194,332	9,009,597
Avgcipub	167	26.662	22.068	1.667	130.365
Industry Co-Pub	167	3.467	4.475	0	27
Industry ResLab Co-Pub	167	0.246	1.832	0	23
Onboarddirct	167	0.605	0.490	0	1
Scientist age	167	57.078	7.376	41	73
Male	167	0.880	0.326	0	1
Ttofoundyear	167	1981.138	8.739	1940	1996
Public Institution	167	0.461	0.500	0	1
Nci Compcenter	167	0.515	0.501	0	1
Prior1998patents	167	6.257	6.697	0	27
PCResins	167	0.216	0.412	0	1
PCBio Tech	167	0.683	0.467	0	1
PCMiscel. Chem	167	0.066	0.249	0	1
PCComputer Hard/Software	167	0.060	0.238	0	1
PCSurgery and Med Inst	167	0.102	0.303	0	1
PCOrganic Componds	167	0.323	0.469	0	1
PCDrugs	167	0.377	0.486	0	1

4. Results and discussion

We present the results of six models in Table 5. Our results hold across models and explain 30% of the variance in patent originality. Given the complexity of the research process, the use of patents as a problematic proxy for inventive activity, and the size of the sample, we consider a fit of 30% appropriate. The strongest result is that university funding is, on average, associated with greater patent originality, providing support for H1. The focal point is not if a patent is assigned to a university or not, but its source of funding. Only in cases where the university is the source of funding does

university research maintain its traditional role of pursuing original research.

In addition, we are able to reject that other sources of funding have a positive impact on patent originality. In other words, the coefficient of both private funding and governmental funding is non-significant. As previously noted, a perspective on the economics of innovation considers that the new rationale in governmental funding, based on competitive calls for applications, could distort researcher incentives to explore original paths (see Geuna, 2001). Our study provides the first empirical observation of this effect. Previous concerns about this issue (Geuna, 2001)

Table 5
Regressions.

	Model 1	Model 2	Model 3	Model 4	Model 5
Dependent variable	Originality	Originality	Originality	Originality	Originality
University funding	0.243	0.327	0.34	0.266	0.25
	(2.60)*	(4.10)**	(3.31)**	(2.23)*	(2.23)*
Governmental funding	−0.049	−0.051	−0.031	−0.027	
	−0.86	−0.96	−0.56	−0.46	
Industry funding	−0.039	0.013	0.035	0.05	0.053
	−0.54	−0.19	−0.54	−0.72	−0.76
Nonprofit funding	0.033	−0.043	−0.058	−0.08	−0.074
	−0.35	−0.45	−0.52	−0.72	−0.66
NCI grant	0		0	0	0
	(1.80)'	−1.36	−0.95	−0.91	
AvgCiPub		−0.004	−0.005	−0.006	−0.006
		(3.79)**	(3.94)**	(4.32)**	(4.32)**
Industry Co-Pub		0	0.001	0.003	0.002
		−0.03	−0.12	−0.39	−0.35
Industry Reslab Co-Pub		0.006	0.005	0.004	0.003
		−0.88	−0.72	−0.51	−0.39
OnBoardDirect		−0.126	−0.146	−0.121	−0.126
		(2.22)*	(2.29)*	(1.84)'	(1.88)'
Scientist Age			0.001	0.003	0.003
			−0.25	−0.92	−0.87
Male			0.058	0.075	0.081
			−0.64	−0.79	−0.84
TtoFoundYear			−0.003	−0.005	−0.005
			−0.86	−1.38	−1.5
Public institution			−0.071	−0.088	−0.087
			−1.17	−1.37	−1.38
NciCompCenter			0.016	0.01	0.018
			−0.28	−0.17	−0.35
PCResins				−0.069	−0.059
				−0.47	−0.41
PCBio Tech				−0.166	−0.161
				−1.14	−1.13
PCMisc. Chem				−0.142	−0.136
				−1.01	−0.99
PCSurgery and Med Instrm.				−0.022	−0.021
				−0.29	−0.27
PCOrganic Compounds				−0.084	−0.079
				−1.21	−1.16
PCDrugs				−0.104	−0.104
				(1.83)'	(1.84)'
Constant	0.315	0.561	6.09	9.774	10.27
	(6.58)**	(8.26)**	−0.93	−1.45	−1.56
Observations	167	167	167	167	167
R-squared	0.1	0.23	0.25	0.3	0.3

Robust *t* statistics in parentheses
' Significant at 10%.
* Significant at 5%.
** Significant at 1%.

combined with our finding suggest that if a goal is to allocate resources to purely curiosity-driven research (which could mitigate the path-dependency of a system), a government should leave freedom to universities. The non-significant coefficient of NCI grant status further strengthens this implication: Funding made available for cancer research is not supposed to run the risk of being employed in dead-end projects.

We also find that legal status of the funding agency is not important. Non-profit organizations have different strategic and financial constraints from private organizations. According to our findings, the net effect does not point toward creation of original knowledge.

We now turn to variables which control for the talent of the scientist. The negative and significant impact of average ISI citation number per publication of an author suggests that originality is not necessarily always a breakthrough in the scientific paradigm. On the contrary, if path dependency is not a problem per se, original projects turn out very frequently to be unsuccessful or to reach a dead-end. Two explanations could shed light. First, original research could be more risky and have a higher rate of failure. Second, because of its originality, the peer group might fail to recognize

its importance. In both cases, more original research will receive fewer citations. To our knowledge, there is no strong evidence of this effect and our empirical findings identify an interesting path for future research. Future research could examine, for example, if star scientists might actually contribute more or less to research than expected by policymakers. Another related question is the relationship between publication productivity and research productivity, which could differ by field of study.

The variables controlling for the linkages of a scientist with her institutional setting corroborate the idea that originality is stronger for scientists focused on university work only. If a scientist sits on a board of directors or an advisory board, she will produce less original patents. Co-publishing with a private company or with a research lab and having a direct affiliation to a university or a NCI center does not have a significant effect.

Dummies for the main technological class of the patent are included in Models 3–5. They do not report a significant coefficient with the exception of the dummies for "drug and medical," which are negative. A highly applied field with routinized innovation, such as pharmaceuticals (Nightingale, 2000),

M. Guerzoni et al. / Research Policy 43 (2014) 1697–1706

shows little originality. Finally, we find no impact of age and gender.

Overall, we can conclude that university funding is associated with greater patent originality. This could be due to lack of incentives in privately-funded research to explore the scientific and technological space outside existing technological trajectories.

The findings of this study highlight two important points. First, we argue that when possible, data should be broken down at the micro level process of discovery and examined at various phases during the innovation process. The nuances related to funding sources could exist for other inputs and steps during a given innovation process. Second, originality could be more important than quality as the proxy for the primary role of the university in generating knowledge, as opposed to technological lock-ins.

On the other hand, we should warn policymakers that the changed rationale for funding allocation in some developed countries could have unintended consequences, affecting incentives for originality. The new task assigned to the university to generate more knowledge, which can be directly applied by the private sectors, appears to be fulfilled. However, the traditional role of the university to provide basic and original research is limited to those projects directly funded by the university. Partly, this could be the intended consequence of the creation of more linkage with industry. An important related question is whether government funding is intended to reduce originality and favor path-dependent innovation processes, or if this is an unintended consequence of greater use of competitive funding allocation schemes for research.

It is important to note that path-dependency is not harmful – on the contrary, it offers an efficient way to organize the process of discovery. Thus, there is a trade-off between an efficient process of discovery which might lead to lock-in situations, and a costly process of trial and error in original research which might lead to the emergence of new technology and industries. The balance is a challenge for policy, but insight can be gained from careful analysis of both processes.

As a caveat, we should point out that incentives related to funding opportunities are of a more complex nature than what this data can grasp; thus, the vast set of possible effects cannot be fully disentangled here. Our results call for more empirical research on this question and for a strong micro-level theoretical framework which links researcher incentives and funding source.

5. Conclusion

Pakes and Griliches (1980: p. 378) point out that "patents are a flawed measure (of innovative output); particularly since not all new innovations are patented and since patents differ greatly in their economic impact." Similarly, in his *Journal of Economic Literature* article on the use of patents as a measure of innovative activity, Griliches asks, "Patents as indicators of what?" (1990: p. 1669), and after sifting through a large literature concludes: "Ideally, we might hope that patent statistics would provide a measure of the (innovative) output [...] The reality, however, is very far from it. The dream of getting hold of an output indicator of inventive activity is one of the strong motivating forces for economic research in this area" (1990: p. 1669). He then draws a line for future research and hopes for the construction of "more relevant "quality-weighted" inventive output measures" based on patent citations (Griliches, 1990, p. 1707). More recently, Jaffe et al. (1998, 2005) addressed Griliches' (1990) concern about the use of patents by developing methodologies to measure the degree of originality associated with a given patent. In fact, a growing body of empirical work confirms Griliches' (1990) assertion about the inherent variability of patent originality.

Patent originality has been long recognized (Nelson and Winter, 1982; Dosi, 1988) in fostering the emergence of new technologies

and industries: although originality is not a sufficient condition of the generation of new industries and it might be likely to end up with failures, the constant attempt of original path is one of the key triggers in the evolutionary process of creative destruction. However, while significant literature measures the impact of patent originality on firm performance, our study is among the first to examine the funding context as a condition which could affect patent originality.

The literature has identified two basic types of research activity. Curiosity-driven research has usually been carried out in the university, while research in the private sector or financed by the government has usually been driven not by curiosity, but by the needs of society (Geuna, 2001). The changing rationale for funding in universities, as occurred in the last decades both in US and in Europe, enabled the coexistence of both types in academia. If this is the case, a relevant explanatory variable is whether – even within university – research has been performed in the usual academic context or closer to the private sector. In order to disentangle these, we examine funding source, which could reflect different rationales and to some extent, proxy the research context in which a project is being carried out.

The hypotheses and empirical results in this paper suggest that research supported by industry tends to be associated with less original patents. Research supported by universities, which has less of an applied focus, tends to be associated with more original patents. This evidence suggests that the alleged decreasing originality of the average academic patent could be spurious and the origin of funding should be controlled. Moreover, this result highlights the importance of the role of the university in creating original knowledge, which is a goal to be pursued within universities not achievable anywhere else.

An important qualification of these findings is that they apply to a limited area of science and technology. Indeed our data describe a specific sector which fulfills some assumption we made. We were able to exclude the possibility of reverse causality based on the nature of this data; doing this for other fields of study might not be possible.

Our study provides initial insights on the relationship between patent originality and funding source, a previously unexamined question. We find that the source of funding is indeed important, and we hope that future research will further examine this question in line with deeper investigation into scientific and research context.

References

Adams, J.D., 1990. Fundamental stocks of knowledge and productivity growth. Journal of Political Economy 98 (4), 673–702.
Agrawal, A., Henderson, R., 2002. Putting patents in context: Exploring knowledge transfer from MIT. Management Science 48 (1), 44–60.
Aldridge, T., Audretsch, D., 2011. The Bayh–Dole act and scientist entrepreneurship. Research Policy 40 (8), 1058–1067.
Arrow, K., 1962. The economic implications of learning by doing. The Review of Economic Studies 29 (3), 155–173.
Audretsch, D., Aldridge, T., 2006. The knowledge filter and economic growth: the role of scientist entrepreneurship. Ewing Marion Kauffman Foundation, 67.
Baker, D., 2008. Financing drug research: what are the issues? In: 2008 Industry Studies Conference Paper.
Cohen, W.M., Levinthal, D.A., 1989. Innovation and learning: the two faces of R & D. The Economic Journal 99 (397), 569–596.
Cohen, W., Nelson, R., Walsh, J., 2002. Links and impacts: the influence of public research on industrial R&D. Management Science 48 (1), 1–23.
Collier, R.B., Collier, D., 1991. Shaping the Political Arena: Critical Junctures, the Labor Movement, and Regime Dynamics in Latin America. Princeton University Press, Princeton, NJ.
Crespi, G.A., Geuna, A., 2006. The Productivity of UK Universities (No. 147). SPRU-Science and Technology Policy Research, University of Sussex.
Czarnitzki, D., Glänzel, W., Hussinger, K., 2007. Patent and publication activities of German professors: an empirical assessment of their co-activity. Research Evaluation 16 (4), 311–319.

Czarnitzki, D., Hussinger, K., Schneider, C., 2011. Commercializing academic research: the quality of faculty patenting. Industrial and Corporate Change 20 (5), 1403–1437.

David, P., 1985. Clio and the economics of QWERTY. The American Economic Review 75 (2), 332–337.

Dosi, G., 1982. Technological paradigms and technological trajectories: a suggested interpretation of the determinants and directions of technical change. Research Policy 11 (3), 147–162.

Dosi, G., 1988. Sources, procedures, and microeconomic effects of innovation. Journal of Economic Literature 26 (3), 1120–1171.

Ertman, T., 1996. Birth of the Leviathan: Building States and Regimes in Medieval and Early Modern Europe. Cambridge University Press, Cambridge.

Garfield, E., 1979. Citation Indexing: Its Theory and Application in Science, Technology, and Humanities, vol. 8. Wiley, New York.

Geuna, A., 1998. The internationalisation of European universities: a return to medieval roots. Minerva 36 (3), 253–270.

Geuna, A., 2001. The changing rationale for European university research funding: are there negative unintended consequences? Journal of Economic Issues 35 (3), 607–632.

Geuna, A., Nesta, L., 2006. University patenting and its effects on academic research: the emerging European evidence. Research Policy 35 (6), 790–807.

Goldfarb, B., Henrekson, M., 2003. Bottom-up top-down policies towards the commercialization of university intellectual property. Research Policy 32 (4), 639–658.

Griliches, Z., 1990. Patent statistics as economic indicators: a survey. Journal of Economic Literature 28 (4), 1661–1707.

Gulbrandsen, M., Smeby, J., 2005. Industry funding and university professors' research performance. Research Policy 34 (6), 932–950.

Hacker, J., 1998. The historical logic of national health insurance: structure and sequence in the development of British, Canadian, and U.S. medical policy. Studies in American Political Development 12 (Spring), 57–130.

Hall, B., Jaffe, A., Trajtenberg, M., 2001. The NBER Patent Citation Data File: Lessons, Insights and Methodological Tools. NBER Working Paper 8498.

Henderson, R., 1993. Underinvestment and incompetence as responses to radical innovation: evidence from the photolithographic alignment equipment industry. The RAND Journal of Economics 24 (2 (Summer)), 248–270.

Henderson, R., Jaffe, A., Trajtenberg, M., 1998. Universities as a source of commercial technology: a detailed analysis of university patenting, 1965-1988. Review of Economics and Statistics 80 (1), 119–127.

Jaffe, A.B., Fogarty, M.S., Banks, B.A., 1998. Evidence from patents and patent citations on the impact of NASA and other federal labs on commercial innovation. The Journal of Industrial Economics 46 (2), 183–205.

Jaffe, A., Trajtenberg, M., Romer, P., 2005. Patents, Citations and Innovations: A Window on the Knowledge Economy. MIT Press.

Kilger, C., Bartenbach, K., 2002. New rules for German professors. Science 298 (5596), 1173–1175.

Levin, S., Stephan, P., 1991. Research productivity over the life cycle: evidence for academic scientists. The American Economic Review 81 (1), 114–132.

Lichtenberg, F., 2001. Are the benefits of newer drugs worth their cost? Evidence from the 1996 MEPS. Health Affairs 20.5, 241–251.

Lichtenberg, F., 2007. The impact of new drugs on US longevity and medical expenditure, 1990–2003: evidence from longitudinal, disease-level data. The American Economic Review 97 (2), 438–443.

Lipset, S.M., Rokkan, S., 1967. Party Systems and Voter Alignments. Free Press, New York, pp. 1–64.

Lindsey, D., 1989. Using citation counts as a measure of quality in science measuring what's measurable rather than what's valid. Scientometrics 15 (3), 189–203.

Malerba, F., Nelson, R., Orsenigo, L., Winter, S., 2007. Demand, innovation, and the dynamics of market structure: the role of experimental users and diverse preferences. Journal of Evolutionary Economics 17 (4), 371–399.

Mansfield, E., 1991. Academic research and industrial innovation. Research Policy 20 (1), 1–12.

Marco, A., 2006. The dynamics of patent citations. Economics Letters 94 (2), 290–296.

Markman, G., Gianiodis, P., Phan, P., 2008. Full-time faculty or part-time entrepreneurs. Engineering Management, IEEE Transactions on 55 (1), 29–36.

Martin, B., 2003. The changing social contract for science and the evolution of the university. In: Science and Innovation: Rethinking the Rationales for Funding and Governance. Edward Elgar, Cheltenham, pp. 7–29.

Martin, S., Scott, J., 2000. The nature of innovation market failure and the design of public support for private innovation. Research Policy 29 (4–5), 437–447.

Merton, R., 1973. The normative structure of science. The Sociology of Science 267, 275–277.

Mowery, D., Nelson, R., Sampat, B., Ziedonis, A., 2001. The growth of patenting and licensing by US universities: an assessment of the effects of the Bayh–Dole Act of 1980. Research Policy 30 (1), 99–119.

Mowery, D., Ziedonis, A.A., 2000. Numbers, quality, and entry: how has the Bayh–Dole Act affected US university patenting and licensing? Innovation Policy and the Economy, 187–220.

Mowery, D., Ziedonis, A.A., 2002. Academic patent quality and quantity before and after the Bayh–Dole act in the US. Research Policy 31 (3), 399–418.

Nelson, R., 1959. The simple economics of basic scientific research. The Journal of Political Economy 67 (3), 297–306.

Nelson, R., Winter, S., 1982. An Evolutionary Theory of Economic Change. Belknap Press, Cambridge.

Nightingale, P., 2000. Economies of scale in experimentation: knowledge and technology in pharmaceutical R&D. Industrial and Corporate Change 9 (2), 315–359.

Pakes, A., Griliches, Z., 1980. Patents and R&D at the firm level: a first report. Economics Letters 5 (4), 377–381.

Roberts, Royston, M., 1989. Serendipity: Accidental Discoveries in Science. Wiley-VCH, Hoboken, NJ.

Sampat, B., Mowery, D., Ziedonis, A., 2003. Changes in university patent quality after the Bayh–Dole act: a re-examination. International Journal of Industrial Organization 21 (9), 1371–1390.

Schumpeter, J.A., 1942. Socialism, Capitalism and Democracy. Harper and Brothers, Oxford, UK.

Solow, R., 1967. Some recent developments in the theory of production. In: The Theory and Empirical Analysis of Production. Columbia University Press, New York, US, pp. 25–54.

Strandburg, K.J., 2005. Curiosity-driven research and university technology transfer. Advances in the Study of Entrepreneurship, Innovation & Economic Growth 16, 93–122.

Stuart, T., Sorenson, O., 2003. The geography of opportunity: spatial heterogeneity in founding rates and the performance of biotechnology firms. Research Policy 32 (2), 229–253.

Toole, A., Czarnitzki, D., 2007. Biomedical academic entrepreneurship through the SBIR program. Journal of Economic Behavior and Organization 63.4:, 716–738.

Thursby, J., Fuller, A., Thursby, M., 2009. US faculty patenting: inside and outside the university. Research Policy 38 (1), 14–25.

Thursby, J., Thursby, C., 2011. Has the Bayh–Dole act compromised basic research? Research Policy 40.8:, 1077–1083.

Trajtenberg, M., 1990. A penny for your quotes: patent citations and the value of innovations. The RAND Journal of Economics, 172–187.

Trajtenberg, M., Henderson, R., Jaffe, A., 1997. University vs corporate patents: a window on the basicness of invention. Economics of Innovation and New Technology 5 (1), 19–50.

Zucker, L., Darby, M., 1997. Individual action and the demand for institutions star scientists and institutional transformation. American Behavioral Scientist 40 (4), 502–513.